Classic Motorcycles

32 GREAT BIKES AND THEIR ROAD TEST REPORTS

LESTER MORRIS

Copyright © 2022 Lester Morris

This work is copyright. Apart from any fair dealing for the purposes of private study, research, criticism or review, as permitted by the Copyright Act 1968, no part of this book may be reproduced, stored in a retrieval system or transmitted in any form or by any means, electronic, mechanical, photocopying, recording or otherwise, without the prior written permission of the publisher.

Lester Morris – Classic Motorcycles: 32 great bikes and their road test reports

ISBN: 978-0-6489619-8-7 (paperback)

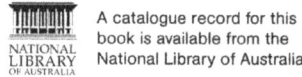

A catalogue record for this book is available from the National Library of Australia

Photography credits

Many photographs are the property of the author, who also acknowledges and thanks the photographers who gave permission to use their work:
Bill Forsyth, Graham Munro, and the late Ray Ryan.
Some images are from historic catalogues and every effort has been made to trace those copyright owners. Please contact the publisher if you believe there has been an infringement of copyright.

Cover and internal design: Ronald Proft

DELPHIAN
BOOKS

Delphian Books
Unit 1, 29 Mile End Road, Rouse Hill, NSW 2155
delphianbooks.com.au

Contents

Foreword:	v
Introduction:	vii
BSA Gold Star: A history of the Gold Star award, and road test of three 'Goldies' from 1938-56.	2
ARDIE: A real Gem from 1933. A Genuine Gentlemen's Luxury Tourer, a type unknown today.	14
BMW R69 and Sidecar: The ideal combination: sports German tourer, with great, comfortable sidecar.	22
ARIEL Leader: Ah, how sad for what could – and should – have been. In particular the 700cc OHV version.	32
ARIEL Square Four: Ten to 100 miles an hour in top gear? Try that with a modern motorcycle!	44
NSU 250: A very trim German OHC machine, with a performance many a 350 would love to have.	54
HENDERSON Outfit: First road-going solo motorcycle to achieve 100mph, way back in 1922.	64
NORTON Inter: Road going version of the mighty Manx Norton road-racer. 'Featherbed' frame as well!	74
TRIUMPH Bandit: Great 100mph DOHC twin 350. Shot down in flames by dumb BSA Board members.	84
BMW R50S: Fast Super Sports model, and the rarest of the rare, with only 1700-odd built in three years.	96
VINCENT Rapide: Forerunner of some of the most eagerly sought-after Classics.	106
VINCENT Black Shadow: Similar to above, if more potent, much quicker, and even more sought after.	112
DKW twin: Pre-war 500cc twin two-stroke, with electric starter and great overall performance.	124
MUNCH Mammoth: Bespoke 1300cc Monster, with much more power than anyone would ever need.	134
SUNBEAM S7: Another Gentlemen's Tourer, if a more modern one, but not very successful.	146
INDIAN outfit: Made in the hundreds of thousands as a 1200cc side-valve, and a great work-horse.	156
BSA A10: The type of 650cc twin which once made England great. Several factories built one.	166
MATCHLESS Silver Hawk: Fifty years ahead of its time, this 1930s OHC Vee-Four was a great effort.	176
ZUNDAPP German outfit: Almost 20,000 supplied to the German Army during WWII. Impressive!	188
RUDGE Special: Four-valve head, and a fine performance from this 500cc pre-war single.	200
VELOCETTE Thruxton: Super Sports 500. Very quick, handled perfectly and a joy to ride swiftly.	210
SCOTT Squirrel: Two-cylinder 500cc twin, water-cooled and fine performer. Pity about the ride!	222
ZUNDAPP K800: 'Flat' side valve four-cylinder, very low centre of gravity; unapproachable in corners!	232
BIMOTA Suzuki: Marriage of fine DOHC Suzuki engine in one of the finest frames ever built.	242
BROUGH Superior: The Rolls Royce of Motorcycles? It certainly was – in the 1930s.	252
NIMBUS: Gentle Danish 750 OHC four cylinder. First motorcycle made with telescopic front forks.	260
LEVIS: An 'ordinary' pre-war 500 single, with an extraordinary, unique rear suspension.	270
BENELLI 6: Great six-cylinder, 750cc OHC Superbike from Italy. First rate machine.	278
TRIUMPH T100: First post-war 500cc twin from 1946. Very swift, if fairly basic.	288
MOTO GUZZI Falcone: Horizontal cylinder 500cc single, almost unaltered in nearly 60 years.	298
ZUNDAPP K600: Flat twin 600. Famous for annual 'Green Elefant' Rally in 'snow-bound' mid-winter.	308
EVER ONWARD: Great 'Bitza' 500 single, with B&S sleeve-valve engine. What was that again?	316

Foreword

I still recall with amusement the time I was walking past a travel agent's window when I suddenly pulled up. That cardboard cut-out in the window looked awfully familiar and yes, it was Lester Morris. His alter ego was, I think, demonstrating somehow that British Airways seats were comfortable.

Now I do realise that accusing someone of being a cardboard cut-out might be considered an insult rather than praise, but think of it this way: how many people do you know who really have made appearances that way? Only famous ones, I'll bet, like in my case maybe Wayne Gardner.

And in Lester's case, an appearance as a flat airline passenger is only an outlier of his many talents. I won't go into detail about those many talents, or the ways in which their application has enriched the Australian cultural scene. Well, all right, here's one: how many motorcycle reviewers have also trodden the boards in panto as the Widow Twankey?

Lester's motorcycle reviews engage the attention not only because he has extensive background knowledge of both the history and technology incorporated in his subjects, but also because his gentle humour often softens the inevitable headshaking of his criticism. Make no mistake, Lester does not spare the guilty when it comes, for instance, to designers, even such acknowledged giants as Edward Turner. Neither, though, does he fail to allocate praise where it is due.

Take his comments about the pretty little Triumph 350 Bandit, which never made it through its teething problems.

'The Bandit power-plant was *initially* designed by the recently retired Edward Turner, who had designed the first 500cc overhead valve vertical-twin Triumph in 1937 and, just as happened with that first 'Speed Twin', which initially had its own share of serious problems, it was up to two of his trusted associates, initially Bert Hopwood and then the brilliant Doug Hele – the latter considered by many to be much the brighter of the two! – to turn the troublesome, poorly designed little Bandit into a viable motorcycle.'

As Lester points out, the failure of the Bandit can be sheeted home to the 'fossilised', in Lester's word, BSA board, not to Hopwood or Hele.

Using first-hand experience in the industry he also outlines the market's reception of the various motorcycles he describes, although he never pretends to know what is essentially unknowable: why some were a success, when others failed. When he does comment on that question he does it, once again, from industry knowledge not from his imagination, as far too many writers do. He also uses his experience to place different motorcycles' importance accurately in history.

It is a pleasure to read Lester's descriptions of such aspects of a bike as working on it and actually riding it. He has the practical, not only the theoretical, background to give highly convincing accounts of both. How can you argue with comments like 'once or twice I whanged the throttle wide open for several seconds at my 7000rpm rev limit in fourth gear and the bike responded immediately, leaping away with a renewed vigour I would have sworn could not be there.'

Take a look at the Contents page of this book, and you will see that it contains a treasure trove of machinery. From the inevitable Vincent Black Shadow to a surprising NSU 250 by way of the classy Moto Guzzi Falcone and delicate (my term, from personal knowledge) Scott Squirrel it is a list to make the most experienced motorcyclist blind with jealousy. Imagine having ridden all of those wonderful and dreadful, and everything in between, machines! Buy the book; this is the closest you will come.

J Peter 'The Bear' Thoeming

Introduction

'A motorcycle is a bicycle with a pandemonium attachment and is designed for the special use of mechanical geniuses, daredevils and lunatics.'
So said George Fitch, in the Atlanta Constitution, 1916.

Recently restored 1901 Triumph bicycle, with Minerva engine and belt drive, ably demonstrates the above.

We should feel sorry for poor old George, who had clearly never enjoyed the freedom of being pounded vigorously over his nation's seriously pot-holed, dusty roads on a very early, crude example of a 'modern day' motorcycle. On the other hand, he may have been more right than wrong, for most of the very early machines he so eloquently described were probably cobbled together from an odd assortment of bits and pieces by the very people he describes as *'mechanical geniuses, daredevils and lunatics'*, the resultant powered two-wheelers – their tiny, under-powered engines bolted onto bicycles as *'pandemonium attachments'*, providing several forms of **sub-basic** transportation.

As we shall shortly see, most of the examples of latter-day classics within these pages began their careers in that fashion as very simple runabouts, roughly 'designed', as Fitch suggests, by some of the odd characters he described so well in his summation. He must have seen many of these God-awful machines lurching flatulently about the countryside when they were brand new, their clearly terrified owners clinging onto the handlebars for their very lives or, quite often, being pelted off of the ill-sprung, haphazardly designed, badly handling, under-braked pushbikes which were never intended to be powered by anything other than a set of flailing human legs.

Had George lived for another 40 or so years he might well have enjoyed (?) the opportunity of seeing the enormous advances in motorcycle design which naturally followed as simple evolution decreed, in much the same way as 'Modern Man' has undergone a similar transition from our neck-less, flat-nosed, hairy, ape-like ancestors to something a little better to look at, and with a little more common sense (?). By no means perfected in the mid-1950s for George to admire, even though some may argue otherwise, motorcycles in that era had clearly improved greatly over the design and outward appearance of some primitive examples of *Homo sapiens* which had been creeping about prior to that time.

If poor George had survived to that time, he may then have had the opportunity to perch his terrified backside onto a much more modern bicycle, and then ridden off for a squirt into the countryside, to perhaps change his odd mind as he found he actually enjoyed the experience: or not, as the case may be.

Some of the *Classic Motorcycles* described within these pages survived their maniacal birth pangs and were vastly improved in later years, many of the *'mechanical geniuses'* who designed them by now long gone, the motorcycles now holding their collective heads on high as prime examples of some of the finest motorcycles to have ever been built; whether they were perfect or not. Some of the 'lunatics' whom George describes are thrilled and delighted to be still riding many of those machines about on an almost daily basis. Long may those Lunatics live, and long may their trusty old irons do so as well.

One might ask the entirely legitimate question as to what the ingredients are which go into making a Classic Motorcycle in the first place: indeed, a Classic *Anything*. There is apparently no format which can be applied, at least none of which we are aware, for these sometime-rare motorcycles seem to slide into the loosely defined Classic category with little rhyme and no obvious reason. Of course, one man's Classic motorcycle may be another's shocker, but that is one of those intangible things which, themselves, evince little rhyme and no discernible reason. Some people may harbour the mistaken belief that a motorcycle which is an Oldie must be a Classic Motorcycle simply because of its age, but an '*oldie*' may not have been a '*goodie*' even when brand new and would certainly not have improved with age – unlike, say, a fine wine, a good joke or a great opera singer would. Or might!

Again, in making my selection and including them in this book, I am well aware there are many other machines which are not included, and which certainly enjoy the appellation of '*Classic Motorcycle*', but there must be a limit somewhere to the number which can be accommodated in a publication such as this, and your favourite may not have been included. Let me say that anyone may question why some of the motorcycles featured herein have been included *at all*, and this is entirely as it should be. Among others I would like to have included is the very trim 350cc Vee-twin, shaft-drive Victoria 'Bergemeister' from Germany – with is four-speed, chains-and-sprockets 'gearbox' – the British 350cc flat-twin Douglas 'Dragonfly' from the 1950s; the amazingly stable, 'Hands-Off' 1920s hub-centre steered 'Neracar' from America, and elsewhere under licence; perhaps a 1908, 443cc, shaft-drive, four-cylinder Belgian

Riding (hands off) on the bumpy Montlhery circuit in France, the photographer ably demonstrates the incredible stability of hub-centre steering. Why this type of steering has not been adopted for motorcycles totally escapes me.

FN with its 'kind-of' *telescopic* front forks, but I simply couldn't find any of them which were able to be ridden *at that time*: or, indeed, at any time thereafter. I do know, of course, that these machines are out there: somewhere.

There may not have been room for them in this book, anyway, but if I can find any one of them, and a long list of other genuine Classics I really want to ride – let's say, among others, the 1950s OHC 500cc Jawa twin; a Vee-twin Crocker (an American Brough Superior); the great 1930s 500cc OHC Excelsior 'Manxman' and a few other favourites of mine – then there may be another *Classics* book in the offing. But don't hold your collective breaths, for these machines, and many more great machines I would love to ride, can be found in any of the four corners of this earth if one knows where to look for them, or if someone offers all/some of them for appraisal. I will see what transpires at

Above: Four-cylinder FN, shaft drive motorcycle, circa 1908, which needed bicycle pedals to start the engine.

another date, if anything!

However, several motorcycles in this book are, without question, first-class Classic machines, popular examples of which include the Vincent Rapide and Black Shadow siblings; Ariel Square Four; BSA Gold Star; the Scott Squirrel; Rudge Special; R69 BMW/Steib outfit; Velocette 'Thruxton'; Brough 'Superior'; the extremely rare R50S BMW; OHC Norton International and the advanced 1930-35 OHC four-cylinder Matchless Silver Hawk. Others featured within these pages are either rare, virtually unknown, 'second level' classics, or otherwise deserving, and they are all gleefully included for a variety of Very Good Reasons, all of which are – or should be – of more than a passing interest.

Some very interesting machines herein include the ill-fated, prototype 350cc DOHC Triumph Bandit vertical twin from 1970, the marvellous 1933 RBK503 Ardie; Henderson 1300cc Big Four; WWII Wehrmacht Zundapp outfit; Moto Guzzi 'Falcone'; 1939 500cc DKW two-stroke twin, with its electric starter; Denmark's 750 OHC four-cylinder Nimbus; the monstrous TS1300 OHC Munch Mammoth; the swift NSU 250 and several other oddities. All of these little-known machines which I rode certainly justify their inclusion within these pages when one reads the various texts to discover – perhaps to their surprise – what these rare motorcycles have, or had, to offer at the time, and just why they were included in this list of latter-day, in-depth road test reports.

When I say **'latter day'** and **'in-depth'** I mean reports which may not have been published when some of these earlier machines were new, but were finally published with my by-line in a variety of specialised Australian magazines from 1972 until well into the 1980s. **In-depth** means details of the long history of some of these machines, and much of their development, which too often means somewhat long, 'wordy' dissertations upon some of them. Most of those road test reports were featured in the deservedly popular Australian *Two Wheels* magazine, or the lesser-known, if equally memorable Oz publications, *Classic Motorcycles, Bike Australia, Cycle Australia, Classic Bike, Revs* or *The Bike Book* and two or three other, lesser-known publications. All of these reports were written by myself, the machines loaned by proud owners who all seemed to me to be happy for someone they may have never met to jump upon their precious machines and ride off into the sunset.

My swift disappearance upon these machines was never attended by a written or implied guarantee that the rider, or indeed the priceless machine, would ever return unscathed. This was never to be the case, of course, but two of the machines I rode broke down during the test rides; a late model DBD34 Gold Star BSAs magneto totally giving up the ghost at the very end of the report – and unable to be repaired at the roadside – the 1935 Matchless Silver Hawk needing some of its clutch-spring sleeve-nuts to be found, located in the oil at the bottom of the alloy primary-drive case and nipped up again before I could ride the motorcycle away.

I trust I might have been well enough known (even in those far-off days) as a long-serving motorcycle writer and commentator for these trusting owners of rare and valuable machines to allow me to take their pride and joy out of their hands for some time to conduct the various tests and to have this odd person photographed riding their bikes about. It may have been an anxious time for the owners of these precious machines and might not have been much of a buzz for these fellows, but it certainly was a great buzz for me!

At the time, I thanked the owners of those precious machines for allowing me to ride their rare, well-restored motorcycles, as well as for some of the priceless information they imparted. This wasn't always on the technical details of design and/or the materials from which the various components were made, for I knew the Tech Specs well enough with the better-known machines I rode, but the information on just who, how, when, where or why the owner/restorers found those machines in the first place was of great interest. I was always well aware of the enormous amount of work involved in restoring those rare and interesting machines;

not to mention the enormous amount of time involved or even, more importantly, the expense which was naturally incurred. Most of this more personal information is included in the various reports for everyone to read and (hopefully) to wonder at, for I found the stories of world-wide searches for rare spare parts as well as the painstaking, time-consuming process of hand-making many components which were simply not available anywhere on earth, to be of enormous interest.

Bearing in mind the local laws regarding the compulsory wearing of approved motorcycle helmets, I tried to wear some of the clothing which might have been worn by motorcyclists in the various eras, as in the case of wearing a German uniform when riding the WWII Afrika Korps Zundapp outfit, or plus-fours with flat cap and goggles when riding the 1935 Matchless Silver Hawk on a very quiet back-woods road outside of the small hamlet of Kilmore in Victoria. It was the same when riding the 1939 DKW two-stroke twin and the rare, flat-four 800cc Zundapp, but those more 'informal' shots could only be taken on rarely used, quiet country roads when there was no-one else – Police or otherwise – about. But some of the bikes had to be ridden and photographed later, often on major roads, which meant that an approved helmet had to be worn at those times. I might also add that, when riding those rare machines, I of course wore the right type of protective clothing as well if I was not being photographed. This hopefully accounts for the odd variety of clothing worn in photos which illustrate the various reports.

As I have mentioned, the bikes were very rare when those road tests were originally conducted and with the passage of time those bikes (and, sadly, some of their owners) have disappeared, which meant that to find other examples to photograph anew proved to be an almost impossible task; in its own way perhaps every bit as daunting as chasing up rare and expensive engine and frame parts. This meant that I had to dig out what I could find of the old material, which proved to be a task which, again, was very time-consuming and not always successful. As an example, I could find only a couple of photos from the original Black Shadow Vincent report, which was published in *Two Wheels* in 1979: a couple of those earlier photos are included in that story, along with a bunch of new ones. I was very fortunate in discovering a pristine example of a 'Shadow' in Sydney's Blue Mountains, enjoyed the owner's permission to ride the bike for a couple of hours, and for the ace photographer **Bill Forsyth** to capture everything I needed. Naturally, with the text written and already published, I didn't need to ride the machine for anything other than to secure a series of new photos, but I still enjoyed a great blast on this most marvellous of Classic motorcycles. The Black Shadow remains a firm favourite of mine, even though I can't find the space for one in my garage. That is my excuse anyway, but I must also say that I wish the necessary photographs of the other motorcycles were as easy to obtain as the 'Shadow' photos were!

It could be argued, and with some justification, that the original, semi-automatic 'commuter' **50cc OHV Honda 'Super Cub' step-thru** from Japan must be a true Classic Motorcycle and ought to have been included in this list, if only because that little machine became such an enormous success, and was very instrumental in placing the whole world back on two wheels. This was only a matter of a very few years after (or in some cases during) the disastrous collapse of almost the entire motorcycle industry world-wide which began during the mid-to-late 1950s. It was a frightful time, for the decade which followed was to see almost all of the once-great and famous motorcycle factories from England and Europe simply disappear. Most of them were British, and most of them never recovered. Apparently, nobody thought to tell the Sleeping Giant Honda about this, for the little commuter Super Cub arrived in Australia, hot off the assembly line, near the end of August, 1958, only a matter of a few months or so before its introduction into America and other International markets. Shortly thereafter a more efficient overhead *camshaft* engine was employed, which was then enlarged to 70cc, 90cc and 110cc capacity, the

little bike enhanced by an electric starter almost as a matter of course.

The 1958 step-thru *(pictured above)* wasn't the first machine from Honda to arrive in Australia before anywhere else on earth because in April, 1958, a small batch of just twelve of the more interesting, overhead-camshaft, two-cylinder, 250cc C71 'Dream' motorcycles, fitted with electric starter, four blinkers, twin mirrors, and fully enclosed rear chain to ice the Honda cake, arrived in Sydney. This happened more than a year before the machine became known in any country outside of Asia. Weeks later, a 305cc version of the 250 appeared, with a 125cc OHC twin-cylinder model called the 'Benly' arriving some days later again. A very sporty 125 twin arrived even later in 1958, and it proved to be a little fire-cracker of a machine, even though it didn't always go quite where it was pointed, for its skinny tyres loved to be controlled by Sydney's steel tram-lines rather than the person riding the bike. Therefore, it was not just the 50cc commuter machine which saved the industry, for it was aided and abetted by the earlier, more sporting machines from Honda which preceded the little marvel and sent it on its way to greatness.

In 1963, just five years after the first Super Cub was launched, one of the most successful advertising campaigns in history was mounted when the famous **'You Meet the Nicest People on a Honda'** colour brochure was launched in America, which simply raised the profile of the machine's *rider*, rather than the bike itself. That campaign helped Honda's Super Cub, and its later iterations – as a so-called 'farm bike', postal service delivery machine and a great many small, if brisk performing, commuter machines – to achieve the miracle of more than **100-million variations** of that original Honda being built and sold over those many years! This is far and away the greatest number of motorised vehicles of any kind to have ever been made. It's a safe bet that no powered vehicle, regardless of what it might happen to be, and how many wheels it may happen to be perched upon, will ever approach that incredible figure.

Honda has done it all again, for the company has re-introduced the Super Cub as a 125cc OHC machine which is modern in every way, but still entirely recognisable as a *latter-day* Honda Super Cab, and it bids fair to become at least as highly successful as that first commuter, which was built some sixty long years earlier. We sold quite a number of the first shipment of Cubs to nurses (and some impecunious Doctors as well) who worked at a local hospital while I worked in a nearby, outer Sydney suburban motorcycle store, the little Cub thus earning our nickname of the 'nurses' bike'. Wonder how many nurses are going to be seen flashing about on that new Super Cub?

I confess I owned, and rode, a 70cc OHC Honda Super Cub for a few years in the early to late 1970s, which was looked down upon as the butt of many a joke by other motorcycle journos, but the little bike was very handy to have when

I was busily engaged in writing numerous road test reports – including some which are included within these pages. I could leave the little machine behind in a local warehouse, or hidden in the service centre of a major distributor, as I rode off on a much larger motorcycle I would have for several days while conducting the test report. Better than leaving the family car at the importers, then arguing about this with my controller who wanted the vehicle to stay at home for her own use.

Unhappily, as something of a *'Purist'* – did somebody say 'snob?' – I cannot list the historic little Honda Super Cub as an all-time Classic Motorcycle within these pages (except here, of course), even if it does truly deserve that appellation, perhaps more so than some of the machines which are detailed herein. But at the very least we must acknowledge its outstanding place in the history of motorcycling, for that most marvellous little, bullet-proof machine, which helped carry our flag on high and was almost entirely responsible for the Phoenix-like rebirth of motorcycling worldwide, must be given the credit it so richly deserves. *I trust I have managed to do just that!*

Let's not pursue this, but there is now a whole raft of *much more modern* motorcycles which will one day enjoy Classic status, and some day, someone, somewhere will realise this and produce a book such as this which will include some of them. That will be for another time and another author, I feel, although I must say I have ridden most of these *'Neo Classic Motorcycles'* myself and reported upon them in a variety of motorcycle publications. Those motorcycles will of course include the 900SS Ducati Desmo Vee-twins; Harley's Bi-Centennial 'Sportster'; the R90S and early K-series BMW; the first CB750 Honda Four from 1968 and its later sibling, the 1978 six-cylinder CBX1000; the very swift 1972 DOHC, 900cc K1 Kawasaki; Triumph's three-cylinder 750cc OHV Trident; Kawasaki's huge, shaft-drive OHC K1300, a great six-cylinder machine; the flashing, four-cylinder, DOHC, shaft drive MV 'California'; the exciting Suzuki Katana; Honda's advanced flat-four, OHC C1000 from 1974; the three-cylinder 1300cc Laverda 'Jota'; the more 'pedestrian' Moto Guzzi 850T, and a host of others.

Add a couple of those 'others' I haven't mentioned to the list of those eighteen newer Classics and there are enough of them to be of interest to modern-day motorcyclists who may never have heard of some of the bikes I have just listed – much less those Classics detailed earlier within these pages – and the clear possibility of another book on Classic Motorcycles emerges, if from a brand-new generation: perhaps a brand-new perspective. I have ridden each and every one of those machines listed above and reported upon most of them in a variety of motorcycle publications but, creeping up to some 90 years of age at the time these words are being written, I'm not too sure about my attempting to shuffle them into a list in the preparation for another book of this type, much less chasing them up for a new series of photographs. At least not right now, if at all! But then again, the more I think about it…?

WITH THANKS:

My niece, **Ruth Maggie Morris,** from Nairne, South Australia, an Adelaide suburb, worked her magic upon many photos and illustrations which were featured in original road test reports published around 40–45 years ago in a variety of top-flight Australian motorcycle magazines. This was done by the digital processes she had learned during her studies at Adelaide University. I thank her most profusely for her great efforts, because of the chronic shortage of original material. There was a fair amount of the original, unpublished material still available, of course, courtesy of several great photographers, namely **Graham Munro, Bill Forsyth**, and friends of the late **Ray Ryan**, along with one or two others I only met very briefly at the photo shoots, and whose names I cannot remember. It was, after all, many those long years ago, but I do apologise to these nameless few, whose works, as ever, have always greatly enhanced the printed word.

My long-suffering wife, the lovely **Lyn Morris,** deserves my unfailing thanks – indeed gratitude – for her time and generosity in typing much of the text herein and for her energy and expertise in finding, and then placing, the numerous photographs which grace this tome after my instructions(?) as to where they ought to go. Many of these photos were to be found scattered about in a bewildering number of odd locations throughout my computer, as well as many without, then downloaded and placed into position with the appropriate captions. How she found many of them, and was able to move them to my designated, clearly marked, positions (so that Ron and Kristina Proft – see below – could slot them into their allocated places) is beyond me.

I must also salute **Scott Kitto**, of *Memories Studios*, Quakers Hill, who used his skills in the complete 'renovation' of old and/or badly faded, original photographs to make them look almost like new – a very neat trick. He was presented with a load of sub-standard material, including postage-stamp sized pictures on proof sheets, which were then expertly rendered to look like newly printed, full-sized photos. Then, and by no means the last or the least, the lovely **Kristina Proft**, and husband **Ron** of *Delphian Books*, Rouse Hill, whom I found almost by accident. Ron was responsible for the final design of the book, as well as its cover, and they have done a great job. Without those great professionals, the book would not have looked up to standard, or may not have been published in the first place.

Lester Morris, Sydney, Australia, 2022

A group of the boys were whooping it outside the premises of Alcock Engineering in the small, South Coast village of Bega, New South Wales, circa 1912. And what a great shot of some fine machinery from an earlier generation to those featured within these pages.

The motorcycles are: Left-to-right – Speedwell, Rudge Multi, Sunbeam, another Speedwell, Triumph, Ariel, Indian and a single-cylinder, shaft-drive Belgian FN. I mention the FN specifically for a number of reasons; firstly, most FN were four-cylinder machines (see photo of the FN Four in the Introduction, on page viii), and the man sitting on it is a dead-ringer for this book's author, Lester Morris. Of course, he is not the author, but is an 18-year-old youth named Ben Morris, fated to become the author's father more than 20 long years later; hence the remarkable likeness!

He didn't live in Bega, but had just arrived, having driven from Sydney in the first motorcar to drive into the village. He was strolling by, and as no-one was seated on the FN, he decided 'why not' and climbed aboard the machine. Three years later, Ben Morris was to make history by arriving on Gallipoli just after dawn on 25th April, 1915, Day One of the WWI fighting, as an unarmed, 'front-line' stretcher bearer, the most dangerous job of all, with a life expectancy of 14 days! However, he survived for 14 weeks before being wounded by shrapnel and was then sent back to Australia.

BSA 500cc OHV 'Gold Star'

A POTTED HISTORY: 1938 – 1956
DBD34 MODEL

Val Page was probably the most gifted of all the British motorcycle designers, a man who enjoyed a 40-year plus career while being employed at various times by several of Britain's best-known engine and/or motorcycle manufacturers. As a young man finishing his apprenticeship in the 1920s, he was instrumental in developing the famous, all-conquering J.A. Prestwich (JAP) speedway engine and the experience he gained in carburation, cam profiles, port shapes, valve angularity and gas flow during that project stood him in good stead when he later designed the sporty, single-cylinder Red Hunter Ariels and the overhead valve Triumph singles which were made in 250, 350 and 500cc capacities. The staid-looking OHV Triumph machines he designed as roadster and commuter models were tarted up by Edward Turner in 1937 and designated Tiger 70, 80 and Tiger 90, the new nomenclature hinting at their respective top speeds.

The changes were mostly cosmetic, for the fundamental designs remained essentially the same, but the new, brightly coloured machines with the upswept exhausts and exciting silver paint jobs looked very swish and became fairly popular as sports mounts. The 'new' 500cc Tiger 90 in particular, which was once the 5H roadster, benefited greatly from Page's cleverly designed, nigh-perfect port shape and over-large valves, and was initially quite a decent road iron in its guise as the apparently 'pedestrian' 5H; all it needed for greater acceptance as a sports mount was the all-new paint job and mild tune-up which Turner had bestowed upon it.

Page had by then moved to BSA and, among many other things, set about improving the performance of the company's staid 500cc roadster by again employing much of the expertise he had gained over many years in other factories. In 1937, Page totally redesigned the 500cc Blue Star plodder (which had recently been endowed with foot gear-change gearbox) and morphed it into the more sporty 500cc Empire Star, the bike soon to make history as the forerunner of what is assuredly the most successful of all British five-hundred singles – the immortal **Gold Star BSA**!

As an introduction to the all-new Empire Star five-hundred, a trial run of 800km on the banked concrete 'saucer' track at Brooklands was organised in 1937, the bike running hard for 500 miles (800km) at an average speed of 70mph (130km/h), a performance which, however impressive, was thoroughly upstaged later in 1937 by a recently retired road racer named Wal Handley. A top-flight racer, Handley had won four Isle of Man road-race events in previous years, including the first ever Junior/Senior double in 1924 – among many other victories – and was thus easily persuaded to climb aboard a specially tuned Empire Star BSA to contest an insignificant, mid-week, three-lap event on the dangerous, broken-up, pot-holed Brooklands track. The bike was a highly tuned special, with enlarged ports, racing cams, large-bore TT race carburettor – calibrated to burn alcohol fuel – a very high 13:1 compression ratio piston, and carefully tuned exhaust system.

He easily won the short event, averaging 102.57mph for the race (his top speed on the rim of the track's steep banking was just under 108mph) which allowed him to be the recipient of the British Motorcycle Racing Club's special **Gold Star** lapel pin which was awarded to anyone who bravely lapped the bumpy track at an average speed of at least 100mph.

There could just as easily have been a Gold Star New Imperial, Gold Star Norton, a Gold Star Rudge, even a Gold Star Excelsior, for the latter – fitted with one of Page's earlier JAP engines – was the only *250cc* motorcycle to claim a 100mph lap and therefore the coveted Star, but it was BSA, with its image of staid reliability rather than sporting prowess, which immortalised the Gold Star. In so doing, the company introduced a machine which was, as it evolved over the years, at its best, probably without peer among other large-capacity, single-cylinder motorcycles.

Just one year after Handley was awarded his Gold Star the first, Page-designed, *all-alloy* Gold Star BSA appeared in the 1938 BSA catalogues, still alongside the Blue Star/Empire Star from which it evolved, but there were many differences between the machines apart from the former's defining alloy head and barrel.

During its heyday the Gold Star BSA, in both 350 and 500cc forms, was all but invincible on three continents; it twice won a World Championship in Scrambles (read Moto Cross) races; it won numerous Gold Medals in the highly competitive International Six Day Trials; it was usually hard to beat in the uniquely British Observed Trials events; it ran to major places in the Daytona 200 and it was often the bike to beat in flat-track, TT and short-track events in America, as well as similar 'short circuit' events in Australia. It also won more than its fair share of long-distance races on British airfields, and the occasional (if in fact, quite rare) Speedway machine fitted with a Gold Star engine was also very successful.

To be sure, the International Norton, with its wonderful 'Featherbed' frame, and the all-alloy Triumph twins, sometimes gave the much later model Gold Star BSA a run for its money during the early and mid-1950s, and into the early 1960s. The sports Velocette 'Thruxton' models were a very hard nut to crack as well, but later model Goldies were far more versatile in every respect than any of them, and this clearly shows in their astounding list of successes.

In Australia, an overhead valve Gold Star BSA won at Bathurst when the Victorian rider Trevor Pound easily won the 1959 Junior (350cc) Australian GP on the Guilfoyle BSA – surely the world's fastest 350cc Goldie – which gave a great deal in added weight away to its much lighter rivals, the highly specialised overhead camshaft – and sometimes *double* overhead camshaft – road racing Manx Norton, KTT Velocette and 7R AJS machines.

The BSA swept all before it in the Clubman's 350cc races on the Isle of Man and other race circuits from 1950 to 1956, and easily won in the 500cc Senior class several times against spirited opposition from the other British factories as well. And all the while, the Gold Star BSA looked almost the same (at least externally!) as it evolved, while it retained a similar state of engine tune for high-speed events and long-distance touring. In fact, it was only the detailed cam profiles, length and diameter of exhaust pipes and race-tuned megaphone or road-going 'muffler', compression ratio, carburettor and gearbox ratios which distinguished one competition model from another, the high-speed road-burner from the more sedate (?) tourer.

Contrast this list of achievements with the best of today's breed, where specialisation is the name of the game and you need a different motorcycle for almost every venture from

The original 1938 BSA Gold Star, with alloy head and barrel, Amal TT carb and mag-alloy gearbox shell, but still with girder forks and rigid frame. A real 'goer', but probably up-staged by new, 1938 500cc Triumph twins.

shopping to commuting and very certainly in the many different forms of motorcycle sport. It could thus be argued that there was never a machine made in any country on earth which was as versatile as a well-tuned Gold Star BSA, even though the factory always employed that 'simple' single-cylinder, pushrod overhead valve engine.

That first ever, 1938 Gold Star BSA looked superficially not unlike the sibling from which it evolved, but there were many differences apart from the obvious alloy head and barrel on the sportier model. The cast-iron 'Blue Star' model employed a separate tower to house the pushrods for the overhead valve gear, while the new sports model had a tunnel cast into the finning of the head and barrel on the engine's right side to enclose the pushrods, the lower section on the barrel covered by a small plate to allow access to the tappets for inspection and adjustment. Photos and drawings from the time show the tapered housing to be uninterrupted, but within three months this was modified to incorporate a pair of bolts which clamped the two castings together at the junction of head and barrel, almost certainly to overcome an oil leak at that area in the pushrod tunnel.

The Amal 10TT race carburettor with which the new Goldie came equipped had no air filter, of course, and was as much a pointer to the new sports machine as the alloy castings were, but a lightweight frame with no sidecar lugs was apparently also part of the new bike's design, as photos from the period clearly show. However, there are also photos from the period which show the *Empire Star* BSA frame with no sidecar lugs on its frame either, and there were rare 1938 *Gold Star* models with sidecar lugs which are clearly visible.

The lightweight magnesium alloy gearbox was not so obvious, but the petrol tank with its tank-top toolbox was, though this was changed in 1939 to adopt the small instrument panel so beloved by enthusiasts.

The frame was unsprung at the rear, with front suspension by girder forks which were as universal then as telescopic forks are today. They looked a bit agricultural, but the skinny-looking forks, with their external springs and handwheel adjustment for friction damping, could be quite effective.

Oddly, that first BSA Goldie wasn't quite the success it might/should have been, probably because the all-new 500cc Triumph Speed Twin, which was also introduced in 1937 and refined the following year, had set the motorcycle world on its ear. The well-received twin-cylinder Triumph thoroughly up-staged the new sports BSA as a headline-grabber, and this was probably the reason for the 500 single's somewhat quiet debut.

Pre-war Goldies were a bit sparse on the ground in Australia as well, for that matter, but there were enough of them about for several of them to have survived the war and the years that followed, and for most of them to bask in the adulation they may not have received when they were brand new.

One man who could trace the evolution of the Gold Star BSA from its inception in 1938 to its last gasp in 1963 was Wal Cribbin, an engineer from Parramatta, who rejoiced in the fact that he had examples of the first Goldie from 1938, an evolutionary plunger-framed model from 1951 and the swing-arm machine from 1955, the design of which remained, with only detail modifications, until the machine's demise.

One could say that the proud possessor of a well-restored 1938 Goldie was fortunate, and doubly fortunate, to have one of the even better, sprung-frame versions of the 1950s. To have three prime examples, including the last is, for the serious enthusiast, to be thrice blessed!

The three machines are in showroom condition, the 1938 model, Wal's personal favourite, registered as a vintage machine and ridden, at the time of this report, almost as daily transport.

Lined up together, the three machines are very obviously from the same mould, for the engines are very similar, the gearboxes and some cycle parts on the post-war models virtually identical. But, just as the first M24 Gold Star differed in many ways from the M23 Empire Star, the three

Post-war, 1951 Goldie, now with very handy plunger rear suspension and first-rate telescopic front forks. A far better ride, assisted by sprung single saddle. The machine employed a larger front brake and different bore/stroke measurements. My favourite of the three.

models are quite different under the skin.

Bore and stroke dimensions of the pre-war Goldie were 82 x 94mm, the engine a typical long-stroke design with a compression ratio of a high 7.8:1, the engine developing a respectable 28BHP at 5250rpm. There were some minor detail changes to the 1939 model, with the 1940 500cc Gold Star the last of the line for 10 long years. The Gold Star BSA re-appeared in England in 1948 as a 350, with bore and stroke of 71 x 88mm, again a long-stroke engine but with a better designed set of head and barrel castings, the pushrod tunnel much neater and the rough-cast bosses for the clamp bolts gone.

The late 1949/early 1950 BSA Gold Star was available as a 500 again, its engine dimensions much more modern with bore/stroke of 85 x 88mm – very nearly 'square.' A 10TT carburettor very similar to the pre-war machine was fitted, and the crankcase and timing case castings were almost identical to the earlier machine. The tried-and-true Lucas Mag-dyno unit was again employed, these dual instruments almost universal on British singles. The Cribbin 1951 model enjoys the benefit of the much more modern suspension system with the adoption of telescopic front forks and the plunger rear suspension so popular on British machines in the 1950s. A single sprung saddle takes care of the odd nudges the suspension's 3 inches (80mm) of limited movement cannot handle. Though undamped, but grease lubricated, the plunger rear suspension was certainly a giant leap ahead of the pre-war rigid frame, even considering its comparatively short range of movement.

The front brake on the 1951 machine was a hefty 8 inches, employing the same alloy backplate unit as fitted to the much heavier twins, the front wheel wearing a steel rim of 21 inches diameter with a 300 x 21" ribbed front tyre. The pre-war Gold Star employed a 300 x 20" front hoop, but this size was slowly phased out by BSA after the war.

Wal's 1955 BB34 was again removed from the previous year's model, for it was at last fitted with the swinging-arm rear suspension adopted two years earlier on other BSA models. There were in fact some out-and-out racing BSA Gold Star machines fitted with the swing-arm frame from late *1953*, and there were some more lightly tuned 1954 Gold Stars fitted with swing-arm rear suspension, but the later frame did not appear in Australia in any real numbers at that time. An extra 40mm of rear wheel, hydraulically controlled suspension was realised with the later frame design, but was largely negated by a nearly rock hard dual-seat which allowed for very little give.

My personal preference is for the plunger rear suspension Goldie, provided of course the near-ubiquitous sprung saddle is used, even if the bike does move about a bit more and chatter happily over uneven surfaces at speed. What happened with the latest Gold Star was that, along with the 'better' swing-arm frame came a slight lengthening of the machine's wheelbase from just under 55 inches to just under 57 inches, and with it a touch 'slower' – albeit quite subtle – handling. Again, the bike was just 4 pounds heavier at 380 pounds, but much of the weight seemed to be attached to the steering head by some strange alchemy (or a change in the steering head angle) for the bike was very obviously heavier to steer at low speeds, particularly in traffic. There is no doubt the heavier duplex frame with its full-cradle engine support was a more rigid assembly and removed much of the gentle 'weaving' for which the earlier Gold Star was noted, but overall, I much prefer the feel of the earlier design.

Piston slap had been almost a feature of the BSA 500 singles for some time and, while by no means detrimental to the machine's welfare, it was noisy in the cast-iron engines and – to be kind – quite intrusive in the alloy models where the castings actually amplified the noise. This forced the adoption of a shorter connecting-rod in 1954, a reduction of almost 1 inch when the 6½ inch rod was fitted. The gudgeon eye was lowered in the piston and this meant more meat above the pin, with a touch less rocking action and thereby a somewhat quieter-running engine. At the same time the 500cc Goldie employed an improved oil feed to the big-end assembly, and adopted flywheels which were more oval in shape: the reason for the latter modification has never been fully explained.

BSA took advantage of this major design change to adopt a much larger alloy barrel with much heavier fins, with a more heavily finned cylinder head to match. The engine, which looked much more purposeful, was still instantly identifiable because the crankcase and timing case castings remained virtually identical to the earlier models – including that first machine nearly two decades before!

Nor did the modifications end there, for shorter, more solid-looking Duralumin-alloy pushrods *without tappets* were adopted, the necessary valve-lash adjustment effected by eccentric rocker spindles. Adjustments could be carried out simply by slackening off the domed rocker-spindle nuts and turning the other end of the eccentric spindles with a wide-bladed screwdriver. For some reason, I suspect to allow for ease in lining up the pushrods when re-assembling the engine, the plate formerly used for tappet inspection and adjustment still sat demurely screwed to the base of the pushrod tunnel.

To take advantage of the lighter, tappet-less pushrods and allow higher engine speeds and thus more power, the later Goldies employed shorter, lighter valves, with a larger diameter head for the inlet and special material for the exhaust valve. Nimonic-80 was sometimes used for the exhaust, and there were some machines with sodium-cooled stems, the hollow valve stem filled with sodium and then sealed. These special valves were intended for use with very high compression ratios and alcohol fuels, especially in long-distance races.

In a further attempt at lightening the overhead valve train, the shorter valves springs, which were also shot-peened to relieve surface tension, were retained by light alloy valve collars and lighter collets, the latter firmly located by thin circlips.

A late model Gold Star BSA, depending on its state of tune, but assuming it to be in Clubman racing trim, could crank out just over 40BHP at a very high 7000rpm. The engine was said to be safe for short bursts to 7500rpm but was on the edge of its reliability after that.

With megaphone exhaust and full development, running a high-comp piston and methanol fuel, the best Goldie might push out close to 50BHP, by any standards a fantastic achievement for a pushrod 500 single, for it was then almost on par with the power output of the racing OHC Manx Norton.

BSA singles always leaked a film of oil from the timing case breather – in fact both the pre-war and 1954 models Wal owns leaked a few drops from this breather on our test rides – but BSA addressed this problem with a new rotary breather fitted into the timing case and driven by the magneto gear on the late models. The disc was held into the cover by a spring and was 'timed' to breathe into an outlet pipe under the timing case. Rather than a direct drive from the magneto gear to the rev-counter gearbox, a slot in the outer face of the disc engaged with the drive spindle on the little 'gearbox'.

A new-style gearbox with neater shape and more efficient gear selection was used with the swing-arm frame models, while the pressed-metal primary chain-case from the earlier models was finally abandoned in favour of a trim alloy case which looked a whole lot better and was at last free of oil leaks. The clutch was also vastly improved, both in its efficiency and the smoothness of its operation.

These changes, by no means as minor as they may have seemed, remained with the Gold Star till the end of its days (which, unhappily, were not far off), the latest models rejoicing in large, full-width, 8-inch front brakes, clip-on handlebars, rear-set footrests and reversed gear-lever. The exhaust system was carefully tuned and remarkably efficient, while carburation was looked after by a huge 1½ inch Amal Grand Prix carburettor with a long, wide-open bell-mouth which seemed large enough to catch unwary pigeons.

Wal Cribbins's 1955 Gold Star has the later sports/racing 'Clubman' exhaust system fitted, along with its attendant GP carburettor, the 2-inch diameter exhaust 'drainpipe' carefully tuned for length as it curves neatly across the timing case and exhausts into a tuned megaphone which is 'hidden' within the impressively long, tapered muffler. There are a series of baffles at the tail-end of the long muffler just after the in-built megaphone, and they do take the edge off the exhaust a bit, but when someone a block or two away starts his Clubman Goldie in the morn for a pre-dawn rasp into the countryside you are bound to know all about it

The Cribbins BSAs are not entirely original, but similar modifications have been affected the world over to enhance a bike's performance, and are just as acceptable in this country. The 1938 Gold Star has a 1939 petrol tank fitted, and it has had the much later Amal Concentric carburettor fitted in the interests of easy starting and much more civilised road manners. Both bikes will start in a kick or two, and both idle (almost) like well-oiled Swiss watches. Gold Star BSAs were *never* renowned for this, for the specialised racing Amal Carbs had no idle jetting and no throttle-stop screw adjustment, so were very difficult to start without the right drill and were never happy idling.

They were never terribly happy running slowly either, for the 10TT was an unashamed racing carburettor and was never intended to be used often – if at all! – in cut-and-thrust traffic conditions or in day-to-day commuting; the more efficient, huge GP carburettors were, arguably, more temperamental and even less suitable to slow running.

To say the simple Amal Concentrics have transformed the two earlier Goldies might be pushing things just a bit, but no Gold Star BSA in my experience has ever showed much liking for quietly plonking away at idle speed.

The pre-war M24 Goldie feels to be the quite light bike it is and shows its tendency to be even lighter at the steering head, with the tendency for the bike to flop into corners which was always so typical of the low-slung frame and girder front forks. The girders rattle a little over bumps, while the rear stand, which springs up behind the rear guard, adds its own harmonics to a bike which is a delight to see, and pleasant to ride. Naturally it graunches into gear as they all did, but the modified clutch, which is from the later, Val Page-designed Army BSA M20 model, is light and progressive, the standard gear ratios well suited to the engine's grunt.

On the other hand, the plunger-sprung 1951 model proved to be a delight, with its more stolid feel by virtue of its extra weight, and the undoubted comfort of its much more modern suspension system. The ZB34 was fitted with the semi-close ratio gear set and was not quite so easy to move away from rest, needing just a touch

The final iteration in 1956, with longer-travel, swing-arm rear suspension, not helped by firm dual-seat. Fitted with a huge, 1½" (38mm) Grand Prix 'full-race' carburettor, sports cams, high-compression piston, tuned exhaust, and high-geared, close-ratio gearbox. A very swift machine, indeed!

more of clutch and a squirt more of throttle. I'd bet it has a racier cam as well, because it was typically a little hesitant just off the idle, but came good with a very satisfying rush as soon as the engine speed began to pick up.

Unhappily, the rides were all too brief, for Wal's time was limited and it was raining heavily as well – which didn't help the photographs – so there was no chance to squirt the machines as they deserved (and clearly wanted) to be squirted. But I was able to put a later model, a 1956 DBD34 Gold Star BSA, well and truly through its paces at another time and in another place, which was something else again. The last of these Gold Star models were finally made almost to 'Special Order', and were usually available only in Clubman-racer trim with all the go-fast bits which were not always specified, including the ultra-close ratio gearbox which could be such a pain in traffic. You could ride one of these latest models as daily transport if that was your wish, but that was not where these machines really shone, because you really had to learn how to come to grips with the starting procedure for the big GP carburettor, and how to handle the large Amal when the bike was finally underway.

While the Cribbins 1955 model was fitted with the standard, swept-back exhaust and mega 'silencer', and with the big 1½ inch GP fitted especially for us; it usually wears the large 38mm Amal Concentric, a much more civilised instrument. It also carried some of the special items which were so readily available when the Goldie was new, but for which one sometimes had to wait weeks after a machine had been ordered. However, it was not fitted with the rear-set footrests or reverse gear lever fitted to the later DBD34 models.

The most popular Gold Star cams were the *65-2448* inlet and *65-2450* exhaust combination, and these were used for Clubman racing or high-speed touring, while there were other cams which could be specified for Scrambles, Trials, GP events and so on. There were at least five sets of gear ratios from the ultra-close to ultra-wide, several compression ratio pistons, and countless fiddly bits. I am sure, by the way in which it performed in a later Gold Star test report, the 1956 DBD34 which I borrowed from Col Brenchley's Aladdin-like, cavernous garage for a later ride, and subsequent report, had these cams fitted.

Among the 'fiddly bits' with which the Brenchley DBD34 Goldie came equipped was the powerful after-market twin-leading shoe front brake made by the British specialist tuner Eddie Dow, which was augmented by a much more acceptable, longer and more softly padded dual-seat. The bike came equipped with rear-set footrests, clip-on handlebars (and genuine thumb-squashers-on-the-fuel-tank at that!) and reversed gear lever. The latter meant that gear changes were the opposite of normal BSA, and were now 'one down and three up', the same as the Triumph pattern. It took some getting used to, but as ever the gear changes could be made as fast as hand and foot could move.

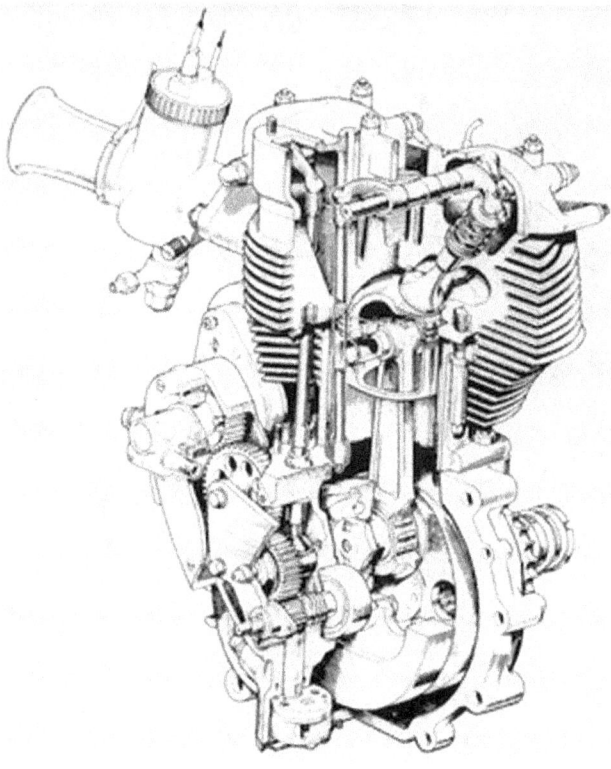

Deceptively 'simple', pushrod, 500cc OHV Gold Star BSA engine, fitted with this huge, 38mm AMAL Grand Prix carburettor, was probably the most successful single-cylinder engine of its type. At its best it could be tuned to run on very high compression ratios, burning alcohol fuel and producing almost as much power as the venerable 500cc OHC Manx Norton race engines.

It would be better for both rider and machine if the owner of a late model 500cc 'full-house' Gold Star BSA was to live in either a large country town or on the fringes of a large city, where the rider could very quickly get out of town and onto a major road in the open air to enjoy the best that this highly-tuned machine could offer, for it is certainly not at its best within the confines of any sort of city traffic, be it heavy or light.

Because of the great front brake and the high-mounted footrests, the Brenchley Gold Star was a real gem out on the open road, where it could be pelted hard into a series of fine, fast corners or tight Ess-bends with great enthusiasm, often after playing 'Boy Racers' by diving late into them under heavy braking and quickly slipping down through the ultra-close ratio gearbox. Slow corners need a juggling act between throttle and clutch to keep the engine on the boil, but once the clutch was fully home, the bike would pull away with all the grunt of a large express train, in particular on steep uphill stretches, where it would dig in and drive hard to make light of even the heaviest gradients. What a joy it was to ride that frisky bike hard on the open road, which is its true domain.

The low, clip-on handlebars on the later Goldie did no favours at all to the heaviness of the steering at low speeds, but the heaviness disappeared entirely at much higher speeds, while the excessive weight usually forced upon wrists and reproductive organs also disappeared as wind pressure at those speeds with the unstreamlined machine forced a more upright riding position which eased the problem quite perceptibly.

Starting from rest, uphill and with a pillion passenger while pulling the tall 8.7:1 first gear, was a daunting prospect – I only tried it just once, and then only to see what it would be like! – the 1956 Goldie capable of more than 60mph in first gear if you wound it well out before you needed to slot into second! Unlike the ZB34, the more highly tuned DBD34 machine needed an even greater fistful of throttle and some very judicial use of the clutch if it was to make a smooth getaway – even when ridden solo – and this was no easy thing to do in heavy traffic.

Top speed *on the road* with a fully-equipped Clubman Gold Star BSA was in excess of 110mph in the old money, which made the DBD34 possibly the fastest pushrod 500cc single-cylinder motorcycle in the mid-1950s to early 1960s, while only just shading the very swift *Velocette* 'Thruxton' 500 single; itself a marvellous machine with an outstanding open road performance.

There was probably never a motorcycle

The Brenchley DBD34 Gold Star was some performer, set up almost entirely as a 'road-going' racer with all the engine 'go-fast' bits, allied to 'Boy Racer' clip-on handlebars, rear-set foot rests and reversed gear leaver. Here it is moving very swiftly into a glorious, sweeping left hander. In this guise it was not the most comfortable machine to ride, but who cares? The Goldie was such an exciting machine to ride hard, and that was all there was to it!

for which such a wide diversity of special equipment was available ex-factory, if not always ex-stock, and the machine – which sold in reasonable numbers – was quite a popular racing motorcycle in this country, as it was in probably every other country on earth. More so as a 350, if only because riders could compete on the same machine in both the 350cc 'Junior' and 500cc 'Senior' events on the same programme, and in the so-called 'Unlimited' class as well – if the starting line-up in the latter event was bit light on and needed to be padded-out, it should be said.

Our thanks were given to **Wal Cribbins** for loaning us three well-prepared examples of the evolution of the Gold Star BSA, a machine ahead of the game in its time, and a machine still winning its fair share of races around the world in Classic race programmes. I must also thank **Col Brenchley**, for the loan of his 1956 DBD34 model for a later test ride, that final evolution of a machine which was to remain almost unaltered from that date until the last Gold Star BSA was seen, quite sadly, to be wheeled out of the British factory in 1963.

Here is a serious, full spec 500cc Gold Star BSA racer from the 1950s. At its best this machine was unapproachable in Clubman racing, but it could give a good shake-up to some GP machines on the tighter, more twisting circuits. With a full fairing, race cams, high compression piston, that massive carburettor and tuned exhaust it was capable of over 130mph in the old money.

The giant company, Mahindra of India is now building an all-new Gold Star BSA. The water-cooled, multi-valve single is now a full-blown 650cc DOHC design, featuring disc brakes all round, while producing 45BHP, about the same as the racing DBD34, 500cc single above. With some very judicious tuning, the engine could produce 60BHP, which would make this machine a real flyer!

TECH SPECS

(Brenchley 500cc DBD34 BSA)

Make: BSA

Model: DBD34

Year of manufacture: 1956

Type:
All-alloy overhead valve air-cooled single-cylinder four-stroke. Valves controlled by Duralumin pushrods, from cams at base of cylinder to rockers carried on eccentric spindles. Bolted up crankshaft, with caged roller big-end, ball and roller main bearings.

Bore x stroke: 85 x 88mm

Capacity: 499cc

Claimed power @ rpm: 38BHP @ 7000rpm

Compression ratio: 8:1

Carburation: 38mm Amal GP Race carburettor: no air filter.

Ignition/Lighting: Lucas Mag-dyno instrument: magneto ignition; incorporating 6-volt generator.

Transmission: Single-row, ½" x 5/16" primary chain in alloy, semi-oil bath chaincase to the separate four-speed gearbox, with final drive by chain.

Gear ratios (overall):
1st – 8.7:1; 2nd – 5.99:1; 3rd – 4.96:1; 4th – 4.52:1. Right foot change, one down, three up (with reversed gear lever).

Frame:
Brazed tubular steel, with duplex down-tubes and full-cradle engine support.

Suspension:
Front – BSA pattern telescopic forks with coil springs and two-way damping.
Rear – swing-arm, with combined Girling spring/damper units, with three-way adjustments.

Wheels, brakes:
Front – Dunlop alloy rim laced to hub containing Taylor-Dow twin-leading shoe brake plate operating in BSA 200mm drum brake.

Rear – Alloy rim laced to standard BSA hub containing 155mm single-leader drum brake.

Dimensions:
Wheelbase – 1350mm;
Ground clearance – 125mm;
Seat height – 760mm;
Weight – 174kg; Tank capacity – 19 litres.

Performance:
(from original DBD34 road test, June 1955)
Top speed – 185km/h;
Standing-start, ¼ mile – 13 sec;
Braking (from 50km/h) – 8.8 m;
Fuel consumption (overall) – 14.5km/l.

1938/1951/1955 Machines loaned by:
WAL CRIBBINS, Sydney, for purpose of historic, direct comparison.

The 1956 Machine loaned by:
COL BRENCHLEY, Sydney, for later road test report.

1933 Ardie HBK503 'Meran'

500cc OHV 'GENTLEMEN'S TOURER'

It is true to say that, in these days of computerised motorcycle design, and more than a little input from robot, or at least hands-free assembly of some very complex machines, there will never be another motorcycle quite like the 500cc, single-cylinder, **1933 Ardie HBK503 'Meran'**. In fact, even when the machine was built in Germany, there would have been very few motorcycles which carried anywhere near as much additional bolt-on, luxury material as this bike had. It fairly bristled with a huge assortment of oddments which were clearly bolted on some time after the base machine was assembled.

Many of the additions were necessary, but by no means all of them were, for the 500cc single cylinder German Ardie was what they referred to in those days as the '*Compleat Gentlemen's Luxury Tourer*', the likes of which are nowhere to be seen today – even if you add the huge Honda Gold Wing juggernaut and a host of long-wheelbase Cruisers to the mix.

Just one of many examples of the extra mile the builders of this extremely rare motorcycle went to is the addition of a large, heavily chrome-plated metal box affixed to the top of the wide, large-capacity fuel tank. In passing, the tank carries no fewer than **two** tank caps at the front and on opposite sides, assumedly to make it easy to fill the tank no matter which side the petrol-pump hose happens to be on! Mustn't scratch the tank, and thus mar the pristine chrome or pale olive-green paint job, must we!

The shallow box is hinged at the front and would carry a pair of stout gloves and perhaps a sandwich or two (or even a hip flask, if required) but it also displays a simple instrument panel consisting of an eight-day clock and an ammeter, with a glass compartment on top of the box to allow a touring map, or a shopping list, to be clearly seen. The very handy, solid box was obviously fitted to the tank as a standard accessory, for it screws in place as if it was always meant to be there, and it sits firmly atop a moulded rubber mat. The speedo and odometer sit in a tiny, postage-stamp sized glass window on top of the rear of the headlamp shell, and is of course illuminated at night.

A very substantial, clamp-on, moulded grab-handle is attached at a special point mid-way along the left upper frame rail which is there to assist a gentleman in lifting the bike onto its centre stand; naturally, the handle is heavily chrome plated, it fits into the palm perfectly and is ideally positioned to greatly assist the rider in easing the bike onto the stand. The 'humble' Ardie centre-stand is a thing of joy for it employs an easily accessible, rubber-tipped lever to stand upon, which utilises a fulcrum action to allow a rider to effortlessly haul the bike onto the stand's egg-shaped, double-curved, 'roll-on' legs. A Gentlemen's Grand Tourer indeed, for the bike can *almost* be heaved onto its centre stand with the rider still seated; if the rider's legs happen to be long enough!

I won't be quite so bold as to say the Ardie is the most beautiful motorcycle I have seen, for it comes from the hand-built era of nuts and bolts and not terribly flowing lines, but it certainly comes very close indeed to being a thing of beauty, for it sparkles in the sunlight with its light ivory/olive green colour scheme and heavy chrome plating as few machines can hope to do in this era of mass production.

Another area which bristles with great attention to detail is in the machine's rear suspension, of which there is none – at least not at the rear wheel itself. If there is no rear suspension, one could *almost* say it is not necessary, for the rider's single, soft rubber saddle is hung from its nose, cantilever-style, with a single, horizontal spring directly beneath it, which is able to be adjusted to a rider's weight by the agency of a large, chrome-plated 'wing-nut' which can be easily screwed in or out to provide an infinitely variable degree of suspension to the seat. Of course, the spring is entirely invisible, for it resides inside its very own chrome-plated sleeve, away from prying eyes.

As a matter of interest, the cantilever-mounted sprung saddle was adopted by several other German factories in much later years, including Hoffman, NSU, Victoria, Zundapp and as a standard fitting on all BMW machines from the 250cc single cylinder up to the sports R69S 600cc twin. However, most German motorcycles were fitted with dual-seats when specified for export.

It is not only in the near perfection of the Ardie's total restoration that beauty is to be found, for the machine has been restored to no more than its original showroom condition. It's in the fact that the Ardie was well removed from its fellows some 90 years ago, when it was first built. It bears no comparison to modern motorcycles.

But if the Ardie looks as though it has just come from the showroom floor then it didn't get that way by accident. The rare machine enjoyed a very chequered history before it landed on these shores, for it was badly in need of a complete restoration before it could even be fired up and ridden. The story is an interesting one – and there are as many of these types of stories as there are classic motorcycles.

Enter Heinz Sommerfield, of Hamburg (Germany), who is a collector who owns an identical model. Heinz's spotless RBK503 has won prizes in Veteran and Vintage rallies all over Europe. He visited Australia in 1976 and brought the bike with him, riding it from Fremantle to Adelaide, then Melbourne, and finally to Sydney.

I will repeat that: A German enthusiast, riding one of the very few, almost unknown examples of a 1933 Ardie RBK503, rode that priceless motorcycle a third of the way round Australia, *that's almost 4,500 kilometres*, with every confidence in the bike's ability to do so – and he made the long journey with no problems whatsoever.

Sommerfield returned to Germany vowing to return someday and was amazed to discover yet another RBK503 in Germany. These machines are now just three Merans known to exist in those two Nations, although there are a very, very few recently discovered in, of course, America. Heinz decided to send the latest discovery all the way to Australia, to the enthusiast Vin Minogue in Melbourne for a complete restoration, so he could return to Australia to ride the Ardie in the International Veteran and Vintage Rally in 1978.

The bike arrived in November, 1977, in a 505 kg crate. It was found to be in a very sorry state indeed, the engine literally worn out, the cycle parts and general paint work almost beyond redemption. Working every free moment he could afford, it took Vin just over a year to restore the bike. He put more than 1000 hours into the project, and relied on a great deal of highly specialised help from craftsmen in various trades.

Virtually every nut and bolt had to be replaced, with more than 300 items rechromed. Many items were made from scratch. The paintwork is an exact match to samples sent from Germany, with every item on the machine restored as near as possible to the original, for of course nothing was available from Germany for the engine, tinware, numerous 'add-ons', or running gear.

Unhappily, the bike could not be finished in time for Sommerfield to ride it in the international event, but he came anyway, arriving in time to help with some of the detail work and offer some valuable advice before he flew back to Germany. The bike was finished in March 1979.

According to Vin Minogue, via Heinz Sommerfield, the bike is authentic in every detail, right down to the (natural) adoption of metric nuts and bolts – which were not easy to obtain in 1979 – and the unusual colour scheme. To detail the work which went into the restoration would fill this report twice o'er but it should be sufficient to remark that I have yet to see a better example of the restorer's art, or a machine which is such a thing of beauty in its natural state.

The Ardie's open road performance is a revelation in easy, relaxed touring. The old, slow-revving engine fires up at about every 10 metres, but is able to take the steepest hills in top gear with a touch more throttle. The bike belongs very much to a more relaxed era, but can still show a very brisk turn of speed if you care to screw the throttle open a notch or two.

The engine idles with more than a touch of vibration – in fact nearly all the 'loose' bits jump and rattle about – but the moment the bike is underway the old thumper evens itself out well. The owner claims the bike will effortlessly cruise all day at 110 to 120km/h, which I don't doubt for I found the engine to be much smoother once underway than many modern multi-cylinder machines. This is very unusual for a large-capacity single cylinder motorcycle.

Hand gear change was very much in vogue in the mid-1930s, and the Ardie of course comes so equipped. The chrome-plated gear lever, as the cliché goes, falls easily to hand, but hides coyly behind the right knee-grip rubber on the petrol tank. The lever pulls up and back for first, then down through the gear-gate for the next three gears.

It's possible, at slow speeds, to slip down from top into the lower gears, but it needs a walking pace to select first gear silently. Each gear engagement announces itself by a 'notchy' click through the hand lever, but there is never a suggestion of a gear not engaging, even though it cannot be selected as positively as on the later, 'positive-stop' foot change machines.

The only hassle is first gear, which cannot be selected at rest unless the machine is rocked forward slightly as the lever is pushed home. Minogue assures me it has always been like that, but it is a bit of a drag for it lets everybody know it has been selected by an alarming, loud graunching sound. Once underway the gears all select without drama, including the offending low gear.

Finicky attention to minute detail is a feature of the German machine. Its colour scheme of deep ivory (and just a hint of milky green), with dark green and white pin-striping and lashings of heavy chrome, must have been unusual when many of its contemporaries were finished in black-on-black; albeit with their own fair share of chromium plate. While the bland specifications of the Ardie Meran may appear unexciting by modern standards, this cannot detract from a machine which looks like a Concourse winner from every angle, and which doesn't disappoint no matter

Even though the machine displays the usual 'nuts-and-bolts' design of the 1930s, it is covered with numerous luxury inclusions. Note the heavy, cast-steel Ardie tank nameplate, the 'flip-up' container screwed to the top of the tank, and the Classic, long gearchange lever, its gear-gate hidden behind the rubber knee-pad on the fuel tank. Also, the easy 'roll-on' centre stand, auxiliary clutch release foot-pedal and well-drilled heat shield on the upswept exhaust pipe.
Finally, the rear suspension unit for the cantilever-mounted, rubber single saddle. The horizontal chrome slider contains a long spring, adjustable for rider weight by a large wing-nut, with a close-fitting rubber 'snubber' inserted to control spring oscillation.
Great stuff!

how detailed the examination.

The Ardie power-plant – as a perfect example of this point appears to be a fairly ordinary 500 single; but even here the bike springs a surprise. Made by Augustus Bark, of Dresden, the pushrod OHV engine employs an 84 x 90mm bore/stroke configuration, with a single cam to operate both valves *via* simple, flat cam followers and a pair of long pushrods. The single-lobe camshaft is gear-driven in the base of the timing case from a normal half-time pinion which is keyed to the end of the crankshaft.

An exhaust-valve-lifter lever is mounted on top of the right crankcase, close by the upswept exhaust pipe. This allows the slow-revving single to be kicked over with ease; although it would be easy enough anyway, thanks to the engine's rock-bottom 5.8:1 compression ratio.

Sited outboard of the circular timing case is the external magneto. It is gear-driven from the camshaft, as is the horizontal, shuttle-type oil pump which lies directly beneath it. The magneto is fitted with manual advance/retard control by cable from the left handlebar. The advance/retard is not just for easier starting; a slight retardation of the spark allows even better pulling from low engine revs in the higher gears.

The engine appears to be a wet-sump design, but closer scrutiny reveals a dry-sump system with the large oil container cast as part of the crankcase, though it's carried ahead of the crank chamber and wrapped beneath it. Well ribbed, more for appearance than an aid to cooling or increased strength, the oil container's position imbues the engine with a solid, strong look.

The design is reminiscent of the lubrication system used so successfully on the later Royal Enfield singles. A large metal cap on the container's left side allows the lubricant to be replenished, with the oil pump pick-up-point – just ahead of the magneto on the engine's right-hand side – fitted with a screw-in wire-mesh filter.

Oil is pumped under pressure to the timing side main bearing, then to the timing gears (including the magneto and pump drives) and along the hollow main-shaft to the caged roller big-end bearing. An external pipe carries the lubricant from the base of the timing case to the main bearings on the drive side, via an oil union at the base of the cylinder and a series of internal drill-ways.

A thin, external oil line between the pushrod tubes conducts lubricant from the top of the timing case to the overhead valve gear, the oil returning to the case via the pushrod tubes, incidentally lubricating the tips of the cam-followers which locate the ball-ends of the two long pushrods. The base of the twin, chrome-plated tubes slide up to allow easy access to the tappet adjusters located on the *bottom* of the pushrods: not unlike the late, lamented pre-war 500cc Tiger 90 singles. This feature, along with the detachable end cover over the contact breaker points and the simple horizontal carburettor, makes for very easy 'home' maintenance indeed.

The engine is inclined forward at about 15 degrees in the frame, cylinder head and barrel being heavily cast iron. The head features dual exhaust ports feeding a pair of fat upswept pipes with heat shields attached. The whole design is a masterpiece of symmetry, while still displaying the solid 'nuts-and-bolts' engineering which was so typical of the era. Again, as we have noted, part of the design philosophy of the era between the Wars, the semi-unit construction four-speed gearbox design employs the ubiquitous hand gear change.

Primary drive to the damp clutch is on the engine's left side by 9.5mm x 5.5mm duplex chain, the same size (Imperial $^3/_8$" x $^7/_{32}$") as the chains fitted to British BSA twins of the 1950s. The generator drive is from the same side and also by chain – between the primary-drive sprockets. The entire drive assembly is contained within a matt-finish, aluminium alloy chain case.

Typically, the engine sprocket employs a cam-and-spring shock-absorber unit, and the primary-chain case has a drain plug to ensure the oil level is not above the lower run of chain, for the clutch (which is essentially dry, or at best 'damp') would slip if too much oil was used in the primary drive case. The oil is there only to lubricate the chain.

The final drive chain is also totally enclosed, and well lubricated by a special pipe which carries condensed oil mist from the crankcase breather onto the front run of chain as it rounds the final drive sprocket. Though totally enclosed and well-sealed, the rear chain-case is not an oil bath. On checking, I found the rear chain very well lubricated but not a drop leaked from the case to spoil the showroom glitter of the old warhorse.

The Ardie is fitted with a free-wheeling device in top gear which is quite probably unique in motorcycling. Try as I may I couldn't nut out how the odd thing worked. But with no less an authority than the brilliant Australian engineer/designer Phil Irving also stumped by the device, I am in very good company.

Of course, the device has only been viewed on the machine with half of its workings visible, but it remains a mystery nonetheless. It works, and works well for one can feel it engage and disengage, which is probably all that matters. The device is fitted on the final drive sprocket. You can see a collar and couple of spines, the sprocket and chain, and nothing else. On the overrun, shutting the throttle in heavy traffic or descending steep hills while in top gear – where the rear wheel would normally 'drive' the engine – the free-wheel device disengages and allows the bike to run along without benefit of engine braking (I assume conserving fuel is the prime function). When the throttle is opened again, drive is resumed.

Because of this odd device the Ardie needs good brakes, particularly when descending steep hills, but the bike is well served in this area by a pair of 30mm wide, 203mm (8") drum brakes. Naturally, changing back to third gear allows full engine braking when required, and the other gears can also be used.

The brakes are coupled, with the foot lever controlling both front and rear, or the handlebar lever applying the front brake on its own. The rear brake pedal operates a small crank which pulls the rear rod into operation, at the same time as it pulls the world's longest front brake cable to apply the front anchor. The levers are a little spongy in general feel, but allow a progressive control nonetheless.

To save the embarrassment of being pelted up the road if you are forced to brake hard when cranked over halfway round a corner, there is automatically more pressure on the rear brake, and you can always use the front brake lever as a manual override if you need both brakes applied (while upright of course!) in an emergency. At no time was the fact that the coupled brakes being controlled by the less sensitive foot lever was evident, and there was never any drama when braking hard to test their effectiveness. I didn't apply the brakes heavily while cranked over, of course, but Vin Minogue – the bike's restorer/owner – assures me he has covered many hundreds of miles to rallies and competed in various gymkhana events without undue drama.

If the overall engine design is not very remarkable, the frame and cycle parts are something else again, for most of these components are hand made with great care and attention. The fuel tank is a work of art, with its strong wedge shape and beautiful finish of heavy chrome panels relieved with deep ivory-green and dark-green pin-striping.

As I have noted, the tank's top has twin petrol caps and the small, lockable box in which the itinerant motorcyclist of the period could carry a pack of sandwiches and perhaps a banana and some cigars. It isn't deep enough to carry an apple, though you could probably squash a pear in there if you tried hard enough. The tank box's clear 'window' carries a map of Murrumbeena in it, as a reminder of the suburb where Vin Minogue used to live.

Handlebars are neat and uncluttered, with little more than the usual clutch and brake levers, but also employing a small lever on the left-hand side to control the magneto's manual spark advance, with a matching lever on the right side for the air slide in the carburettor. A small trigger lever on the left side carries a cable into the headlamp shell to control the position of the lamp's reflector. *Reflector?* Yes, the headlamp has a single-filament bulb and can only be dipped, or

A true 'Gentlemen's Tourer', a type of motorcycle unknown to today's riders. The Ardie, with its dual exhaust ports and upswept exhaust, was a real joy to ride. Everything in its rightful place, the bike smooth and silent, with a handy performance if you screwed the wick up a notch or two: the 1930s rider would have loved it! Note the perfectly placed handgrip and large leverage arm for pulling the bike gently onto its 'roll-on' centre stand.

raised, by moving the entire reflector within the headlamp shell! Some pre-war Morris 8/40 cars – among many others – had a similar system, but the 8/40 was *electrically* controlled by rheostat from the dipper switch.

The Ardie is very much a product of its era, which is why the suspension consists of simple, dual-spring girder forks up front and no rear suspension. Hand wheel adjusters on the sides of the girders apply pressure to fibre discs in the friction dampers which then exert some measure of control over the action of the dual fork springs; but they could never be as smooth as the later telescopic forks in their action.

That the tail end of the German beauty is extremely comfortable is thanks to the single saddle being supported at its nose and having that built-in cantilever suspension system. The horizontal spring contained with a pair of chromed sliding members, is said to allow just over 20 cm (that's all of 8 inches!) of movement. This proved to be more than sufficient to soak up every type of road bump with an ease I found hard to accept, although the rear wheel could skip about a bit over heavy corrugations – and Melbourne's tram-lines!

There is no doubt the sprung saddle was far more comfortable than some swinging-arm rear suspension units currently in vogue, though I'll admit the rear wheel spent some of its time in the air over really rough going, particularly under heavy braking! But with the sprung seat working in conjunction with a set of old girders which were also more comfortable than they had any right to be, the 90-year-old Ardie remains amongst the most comfortable **Classic** machines I've ridden for some time.

It must be said that the front forks chattered a bit over rough going, and the handling was sometimes a bit uncertain, but it was a small price to pay for a delightful ride on a genuine Luxury Tourer. Perhaps the only disadvantage of the sprung saddle is that you feel a little insecure in the beginning, simply because the saddle mounting is essentially very flexible. But a few moments spent bouncing over the rough roadways soon brings the advantages of such a system into sharp focus.

The engine is low slung in the frame, with much of its mass below wheel-spindle height. This allows for a low centre of gravity and a low saddle height, which encourages quite high cornering speeds – if the road surface is smooth and the whim moves you that way.

The frame is another work of art, having no fewer than 12 forged lugs into which the various frame tubes are brazed without a single blemish. It's almost as though the many joints which hold the solid duplex-tube frame together were securely *glued* in place.

Little touches of luxury abound – from the chromed hand wheels which apply pressure to the front fork friction dampers, to the forged-steel linkages which locate the girder forks to the frame, to the large metal tank badges and the heavy, personalised steering damper knob. Perhaps it isn't possible to hand build such a machine in the more frantic 21st century – but if that's progress…?

Both front and rear mudguards are deeply valanced, probably to keep the shine on your brogues; the guards themselves are both wide and deep and finished without a blemish.

Witness the stays with which they are mounted to the frame. The stays are tubular and attached to the *outside* of guards in tiny indentations, further located by smart looking, cast-steel chrome-plated saddles and locked by chrome-plated, captive studs and chromed 'acorn' nuts. The rear section of the rear guard detaches (but leaves the valance behind) by unscrewing a pair of hand-levers on the side and swinging the blade clear to allow wheel removal.

Between each pair of rear-guard stays are neat, lockable toolboxes which sit on either side of the guard, directly above the upswept mufflers. They just may carry the odd champagne flute to complement the sandwiches and squashed pear.

Apparently, there were some examples of other Ardie motorcycles which were fitted with the English JAP engine, and there were many other Ardie models made over the years from the factory's inception in 1919 to its demise in 1958. In the early 1930s the factory made many machines with aluminium frames; machines from as small as 125cc to huge 600cc singles. The factory started production with a 350cc two-stroke machine in 1919, and ended coincidentally with a 350cc two-stroke twin in 1958.

I have yet to see another example of the marque – its rarity would certainly see to that – but if I did stumble upon one, and it was as good as the RBK503 Ardie Meran, it would be some motorcycle!

TECH SPECS

Make: Ardie

Model: RBK503

Type:
Single-cylinder 500cc pushrod overhead valve four-stroke, with two-valve head, dual exhaust ports and twin, 'upswept' exhaust pipes and mufflers, cast-iron head and barrel. Engine and gearbox are semi-unit construction.

Bore x stroke: 84 x 90mm

Compression ratio: 5.8:1

Power @ rpm: 22BHP @ 4600rpm

Carburation:
AMAL 29 Type, $1^{1}/_{16}$" bore.

Electrics:
Magneto ignition. Bosch 6-volt/45-watt generator. Wet lead/acid battery.

Primary drive:
By duplex, 9.5mm x 5.5mm chain to four-speed hand-change gearbox. Gear rations unknown.

Frame wheels, brakes:
Single down-tube, 'full cradle' tubular steel frame, 19" wheels, 350 x 19" ribbed front, 400 x 19" block rear tyres. Large, 8" x 30mm wide, coupled drum brakes front and rear. Front suspension by girder forks, with no rear suspension, but has a rubber, cantilever-hung single saddle suspended upon a horizontal, fully adjustable, long-travel, enclosed coil spring.

Dimensions:
Length – 2160mm; Wheelbase – 1410mm; Width – 770mm; Saddle height – 710mm; Fuel tank capacity – 14 litres. Fuel consumption (suggested) – 3.9 l/100km; Weight – 175kg.

Top speed (claimed): 135km/h.

Machine loaned by:
VIN MINOGUE, Melbourne.

1960 BMW 'Sports' R69/Steib sidecar

600cc HORIZONTALLY OPPOSED OHV TWIN CYLINDER

In late 1913, the brilliant young engineer Max Friz designed a modern-looking, water-cooled six-cylinder overhead camshaft aircraft engine, the engine finally built in 1917. It was later used in German fighter planes during the latter half of the First World War: one of the pilots who flew in those aircraft being an infamous WWII Nazi called Hermann Goering. The new powerplant employed six separate cylinders, with the overhead camshaft driven by vertical shaft and bevel gears. To allow the aircraft which used the engine to fly at higher altitudes than normal, Friz designed a special butterfly-control for the venturi in an all-new carburettor, the aircraft then creating a new high-altitude record. Clearly, this also enabled those aircraft to be capable of surprise attacks from above upon enemy aircraft which were restricted to flying many thousands of feet below them.

The engines were built by a German company which had an almost tongue-twisting name, but a name which (almost incidentally) included the initials BMW. The company was a large industrial one, initially called – among other things – the *Rupp Motoren Werke*, but, as it was established in the city of Bayreuth it was later to be called the *Bayerische Motoren Werke*, to remove it from the other industrial factories to which it was aligned.

Just after the war, Friz 'designed' a side-valve flat-twin engine with external flywheel, which looked like an identical copy of the British Douglas motorcycle engine, with its pots similarly in line with the frame, one cylinder facing forward, the other to the rear. It was said to be originally intended as a stationary engine, but it was later fitted with a three-speed gearbox and was used to power a few little-known German motorcycles. Later still the engine/gearbox unit was used to power the better-known *Victoria* motorcycle and finally the *Helios*, the latter motorcycle initially made by BMW.

In 1923 Friz designed an all-new motorcycle, again utilising the 'flat-twin' design, this one with the horizontally opposed cylinders mounted transversely *across* the frame, the 486cc side-valve motorcycle employing a three-speed hand-change gearbox, with shaft final drive and front suspension by trailing link with a quarter-elliptic leaf spring. This time, it was not just the engine which was designed by him, for the entire machine was his creation from stem to stern. One of the most remarkable features of the new engine's design was the simple lubrication system which – with only minor modifications – continued over the decades until the all-new BMW flat-twin engine was designed in 1969. But it seems odd that this man should turn his talents to motorcycle design, for he was by then on record as stating very firmly that he simply did not like motorcycles at all!

However, the 1923 side-valve R32 BMW was (like the Helios engine before it) something of a copy, because it echoed very closely the British **overhead** valve 400cc flat-twin ABC motorcycle built some three years earlier by the eccentric genius Granville Bradshaw, the Bradshaw machine also featuring a three speed, hand gear change and leaf springing on the front, but with chain rear drive and an early type of swing-arm with leaf springing on the rear as well.

Max Friz was not to know this at the time of course, but that first R32 BMW was to firmly establish the BMW name – in fact to arguably establish the company *itself* – as it was never established before. He was originally a senior director of BMW and remained at the helm for many years thereafter. Quite apart from its car manufacturing arm, BMW has become one of the most famous, and highly successful, motorcycle manufacturers of all time. And in all those long years, the German factory has continued to this day (and probably well beyond!) to build the horizontally opposed twin cylinder motorcycle engine in a variety of sizes and styles, and by the hundreds of thousands at that.

'Flat twins' were made in many guises from 600 and 750cc side-valve and overhead valve machines for use during the 1939-45 hostilities to the DOHC Rennsport road racers. The pre-war machines from 1933-on adopted telescopic front forks, the later models with plunger rear suspension, while the viciously swift, if ill-handling, shaft drive Rennsport racer of the 1950s adopted the then-standard Earles front forks with swing-arm rear suspension. Among other famous BMW flat-twins were the more 'ordinary' R50 500cc roadster, the rare R50S sportster from the 1960s to the 600cc R60 which was mostly intended for long-distance touring or sidecar use. Finally, to nippy 35BHP sports 600cc R69 and more highly tuned R69S which produced a very handy 45BHP.

The R60 BMW was often used to tow a sidecar about, but it was equally popular as a solo tourer. However, the German machine was just one of many motorcycles which were intended to be sidecar mounts, for many factories specified more than one machine in their range as 'specialised' sidecar machines. Such British machines as the overhead valve Panther 600 and 650cc singles; side-valve M20 and M21 BSAs; the VB Ariel, a 600cc side-valve; Norton's 600cc side-valve 16H and overhead valve Model 19 singles, were just some of many motorcycles to be listed as specialised sidecar machines, while the big 1000cc Vincent employed dual rear sprockets as standard, a solo size on one side of the rear wheel and another – four teeth bigger – for sidecar use.

Like the BMW motorcycles of that era, the Vincent 'Girdraulic' front forks were adjustable – by means of an eccentric mounting spindle for its lower spring units – to alter the trail angle when it was to be used to haul a sidecar around, while the frames of many other British and European machines of 500cc and larger were fitted with sidecar mounting lugs as a matter of course. In those days, sidecars were a cheap and reliable means of transport, but the most exclusive outfit of them all was certainly the **BMW/Steib** combination, which usually saw an R60 hitched to a German Steib. The sidecar body was available as either the shapely and fashionable 'launch' type for general use, or the more sports-like model with a body like a sausage-shaped, miniature, aluminium Zeppelin. The two went together as though designed and built in the same factory – which many people still think they were.

BMW was happy to have its nameplate attached to the Steib sidecar body and to call it their own, the outfit often sold as a complete unit (it was listed in contemporary catalogues that way) but the Steib was not made by, or in, the BMW factory.

Very, very few of these outfits ever made their way to Australia, for they were far too expensive for all but the well-heeled enthusiast – and there were even *fewer* of them! – but I really enjoyed a very satisfying outing with the subject of this report; not an R60, but the sports, **R69 BMW/Steib,** fitted with the very flash, sleek Zeppelin body.

The R69 was a 1960 model, a very critical year for BMW for it was just one year after the factory toyed with a decision to halt entirely – or at least dramatically reduce – the production of motorcycles, the company still in financial difficulties and on the verge of going out of

The smooth lines of the BMW/Steib sidecar on display. Note the Earles-type pivoting front fork, ideal to withstand the side-thrust loads while cornering a motorcycle outfit. The sidecar could greatly benefit from having the Steib windscreen fitted, although it has the original Tonneau cover, which can provide some help.

business entirely. There were, in fact, just 2,594 of the R69 models built in the years 1955-1960, a very small number in anyone's language. Only a sudden injection of bank funds allowed the continued production of motorcycles, as their aircraft manufacturing facility was sold and a new range of small cars began to take off in fine style. Just a small trickle of bikes came into Australia, for the market was still very depressed at that time, but the New South Wales Police adopted the R60 – the sidecar model – for pursuit and patrol duties in that very year, which may have helped, in some minor way, to justify the German factory's decision to press on.

It may be significant to note that the BMW market was stronger in Melbourne at the time, because Steib combinations were simply not seen in NSW at all, and I can remember just one R69 doing the rounds – though the later R69S Super Sports models were to be seen here and there; as they still are to be seen on occasion. Though outwardly similar to the other BMW engines of its era, there are several essential differences in the R69 specifications. Quite apart from the two deeply grooved 'fins' atop the rocker box (the 'standard' BMW machines all have six smaller fins) the heavy crankshaft is supported on *three* main bearings, where two were normally used. The R69 included a substantial self-aligning bearing on the clutch end with bronze cage and spherical rollers – with their larger bearing surfaces – and a heavy-duty ball-bearing at the front of the engine. A smaller outrigger bearing helps support the crank and provides additional rigidity. Typical of its era, the pressed-up crank is fitted with caged roller big-end bearings.

As a point of interest, and contrary to popular, expert belief, even though they are superficially very similar, the crankshafts fitted to each BMW twin are subtly different. For example, the crank for the 500cc R50 is different to the later R50/2, and is different again to the rare Sports R50S, while the R60 is as different from the R69 as the R69 is different to the R69S. It's confusing to say the least, and no, they are **not** interchangeable, but the reason for these slight differences seems to be simply because of the difference in power output from the later and/or more highly tuned engines.

On the R69 models, the valve rockers are supported on crowded needle rollers instead of the more usual bronze bushes, the overhead valves controlled by quite thin pushrods. The higher-compression alloy pistons are usually three-ring type, but occasionally four-ring pistons were used.

Unlike the later /5 series, which appeared from 1969 with the newly designed engine, the camshaft is carried *above* the horizontal twin engine and is driven by a large gear which in turn is driven by a very solid-looking half-time pinion on the crankshaft. In the interests of quiet running, the gears were machined as carefully matched pairs, and they were available in no fewer than 11 different sizes!

The magneto is driven from the end of the camshaft, the contact points with a built-in automatic advance of 20 degrees, with another 10 degrees available on the R69S models only, by means of a manual lever on the left handlebar. The 6-volt Noris generator is driven from the forward end of the crankshaft, outboard of the cam and oil-pump drive gears.

Directly below the crankshaft gear a smaller alloy gear is driven, its spindle fitted with a small gear which in turn drives the oil-pump gear which supplies lubricant from a large sump carried underneath the crankcases. Oil is pumped under surprisingly low pressure to the main bearing, where specially designed oil 'slingers' direct the lubricant to the big-end journals, from where it is flung centrifugally about the crankcase's cavernous interior, and conducted by oil galleys and drillings to other engine components. It is seemingly a crude system, but very effective, and served a variety of BMW engines well for almost half a century.

At the rear and atop the large alloy engine casting, sits a large-capacity air-filter with metal gauze element fitted. It feeds the two 28mm Bing carburettors which sit neatly behind the twin cast-iron cylinders. Cylinder heads are light alloy, heavily finned, with their 'double-finned' detachable rocker covers.

The four-speed gearbox bolts to the rear of the large crankcases, the engine-speed clutch interpolated between them, and final-drive by shaft contained, in the style of the later BMW models, within the right-hand rear suspension swing-arm.

Engine dimensions are almost square, with a bore and stroke of 72 x 73mm respectively, which gives a capacity of 594 cm, while the compression ratio of 8:1 allows the lightly stressed engine to push out a handy – for its day – 35BHP at a high 6800rpm. A series of large alloy castings surround the electrics and air filter, making for a neat and compact engine design, long the hallmark of the horizontally-opposed 'boxer' twin BMW.

The frame is a work of art, with oval-section, tapered seamless-steel tubing (with round-section tubing interpolated at high stress points), castings and forgings skilfully welded to make a box-like, rigid assembly which is at once low-slung and quite long. Duplex tubes surround the power-plant and contain it, to curve up at the rear and return to the steering head, with heavy gussets for swing-arm mounting and steering head, while a large, fabricated boss helps attach the swing-arm unit to the frame.

The unusual manner in which the rear shock absorber units are fitted – they mount half way up the shock's length, as well as at the top – allied to the short, dumpy Earles front forks adds to the general low-slung appearance of the bike, while adding great rigidity and torsional stiffness.

One major advantage of the Earles forks is that they can easily have an adjustment built in to allow for variations in fork trail angle; not an essential ingredient, but very handy if the bike is to be used with a sidecar attached. In BMW's case the top mounting point for the short spring/damper units which serve as front forks has two holes drilled in it, while the long pivot fork which tucks well behind and below the steering head is similarly endowed so that the two different settings allow for an almost ideal trail angle for sidecar use.

The difficulty with driving sidecars is that, unlike most solos, the outfit behaves entirely differently on left and right-hand corners with a different technique required for each, and the easier it is to simply turn the handlebars around the easier the job becomes. It is an over-simplification to blandly state that the 'shorter' sidecar trail angle is akin to fitting the unit with power steering, but that is just about what it amounts to and this, allied to less tendency for the handlebars to shimmy about in sympathy with the movement of the sidecar wheel over bumps, makes the chore of steering with a 'tiller' much, much easier. Simply put, to equip a sidecar outfit with the correctly adjusted trail angle is to transform its handling and comfort beyond measure.

Steib's sidecar fits the BMW frame as

As comfortable a cruising combination as anyone would ever want. Note the pivot point, just ahead of the Art Deco sidecar mudguard, to provide for the independent springing for the sidecar body. The guard's grab-handle, with its clearance and tail lights, provided an easy way to slip into the close-fitting sidecar.

though it grew there, with four sturdy mounts which attach to the frame directly below the cylinder and to a sidecar lug on the left duplex down-tube under the steering head at the front and at a major frame junction near the gearbox at the rear. There is a slight 'lean-out' of the motorcycle in relation to the sidecar, and this is usually built-in to help overcome the tendency for the outfit to run down the camber of a road, though of course the long, threaded mounting-bolts allow for an infinitely variable adjustment to this necessary evil.

The alloy body of the sports Zeppelin is flexibly mounted to its chassis by a pivot-point either side of the sidecar nose, which holds the body remote from road shocks as it is suspended at the rear on a pair of light spring/damper units which fit from the base of the chassis to the top rear of the sidecar body. This allows the sidecar body to 'float' within its solid chassis, while the sidecar wheel enjoys a torsion-bar suspension system of its own, not only – I suspect – to help provide the sidecar with its saloon-car ride, but also to help insulate the bike's rider from road-shocks generated by the sidecar wheel.

A tonneau-cover is fitted on this outfit, but is not very successful at keeping out Melbourne's chill. A windscreen would be much more preferable, and in fact was usually fitted when ordered, for the sidecars were very much a hand-built affair, with such niceties as hydraulic sidecar-wheel brakes, launch bodies, cramped dickie-seats (for legless people) and many other variations.

This example had a very well-padded seat and backrest, the seat cushion at a steep angle to flex the knees and stop a passenger's heels from drumming on the sidecar floor, while a surprisingly capacious boot takes up the entire area from the backrest to the rear of the sidecar body. A lockable lid over this compartment is fitted with a neat alloy grill to locate a large suitcase or carry-bag, while a fold-up rear carrier fits to the rear of the motorcycle itself. Loaded to capacity, these brackets and open spaces would allow plenty of luggage to be carried on a camping or touring holiday. Or for a picnic

Of course, the Steib sidecar body came equipped with a quite large boot, and rear carrier, with in-built slots for two straps to retain the Fortnum and Mason picnic basket(?) Note: One of the pair of spring/damper units, which form the sidecar suspension, which is totally independent of the sidecar wheel's torsion bar springing. The sidecar rides like a well-sprung saloon car.

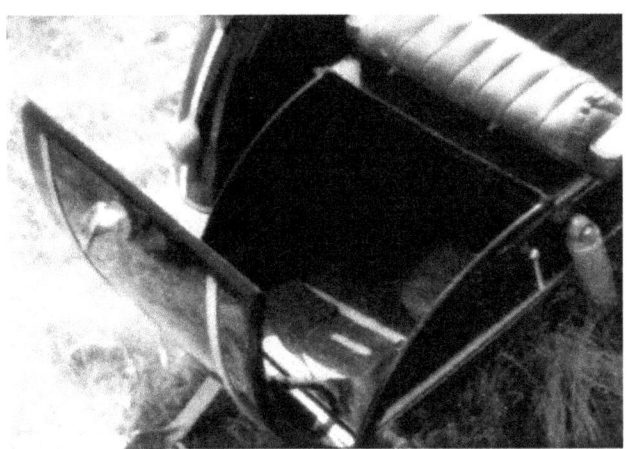

Here is the boot fully open, ready to take the champagne and the three special flutes – mustn't forget the pillion passenger – along with (perhaps) a few un-necessary tools and some books, possibly a tartan blanket and a small, fold-up umbrella?

somewhere, if a picnic hamper was carried in the boot with, say, a small keg on the rear carrier!

The sidecar wheel is interchangeable with both motorcycle wheels, which are themselves interchangeable front-to-rear (a most unusual, but distinctly German, practice), while the sidecar wheel is covered by a well-sculptured, flowing mudguard which is deeply valanced and surmounted by a streamlined alloy grab-rail with 'clearance' lights fitted front and rear. The guard unclips from the front and swivels clear to allow for easy removal of the wheel.

The Steib sidecar augments the lines of the R69 BMW beautifully, making a homogenous outfit which turns heads at every level. It looks like, and very definitely is, a gentleman's carriage. At least for those of us who prefer our transportation to be via two, or sometimes three wheels.

As you would hope, the ride is at once smooth and very, very comfortable, the sidecar gliding over road irregularities and broken surfaces with nary a whimper. I took a ride for a few clicks in the sidecar to check its comfort and emerged suitably impressed, but not much can be said of comfort during inclement weather, as the chair is draughty in the extreme without Steib's trim, sporty windscreen. The feeling, in Melbourne's damp, chilly winter weather is tantamount to sitting in a half-filled, tepid hip-bath, with a large and noisy fan tuned up to full-blast ahead of you, a rock band playing loudly in your right ear, while someone beats you periodically about the helmeted head with a damp, sand-encrusted chaff-bag!! What a huge difference a windscreen of any make or model would make to passenger comfort while sitting in that otherwise great sidecar!

At first acquaintance, the BMW's awkward 'sideways' kick-starter, mounted on the machine's left side, makes for some difficulty in kicking the bike over at the best of times – there is, of course, no electric starter fitted – but with a sidecar attached there is little room between the bike and the sidecar body, but like most things, a little practice and the knowledge that you won't tear the heel off your boot or fracture a fetlock in the exercise at the end of the swing helps ensure a never-fail first-kick affair!

There's very little 'torque-reaction' rocking at idle – the third wheel takes care of that – and the engine runs smoothly at most speeds above a brisk idle. Traditionally, the bike selects first gear with a crunch that would make the horn redundant as a warning device, but the old trick of merely stroking the clutch lever and actually changing gear as the clutch is about to be re-engaged makes for silent upward (and, very occasionally, downward) gear changes to be made when on the move. As usual, because of the engine-speed clutch, it is better if the gear change is made somewhat casually, for this is a gearbox which prefers not to be hurried.

Happily, the engine is punchy enough to pull well even up hills after a leisurely gear change, for there is a handy reserve of torque build-up in the large flywheel as the engine digs in without 'pinging' and pulls strongly from quite low engine speeds; helped, of course, by the sidecar gearing, which was an option in the crown-wheel-and-pinion final drive encased so neatly in the rear hub. Solo gearing was 8/25 teeth for the driveshaft pinion and crown-wheel respectively, while sidecar gearing was 6/26. For servicing, the quick-detachable rear wheel slips off its splines in no more time than it takes to remove one nut and wriggle the wheel free.

As usual with a sidecar attached, the handlebars have to be (almost unconsciously) turned ever-so-slightly to the right when taking off from rest, and again when upward changes are made on the move, and this overcomes the tendency for the bike to try and drive itself round the sidecar. The amount of sidecar-wheel lead, that is the sidecar wheel's location in relation to the motorcycle's rear wheel, makes a noticeable difference to this phenomenon, but the tendency remains, and in fact it is necessary to hold the 'bars with a very slight pressure on the right side to maintain the machine in a straight line on flat roads.

But what a joy this becomes on left-handers, because then the drill is to attack the corner a gear lower than one might do on a solo but under full power to take full advantage of all the power driving from one side of the vehicle. The tail-end will step out a little with this treatment and you sometimes need to apply just a few degrees of opposite-lock and shift about one-third of your body weight towards the chair, and ... well, anyone who has pushed a sidecar hard and fast over a switchback series of corners can tell you what a great joy this is, particularly when the last of the series of corners (as it was in this

'Wring its neck!' shouted the incumbent owner/passenger, Bill Rylett, in the sidecar, which I was delighted to do. Here, both leaning into the corner, we attack this swift left-hander just after a 'late-apex' approach and under full power, while applying a couple of degrees of opposite lock. This was to correct a rear wheel which was just beginning to step-out nicely, the sidecar wheel just skimming along the road surface. The bike never missed a beat. All three of us, the bike's operator, the sidecar passenger and his faithful dog (who is watching me very, very closely for some reason) joined with the outfit itself in enjoying that great corner!

test) is an open, fast left-hander!

It doesn't make a whole lot of difference whether anyone is in the chair or not, if the power is kept full-on the sidecar wheel either remains glued to the road or skims along with a few centimetres of daylight underneath it. Yes, it is safer with someone in the chair if you are going to drive it like this, particularly if you find a left-hander a bit tighter than you thought it was going to be, or if you have to button-off the power through the corner for whatever reason, because you can be in very big trouble if you have to do that with no weight in the chair.

If this happens, you can be assured the sidecar wheel will be a metre in the air in double-quick time and you'll find yourself cornering the thing like a solo... except that you have the *right* footrest on the road and the handlebars turned several degrees to the left. From my own experience I can tell you that you can still scratch around, but it's pretty exciting stuff, and definitely not for the novice!

Right-hand corners are approached quite differently and here the drill is to dive into the corner deeper and faster than usual and either ease off the power slightly as you turn the bars or even lightly apply the brakes. This tends to stop the bike rather than the sidecar, which then obligingly pivots round the bike and just as obligingly zips round the corner. Easy isn't it? Try it sometime, it's very much harder than you think!

You can drive the outfit hard through right-handers of course, and here the technique is different again, because the tail will step out and tighten the corner, while you happily steer into the slide and press-on under full power. Some of the earlier carburettor designs wouldn't allow this, because fuel-surge in the float-chamber would tend to put the fire out.

The Bing carburettors with which the BMW is equipped have part of the base of the carburettor body moulded to allow fuel to more fully surround the main jet, so fuel surge, at least under reasonable cornering speeds, was no problem. The alteration to the trail angle also made the chore of cornering briskly a whole lot easier, the 'power steering' making light work of moving the handlebars about once underway, though steering was of course heavy when wheeling the bike around in the garage or parking area.

Twin-leading shoe front brake and a similar-diameter rear brake were always very efficient on the Earles-fork models, the drums of very large diameter and the shoes very wide. A parallelogram-linkage built into the front suspension system works as an anti-dive mechanism, the forks tending to rise when the front brake is applied, while the weight-shift tries to push them down again. Though mechanical in effect, the system is simple and very effective, making a technological over-kill of today's highly sophisticated hydraulic systems which are currently all the rage on many Japanese machines. However, suspension movement in the front forks is compromised to some degree.

Brakes are powerful indeed, but of course as the preceding techniques indicate, there has to be a certain movement of the handlebars to the left to compensate for heavy braking, just as the opposite obtains when accelerating.

Again, the movement of the sidecar wheel over large road irregularities can move the handlebars if the motorcycle rocks side-to-side, but an effective coarse-thread friction steering damper can be nipped up a touch to overcome any tendency for the handlebars to shimmy over rough surfaces.

Most touring BMW machines imported in the mid-1950s had dual-seats fitted, but the sportier models usually had the marque's rubber-covered, sprung, single-saddle fitted, the pillion seat attached to the rear guard and flexibly mounted to the rear of the saddle. This allowed for the absorption of any heavy bumps the supple, comparatively long travel suspension system may not have been able to deal with, and it did it in a way which was, and remains, impossible with even the best and most comfortable dual-seat. In all, the R69 rides and handles almost impeccably, even by the most modern standards and, as we have remarked, is comfortable in the extreme.

Happily, the BMW's owner, Bill Rylett, who used to terrify Melbourne's matrons with his fire-engine red Munch Mammoth TS1200 in the 1970s, accompanied me during much of the test, and his weight (and that of his faithful dog) helped keep the sidecar wheel honest during some pretty brisk riding. Bill suggested I push the bike hard on occasion to get the best out of it, and of course I was happy to oblige. The engine is a comparatively low-revving one and is immensely strong, so it lapped up this punishment with ease, the well-sprung, torsionally rigid frame assembly also lending its strength to overcome the high side-stress loads of cornering a heavily laden outfit at speed.

The bike is not quite in showroom condition, for it is used almost daily as basic transport, but it is still very clean and absolutely oil-tight, the design is honest and hard-working, harking as it does back to the 1930s, and the German-Gem has very definitely survived the test of time. It was restored some few years earlier, and looked almost as if it came off the production line just a few months previously, instead of more than half a century earlier.

The R69/Steib combination is a genuine Classic and deservedly so marking, as it does, the German make's near-demise and yet pointing the way to a future the factory seemed, at that time, never to be able to enjoy. It was a privilege to ride the bike and to be allowed to pelt it through its paces with the owner's approval and consent. Usually, this type of machine has to be ridden with due deference to its rarity, status and condition, but to say that the encounter was a highlight – if an all-too-brief one – of an even rarer visit to our Southern-most capital, is almost an understatement.

TECH SPECS

Make: BMW

Model: R69 (w. STEIB sidecar)

Years of manufacture:
1955-1960: **R69**: 2,956 units.
The 42BHP Sports **R69S,** 8,361 from 1960-1966: (11,317 all told)

Type:
Horizontally-opposed twin-cylinder four stroke, with pushrod-operated overhead valves. Alloy cylinder head, cast-iron cylinder barrel. One-piece steel con-rods with caged roller big-end bearings, the crankshaft supported upon ball and roller bearings. Lubrication through dual gear pump, by forced feed and oil slingers.

Capacity: 594cc

Bore x stroke: 72 x 73mm

Compression ratio: 7.5:1

Power @ rpm: 39BHP @ 6800rpm

Carburation:
Two Bing 26mm, with paper pack air filtration.

Electrics:
Bosch Magneto ignition, with Bosch 6-volt generator to lead/acid battery.

Transmission:
Four-speed gearbox bolted to rear of engine, with direct drive through single-plate clutch to four-speed, foot-change gearbox, the final drive by enclosed shaft through bevel gear and crown-wheel: ratios – 8/34 (sidecar).

Gear ratios (internal):
1st – 5.33:1; 2nd – 3.02:1;
3rd – 2.04:1; 4th – 1.54:1

Sidecar gear ratios (overall):
1st – 22.50:1; 2nd – 12.83:1;
3rd – 8.67:1; 4th – 6.54:1.

Solo gear ratios (overall):
1st – 16.95:1; 2nd – 9.6:1;
3rd – 7.8:1; 4th – 4.9:1.

Frame, suspension, wheels, brakes:
Double loop, full-cradle, tapered-tube steel frame, reinforced at steering head, swing-arm and rear gearbox mounts, and top mount for rear suspension units. Sidecar wheel sprung by separate spring/damper unit, with sidecar body suspended independently at its rear by telescopic spring units, pivoting at front from within chromed, tubular steel surrounds.

Earles-pattern front forks with short, two-way damped, hydraulically controlled spring-damper units, rear by swing-arm with two-way damped spring-damper units, three-way adjustable for weight and damping. Alloy rims are 18" diameter, laced to full-width hubs with two, 200mm (8") drum brakes, front Twin-Leading-Shoe, rear Single Shoe. Block pattern 350 x 18" front tyre, 400 x 18" rear.

Dimensions:
Length – 2125mm; Width – (solo) 722mm;
Height – 980mm; Wheelbase – 1415mm

Weight:
(Solo) 202kg; (with sidecar) 324kg.
Fuel tank capacity: 17 litres:
Usage: 3.6L/100km (solo).

Machine loaned by:
BILL RYLETT, Melbourne.

1958 Ariel 'Leader'

250cc TWIN-CYLINDER TWO-STROKE

By the late-1950s, motorcycling worldwide was at its lowest ebb, with many once great motorcycle factories, both in Britain and the Continent, closing their doors, or severely curtailing their activities, with many of the most famous factories on earth simply vanishing forever. The Japanese had arrived in very small numbers in early 1958, when Honda – virtually unknown outside of Japan at the time – was imported into Sydney by the now long-defunct Bennett and Wood empire.

The Australian company Bennett and Wood, which was at one time one of the biggest importers of motorcycles and Lucas electrical component parts in the Nation, was the first company outside of Asia to import Honda motorcycles, even as their range of BSA motorcycles were quietly slipping down into the dustbin of history. The importation of the new Japanese machine began quietly enough with a shipment of less than twenty 250cc twin cylinder C71 motorcycles. But if BSA was in strife, then one of its companies, Ariel Motors, was no better off; in fact, it was going backwards at a much higher speed. The problem was simply that the British factories in general, and Ariel/Triumph/BSA in particular, had been caught asleep at the wheel, with most of the designs of their 'tried-and-true' motorcycle designs, stolid and reliable though they were, harking back to pre-war times.

Ariel's 'old-fashioned' designs included the sports Red Hunter 500cc singles, the 650cc BSA-clone 'Huntmaster' twins, and the most impressive of them all – if not quite so out-dated, as high-performance Japanese multi-cylinder machines were to clearly demonstrate a decade later – the unique, four-cylinder 1000cc Square Four, which tragically left the Ariel catalogue in 1959. It had its shortcomings but was still a fine motorcycle which had endured many revisions to the original design which appeared as an exciting, four-cylinder 500cc overhead camshaft sports mount in 1930. Great though the Big Four was, and it certainly deserved a better fate, it seemed to be no more acceptable to motorcyclists than any other British machine available to the buying public at that time.

But the decision to abandon the *entire four-stroke range* was made by Ariel at the very end of 1954, as it looked instead to what was by then a reasonably brisk market in motor scooters, which it was hoped might kick the motorcycle movement back into life. These were desperate times indeed, the company not considering the design of just a 'simple' motor scooter, because there were several manufacturers about who were making a large variety of those small machines. One of the later ones, and certainly one of the best, was the four-stroke, 250cc twin cylinder Triumph Tigress/BSA Sunbeam designed by Edward Turner in 1958 and made by Ariel's parent company, Triumph/BSA. Its smaller sibling, the Tina was 'powered' by a single-cylinder 175cc two-stroke engine which was originally used in the later BSA Bantam motorcycle.

It was the last time the venerated old Sunbeam name was used: or, more fittingly, resurrected, for it appeared upon the front apron of a different coloured, badge-engineered scooter which was built on the same assembly line as the Triumph Tigress. But what the parent company *really* wanted was a lightweight *motorcycle,* a two-wheeler not unlike a scooter; in effect a new machine which might encourage people to return to motorcycling – in particular, of course, to a machine bearing the company's Ariel nameplate.

Enter Val Page, the gifted, recently retired, English designer, who had originally joined Ariel from J.A. Prestwich (JAP) as far back as 1927, but had then moved about through a variety of other factories over the years. Page, in company with the equally clever engineer Bernard Knight, was given the brief to design something – *anything!* – in a bid to stave off the seemingly inevitable closure of the factory. They apparently enjoyed *carte blanche,* for the two men finally came up with one of the most brilliantly conceived lightweight motorcycles in British history, a machine which remained a closely guarded secret, but which finally looked as though it might deliver the goods, for it was a motorcycle which should have been able to appeal to motorcyclists everywhere, in particular to the huge market in America. The amazing new motorcycle could have done all that, and perhaps should have done all that and more, but sadly, in the end, it simply did not.

The machine which should have become Ariel's saviour was the space-age – almost 21st century? – twin-cylinder 250cc two-stroke **1958 Ariel Leader**, a machine which took all of four long years to design and fully develop and which was entirely unlike anything which had ever been built by a British motorcycle factory. It did, however, seem to owe some of its basic design to the 1929 Ascot-Pullin, a 500cc machine which, like the Ariel Leader, employed a series of impressive, two-tone metal pressings which completely concealed the power-plant, while providing some additional weather protection to the rider.

The new two stroke twin also owed something to the equally space-age, 250cc OHV Italian Aer Macchi 'Chimera' (Dream), which preceded the Leader by some five years. The Italian machine, with its horizontal cylinder, employed a close-fitting cowl over the cylinder head and barrel, and also had its entire power-plant enclosed within a series of very fetching metal pressings but, unlike the all-enclosed Ariel, there was no attempt made to provide weather protection for the rider.

The new Ariel Leader almost broke new ground for it glorified in a lovely two-tone colour scheme of either scarlet and pale blue, pale blue and ivory, mid-blue and cream (incidentally, two of the colour schemes adopted by both Ascot-Pullin and Chimera), or the occasional Admiralty grey and cream, with total enclosure of engine and gearbox by large metal pressings which were attached to a most unusual frame: if it could be called a frame, because it was as unlike the traditional, 'pipe-tube' motorcycle frame as it was possible to be.

The Leader also featured optional pressed-metal panniers, in matching colours, and it came with a pair of large, integrated leg-shields as standard ware, which were topped by a wide instrument panel incorporating a large Perspex windscreen, the latter attached to a wide, deep instrument panel. The impressive panel accommodated a speedometer, ammeter, headlamp and ignition switches, and – again as an optional extra – an eight-day clock! There was also a small lever in the centre of the large panel which could be used to adjust the angle of the headlamp if a large pillion passenger was to be carried.

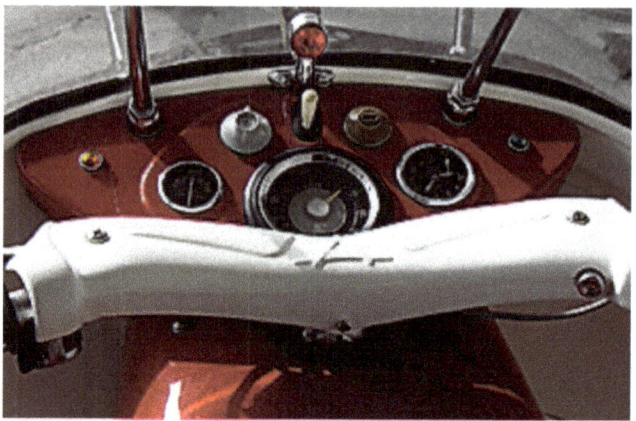

The Leader's instrument panel included an ammeter, speedometer, eight-day clock and headlamp switch. The pressed-metal handlebar cover includes the horn button (right) and the blinker switch on the left side.

The headlamp was mounted to the front of the wide faring and was embraced by a very smart-looking streamlined cowl, which lent its own shape to the very pleasing lines of the most futuristic-looking motorcycle. Ariel was also ahead of the game in sporting a set of over-large blinkers, which were also listed as extras: this was the first British motorcycle to be so equipped.

Neat cowling over the headlight, with the first set of blinkers to be fitted to a British motorcycle.

The 'fuel tank' was not a fuel tank at all, but rather a large compartment which opened at the top with enough room to accommodate an open-face helmet and still have space left over for gloves and a few other accessories. The small fuel tank was to be found lurking underneath a long, flat, softly padded dual-seat which was hinged to provide access to the tank, the machine's 6-volt battery, and some electrical ancillaries. A trim mudguard sat atop the rear wheel to keep road grime from finding its way into the under-seat compartment. In similar fashion to the Japanese Honda machines which preceded the Leader into Australia a few months earlier, the dual-seat was covered in a red or blue material which matched the machine's colour scheme: or, sometimes, in plain black.

But it was the most unusual frame which was one of the most striking features of the machine, although it could not be seen with all the protective panels fitted. The 'frame' was a lightweight, immensely strong and torsionally rigid box-girder, 'monocoque', or 'beam', design which was made from two, large, mirror image, 20-gauge metal pressings which were jig-welded together down its 'backbone' and belly, with several other strengthening panels attached, including several cross-bracing ribs under the large seat. There was a wide, substantial box-section bracket solidly attached to an area just under the frame's centre, from which the two-stroke engine depended, bolted firmly to the special bracket as if hung by the scruff of its neck at the front, and the seat of its pants at the rear.

Though well enclosed, the power-plant could still be easily accessed for changing spark plugs and other simple maintenance, while most of the power-plant could be dismantled without removing it from the frame. The steering head was enclosed within a section of the frame which was in effect wrapped around the tubular stem, imbuing that highly stressed area with immense rigidity. It must be said that the odd-looking frame was not entirely unique, for its design parameters owed more than a little to the trim little LE Velocette, a small commuter motorcycle with a smaller, similar beam-type frame which had appeared on the scene almost 10 years earlier.

The new Ariel's small, 16" wheels, with their very swish white-walled tyres, were partly enshrouded by deeply valanced mudguards, the front guard in particular being quite substantial, and with good reason, while a large, separate 'wrap-around' panel was attached to the rear of the impressive frame, where it was clearly intended as a large, multi-purpose rear mudguard. It was firmly bolted to the main frame, while being hinged at the back to allow access to a rear wheel which was all but invisible. The carefully designed pressings at the rear of the bike added their own smooth contours to the finely sculpted, sweeping lines of the motorcycle. The guard assembly helped ensure rigidity to the machine's rear end and was in effect cantilever-hung, but it had no rear stays to which the twin mufflers might be attached. This was attended to by attaching a pair of angled, chromed rods from the ends of the two long, tapered mufflers to the base of the large rear fairings, at once adding even more rigidity to the guard itself as well as providing a secure attachment for the mufflers.

With the tail-piece hinged clear, the quick-detachable rear wheel could be removed by the simple ploy of removing the axle and sliding the wheel off its splines, without disturbing either the brake drum or chain drive assembly. The slim rear mudguard is a close fit over the rear tyre, but does not need to be detached when removing the wheel.

These unusual muffler mounting stays were used because there was no other way to provide the essential support for them.

35

As if to add to the unusual appearance of the advanced machine, the oddly shaped front forks were totally unlike anything which had ever been seen before. Two entirely separate 'legs', again consisted of 20-gauge metal pressings, instead of the more standard telescopic forks, were butt-welded together and thus strongly braced, before being welded onto a very solid and well-strengthened horizontal cross member. In the centre of this cross bridge-piece sprouted a very strong single tube, very similar to the type found on bicycles, which was inserted through the steering head stem, with its attendant bearings, to be firmly clamped to the fabricated handlebars.

The odd forks were of the trailing-link type, the suspension pivot points carried at the forward end of the suspension system, well ahead of the front axle, the suspension's spring/damper units and other working parts totally enclosed within the large pressed-metal shrouds which imbued the forks with the appearance of a pair of large, truncated golf clubs. On either side of the top of the fork bridge-piece a pair of neatly enclosed nuts could be unscrewed to allow the two spring/damper units to be easily removed for repairs or replacement.

Because of the short front fork assembly, unsprung weight was thus greatly reduced, the short, fully enclosed suspension units working perfectly to absorb most road shocks with ease, their working parts and lower mounting sites for the suspension accessed by detachable, chrome-plated panels. An unusually thick front axle was employed to help ensure the wheel's integrity in relation to the beam frame – and the rear wheel – throughout the entire range of front suspension movement. In short, if they looked a bit like 'ordinary' front forks with a fancy cover over the end where the sturdy front axle was fitted, then they were clearly totally different, but still very effective.

As part of the clever front-end design, and to augment the thick front axle's contribution to an uncompromisingly strong front assembly, the deep, heavily valanced front mudguard was very firmly secured to the two fork blades and was obviously immobile, for it was 'unsprung' and didn't move with the action of the front wheel. This added its own bulkiness, and additional stiffness, to the front end, removing much of the stresses from the top bridge-piece while further ensuring the rigidity of the two fork legs in all planes.

At the rear, the chain drive was totally enclosed, the two double-acting Girling spring/damper units almost concealed within the very neatly styled rear guards. Again, flying in the face of convention, the rear suspension's swing-arm pivot points were actually mounted *onto the rear of the unit-construction engine castings instead of the frame*, just inboard of the large alloy engine side covers. The brilliance of the odd design quirk in having the swing-arm pivot point mounted to the *engine* instead of the frame becomes obvious, for the suspension is then *co-axial* with the final drive sprocket, which ensures that there was to be no variation in the tension of the ½" x ⁵⁄₁₆" final-drive chain over the entire movement of the rear suspension. Though almost unique, it was a brilliant concept, which allowed for smoother running and less stress on the slim rear chain, with the bonus of a longer chain life.

Ariel had always used Burman gearboxes for its range of motorcycles, specifying either the lightweight CP type or the heavier BA type, depending on the model, so it made good sense to design the unit-construction gearbox to accept the standard four-speed Burman CP gearbox internals. It would be far more economical to do this than to spend the time and money on designing an entirely new gearbox. All that was necessary was to have the interior of the gearbox shell, and the outer cover where the gear lever and kick stater were attached, designed in such a way that the Burman gearbox parts would slot straight in.

It has been suggested by some that the designer pinched his ideas from the by-then defunct Adler two-stroke twin, because there were some similarities, in particular the same bore/stroke dimensions of 54 x 54mm, but the engine, which was canted well forward in the frame at 30 degrees to take maximum advantage of the cooling air-flow, was very different in many areas. Quite apart from the Ariel's unusual swing-arm pivot points, the heavily finned alloy heads were designed to complement the strange-looking, deeply spigoted cast-iron cylinder barrels. As a result of this design, the barrels seemed to be very short and were extremely heavily finned at the exhaust ports, again to allow for maximum heat dissipation.

Lubrication was by petrol with an oil mix of about 16:1, which was perfectly adequate in view of the lightly stressed engine, and acceptable at the time because the later, Japanese-inspired positive-feed lubrication had not yet arrived; in fact, the *first* of the new range of Japanese two-stroke motorcycles from Suzuki, and later Yamaha (both of whom *did* pinch their design parameters from the German Adler 250 twin), which arrived around 12 months later, employed the same 'petroil' lubrication as the Ariel Leader. It must be pointed out however, that the 250cc two-stroke GTP Velocette, and the Villiers engine company, had both employed positive, pressure-fed oiling in two-stroke engines way back in the early 1930s, though it was never employed in Villiers two-stroke engines after the war. No-one, anywhere, seems to know why Villiers did that, for it was clearly a backwards step!

The Ariel has only one carburettor and a small one at that, a 5-series Amal with a bore of only ⅞"; great for just tootling about, but not very inspiring if you were serious about giving the bike an enthusiastic work-out. Perhaps the machine might have been better served had it employed twin carburettors of a somewhat larger bore size, which would have resulted in a much more spirited performance.

Bolted to the top of the crankcase under the large boss which suspends the engine, the carburettor's inlet tract is tortuous, for the cast-in manifold branches immediately into the two separate ports for the two separate cylinders. Because of the manner in which the two cast-iron pots are fitted, they are very short externally, the extremely heavy, horizontal exhaust finning at some 30 degrees across, to compensate for the angle at which the motor is inclined in the frame.

The machine's ease of maintenance is all but unheard of today, and it was also unique in 1958 when the machine magically appeared on the scene, unheralded and unannounced, as the industry was in its death throes. The all-new, unprecedented Leader startled all of us back then, as the first Honda motorcycles assuredly did, the Ariel Leader continuing to turn heads to this day. It was thought – in fact actually *said* by many of us at the time – that this new challenge to the company's dwindling fortunes just might work for the company.

Ignition was taken care of by two separate coils, with twin contact breaker points under a small cover at the left side of the crankshaft, with a 6-volt alternator on the opposite end, and these needed to be removed to allow the two-piece crankshafts to be removed one piece at a time (the assembly pulling apart from the middle, through its hollow crankshaft and integral locking bolt and tapers) by courtesy of a very special tool. It was a very clever design feature to couple the two separate main-shaft ends, similar to the system used in the 250cc British Excelsior 'Talisman' and the German Adler twin's crankshafts. These shafts are usually joined by a serrated Hurth-coupling or male-and-female double tapers and keyways.

The crank was supported on three main bearings, with a large, double-lipped oil seal next to the centre main bearing to separate the two crank chambers and retain the combustible gases.

Inboard of the points assembly is the primary-drive sprocket, which sits in its own oil bath and takes its drive directly to a multi-plate clutch containing a *'cush-drive'* shock absorber unit made from a plastic, Neoprene-like material.

This was current practice on some British machines in the 1950s, but the fully enclosed rear chain was not – though it was a catalogued extra on other Ariels (in particular the Huntmaster 650 twins, and later Red Hunter singles – and was often seen on European machines. Cleverly, a small felt wick in the top of the enclosed primary chain catches oil which then drips from a small jet onto the inside of the bottom run of the enclosed rear chain, providing a form of carefully controlled, semi-automatic lubrication. Provided you keep an eye on the level of oil in the primary drive, the system is simple and maintenance-free.

The Leader engine is mildly tuned, with a compression ratio of 10:1, small squish bands in the alloy heads allowing ping-free combustion, and it pokes out an amiable 17.5BHP at 6400rpm, all great Grand Touring stuff, and very acceptable to its intended owners. Fitted with twin carburettors, slightly modified port timings and slightly higher compression ratio, the engine could easily have developed a sporty 20-plus BHP, which just might – might! – have made it more acceptable to riders in those days. As a point of interest, the Ariel factory made a set of tuning hints readily available which would allow the two-stroke twin to be tuned to push out in excess of 35BHP.

We are talking here, let us not forget, of a very swish and very advanced-looking motorcycle from the middle of last century; a very smart-looking motorcycle for its time, if not for just about any time. The Ariel was rare in its day, for only a dozen of them made it to New South Wales and even fewer to the other States, the model we rode was said to be the specially prepared Earl's Court Show model from 1959, which was not fitted with any of the optional material. A year later, it was suggested a new, prototype **350cc** four-stroke twin-cylinder engine should be adopted as well, and a few were constructed, but money was very light-on, and the idea never left the prototype stage.

The pristine machine I rode for this test report was owned by the Sydney Metzeler importer, John Galvin, of Galvin Marketing. The Galvin Ariel bristles with what appears to be additional chrome plating, even extending to the dome nuts on cylinder heads, with many, many external components said to have been specially made for the model, or buffed and polished for the occasion. But Galvin told me he was horrified to discover that every Ariel Leader to come into the State was similarly finished, and all have pretensions of being the 'exclusive' Earl's Court Special. Be that as it may, the Leader is a great-looking machine, and holds its own in any company today, as it showed the way to others all those years ago.

But in terms of sheer performance, the Leader shows the way to nothing today, for it was very much a casual performer with a top speed which was just over 75mph (125km/h). It would thus be hopelessly out-classed by a hard-ridden modern-day 125, and it wouldn't see which way a sporty 250 went.

But the machine was always intended to be a Gentlemen's Tourer, and there is no doubt it fits the bill very well, from its stately sit-up-and-beg, comfortable riding position to its modest performance and its fine road manners. It fairly screams for those two carburettors, or, at the very least, a larger bore instrument than it currently has, and a fifth gear would work magic, but the manufacturers could easily have designed the Ariel Leader as a sports mount if they had so desired. Clearly, they did not, and that's all there is to it. There was, however, a stripped-down 'Sports' model, called the Arrow, which was soon to follow:

Inevitably, the 'naked' Ariel 'Arrow' felt the tuner's heavy hand upon it many, many times o'er and was ridden with some verve by many top-flight road racers, winning very many races during its short lifespan. At one time, the Ariel factory issued a set of tuning specifications, in which a learned amateur could descend upon a very ordinary, hapless Arrow and in time, following the detailed instructions very diligently, could end up with a machine developing more than twice the original power and which could then be ridden to very many race wins in Clubman-style road racing.

The Ariel two-stroke engine employed the near-classic 54 x 54mm bore-stroke ratio, but was initially strangled on the 'Leader' with a single, 6-type carburettor of just ⅞" bore – as in the road test report – which produced a mere 17.5BHP at 6500rpm. The introduction of the more highly tuned 'Golden Arrow', with its slightly higher compression ratio and carburettor of 1¹/₁₆" bore, saw power jump to 20BHP at the same engine revs – a handy increase of almost 20%.

I have no access at all to the Ariel race specs, but I have seriously tuned two very ordinary, 200cc 'commuter' Villiers two-stroke engines, which were very successful in early kart racing. These engines developed more than three times the power they produced in their original state. I am thus very aware that, if an enterprising owner were able to grind away the base of the cylinder head substantially to a very much higher compression ratio and adopt a larger diameter, twin carburettor set-up, this would increase the power again, and quite substantially.

If one was capable enough to pull the engine down, there was some room inside the crankcase castings to screw in a couple of suitably thick aluminium discs to the sides of the cases to increase the crankcase compression ratio, making the transfer of gases faster and thus much more efficient, while a little could have been shaved off the faces of the connecting rods to allow the more efficient flow of inlet gases into the crankcase. It would also make for a better feed of oil to the big-ends, while the rods could also be highly polished, in the interest of even better gas flow past them.

Nor does it end there, for a small raising of the *inlet face* at the base of the pistons would allow for an earlier opening of the inlet ports - plus a longer 'dwell' because of the later closing - which would allow even more gas to be introduced into the crankcases, with a corresponding higher power output.

There is even more to do but, in standard trim, the Ariel was seriously under-braked, so a much larger, more efficient pair of brakes would need to be laced in the wheel rims, or – even easier - a pair of the same sized wheels with larger brakes could then be adopted.

Sadly, the Ariel 'Arrow' was equally as unsuccessful as the Leader.

And now, speaking of which, back to the Leader! It is very low slung, with little cornering clearance – which isn't helped by the small 16" wheels – and it cannot be ridden with enthusiasm through corners at anything like the speed its nice handling would otherwise allow. Naturally, it is fitted with Metzeler tyres, but their superior grip is wasted because of the lack of cornering clearance. The front forks work very well, particularly on uneven surfaces, but are just a bit too firm on very smooth roads (when you can find them!). The rear end can sometimes be a touch too choppy for my liking, but is nonetheless very effective, adding greatly to the taut feel of the bike.

The gear change is a bit odd, with too much travel in the lever by modern standards and the four-speed gearbox could be a little uncertain at times when selecting third and top gear. This was a surprise in view of the machine's Burman gearbox internals, which have never shown this trait before. Naturally, I was quite at ease with the right foot gear-change lever, but I found that fairly slow gear changes were the way to go, otherwise it was easy to miss a gear or find

The 'naked' Sports 'Arrow', with higher compression ratio and larger carburettor was every bit as unsuccessful as the original Leader. The Yanks disliked it with a passion!

The only photo I have of me riding the bike. With a careful eye out for possible traffic we are just about to launch ourselves into a gap in the main road traffic. Even though the Leader was no ball of fire performance-wise, it was still a fine machine to ride, fulfilling its stated role as a genuine Luxury Tourer.

several neutrals, which were never part of the original Burman design.

Clutch action is spongy but efficient, the lever feeling almost as though it isn't connected to anything. Oddly, the throttle must be opened up and the engine well on song before you can release the clutch, otherwise the engine bogs down and the bike refuses to take off. It's a little like a sporty two-stroke in that regard, which is a surprise, particularly in view of the engine's mild state of tune.

The starting drill was simple, and had to be strictly adhered to if the bike was to fire up in a kick or two. First the choke, a small nylon rod which stuck out of the engine cover on the left, is pulled out, then a couple of kicks with ignition off, then just a couple again with the ignition *on*, and the engine would fire up without hesitation and idle quite reliably.

There was a sort of unintentional automatic choke withdrawal, which occurred when the throttle was opened up as the engine warmed to its task. Well, it may not have really been automatic, because engine vibration would close the choke off when the little nylon button moved back to its original position as though shoved slowly back by an unseen hand. The engine vibrated much more than I thought it should have, though it was not uncomfortable. There was some vibration through the footrests, and some at the handlebars when the bike was pushed hard through the gears, but it was very well behaved on the over-run or when cruising along in high gear.

Such is the wide spread of power that you could change into top gear from as low as an indicated 25km/h, and the bike would pull away *gently* if you eased the throttle open just as gently. Try *that* with a late model, high revving sportster, and see how far you get!

Conversely, if you wanted to squirt it a bit harder, the Leader would happily nudge 90km/h in third and then run up to an easy 110km/h or more in top gear, a speed which I'm sure it could sustain all day if you called upon it to do so. Happily, the rider could also sustain maximum cruising speed all day, because the riding position is armchair-like – a far cry from the modern style where many small-capacity sports machines call upon the rider to assume the 'pseudo/foetal' position.

For some unaccountable reason, the drum brakes were not really up to scratch. They were both on the small side at just 6" in diameter, were spongy in feel and not nearly powerful enough to be very effective. OK, it is after all, a touring machine, but any motorcycle's brakes should be able to pull the bike up with tyre-yelping efficiency if ever they are called to do so. The bike would no doubt have been better served with 7" brakes and wider brake shoes, along with longer brake lever arms which would apply more leverage to the brake shoes. Perhaps it's just as well the bike is such a 'passive' performer, and not more sports orientated?

Weather protection is great, with the large

What a crying shame it all was! Here is the flat-four, 700cc machine, the engine mounted into a lengthened and strengthened 'Leader' frame, with dual headlights and matching panniers. Shaft drive and fan-cooled exhaust, the engine delivering just 25BHP. But with the essential developments in ironing out all the in-built bugs, it could have produced around 45BHP, an ideal touring iron. It was never to be, for it was shot down in flames by the BSA Board, with its penchant for 'stinkin' thinkin'.

windscreen and wide, built-in leg-shields to augment the complete engine coverage, but a rider would still need protective clothing in the wet, simply because there is obviously no wet weather protection when the bike is stationary. The panels are all pressed metal as we've noted, not plastic or fibreglass as you might expect them to be, and they could originally be well augmented with some extras which Galvin, with all his worldly contacts, was unable to find at the time. Its performance in 1959 was acceptable, if not startling, but the bike was not intended to be a sports mount, as we've mentioned. However – again as noted previously – the engine could be highly tuned for racing, or 'sports touring' if that was your preference: much more effective brakes would then be required!

It is history that the Ariel Leader was the factory's final gesture, for the rest of the range hung on for a year or two before petering out. The bike was in production for eight years from 1958 to 1965 – the very years in which the Japanese began their onslaught on the market and turned the motorcycle wheel full-circle. Overall, there were just over 35,000 of the 250cc two-stroke twins, in Leader, the un-clad Arrow, Arrow Sports and the later 200cc version of the Arrow built during those few, turbulent years.

Why didn't it survive? For that matter, why didn't Ariel itself survive, for surely things were – however slowly – improving perceptibly? You would have to ask the decision-makers, the people who decide the fate of men and machines; people, let's face it, like the Triumph/Ariel/BSA Board members who phased out the Square Four, the 750cc three-cylinder Triumph

Trident, the ill-fated, 1000cc four-cylinder Triumph *Quadrant* prototype and the exciting 350cc DOHC Triumph Bandit.

The Leader looked to be a brilliant design, and it was hoped it would restore Ariel's fortunes, but the new Ariel was disliked with some passion in what it was hoped to be its biggest market: America. It was apparent that the Yanks were very much fair-weather riders and it's been said (by them) that they couldn't come to grips with what they considered to be a somewhat 'wimpy' motorcycle, whose bright colour scheme and all-enveloping panels made it look (to them) to be more than a little limp-wristed. The Yanks may have loudly declared that there was little point in having all that weather protection when they seldom rode motorcycles in the wet; or in the snow for that matter, which could be waist-deep in many parts of that country during winter.

To counter this, the Brits built the later 'sports' Ariel Arrow, which was virtually a Leader without any of the metal panels fitted, but it was even less acceptable to the Yanks, for they were then confronted with an un-clad, odd-looking frame which they disliked intensely, because it was unlike anything they had ever seen before: it also drew even more attention onto the similarly peculiar front forks.

As a point of great interest, in late 1960, Val Page, by now past retirement age, designed a very exciting 700cc, flat-four OHV engine, which was laid on its side, the cylinder head to the left, the unit originally intended for the Army to adopt as a stationery power-plant. Cleverly, a few extra powerplants were built in-unit with a four-speed gearbox and shaft drive, which were intended for possible use in high-performance Ariel roadsters, using enlarged and strengthened Leader frames. Two prototype power-plants were submitted – without integral gearboxes, of course! – to the War Ministry, and were approved for use by armed forces, but funding was cut by a new Government, the Ministry of Defence finally deciding against the expensive, four-cylinder design, the project simply withering on the vine.

The engine design was then stolen by BMW for its later K series motorcycles and nothing was heard again about the exciting new Ariel machine. However, at least one complete prototype machine remains which was gleefully ridden for a time and reported upon favourably. It was said to 'run very smoothly, with very little engine noise, if under-powered' A 700cc OHV flat-four Ariel motorcycle now languishes on display at the British Motorcycle Museum. An utter tragedy, if ever there was one, for that machine, had it been fully developed (which would of course take time and money, which the company simply didn't have) may well have saved the company had it finally made its way into the marketplace.

The trim little 250cc *two-stroke* Ariel Leader was probably far too advanced for its era, but if the motorcycle was introduced by a *Japanese* manufacturer **today,** with, say, that flat-four, four-stroke engine, and fitted with all the expected mod cons, instead of being built by the Brits just after the middle of the last century, it would assuredly be hailed world-wide as a brilliant, very advanced design. It would probably be accepted by many thousands of rabid enthusiasts with arms opened wide. ***Perhaps even in America?***

TECH SPECS

Make: Ariel

Model: Leader

Type:
Unit construction, twin cylinder two-stroke, with separate, heavily finned cast-iron cylinders, alloy cylinder heads. Cylinders angled forward 45-degrees in frame, attached by a special bracket behind the cylinder heads and at the base of the gearbox. Single Amal 375 Monobloc carburettor, 7/8" bore. ('Sports Arrow' model employed 1 1/16" Amal 376 Monobloc.)

Bore x stroke: 54 x 54mm

Capacity: 247cc

Compression ratio: 10:1

Power @ rpm: 17.5BHP @ 6750rpm

Transmission:
By oil bath primary chain, through four-speed gearbox, with final drive by light, ½" x 5/16" fully enclosed rear chain.

Gearbox:
Four-speed with Burman internals, right-side foot-change, one up/three down pattern.

Gear ratios:
1st – 19:1; 2nd – 11:1; 3rd – 7.8:1; 4th – 5.9:1

Electrics:
Crankshaft-mounted Lucas 6-volt, 140-watt alternator, wet-cell battery, twin coils-and-points ignition.

Frame, suspension, brakes, wheels:
20-gauge pressed steel, torsionally rigid, 'box-girder' beam frame, with strengthening gussets welded to major stress points, separate rear section includes rear mudguard, to swing-up for QD (Quick-detachable) rear wheel. Front suspension is a pressed steel, fabricated trailing-link type forks, with dual, two-way damped spring/shock units. Rear suspension is by swing-arm attached directly to crankcase castings, with dual, two-way damped spring/damper units. Drum brakes are 6" (150mm) diameter, by 1 1/8" (30mm) wide. Wheels are 16" diameter, with 325 x 16" tyres front and rear, ribbed front, block pattern rear.

Dimensions:
Length – 196cm; Wheelbase – 130cm; Seat height – 73cm; Weight – 150kg; Fuel tank – 13.5 litres; Range (@ 90km/h average) – approx. 370km.

Top Speed: 120km/h.

Machine loaned by:
JOHN GALVIN MARKETING, Sydney.

1955 Ariel 'Square Four'

1000cc OHV FOUR CYLINDER

British motorcyclists were stunned when there was not just one, but *two*, four-cylinder overhead camshaft motorcycles exhibited at the Olympia Motorcycle Show in 1930. One of them was the 600cc Vee-4 OHC **Matchless**, its overhead camshaft driven by bevel gears and vertical shaft, the other was the trim, 500cc OHC **'Square Four' Ariel**, its overhead camshaft driven by chain, with transmission *via* a four-speed, hand gear-change Burman gear box. The Matchless, which was designed by Bert Collier – as a logical progression from an earlier twin-cylinder side valve machine designed by his brother Harry – was to last only six years before it was removed from the Matchless catalogue in 1935, while the Ariel was to survive, after several dramatic computations, until it disappeared in 1959, by then a full-sized overhead valve, all-alloy 1000cc machine which still featured the original, brilliant Square Four concept

The Square Four Ariel was designed by Edward Turner, famous in later years as the designer of the range of Triumph vertical twins, who had sketched his idea for this brilliantly conceived engine on the back of an empty Wild Woodbines cigarette packet in 1928, before he then foisted it around a series of mostly disinterested motorcycle factories. He went firstly to AJS and then to BSA, before the exciting new design was finally picked up by Ariel. Cleverly, the engine took up only a little more space in its frame (which was a slightly modified component from a 500cc single) than a vertical twin of the same capacity might take, the bike followed in 1932 by a 600cc variant, which was originally intended to cater for the demands of sidecar riders, but which was naturally fallen upon with glee by long-distance touring riders as well.

The engine was entirely redesigned in 1936, to emerge in 1937 as the 4F, a pushrod, 1000cc overhead *valve* machine, the engine block and head moulded in cast iron, which made for two things which were less than ideal; firstly, it was much heavier than the overhead camshaft models, and the rear cylinders were prone to over-heating, particularly in Australia, where the high summer temperatures were always somewhat prohibitive. In 1938 the machine was enhanced by the adoption of the Anstey-designed plunger rear suspension – all previous models had no rear suspension – which differed from the few other systems which had recently been introduced by having a small, pivoting 'stirrup' attached just ahead of the springs, which was intended to allow for a minimal variation in rear chain – and rear *spring* – tension as the machine flopped into pot-holes or bounded over bumps.

A further enhancement followed in 1949 when the Mark One was introduced, at long last fitted with the all-alloy head and barrel it so desperately needed, which naturally gave the rear pots an easier life, while incidentally – because of the adoption of coil, instead of magneto, ignition – shaving nearly 45 pounds (22 kg) off the bike's overall weight. However, the two exhaust ports exited the cylinder head via just *one* large-diameter exhaust pipe on each side which was still not really ideal. The Ariel Square Four's final improvements occurred in 1953 with the updated Mark Two, when the aluminium alloy cylinder head and wider barrel were completely

Cutaway drawing of Turner's original Ariel 500cc Square Four engine. Note the chain driven overhead camshaft, the 'overhung' cranks on the front (no main-shafts), the vertical valves and the forward-facing inlet manifold. Cleverly, the helical-cut gear teeth on the front crankshaft's flywheel meshed with the rear flywheel to couple the two shafts, the forward one revolving anti-clockwise. A brilliant, very compact four-cylinder design.

redesigned, the cylinders by now slightly further apart from one another for better air flow and thus better cooling, while still in the huge, one-piece aluminium alloy casting, but also with the exhaust gases now leaving the cylinder heads via *four* separate, thinner-diameter exhaust pipes.

It is in this guise that the Big Four remained until its somewhat premature demise, except for the fitment of a one-gallon oil tank on the last models to be built, just before the manufacture of **all** the four-stroke models was stopped in 1959 in favour of the all-new, Val Page designed 250cc two-stroke twin-cylinder **Ariel 'Leader'**; a machine the company earnestly believed would save their bacon, and a machine which we have just detailed. It is reasonable to assume that the all-new aluminium castings for the 1953 Square Four head and barrel might also have been designed by the gifted Val Page, who was in charge of the design office in Ariel at that time.

Ariel's great engine was, for the most part, quite trouble-free, and would give many, many years of faithful service, but owners of a new Square Four in the mid-1950s needed to be made well aware of some of its short-comings if they were going to get the best out of it. There was a small 'sludge-trap' built into the crankshafts, which needed to be cleaned out every 20,000 miles, if only to save the left-front big-end assembly, which was the last bearing area to be lubricated when the engine was fired up. It is quite different nowadays, because modern, synthetic oils have not only a lubricating duty to perform, but they fulfil the role of detergents as well, keeping the engines they lubricate much 'cleaner', and are much less prone to being compromised by unwanted material clogging up essential oil galleys and internal drillings than the earlier, mineral based lubricants were.

However, it is still a Very Good Idea to continue to check that essential little sludge trap, if not quite as regularly as in days of old.

The cleverly executed 1000cc overhead valve Square-Four (or 'Squariel', as it was called by almost everybody in its heyday) was a dominant engine, and it enjoyed the reputation for many years of being one of the only two machines of its type in the world: if we may the except the rare Danish 750cc OHC, shaft-driven in-line four for the moment. That may seem hard to believe by today's standards, when large-capacity, four-cylinder motorcycles are to be seen everywhere you look, but that is the way it was in the middle of last century.

That unique, all-alloy engine filled its full-

In 1953, the all-alloy OHV Square Four enjoyed its final design, with four short exhaust pipes, redesigned barrels and slightly wider crankshaft to allow for better cooling of the rear pots. There can be little doubt that Val Page was involved in the latest design. This was the only year in which the machine enjoyed the fine 'Wedgewood Blue' paint finish.

cradle frame to capacity like nothing else in sight, but the rare 'square' configuration meant it was still fairly compact, for it was kept mostly within the solid frame's boundaries without hanging outside its confines, which meant that little damage would occur to either engine or gearbox in the event of the bike sliding gracefully along the roadway for some distance on its side – should it ever come to that!

The engine imbued the bike with a very punchy performance, the power output a very handy 42BHP at just 5800rpm, a modest output perhaps by modern standards, and at comparatively low engine speeds, but more than enough to propel the weighty machine to a top speed of more than the Imperial 100 miles per hour. But there was more to it than that, because of the machine's near-miraculous top gear performance. The publicity blurb which accompanied the early brochures proclaimed that the Square Four was capable of a performance in *top gear alone* of 'nearly 90 miles an hour, from 10-100mph' because the engine was so smooth that the bike would pull away from almost a brisk walking speed to its maximum speed without any form of transmission 'snatch' and without changing back into a lower gear; with the proviso, of course, that a rider was very, *very* gentle on the throttle! This is quite impossible to achieve with today's high-revving, far more powerful motorcycles.

We did not explore the upper limits of our test machine's performance too often, but the great engine's smoothness, allied to its wide spread of power, were proven time and time again in heavy traffic, as well as on the open road, because the bike could be kept in its higher gear for most of the time, much like a large V8 automatic car, and would pull away very smoothly and with a pleasing burst of acceleration if the wick was turned up at anything above about 70km/hour. At lower road speeds, it would be even more urgent if stroked back out of top gear and the throttle opened with some enthusiasm. It was a relaxing, easy ride, if a little unwieldy as it weaved enthusiastically about while cornering over ripples at speed; due, no doubt, to its un-damped, short-travel plunger rear suspension, which was not helped at all by a large dual-seat which was firm enough to be almost bullet-proof.

There are still several of these remarkable machines to be found, not only in Australia, but world-wide as well. And we managed to find one for this test – a **1955 Square Four Ariel** of around the same era as many which may have been consigned to the local rubbish tip: if only because their owners may not have been made aware of the critical importance of that half-hidden, trim little oil sludge-trap. The machine was loaned us for this test by long-time motorcycle buff Brian Greenfield, who enjoyed a strong Vincent interest and a collection of unusual bikes, and who was quite happy to allow his pride and joy to be used in this report.

The bike is in essentially original condition, the model moving away from the Wedgwood Blue or, later, Deep Maroon of the newly designed 'four-piper' from 1953, the slightly later model finished in the black-with-red-tank scheme which was used so dramatically at the time on the firm's sporty 500cc Red Hunter singles.

That 1955 model flew in the face of the fashion of the day by continuing to retain the Anstey spring-heel rear suspension system when all the large, twin-cylinder Ariel machines were well into swing-arm rear suspension. The argument for retaining the Square Four's plunger rear suspension was that an over-long wheelbase would probably result, and an entirely new frame would need to be designed and built. The four-stroke Ariels quietly disappeared just four years later, but not before a one-off Square Four prototype was made in the factory with the long-overdue swing-arm rear suspension at last in place.

It was not alone, because there was a 'four-pipe' Square Four power-plant in Sydney which was shoe-horned into a late model swing-arm Ariel 'Huntmaster' frame back in the early 1960s, and there is yet another, this one fitted into that great 'Featherbed' Norton frame. It was called the 'Esquire' and it made its appearance in America several years ago. There may well be – or should be? – many others out there as well.

The front forks, which were common to BSA and Ariel for years, were as good as any available at the time, but the plunger rear suspension was not up to scratch when compared to a modern swing-arm suspension It was, however, probably the best of its type.

A major advantage of plunger rear suspension was purportedly to allow the rear chain tension to remain virtually constant through the suspension's small, 75-80mm range of movement, but the system was un-damped and thus not well controlled, or even rigidly retained. This often allowed the rear wheel to swivel slightly out of plumb in relation to the front wheel as the suspension chattered away, for the rear axle's location was flexibly altered by being mounted in the centre of a double pair of springs on each side.

At the cost of some choppiness in the ride, chain life was extended, but the Ariel's short pivoting stirrup was mounted to the frame at three points on each side, which in turn necessitated far too many bronze bushes, which the factory suggested should be lubricated through several grease nipples at **250 mile intervals!** This figure was stipulated in the Owners' Handbook, but may have often been ignored which, it was said, could result in premature wear.

But if the Ariel frame design may have left a little to be desired, then that most impressive engine remains a thing of beauty. A masterpiece of engineering skill in many ways, including the great space-saving square formation, the well-executed alloy castings of the latest 4F model always dominated the large frame in which it sat so comfortably.

Very much narrower than the current rash of transverse, in-line four-cylinder machines, the Ariel has two quite separate crankshafts for each pair of cylinders, with the shafts coupled on the machine's left side by a large pair of straight-cut gears: the geared cranks naturally revolve in opposite directions, the front anti-clockwise. Because of the trim engine design, the primary-drive chain-case also sits within the confines of the outer perimeter of the engine and frame-rails.

The primary drive sprocket is driven from the extended end of the rear crankshaft, out-board of the rear coupling gear, and it is fitted with the cam-and-spring engine shock absorber unit adopted almost universally. A single row, ½" x 5/16" chain takes the drive to the essentially dry, multi-plate clutch and four-speed BA Burman gearbox, with the chain itself running in the primary case oil bath.

The two crankshafts are supported on the timing side – where the chain-driven camshaft, oil pump and generator drives reside – by plain, white-metal sleeve bearings, while the drive sides are supported on substantial roller bearings. The rear coupling gear sits directly inboard of the primary drive sprocket, with an extra roller bearing carried as an outrigger bearing between it and the sprocket. It should have been an ideal arrangement, for the crankshafts are very well supported with heavy bearings and close-fitting gears on their outer main-shafts but, alas, it was not.

In the interests of a clear passage of air for maximum cooling, the pairs of cylinders were of necessity spaced quite widely apart. This meant that the cranks themselves were not well supported *internally*. Consequently, they could flex at high engine speeds, though the engine usually ran with an almost uncanny, turbine-smoothness. The cranks for each pair of cylinders were set half a revolution apart, with pairs of pistons rising and falling at different times and setting up the classic 'rocking couple' motion, although some of this was cancelled out by the contra-rotating cranks. For this reason, the engine was not a particularly high-revving unit; modern enthusiasts might have been surprised to learn that it pushed out its handy 42BHP at the very lowly 5800rpm.

Shaped like an elongated N with a flange in the middle, each crankshaft has its own flywheel bolted to the centre, but on opposite sides of the flanges so that they in fact overlap each other as they spin in opposite directions inside that huge crankcase casting. The outer ends of the two cranks, just inside the alloy crankcases, have additional bob-weights bolted to them to assist the balance factor of the Big Four. The bob-weights were detachable simply to allow the two flywheels to be threaded along the shafts prior to being bolted in place! It seemed to be more than a little agricultural in design, but it functioned perfectly.

The two crankshafts are located far enough apart to have the long, thin camshaft mounted between them, driven by a single ⅜ x 7/32" chain at the front of the timing case on the engine's right-hand side, the camshaft supported only on its extreme outer ends. An extended shaft on the centrally located camshaft employs a small worm-drive to operate the latest, high-capacity, gear-type oil pump: it replaces the twin-plunger type pump which was used for many years in the Square Four engine as it was in all the contemporary Triumph twin-cylinder machines. The generator fits horizontally behind the large cylinder block, with the car-type distributor mounted vertically from the same point, driven off a skew-gear from the end of the generator, which is driven by the single 'busy' chain within the timing case.

Cam follower blocks pressed into the crankcase between the pairs of cranks locate the pushrods which operate the flat rocker arms, which in turn operate the vertically disposed valves which are staggered to allow the exhaust ports to be on the outside of the very large alloy cylinder head.

Though cleverly designed, the Square Four Ariel combined complex features to add up to an engine which was not the most efficient at high engine speeds – though, to be fair, it was never intended to be a sports machine, for it was clearly designed to be ridden as a long-distance, relaxed tourer; a job it always fulfilled to near perfection.

But perhaps the most unusual aspect of the engine design was the long, probably ill-designed, cruciform-shaped inlet port, which fed mixture to the four pots from either a *single* SU or Solex car-type carburettor. The port ran from the carburettor down the centre of the two pairs of cylinders in much the same manner as the early side-valve Ford 'valley-cover' did, and it was about as effective, because all too often – particularly in the heat of an Australian summer's day, with temperatures which would be up into the high 35-degree Cs, or even higher – the inlet charge might become hot enough to have an adverse effect on the engine's volumetric efficiency.

For the rider who would buy the Ariel Square Four, however, this induction system worked well enough and certainly didn't result in fuel bias to one pot or another, but it could have been a whole lot better. Perhaps a pair of opposing, shorter inlet ports with two separate carburettors on either side of the cylinder might have performed better?

The Square Four was heavy for its day at 435 pounds or 197kg (in comparison, the first CB750 Honda weighed 220kg, the Gold Wing a hefty 260kg) and this was partly due to the Ariel's very large battery, a well-filled, one-gallon oil tank on later models, and the heavy-duty six-volt generator with which the machine was equipped. Coil ignition was standard on the 4F, with a four-cylinder distributor from the Austin 7, Singer 7, Morris Minor, et al., supplied by Lucas.

There was no electric starter fitted, but kick-starting the machine was a breeze, because there was always at least one pot which was full of gas and waiting to burst into life. It is one of the few machines of its era which adopted coil ignition, though it was becoming more and more the fashion, and the starting procedure required nothing more than a twist of the ignition switch

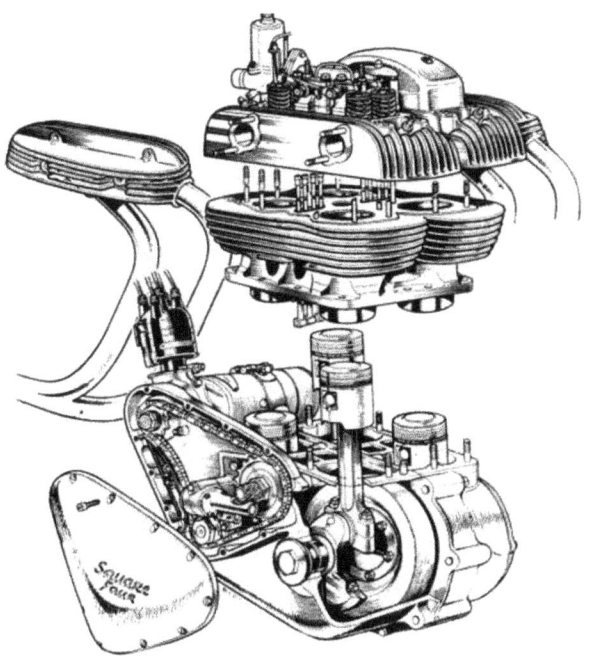

Cutaway drawing of the 1953 engine, which remained un-altered until the bike's demise in 1959 (except for a larger, one-gallon oil tank in later years). Note four exhaust pipes and their alloy covers. Chain inside the timing case driven from half-time pinion on rear crank drives the camshaft, its worm-drive operating the large-capacity oil pump. The chain also drives the generator – and its attendant four-lobe distributor. Note car-type SU carburettor at rear.

and a little muscle on the kick-starter. Oddly, the sound is still distinctly Ariel Square Four, even though many four-cylinder machines have followed its demise.

There was no rev-counter fitted and certainly no idiot lights, the older British bikes making do quite well with a speedo, ammeter and perhaps an ignition switch to match the simple on/off lighting switch. No blinkers either, or starter button, so the handlebar switches are limited to a horn/dipper combination… and that was that! The heavyweight, BA Burman gearbox was separate from the engine, with primary chain adjustment carried out by simply loosening the gearbox mounting bolts and slipping the box back in its slotted mounting bracket.

The clutch action was light and it freed with no drama, with first gear slotting into place with ease. Oddly, the large flywheel effects are not noticeable in the brisk way the bike runs to peak speeds in the intermediate gears, but becomes more obvious when buttoning-off the power in the upper gears. The effect is a little like applying the rear brake – and just as touchy when cranked over! The traditional *'Great British Handling'* is not as evident as it is with many others, due mainly to the plunger rear suspension, and there is a tendency for the rear wheel to hop when braking heavily over bumpy road surfaces. But the suspension is surprisingly comfortable, with long slow-travel front forks working well to make up for some choppiness from the rear plungers.

Brakes proved to be at least adequate. Most of the test was conducted in outer-town areas where the bike was relaxing and at ease with the road surfaces we encountered. Acceleration is quite good, with the big machine able to come on strong through the lower gears whenever the passion arose. It came on so strong on a couple of occasions that riders we passed with ease on the open roads must have wondered what this unknown, odd-looking machine was as they gave the bike the fish-eye when we were all at rest in heavier traffic.

It's a fair bet the Ariel I rode could still reach the Imperial 100mph. Road test reports at the time place the top speed at 102mph but some roughness in the test model would not allow it to pull readily from much below an indicated 20mph in top gear. As I have remarked, it is very much a top gear machine, with mid-range road speeds controlled entirely by the throttle hand and road surfaces, with little recourse to the gearbox,

Always such an easy bike to ride because of its great top gear performance, thanks to a very wide spread of power. Brakes were powerful, the front forks as good as any, if the plunger rear suspension was a little choppy. Top-of-the-line in its day, the Big Four was phased out less than 10 years before the first four-cylinder machines arrived from Japan, to finally dominate the market.

even when pulling out to overtake other traffic. It's all a question of torque, engine speeds and all-up weight of course, but it is in this department that the old war horse really shines. But if you *did* decide to change back a gear and open the throttle wide? Well, what a surprise, for wheelspin could sometimes result in the lower two gears, even if a modern-day 'wheelie' was never on the cards!

In its day the Square Four engine was noted for its turbine smoothness, but the test bike was showing its age, and there seemed to be some wear in the large engine room. Vibration is, in fact, noticeable; it was the wrist-numbing, foot-tingling feeling more often associated with some of the older, big singles, and quite distinct from the more modern high-frequency vibration which can still be noticed. It was, however, not altogether unpleasant.

Oddly, the test machine's engine remained reasonably quiet – the big, alloy Four was a fairly noisy engine to start with – with little but the whine of the coupling gears and some odd clunks and grinds coming from it. Unhappily, the very large, open area inside the cavernous crankcases allowed some amplification of normal engine noises when the machine was new, so it is safe to assume the engine is basically sound, though probably a little more 'loose' than ideal. Any really bad engine-wear would assuredly have made its presence felt very, very audibly.

But the inside of the left muffler tailpipe was just a little oily, and there was some smoke on upward gear changes or when running hard on the road. Mindful of worn crankshafts and (exceedingly rare) thrown left-front con-rods after many miles with minimal attention, I dropped a cautionary word to the machine's owner and left it at that.

The coupling gears were originally fitted with riveted-on fibre discs to help overcome drive noise inherent in the straight-cut gears, but the overhead valve gear ran quietly enough, so the engine was probably not much noisier overall than some later motorcycles with their chattering overhead camshafts and attendant, swiftly revolving, engine parts. An advantage of the Ariel design was to have the mass of a fairly heavy engine carried at a reasonable height in the frame, which in turn allowed for a fairly low centre of gravity. The comparative narrowness of the engine kept the weight within the confines of the frame, which played its part in making the Big Ariel an easy machine to toss about through corners.

It was spoiled, however, by the low-mounted pair of mufflers, so that much of the advantage of its acceptable handling was lost simply because you couldn't crank the machine over to any great degree in tight corners. The plunger frame took the edge off fast cornering at speed anyway, so it again became clear the Square Four was meant to be ridden as a long-legged touring mount rather than a sports machine. In fact, its easy gait at speed on the road allowed some very impressive point-to-point averages, the bike perfectly comfortable buzzing along at an indicated 60-70mph on the open road, and – tight corners apart – able to maintain the pace with ease.

Inevitably, direct comparisons are made almost automatically between the Ariel and its modern counterparts ... and with quite startling conclusions! It came as a surprise to discover that the bike absorbed many road irregularities almost as easily and as comfortably as some later machines which feature – apparently – vastly superior suspension systems at the rear, while the front forks, though not adequately damped, are at least as good as those fitted to some modern machines.

It survives to take its place amongst other examples of an industry which expired at the wrong time, but what form would the Ariel Square Four be if it was still being manufactured, I couldn't help but wonder. It would employ a 12-volt system, an electric starter and probably be water-cooled, with the crankshafts better supported at their centres, be equipped with swing-arm rear suspension, and disc brakes all around. It might retain its overhead valve design, for here was a Classic machine which was unique in its day and it did not need the 'complication' of a double-overhead camshaft design to achieve its stated aims.

The Ariel Square Four engine lived again in later years, when the Healey Brothers, Gregory and Tim, built a very much improved power-plant, which delivered 52BHP – just 10 more than the original - the engine allied to the Burman BA gearbox which was always used in the 'Squariel'. A much more efficient oil pump was used, along with a better oil filter and an added oil cooler. The engine was fitted with higher compression ratio pistons, and an altered camshaft, the engine and gearbox mounted in the swing-arm frame Ariel should have adopted many years before. It came with a double-sided twin-leading shoe front brake and four CB750 Honda-like mufflers. Only 28 of these very exciting machines were built from 1971-77, the expensive road-burner proving to be very popular. Perhaps the brothers could have made many more Healey machines, but they simply ran out of the large stock of spares, and the few engines, which they purchased from Ariel when the company folded in 1959. The Healey was said to weigh just on 162kg, which was lighter than the standard Squariel by around 15kg and was said to be lighter than the much smaller CB250 Honda. The bike was capable of a top speed of 200km/h.

TECH SPECS

Make: Ariel

Model: 4G

Year of manufacture: 1955

Type:
All-alloy air-cooled four-cylinder overhead valve four-stroke. Four cylinders disposed in square formation, with forged crankshafts rotating in opposite directions, connected by square-cut gears. Bolt-on flywheels and balance weights, shafts supported on white-metal plain bearings on timing side, roller bearings on drive side. Camshaft carried between two pairs of cylinders in crankcase, with control to vertical valves by pushrods.

Bore x stroke: 65 x 75mm x 4

Capacity: 997cc

Power @ rpm:
45BHP (31 kW) at 5800rpm

Compression ratio: 7.5:1

Carburation:
Single car-type SU, with felt air cleaner. (Some models used Solex carburettors.)

Ignition: Battery, coil and points.

Lubrication:
Dry-sump with oil carried in separate tank on frame, with high-capacity, gear-type oil pump; separate oil supply in gearbox and alloy chain-case.

Transmission:
By chain from sprocket driven outboard of rear crank coupling gear, to multi-plate dry clutch and separate Burman BA four-speed constant-mesh gearbox, right-foot change, one-up, three-down pattern. The primary chain runs in an oil-bath chaincase, with cam-and-spring engine shock absorber. Final drive is by chain.

Gear ratios (overall):
1st, 11.55:1; 2nd, 7.4:1; 3rd, 5.7:1; 4th, 4.36:1.

Frame:
Single down-tube type, in welded tubular steel, with full engine cradle which bolts to main frame assembly, substantially braced at steering head.

Suspension:
Front: telescopic forks with coil springs and hydraulic damping.

Rear: plunger type, with short trailing links to 'shock' and rebound springs mounted above and below rear axle. Un-damped.

Wheels, brakes, tyres:
Front: steel rim laced to full-width alloy hub containing 7" drum brake, 325 x 19 ribbed tyre.
Rear: steel rim laced to hub containing 7" drum brake, 400 x 18 block pattern tyre.

Dimensions:
Length – 1975 mm; Wheelbase – 1400mm; Ground clearance – 137mm; Saddle height – 760mm; Weight – 197kg.

Performance:
(*Original road test report, 12 July 1956*)
Top speed, 164km/h; standing quarter, 15.1 sec; fuel consumption, 18.2km/litre.

Machine loaned by:
BRIAN GREENFIELD, Sydney.

1955 NSU MAX 'Special'

250cc OHC SINGLE-CYLINDER

NSU began its operations in the 19th century as a sewing machine manufacturer, and by the end of that century became a *bicycle* manufacturer, so it was a natural progression into powered-two wheelers which saw the then-small factory manufacture its first motorcycle in 1901. It followed the trend of the day by fitting a tiny, under-powered engine into a strengthened pushbike frame with rear drive by belt. It was just three years later that NSU manufactured its first motorcar, the German company from then on clearly going from strength to strength as its two and four-wheeled vehicles became more and more popular.

The NSU factory should have made history in 1932, because it was the first automotive company on earth to manufacture a clearly recognisable Volkswagen 'Beetle'. NSU was by then a very large motorcycle manufacturer, but its car making facilities were also quite large, which meant it could be an ideal company to manufacture the prototype of an all-new brainchild from the talented Doctor Ferdinand Porsche. The result of their collaboration was the entirely functional 'Type 32 Volksauto' which was introduced to the public in that year, the car fitted even then with a rear-mounted, air-cooled, horizontally-opposed four-cylinder engine of just one-litre capacity.

Ferdinand Porsche had originally attempted to have a car of this type made by the Zundapp motorcycle factory, and a couple of prototypes were built, but NSU's all-new Type 32 car, with its very distinctive sloping bonnet, remains to this day instantly recognisable as the forerunner of the popular VW Beetle which ultimately sold almost 8 million units worldwide. Zundapp, on the other hand, employed a more typical 'slab-sided' bonnet design, although there were some similarities in the basics.

This NSU car looks more like an early VW than an early VW ever did. Exactly so. The Type 32 'Volksauto' was designed by Ferdinand Porsche and built by NSU in their car facility in 1932, just before it was sold to Fiat, who didn't want to know about it!

The rear end of the NSU Type 32, showing the flat-four, 1000cc power-plant. Very Volkswagen-like, but it faded away not long before the first VW was built in Wolfsburg, Germany, in 1936. The new car used the same flat-four power-plant, but employed a new, ultimately world-famous, body. The factory cornerstone was laid by Adolf Hitler, who greatly assisted Porsche in building their first 'People's Car'.

55

However, in 1932 NSU sold its car manufacturing facilities to Fiat, the Italian automotive giant insisting that the new, streamlined Volksauto prototype should instantly cease development, so that the interesting, in fact *historical*, vehicle would never be manufactured in volume, at least not by NSU, or Fiat for that matter. Thus, the new Beetle almost died at birth, for NSU then turned its attention exclusively to the manufacture of motorcycles for several years. But NSU was to return to making first-rate cars again, and in a Big Way, many years later.

During the Second World War, NSU built the odd-looking – if distinctly functional – HK101 'Kettenkrad' for the armed forces, the peculiar vehicle consisting of a *detachable* motorcycle front-end which could be firmly bolted to a pair of tank-track rear drive units, with 'accommodation' for up to three (or, at a pinch, four) people, including the driver, contained on top of the open vehicle. The unit must have proved its worth, because civilian versions, which were intended for heavy cross-country use on farms and the like, were made for a few years after hostilities ended.

It was said that by 1955 NSU was the largest motorcycle manufacturer in the world, with more than 350,000 motorcycles and scooters manufactured during that year in a variety of types, many of which were Max, SuperMax and SportsMax motorcycles. This was a claim which might have been challenged at the time by the equally large British BSA group if it were not for the fact that BSA was hanging on by its corporate fingertips, before slipping away with most of the rest of the industry – including NSU – in less than a decade later, with NSU making its last ever motorcycle in 1963.

They all fell victim to the Japanese world-wide onslaught, which began very quietly with the importation of a small handful of 250cc Honda motorcycles into New South Wales, Australia, in April, 1958. But the German company had by then won several World Championships in the fiercely competitive 125 and 250cc classes during 1953 and 1954 and added to these triumphs by also establishing several world land speed records, including Wilhelm Herz becoming the first rider ever to achieve over 200mph on a motorcycle, a speed he attained on the Bonneville Salt Flats. Unhappily, NSU disbanded *most* of its road race and record-attempt activities in 1953.

During that period in the mid-1950s, NSU capitalised upon its racing successes by making the small range of lightweight motorcycles, mopeds, the dashing little NSU 'Prima' scooter – under licence to Lambretta – and the popular 250cc NSU Max, a smart-looking motorcycle with a very neat and externally 'clean' engine which made it look like a two-stroke to the uninitiated, but which was in fact a brilliantly designed, single-cylinder, overhead camshaft four-stroke.

Even though the factory had quit international road racing, there were still highly tuned, single cylinder SuperMax racing machines available which were based upon the road-going Max variants, the racers campaigned by private owners and a select few 'factory' riders for some years afterwards, the machines proving to be at once very, very fast and entirely reliable. Many of the race machines were smartly clad in fully streamlined, hand-beaten aluminium fairings, allied to lightweight alloy mudguards and fuel tanks.

There were at least two of the 250cc overhead camshaft single-cylinder Supermax machines raced in Australia, ridden by top-flight riders like Eric Hinton, Jack Forrest and Jack Ahearn, among others, with Forrest winning the 250cc Lightweight event at Bathurst in 1956 by a country mile. Forrest fell on the fast McPhillamy Park corner on the top of the marvellous Mount Panorama circuit on the last lap, but was so far in front of the rest of the field that he was able to remount and still win the event by almost a third of the length of the long, mostly downhill, Con-Rod Straight. The 250cc class was won again on Mount Panorama by NSU, the machines ridden by Jack Ahearn in 1957 and by Eric Hinton in 1959 and 1960. The flashing German motorcycle was finally up-staged in Australia by the all-conquering 250cc four-cylinder Honda ridden by a young Kel Carruthers, the machine sweeping all before it for several years thereafter.

The **1955, 250cc OHC NSU Max** I was privileged to ride for this report was a great example of its type; a trim, neat-looking motorcycle with many design features which made it years ahead of its time and would allow it to stand high in any company even today. The machine remains unique, both in appearance and design. As I have remarked, the thinly finned head and barrel gives it the appearance of a two-stroke engine, yet of course it is not; it appears to have no rear suspension, but it is served by a clever, 'hidden' cantilever system; its engine the only single-cylinder machine to be fitted with *four* connecting rods; the pressed-metal, monocoque frame apparently employs the engine as a stressed member, but it does not. The marque probably pioneered the short-throw, leading-link front suspension with its sprung guard, the design used by other German manufacturers, and which was blatantly stolen by Honda for its first C70 OHC twin-cylinder motorcycles in the late 1950s.

Rather than *advanced* for its time, the NSU suspension system might better be described as *different* – and indeed very effective. The leading-link front forks were more rigid in all planes than modern telescopic forks, because of the NSU's immovable, box-section, pressed steel 'legs', further strengthened by the supporting, high-mounted sprung front guard, the box-section fork legs enclosing the short pivoting-arm and spring/damper units. Essentially soft in springing, the front end of the test machine worked very well as it soaked up most road shocks with ease and managed this without relaying too much shock to the flat handlebars.

A single rear shock, enclosed and out-of-sight within the centre of the pressed metal frame, is connected to a vertical strut on the forward end of the swung-arm, the short, soft movement controlled by springs and hydraulic damper, similar to the system employed on some much late model Yamaha motorcycles. This rear suspension unit is probably over-taxed on the NSU, for it is short and not very well damped; though very comfortable indeed, with a long rear wheel travel because of the forward-mounted spring/damper unit, the tail-end proving to be somewhat choppy over rough surfaces. It could be felt pulling the bike out of line a little when cornering swiftly over bumpy roads.

I stress the machine's extreme comfort, perhaps at the expense of some handling, though there could be few complaints about the manner in which it coped with hard riding. This is helped to an enormous degree by the single saddle, which mounted by its nose and was controlled by a very clever suspension system of its own. A full 75 mm of movement is allowed, and the little seat bottomed on a couple of occasions to prove its effectiveness – but it could have been a little better damped, for movement is controlled by a large spring with a thinner spring inside it and a long rubber snubber.

The inner spring is wound in the opposite direction to the outer and is also close to an interference fit, which is an old trick used in engine-valve control when coil springs are employed. The rubber inserted into the inner spring under the saddle is clearly inserted to provide a form of automatic, infinitely variable, simple damper control.

Mostly it works very well and is enclosed within a neat metal cover mounted within the frame atop the rear cantilever unit. It works very well on undulating roads, but can be caught out over sudden jolts where it will absorb all the energy of the bump and then spring back to position to lift a rider just clear of the saddle. As far as shock absorption is concerned, few machines will ever hold a candle to this system, despite some of its minor shortcomings. A dual-seat was available as an extra for the little Max, and was occasionally fitted, but much of the machine's great comfort might disappear should the great single saddle be replaced with a much firmer dual-seat.

The frame is fabricated from large steel pressings welded down the 'spine' and is immensely strong. The main frame includes the steering head, with the box-section shape at its strongest beneath the seat where stresses are greatest. The rear mudguard – in effect a stiffener to enhance the structure – bolts to the rear of the

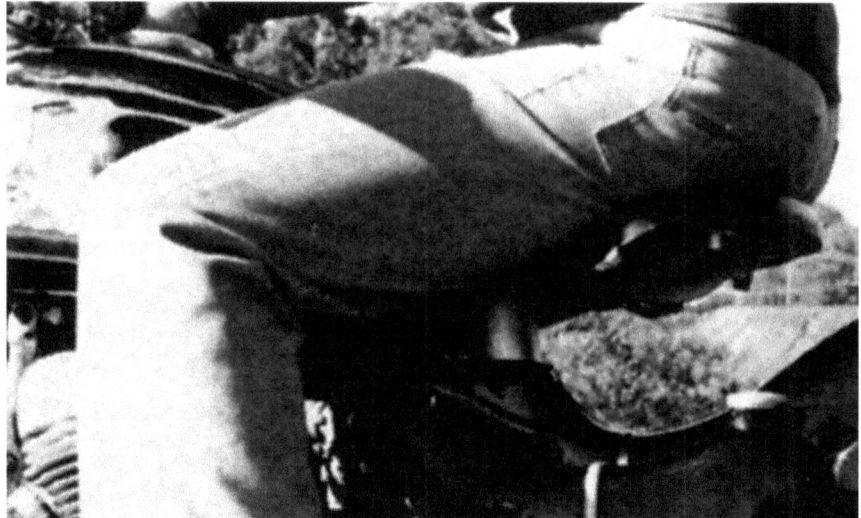

Here is the cantilever-hung single saddle perched upon its vertical suspension system. It added its own dimension to the hidden rear suspension in allowing another level of comfort, as it easily ironed out the shock of potholes and bumps the rear suspension may not have absorbed.

frame just above the fabricated swing-arm, the whole assembly at once rigid and strong in all planes and yet surprisingly light in weight.

Contained within a semi-cradle which bolts to the crankcases about mid-way and with the cylinder head attached by bracket to the lower steering head, the engine does *not* act as a stressed member, though its presence must have an effect on stiffening the assembly. Tidy in the extreme, the engine/gearbox power-unit resembles an alloy 'egg' with an iron cylinder and alloy head sprouting from its top. There is not an extraneous bulge to be seen.

The unit-construction design was not in universal use when the NSU was new, and there were many riders then (as now) who thought the machine was a two-stroke.

In fact, it is a brilliantly conceived four-stroke with a single overhead camshaft driven by eccentrics and connecting-rods, the cam drive carried on the left of the cylinder barrel inside a cast-in tunnel. An eccentric shaft driven from the crankshaft imparts reciprocating movement, through a con-rod, to a similar shaft on the end of the camshaft, while a secondary rod operates from a compensatory eccentric on the same shafts. A **third** rod is carried in the assembly simply to locate the bearing's outer race and to lock the assembly together while a small bob-weight on the end of the camshaft helps the balance factor remain reasonably constant. It was referred to as the 'Ultra Max Drive' which didn't describe the system at all.

The OHC driving rods are quite thin, but resemble engine con-rods though they are longer and have a 'sort-of-big-end' at each end, while the centres of the rods – at the cylinder heads – convert the reciprocating motion to rotating motion and thus drive the camshaft. It sounds

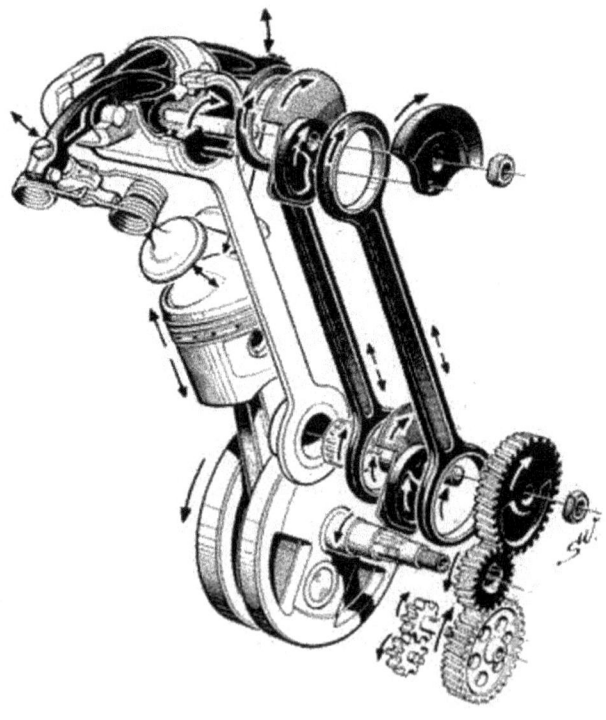

This overhead camshaft drive is unique to NSU. Usually, an OHC is driven by chain, by vertical shaft with bevel gears or by a train of gears. Here is a single cylinder engine, but one which employs not just one, but four connecting rods! The mainshaft's half-time pinion drives a gear which propels the rods to drive the overhead camshaft, and the process can be seen by noting the directions of the various arrows which helps to show how it all works.

complicated, and is damned hard to describe simply, but the system is relatively simple and can be left alone once it is set up and shimmed correctly for valve clearances.

Primary drive is by helical gear from the end of the eccentric shaft, which allows the engine to run in the same direction as the road wheels instead of backwards as is so often the case. The interpolation of a small driving gear on the crankshaft to drive the eccentrics neatly takes care of that, and it also drives a small gear beneath it to operate the high-capacity oil pump.

The crankshaft is a normal, pressed-up assembly with caged roller big-end bearing, the shaft supported on a large, parallel-roller main bearing on the right side, while no fewer than three ball bearings support the 'busy' left side. The engine is over-square, with bore and stroke of 69 x 66 mm, while the compression ratio is modest at 7.4:1. Valves are controlled by hairpin springs.

The electric system is 6 volt and the entire system of generator and ignition carried on the end of the right-side crankshaft.

The little NSU Max has always had a spot in my memory, for it is the first machine I rode in 1959 which had the gear lever on the left side. Riding a long series of British motorcycles with the foot gear-change pedal on the 'correct' (right-hand) side for many years provided something of a problem for me first time out, and I remember exiting a heavily gravelled corner and running into a telegraph pole at less than walking pace while trying desperately to stop the bike by means of its left-side gear lever!

Kick-starting the bike was also a chore in 1959, as I recall, but the fact that the kick-starter was on the NSU machine's left side holds no terrors these days, because the first Japanese machines had their kick-starters similarly mounted – before the advent of electric starters, I might add – so that odd trick had been long learned.

The old, separate-bowl Bing carburettor needs the time-honoured practice of a couple of tickles of the plunger to raise the fuel level in the bowl, and then, with full choke applied, one kick suffices to fire the engine up. It idles quietly and is dead smooth, with the same soft *'thump! thump! thump!'* through the huge pattern muffler that always distinguishes a punchy single – no matter what engine capacity.

But the carburetion is a bit odd coming off idle speed onto the throttle cutaway, and there seems to be little that can be done about it. According to Galvin, the factory specifies a throttle with a cutaway which would do justice to the Hollywood Bowl and at the time of the test there was no smaller slide available. It was a pain in traffic, because once the choke is opened fully the carburettor spits and coughs back at the critical point just as the throttle is opened and the engine threatens to stall every time one moves away from the lights.

In fact, if you have to roll the throttle right off and then open it again on the move, there is a momentary flat-spot before it all chimes in again. As I said, little can be done about this, for different needles and needle positions have been tried without success. A new slide, with a much smaller cutaway to enrich the mixture at that point is needed, and that's all there is to that!

It isn't helped by the adoption of that old German ploy, the straight-pull twist-grip, which is easier on throttle cables but which results in a very slow action. It doesn't serve the bike at all well, simply because it seems to require a giant handful of throttle to get anywhere, and you seem to be rolling it off forever before the bike slows down again. A quick-action twist-grip would have been much better employed by NSU to give the rider the impression of a somewhat higher performance.

In fact, the current, cunning Japanese ploy of fitting quick-action twist-grips seems to imbue smaller machines with the 'feeling' of a higher performance not always borne out in stopwatch figures, and many a tired workhorse in days of yore suddenly enjoyed a new lease of life with the fitting of a well-oiled, 'QA' twist-grip! I know the NSU would benefit greatly by such a fitting, though it would then be non-standard … which would probably never do!

Typically, the clutch lever action is light to the point of being squishy and uncertain, while the gear lever, again typically, requires almost twice the movement of modern machines. To be sure of a clean, fast change you have to actually remove your foot from the rest when lifting the lever into a higher gear.

The engine is very punchy and smoother than most, but the designers have seen fit to equip the machine with a set of very wide-ratio gears. That's okay but the bike would have been better served (and even more so in these days of sports mounts with near-racing performance) if the ratios had been much closer together, with five speeds in the gearbox as well. A glance at the specifications panel will show the huge gaps between the four gears, and this is a pity because the bike is so willing to get up and go. Each upward gear change drops engine speed well down the scale and then one has to wind it all up again … while using that great handful of throttle.

It's a bit frustrating, but cannot take more than an edge off the delightful overall performance of the trim German single, for it can be flung about on smooth roads with an abandon verging on the absurd.

Probably the only real criticism of the machine's suspension could be directed to the limited movement of the front wheel, for it is only deep pot-holes or the broken surface of tar-sealed motocross tracks which disturb the bike's equilibrium – and then, I suspect, it is more the rider than the bike which is disturbed. Over give-and-take surfaces like minor ripples, the bike is amongst the most comfortable this side of road-going LTS (Long Travel Suspension) trail bikes, and the handling is precise and very, very predictable.

The engine would happily run to an indicated 55mph on the old 'Imperial' speedo, and the bike seemed perfectly happy to run to over 70 in top gear (for short periods, might I add, the engine was by no means run-in after a complete rebuild). It came as a surprise to discover that an original road-test article claims the bike managed 64mph in *third gear*, with the engine running at nearly 8500rpm!

This was a monumental engine speed for road bike in the middle of last century, and is

Having noted the deeply valanced and flared front guard I decided to put it to the test by riding the bike through a convenient pool of water, which ended up a little deeper than I had anticipated. We emerged on the other side with boots which were absolutely bone dry. Very handy when riding on wet roads.

certainly a pointer to the efficiency of the odd OHC drive assembly, as well as the strength of the machine's bottom-half. No doubt the NSU Production Racing motorcycles engines would easily buzz to that speed, and assuredly much higher, but it was unusual for a roadster of that age to do so.

Out on the open road, with its uncertain surfaces and occasional bomb-craters, I found the best way to ride the little bike and take advantage of its excellent suspension was to relax my arms and take most of my weight directly upon the sprung saddle, allowing the odd bump to be absorbed by the suspension and the last ounce to be scrubbed off by the seat's springing. It is then you can appreciate the advantage of some form of springing in the saddle itself, rather than rely on the frame's efficiency while perched upon the usual too-firm dual-seat.

Of course, the dual-seat is here to stay, but such German makers as Denfeld and Meier made double seats which were well padded but which also carried a series of springs under the padding to take the edge off the Big Ones. The single, sprung saddle, though of course much more expensive to make these days, could well be re-introduced with great advantage from the points of view of both comfort and safety.

But riding at night required a neat touch on the ignition/light switch because the tumblers were badly worn and an incautious hand would instantly cut the engine when the 'key' was turned to bring the lights on. It took a while to be accustomed to the feel, but once the key was jiggled into the correct position the headlamp was like a death-ray! Far better than some of the 12-volt systems in use today, that 6-volt headlamp lit the road ahead for an unbelievable distance, making high cruising speeds after dark a breeze.

Why the hell they decided to use such a piddling little tail-lamp is beyond me; again, typically German, the lens was about 30mm across and could hardly be seen at all. The stop-light operated only from the rear brake, and there were no blinkers fitted, of course. There were also no warning lights either, except one for the ignition/generator warning, which sat below the single dial speedometer. I would have replaced the rear light with the much larger BMW one: non-standard then, of course, but a German Bosch component nonetheless.

The brakes, if not powerful in the extreme, were well up the task, and certainly in keeping with the bike's performance, though the pedal pressure was unusually firm on the footbrake and light on the hand lever. Contained within very modern-looking full-width alloy hubs, the 185 mm drums employed single-leading shoe operation front and rear.

Chain final drive, on the right-hand ('wrong') side, was totally enclosed, which was, and remains, an unusual feature on a machine of this size: it remains standard fitment on many German machines of the period. Snail-cam adjusters for the rear chain (now finding acceptance on many off-road machines) were standard on the machine.

Air filtration was clever, with the entire frame used as an air-collector with the wire-mesh filter carried in a plenum-like still-air box attached to the oil tank on the machine's left side.

Miserly on fuel and yet possessing a performance which left other 250s – and some 350s – gasping in its wake when the machine was new, the trim little German machine was reasonably popular in its day, carrying on the tradition of sporting lightweights which was so prevalent before the war: if not quite so much after hostilities.

It outshone many of its contemporaries simply because they were by and large a poor lot, with only the C11 BSA (the forgettable) Panther 65, the Royal Enfield in contention from Britain, the 250cc two-stroke Austrian Puch, and R26 four-stroke BMW or two-stroke Adler from Germany to compete against.

Before the war, BSA fielded its Blue Star 250, and there were such little 250cc swifties as the Tiger 70 Triumph, the four-valve Rudge, New Imperial, the OHC Excelsior Manxman, the pushrod Ariel and AJS. The competition was indeed very keen in the class in the 1930s!

Today, there are some swift 250 singles about,

which was probably inevitable because of new legislations to limit the size of motorcycles which may be ridden by Learner motorcyclists, and the field now features several lightweight machines which would have been strange indeed just a few years ago when large-capacity, multi-cylinder motorcycle almost ruled the roost.

If the NSU resurfaced tomorrow with the obligatory five-speed close-ratio gearbox and all the trimmings of the latest machinery – including a Quick-Action twist-grip! – it would surely stand on its merits and be recognised along with the best of Japanese machinery as a fine example of a top-flight, lightweight 21st century German motorcycle. But, in the middle of last century it was clearly well ahead of its time.

This is the factory-built racing version of the NSU Max, which developed 29 BHP at 9600rpm, just over 60% higher than the standard machine! It was usually fitted with an aluminium alloy fairing, which increased its top speed by some 6mph. It was intended as a 'Clubman'-level racer, but was so fast it won many GP events, including a number in Australia.

TECH SPECS

Make: NSU

Model: Max Special

Year of manufacture: 1955

Type:
Air-cooled single-cylinder OHC four-stroke, with cast-iron cylinder barrel and alloy head. Overhead camshaft driven by 'Ultra Max' system of dual eccentrics phased at 90 degrees, via three connecting rods, to valve rockers with tappet-type adjustment and hairpin valve springs. Pressed-up crank with caged roller big-end, crankshaft supported on three ball and one parallel roller bearing. Dry sump lubrication.

Bore x stroke: 69 x 66mm

Capacity: 247cc

Compression ratio: 7.4:1

Power @rpm: 18BHP at 6750rpm

Carburetion:
Bing slide-type, with mesh air-filter and still-air box.

Ignition:
Battery, coil and points, with automatic ignition advance.

Electrical:
Crankshaft-mounted 6-volt 60 watt generator.

Transmission:
By helical gear from left of crankshaft to four-plate clutch with seven springs and cush-drive, rubber shock-absorption, to four-speed constant-mesh gearbox. Left foot-change, one-down, three-up pattern. Enclosed rear chain.

Gear ratios (overall):
1st – 21.6:1; 2nd – 13.73:1;
3rd – 9.53:1; 4th – 6.78:1.

Suspension:
Leading-ink front forks with coil springs and two-way hydraulic damping; rear by pivoting fork, cantilever system with single spring/hydraulic unit. Single saddle carried upon double-sprung suspension, with simple damping by inserted rubber, 'snubber' operating under seat's cantilever action.

Frame:
Fabricated from steel pressings welded down centreline to form spine-type, box-section frame, stiffened by flat-mounted rear mudguard section, engine cradle located at base of crankcases, with bracket from cylinder head to lower steering head.

Wheels, brakes:
Steel rims front and rear, with full-width alloy hubs and enclosed, single-leader drum brakes of 190mm diameter. 325 x 19 Metzeler tyres in block pattern front and rear.

Dimensions:
Wheelbase – 1305mm; Ground clearance – 145mm; Seat height – 75.5mm; Weight – 154kg; Fuel tank – 14.5 litres.

Performance:
(From original road test 1955) Top speed 130km/h (78mph); quarter-mile 21.5 sec; braking (from 50km/h) 9.8 metres; fuel consumption (overall) 27km/l (78mpg).

Machine loaned by:
JOHN GALVIN, Sydney.

1921 Henderson Four 'De Luxe' Outfit'

1300cc SIDE-VALVE FOUR-CYLINDER, WITH HENDERSON SIDECAR

Today, the heavyweight, large-capacity motorcycles with fat dual-seats and forward-mounted footboards are universally referred to as 'Cruisers' and most of them, for some unaccountable reason, seem to be powered by Vee-twin engines. To call them cruisers is as accurate a description of these long-legged touring motorcycles as you would ever wish to hear and the term may be new, but this type of motorcycle is not, for it is described succinctly by Wikipedia as 'a term for motorcycles which mimic the design style of Harley-Davidson, Indian, Excelsior and **Henderson.**' It goes on to say:–'The riding position on a Cruiser places the feet forward and the hands up, with the spine erect or leaning back slightly, ... the 'Western Saddle' riding position, which resembles the riding position used by cowboys in the American West. It allows greater long-distance comfort, albeit *with some compromise of control'*(?) My question mark, underline and italics, for this description is quite accurate, but is ambiguous for I suggest it may well refer – at least in some instances – to the 'compromise of control' of a *motorcycle*, rather than the horse!

It has been suggested by some that the history of the Cruiser motorcycle may go back only as far as 1930, but one of the earliest examples of this type of machine probably belongs to the big **Henderson Four**, the first model of which was made in Detroit, America, in 1912. The first news of the new Henderson motorcycle was actually published in a British motorcycle magazine in 1910, following a letter to that publication from Henderson himself, the letter describing the embryonic machine which was little more than an idea at the time.

That first four-cylinder Henderson owes much to the well-known 1904 FN, for the big American machine's engine was laid-out as an in-line four-cylinder design, which owed much to the design of the earlier four-cylinder Belgian machine – FN, for *Fabrique Nationale* – the European machine having the added features of shaft final drive and an early, crude type of telescopic front fork.

Henderson, however, was not the first four-cylinder machine to be made in America. The distinction belongs to the 1909 Pierce-Arrow; virtually a copy of the Belgian FN four-cylinder machine, a motorcycle which Perce Pierce had ridden through Europe and, in effect, stole for the design of his own four-cylinder motorcycle. However, Henderson assuredly became the best-known and, just as certainly, became by far the most successful.

The 'straight four' was not really a popular design, probably because of engine cooling problems, but there have been several examples of this type of engine employed by other countries as well. The Wilkinson Sword factory – yes, the manufacturers of swords and razor blades, of all people! – built a shaft-drive, in-line four in 1909 and the car maker Vauxhall built a similar machine in 1923, the latter never reaching production, while the mighty Moto Guzzi factory also utilised this design, its fluid-cooled, 1950s shaft drive 500cc GP racer ridden by the ace Scottish rider, Fergus Anderson. However, none of these machines were very successful, with both the Wilkinson and Vauxhall cast in the mould of the Cruiser motorcycle.

The history of the Cruiser was said to be bound up within a motorcycle's design parameters and it is well illustrated in the **1921 Henderson 'Four' K-Model De Luxe** motorcycle outfit we were fortunate enough to discover in Melbourne some years ago. The machine was owned by Wal Maynard of Chadstone and was in pristine condition, glorifying in its standard dark-blue colour, with gold pin striping, the Henderson name still emblazoned upon the petrol tank, the name dominated by that large red X which indicated that the machine was actually built by the Excelsior (Super X) Motorcycle Company.

Although initially made in America by Bill Henderson, ably assisted by his brother Tom, Henderson was actually a Scotsman and an impecunious one at that. The brothers were forced to sell out in 1917 to Ignatz Schwinn, originally a maker of bicycles, who had taken over the Excelsior motorcycle company which was at that time manufacturing the famous Vee-twin machines. Excelsior logos bore the big Red

X which was later to be part of the Henderson logo, Excelsior also marketing some of their own Vee-twins as Henderson machines.

The K-Model we rode was introduced in 1920, but this later, 1921 model was said to include many improvements, though it is outwardly very similar to its predecessor. Detailed modifications to the 1921 model included beefing up the crankshaft and widening the big-end and main bearings to overcome the occasional problem of breaking crankshafts. The crank is drop-forged in high-quality, nickel-chrome steel, case-hardened and precision ground on the four big-end and three main bearing journals. The diameter is 32mm for all the bottom-end bearings, the big-ends 28mm wide, the mains 37mm, with bronze-backed white metal shells employed on bearing surfaces.

The forged, nickel-chrome car-type connecting rods are long and very thin, but are strengthened by adopting the 'old-fashioned' I-Beam shape and are fitted with detachable end-caps which contain the slipper big-end bearings, the conrods employing locking bolts to clamp onto the pistons' gudgeon pins; a practice adopted for many years in automotive circles. The long, three bearing camshaft is also drop forged in nickel-chrome steel and is similarly heat-treated.

As an in-line four, it was the only type of engine employed from Henderson's original designs, no matter who made them, even if some 'Henderson' models – which were essentially *Excelsior* machines – were marketed as large capacity Vee-twins. The four-cylinder engine is a long-stoke design with a bore of 68.26mm and stroke of 88.89mm resulting in an engine capacity of some 1301cc; fairly large for those days. But the Henderson 'Big X' in-line four was a very punchy engine which was surprisingly vibration-free. Pistons are cast iron, to be supplied as an option in 1922 with 'Lynite' aluminium alloy components and at some 95mm are quite long in comparison to more modern designs. The extra length is said to overcome problems of piston slap with its consequent premature wear to both piston rings and cylinder walls.

Cutaway drawing of Henderson 4 interior, showing drill-ways for big-end and main bearing lubrication with the external oil pump and its several oil lines, in front of the engine. Note the drive to gearbox, though large flywheel, with its 'wet' internal clutch assembly.

The pistons employ just two piston rings, but their compression ratio was stated as an odd '58 pounds cold' which hints at about 5.5:1

The crankcase is split horizontally, the lower half also forming an oil sump, the gearbox cast in unit with the engine, the top half of the split casting containing the camshaft and its attendant bearings, along with the engine main bearing housing. The gearbox of course shares the horizontally split casting, while the gearbox bearings are locked into the cases by close-fitting, threaded rings, the bosses for which are machined *into each crankcase half*. This must have entailed very, very close work indeed!

Unusually, the crankshaft is not sited along the centre-line of the cases in relation to the centrally mounted cylinders, but is off-set by 12 degrees towards the timing side. It is said that this allows for less angularity to the con-rods on the firing stroke, while allowing the camshaft to sit along the engine's right side. This means that the lighter-stressed exhaust stroke has a greater rod angularity and this is the reason for machining a notch in the sides of the long pistons and an adjacent area of the crankcase casting. Cleverly, the crankshaft's transverse motion is converted to longitudinal rotation by a bevel gear take-off from the front of the gearbox, with the final drive by chain.

A heart-shaped case at the front of the long crankcase contains the timing gears for the camshaft, while also providing the unusual drive for the four-lobe magneto and the generator on the engine's left side. A flexible drive from the top of the case spins the magneto, while a pulley in the centre of the drive shaft allows for a belt-drive to the generator sited directly above. The flexible coupling is there to allow for any slight misalignment when the external magneto is fitted to its mounting platform.

An externally mounted, two-gear oil pump supplies lubricant under 15psi through external pipes to the base of the engine and through oil galleys direct to the large main bearings. It is routed from there to the big-end bearings, from where it is flung under centrifugal force to the cylinder walls. Another special drilling, which is adjacent to the rear main bearing, conducts oil along the centre of the crankshaft to lubricate the gear selector mechanism and the gears themselves. Most of the other engine components are very effectively lubricated by 'splash' or oil mist, but special drillings allow pressure-fed oil to lubricate the main timing gears and magneto drive bearings. Oil then drains back into the sump through a grid-like 'false bottom' in the lower crankcase half.

Note the ease of maintenance, with easy access to spark plugs, the four-branch inlet manifold, fed by a 1-inch updraught Zenith carburettor. Exhaust pipes hang directly downwards, with a large muffler underneath the footboard.

The four exhaust pipes hang straight down from the side-valve cylinder heads, which looks odd to modern eyes, while the large muffler sits neatly underneath the right footboard. The four 18mm spark plugs hang out in the breeze from the top of the four entirely separate cast iron cylinder barrels, with their non-detachable heads and would appear to be a bit too close to a rider's leg to be comfortable. At the very least, however, the spark plugs are **very** readily accessible. The separate cylinders are thinly finned and this would seem to be a design fault in view of the possibility of over-heating in the rear cylinders, but as each cylinder is cast as a separate component and is thus bolted *individually* to the crankcase, there is a very good air circulation around each of the four pots.

Even though the cylinders are cast in one piece with non-detachable 'heads', there are large screw-in caps directly above the valves which are there to allow for valve and valve seat inspection, or even for work to be carried out on the valves …if an owner was skilful enough, without the necessity of removing a cylinder from the crankcase!

The gap between cylinders two and three is wider than the gap between the other pots and this assists with cooling, but was also due to the long crankshaft's central main bearing, which was ideally situated between those two cylinders. One clear advantage of separate cylinders meant that any of them could be removed on its own without disturbing anything else – if you wanted to do that for whatever reason; or for no reason at all!

The Henderson engine is very low-slung in the duplex down-tube frame, with its centre of gravity well below wheel-spindle height. This is most unusual – if unheard of – in modern, transverse four-cylinder engine designs, because the much more efficient double overhead camshaft engines fitted to most modern four-cylinder machines results in much more 'top hamper' because of the additional weight being carried high in the frame. The very low centre of gravity in the older design was said to imbue a **solo** Henderson with great stability and first-rate handling, even at the extremely high speeds at which the old banger could be ridden. The frame is similarly low-slung, with the perfectly angled, forward-mounted footboards low to the ground, which would assuredly discourage enthusiastic cornering, although this pursuit was

Recently removed from a light aircraft, this Henderson engine has clearly seen some service in the air. The simple screw-in bungs above the valves have been greatly enhanced to make for easier removal allowing routine inspection of valves and valve seats.

probably not indulged in very often 100 years ago, with most of the world's roads still not much better than rutted dirt tracks.

To be sure, Henderson motorcycles were often raced on dirt and board tracks back in the 1920s and the marque won a great many races, but those machines were purpose built, whereas the Model K was very much the old-fashioned Gentlemen's Tourer. As a point of interest, many Henderson engines which had their clutch assembly and gearboxes removed were used in light aircraft and they were very successfully employed because they were reliable in the extreme and were considered to be not only the best-*known* four-cylinder engine at the time, but were considered by most enthusiasts, whether in the air or on the ground, to be the *best* of all the Fours which were in favour at that time.

In passing, there were a number of *two-litre, six-cylinder* Henderson motorcycle made way back in 1924, but they were *said* to have been used a 'test beds', for the engines were originally intended to be used in light aircraft. But you could bet your house on the supposition that there were **many** of them which were put to good use on the open road! There were also several very fancy 'one-off' Hendersons in several colours, which looked more like two-wheeled cars than true motorcycles!

This 1924 six-cylinder machine was said to provide the ideal 'test bed' for the larger, two-litre aircraft engines, but there can be little doubt that there were many sold as complete machines intended for high-speed touring. How long it would take to stop this heavier machine with no front brake has thus far not been recorded.

Described as two-wheel cars, a small number of Henderson bikes received this smart-looking 'art deco', after-market treatment in 1930, with fat tyres and huge, single saddles. As well as jet black, they came in bright red, sky blue, ivory, two-tone pale green and lemon and grey. A marvellous – if rare – transformation if ever there was one!

The Model K has the longest swept-back handlebars I have ever experienced. They come out of the head stock and sweep back at such an angle that the twist-grip throttle control in opened 'inwards' rather than back-and-forth as is normal practice. The left twist-grip is also used: rolled back to retard the ignition timing when kicking the big engine over and then opened up to advance the timing for optimum performance.

It would appear that only those with ape-like arms could be able to turn the bars through their full extent (which would only be required when riding a machine with sidecar attached, of course) but those ultra-long bars, allied to the front fork's trail angle, allowed for a kind of 'power steering' and a total lack of that handlebar 'shimmer' so often experienced when taking one hand off the bars to change gear. This phenomenon can sometimes be present with the best of motorcycle outfits, particularly with the movement of a sidecar wheel over irregular road surfaces, but the big Henderson was very easy to steer and required very little effort, the handlebars almost 'static' over a large variety of road surfaces.

Changing gear on the Henderson is an art all on its own, because there are in fact **two** very long levers attached to the left side of the fuel tank in very close alignment, one of which is used to disengage the clutch, the other to change gears! The bike has a three-speed gearbox, with a separate reverse which is hand operated from the handlebars, independent of the gearbox. With the long clutch lever in the 'dis-engaged' position, the clutch action is smooth and quite precise as the lever is slowly re-engaged to take up the drive.

Gear-changing is thus a very casual affair, with the long clutch lever first disengaging the drive, then the other, shorter lever alongside it shifting the gears, while the long hand lever is then released to re-engage the clutch. Thankfully, there is yet another *foot-operated* pedal on the left footboard to control the clutch, making the process of changing gear very much quicker, but it seems odd that this 'over-kill' of two entirely separate levers should be used for the same

The two levers on the left side of the fuel tank operated the clutch and gearchange, the larger lever operating the clutch. It made for a very casual gearchange, but happily there was an 'over-riding' foot-controlled clutch control as well, which was much, much quicker: just one of many quirks.

operation when *one* would clearly suffice – in particular the much easier, foot operated one!

But the reason for the two separate clutch operating levers soon becomes apparent, for a *second* foot pedal on the left side can be used – in conjunction with a corresponding pedal on the *right* side – to control the rear brake, and this is where the long clutch lever clearly comes into play, for you can use it to disengage the clutch and perhaps change down a gear while you then apply the other (brake) pedal on the left side to slow down. Unhappily, you don't easily stop the bike, because the brakes are not quite up to the job.

If it sounds complicated then it assuredly is, because in fact there are **two** rear brakes which are applied using either of the two pedals; one to take the edge of the bike's speed and the other to slow down and ultimately to stop! Or, of course, you can apply both at once if you are forced to do so, but pulling up remains a fairly casual affair: as for emergency braking? Please don't go there!

The dual rear brake involves a contracting steel band, lined with a flexible, asbestos-like(!) friction material which clamps around the *outside* of the brake drum and is controlled by the right foot, while a lever operated by either heel or toe from the **left** footboard opens up a brake shoe fitted *inside* that same brake drum, almost – but not quite – the same as a normal drum brake fitted with a pair of brake shoes. It's

Keeping a very wary eye on traffic up ahead, groping for second gear was much easier if the foot-operated lever was used. Energy stored in the very heavy flywheel always resulted in a good lurch forward, even before the throttle was opened, which one needed to be well aware of. With no traffic about, the bike would pick up speed very rapidly after every upward gearchange.

all a bit odd by modern standards, but once used to this juggling act, the system of brake, gearchange and clutch control becomes very nearly (if not quite) manageable. It becomes even more so with quite a bit more practice, but it still requires more than a little concentration to get it right every time!

There is, however, no front brake! It isn't unusual because, at that time, there were few motorcycles fitted with front brakes. There were few **cars** with front brakes in those days either and those that employed brakes on all wheels often carried a small triangle on the rear mudguard in which was imprinted a large number 4, or a larger red triangle, to warn following road users that the vehicle up ahead had four brakes and would certainly stop a whole lot quicker than a following vehicle with only two brakes fitted to the rear wheel(s).

A proud boast by Henderson is that the operation of the kick-starter would turn the engine over twice, but a hefty boot on the lever always resulted in the big old engine's magneto firing up in about half a kick, the engine then idling with surprising smoothness. There was no feeling of vibration at the large footboards and none at those long, long handlebars. Much of the engine's inherent smoothness was simply to do with the design of that big in-line four, of course, but the very heavy, large-diameter flywheel just ahead of the gearbox, in which the multi-plate, wet clutch was mounted, would also have damped much of any vibration which may otherwise have been present.

Acceleration was startling, to say the least. Even with the *original Henderson sidecar* attached and its proud owner sitting in the chair, that old war horse took off with a turn of speed which was a surprise and after initially fiddling around with an odd gear-change which dropped the engine revs down to not much more than a fast idle, the bike sprang away again in second gear with a surprising agility. No doubt the energy stored in the bike's thick, heavy flywheel would have helped enormously.

Perhaps it shouldn't have been such a surprise that the engine produced its great torque at not much more than a fast idle, because the Big Four produces its modest power at no more than *3400rpm*, which means that pulling well from low engine revs is a built-in bonus. This was even more obvious in top gear, because the engine pulls its heavy load with ease, even from fairly low road speeds. It would have been nice if it stopped just as effectively!

The bike was actually a very fast tourer, with a top speed recorded in 1921 (on a machine which had over 16,000km on the clock) of over 156km/h, which is just under the old metric 100mph: another Henderson achieved the 100mph 'yardstick' later in the same year. On a stinking hot day, again in 1921, a standard, four-cylinder motorcycle endured a Police-sanctioned run of some 50km on a sandy, desert road in Bakersville, the motorcycle averaging just on 110km/h for the journey. It was a stunning performance for its day, but there is no record of how long it took to pull up again after the test was finished. Furthermore, it is probably no surprise that the Police were happy to be involved in that record run, because Henderson machines were always a favourite as high-performance 'pursuit' motorcycles with a number of police forces in America.

If the bike's road performance is impressive indeed, then so too is the machine's comfortable ride. The heavy-duty front forks are the trailing-link design with the shock and rebound springs directly ahead of the steering head contained in a weather-proof cylinder. The spring action is un-damped, but nonetheless very effective, the large 3.50 x 20" tyres on their wide rims helping to soak up some of the road surfaces' irregularities.

There is no rear suspension, but the newly designed deep-pan 'anatomically correct' single saddle handled bumps, dips, pot holes and other poor road surfaces with an amazing, almost contemptuous, ease. The large saddle is mounted from its nose on a pivot point half way along the petrol tank, with the suspension medium a pair of shortish tension springs at the rear of the saddle base. The long fulcrum thus allows the saddle to move through its long travel almost vertically, instead of prescribing an arc as it would do if the saddle was hung directly from its nose. That large saddle and its attendant suspension was a revelation for, no matter what the rear wheel was doing over 'uncertain' road surfaces, that saddle simply floated over everything with no road shock transmitted through to the seat's incumbent. Because the saddle did such an amazing job in absorbing road irregularities one could have thought rear wheel suspension was entirely superfluous. Had even the crudest form of rear suspension been employed in conjunction with the wonderful saddle, the ride would have been quite extraordinary!

Unhappily, Henderson was to survive for only another ten years, but the name went out with a bang when just two prototype *six-cylinder*,

As a last Hurrah, this 1931 two-litre Henderson was yet another great six-cylinder machine, only two of which were ever made. Thankfully, they both still exist, but at last fitted with a (tiny) front brake, which was finally adopted as late as 1928! Note how front forks run through the front guard, a feature seen again when the new Vee-twin Henderson made a brief re-appearance in the year 2000.

1995cc monsters were produced in 1931 to augment the last of the 'Flying Fours'. At just under two litres capacity and at last equipped with a (small) front brake, what a blast those two machines would have been with an engine of that capacity!

To finish, let me quote *verbatim* from the publicity blurb which was published in an original Henderson brochure I have which accompanied the 1921 model. It could have been written yesterday and sums up motorcycling in general better than many a paragraph which *was* written yesterday!

It says: *'Pre-eminent in the motorcycle world is the new Henderson de-luxe model. It is conspicuously in a class by itself for no other machine combines so many alluring and attractive features. It is the culmination of ten years of constant endeavour to build the very ultimate in motorcycles, a really perfect and finished Four. Extreme speed, surpassing smoothness and motor operation at all speeds, amazing responsiveness to the throttle, complete absence of vibration, shock and jerk, with quietness, cleanliness, dependability and durability to a degree hitherto unknown, are all built into the new Henderson de-luxe model and the result is a motorcycle which dominates the field by sheer weight of inherent worth.'*

I love this last paragraph, for it says it all: its philosophy applies to motor cyclists world-wide **even today**, as it did in 1921 and as it ever shall. It reads: *'Speed makes an essential appeal to motorcycle riders. They like life, snap, pep and fleetness in a machine. Even though they may never ride wide open, they like to know that their machines have a reserve of speed and power. They like to boast to their friends what their machines have done and can do. They like to go out on the road and demonstrate that they 'have the goods''.'* Amen to that!

That anonymous copy-writer summed it all up so very well for, quite apart from extolling the virtues of that old war horse, the sentiments expressed a century ago about motorcycling in general and the motorcyclist in particular, are just as viable today as they have ever been.

Here is another Henderson 'two-wheeled car', just one of many from the late 1920s/early 30s, and what a machine it must have been. As far as we can ascertain, all these Hendersons, which were so greatly modified back in those days, are still in existence today, which should be no surprise.

TECH SPECS

Make: Henderson

Model: De-Luxe

Year of manufacture: 1921

Type:
Air-cooled four-cylinder four-stroke. Cylinders located in-line disposed lengthwise in frame. Lightly finned cast-iron cylinder barrels are four separate castings, L-shaped with non-detachable heads and side-valve location. Screwed-in valve-head cover plugs, removable for valve servicing or replacement. Crankshaft forged from nickel-chrome steel, with three-bearing crank, all bearing journals hardened and ground. Drop-forged steel con-rods, with split big-ends and slipper bearings in white metal-lined bronze shells. Two-ring cast-iron pistons, gudgeon pins located by lock-bolts in little-end eye. Wet sump lubrication supplies oil by double-gear pump under pressure to crankshaft bearings, big-ends and, by centrifugal force, to cylinder walls. Pressure-fed timing gears at front via the crankshaft and to clutch and gears via crankshaft at rear.

Bore x stroke: 68.26 x 88.89mm.

Capacity: 1301cc

Compression ratio: 58 psi cold (approx. 5.5:1)

Power: 18BHP (21 kW) @ 3400rpm

Carburation:
Single up-draught Zenith 25mm through four-branch alloy manifold, with air pre-heated by 'stove' enclosing rear exhaust pipe.

Ignition and electrics:
Simms four-pick-up magneto. Splitdorf generator, belt driven from magneto drive, with Wico 6-volt battery, supplying electric lighting for head and tail lamp.

Transmission:
Direct drive from crank, through large flywheel incorporating multi-plate clutch and bevel-gear drive to three-speed gearbox in unit. Left-hand, long clutch release and gear-change levers, forward for first, back second and third. Two neutrals. There is also a left-foot operated clutch, with separate hand-held lever on left side for reverse gear.

Frame and suspension:
Welded tubular steel frame, with forged lugs at steering head, duplex-downtube connection and engine-mount base. Lugs welded to the inner-side of frame lower rails provide mounting points for the engine. Fuel tank slung beneath upper of the two top frame rails. Front suspension by trailing-link fork, with linkages to centrally mounted, enclosed single spring. No rear suspension, but long-travel deep-pan saddle provides a surprisingly comfortable ride.

Wheels, tyres, brakes:
Dual rear brake, the external contracting type operated by right foot, the internal expanding type by the left heel. No front brake fitted. Tyres 3.5 x 20 inch.

Performance:
Top speed, with sidecar: 75mph; solo machine tested in 1921 at 98mph.

Machine loaned by:
WAL MAYNARD, Vintage MCC of Victoria.

Norton 'International'

500cc OHC SINGLE CYLINDER

The well-revered International Norton saw its genesis in the first-ever, 1927 CS1 (*Camshaft Senior One*) single-cylinder 500cc overhead camshaft machine, the original bike employing the then-fashionable cast iron head and barrel, the entire valve gear exposed to the elements, with the cycle parts almost as basic as any other machine in the Norton catalogue at that time; except for the engine of course and its all-alloy primary drive chaincase. It was a classic 'long-stroke' design, with bore/stroke measurements of 79 x 100mm, the same specifications which existed on the more prosaic overhead and side-valve 500cc engines which were also in the 1927 Norton catalogue. The CS1 overhead camshaft was driven by a pair of bevel gears at each end of a long vertical shaft, which was located inside a chromed steel tube which enclosed the drive components. The CS1 was actually based upon the 500cc overhead valve single, but with detailed changes to the base of the cylinder barrel and crankcase castings to accommodate the overhead cam bevel-gear drive; the cylinder head was, of course, entirely redesigned. The following year, the little-known 350cc version emerged, the CJ1 (*Camshaft **Junior** One*) always the poor little brother, which was never anywhere near as popular as the five hundred.

Naturally, the spare parts bins were loaded with special racing engine components which would allow the new CS1 to be a very a competitive road racer, so much so that in its first ever road race the new single won the 1927 Isle of Man Senior TT in the hands of the great Alec Bennett. The machine went on to secure very many wins and places in the coming years. In fact, that first CS1 formed the basis for the later, more specialised 'Manx' Norton full-on racing motorcycles which were to follow and which dominated the road race scene for very many years, not only pre-war but into the late-1950s as well.

The busy, beautifully crafted, highly polished alloy primary chaincase dominated the bike's left side, the same side from which the long exhaust pipe and funny little barrel-and-fishtail muffler emerged. Unhappily, the great alloy

The great all-alloy primary drive chaincase on the first CS1 Norton, the bike to be called the 'International' in later years. Note the extensions covering the chain drive to the generator at front and a similar chain drive to the magneto just ahead of the clutch. And, yes, the exhaust pipe exited on the left side in those earlier days.

primary chain-case was to disappear in the very early 1930s, to be supplanted by the simple – *and clearly much cheaper* – pressed metal chain-case cover which was adopted across the range of machines and was to continue on the singles and the new twin-cylinder machines for many years thereafter. On the pre-WWII machines the exhaust system had been re-routed and placed on the more 'normal' right hand side of the machine.

Through the natural processes of evolution, the CS1 became known as the 'International' from 1932 onwards after it had been smartened up in a minor design change, along with the adoption of Norton's own 'upright' four-speed

In the 1930s, Norton took a giant step backwards in replacing the primary drive casting on the OHC models (above) with this much cheaper, stamped-metal cover. It was 'sealed' by a 20 x 20mm rubber band around the inside lip of the outer case. If oil ever reached the rubber, it took on a jelly-like appearance which could then allow oil to dribble out of the chaincase.

gearbox in 1935. Up until that time, Norton had used the odd three-speed Sturmey-Archer gearbox, with its hand-or-foot gear change, which used a long lever with a wooden knob on it for changing gear by hand, or re-routed with a kink at the end and a small right-angled knob if used to change gear by foot. Either way, the so-called 'positive-stop' gear change had not until then been adopted (Velocette was the first with positive-stop, foot-gear change on its racing machines in 1929) which meant that many a too-hurried gear change on the 'Inter' was of the 'hit-and-miss' variety.

The all-new, four-speed 'Norton' gearbox which was to follow was actually made for the company by the Burman factory after Norton had bought out the Sturmey-Archer group; meanwhile, Burman continued to make their own 'CP' or 'BA' gearboxes, which they happily supplied in their many thousands to just about everybody else. The new Norton gearbox was employed almost co-incidentally with the adoption of a newly designed all-alloy head and barrel, which followed several months later.

In 1938 Norton employed its own plunger rear suspension unit for some of its five hundred singles, which naturally included the International and Manx Norton racers, but just one year later the road-going (or TT replica, as some called it) International OHC single was removed from the Norton range, seemingly in readiness for the factory to apply itself to an all-out war effort, which saw more than 100,000 side-valve machines of 500 and 600cc – the latter often for sidecar or ammunition-carrying side-***box*** use – manufactured for the Allied forces.

The 'Inter' reappeared in 1947 with the plunger rear suspension and the famous 'Roadholder' telescopic front forks, the engine's bore/stroke dimensions of 79 x 100mm unchanged, the cylinder head and barrel taking a step backwards in being made from cast iron – although, very strangely, the bike could be ordered with all-alloy head and barrel *at no extra cost* – while the valve gear, with its wide hairpin valve springs, remained exposed as before. It was, in essence, very nearly the pre-war 'round-head' Manx racer, thinly designed as a super-sports motorcycle fitted with all road equipment. The 'new' 1947 Model 30, 500cc International Norton was road tested in England by 'Motorcycling' magazine at the time, the report published in the July 3rd 1947 edition.

The machine's pre-war racing heritage was quite obvious when the bike, with full road trim and the rider in heavyweight riding gear, achieved a top speed of just on 97mph, with an elapsed time through the standing quarter mile of just over 15 seconds. This was a remarkable performance for a road-going single-cylinder five hundred in 1947, be well assured of that!

In 1950 the marvellous, McCandless-designed 'Featherbed' frame was created and it was almost instantly adopted for the 1951 350 and 500cc Manx Norton road-racing machines, the all-new frame by now complete with swing-arm rear suspension and of course the Roadholder front forks again. This brilliant frame design seemed simple enough and not unlike many other swing-arm frames which were beginning to appear at the time, but it was the full-cradle design, at once lightweight and rigid in all planes, with extra gusseting at the highly stressed steering head and swing arm mounting points. It was to set the standard by which all other 'pipe-tube' frames have been judged ever since. In one swoop, the new Norton frame – built for them by the Reynolds Tubing Company – made every other component of similar design look positively agricultural in comparison, for nothing in those days (and very few – if any – since then, it must be said) has ever come near it for its accurate, hairline steering and impeccable handling at all speeds and over almost every road surface. It also allowed a reasonable measure of comfort not always to be found back in the early 1950s.

A brand-new twin-cylinder five-hundred, the Norton 7 'Dominator', was introduced in late 1948 and it was soon to be fitted into the all-new frame, which turned the plunger-sprung and fast, if somewhat fairly lumpy, ill-handling twin into a machine with a secure road-going performance in mid-1952 which the earlier

Model 7 Dominator could never have achieved. Without doubt this was all due entirely to the brand new 'Featherbed' frame, the new machine becoming much more popular as a result of its far better road manners.

The International Norton, on the other hand, was never a big seller, but the engine was finally fitted with an all-alloy head and barrel as standard-ware in the early 1950s, the power-plant, with its later, much neater 'laydown' Norton gearbox, at last slotted into the Featherbed frame in late 1952. It remained in that guise for the rest of its short life, the sports OHC machine to leave the catalogues again in 1956, even though – it was said – an International Norton could still be made to special order for anything up to three years after it was 'no longer available.'

Always an exciting, all-round performer, that later machine then enjoyed an almost God-like acceptance from the very few riders who were fortunate enough to have actually owned one of them, for the new bike enjoyed the fine handling which so well augmented the spirited performance of the punchy, overhead camshaft motor.

But there were other things about the model which were not *quite* so endearing, such as the boot-soaking oil leaks which sometimes escaped from the stamped metal primary chain-case and the oil mist which often drifted onto one's trousers from the naked valve gear and its attendant hairpin valve springs. The alloy engine was also extremely noisy in operation, thanks to the large alloy head and barrel castings, which tended to amplify the whine from the two sets of bevel gear drives to the overhead camshaft, allied to the chatter from the exposed valve gear and more than a little piston slap; the latter quietening down somewhat as the engine warmed up. It has been suggested by some wags and with some accuracy, that a 'silent running' International Norton probably had something radically wrong with it, which might swiftly result in the emission of some very expensive *non-standard* noises before suddenly expiring!

Perhaps my most vivid recollection of the sporty Inter was the window-smashing exhaust noise, which heralded the approach of the bike long before it was ever visible to the naked eye. We had a brand-new 1956 International Norton on the showroom floor of the Sydney Suburban motorcycle store in which I worked for a few years and it became what we called a 'Happy Birthday Bike' because it sat there for more than a year before it was finally sold to a large, red-headed fireman. This man thrashed the bike mercilessly, so it was often in for more than the simple routine servicing and, as I would always do with any machine which had just been serviced, I road-tested the Inter several times after it left our service centre before handing it back to its eager owner. Its 'hearty' exhaust note might have been music to *my* ears, but this was perhaps not quite so acceptable to the casual bystander.

The machine I was able to borrow for just two days to conduct this test report was also a **1956 model 30 International,** the last year of its 'volume' manufacture. It belonged to the late Barry Ryan, a Montesa and Triumph dealer from Parramatta, an outer Sydney suburb. Barry picked the bike up on a trip to the UK, with the intention of refurbishing the machine during whatever spare time he may have had available. He had seldom enjoyed the luxury of any 'spare time', so the machine remained in much the same condition as it was when he brought it back to Australia.

As soon as I clapped eyes on the bike's flat 'muffler' I was reminded of the time I rode a brand-new Inter to a Sydney Motor Registry in 1953, only to be pulled over and booked by the Police: no, it was not for speeding, as might popularly be supposed, it was for excessive noise! The officer was in no way interested in hearing that the machine's so-called 'silencer' was in fact a bog-standard fitting and had not been 'enhanced' in any way. The standard muffler fitted to the Inter was (seemingly) exactly the same as the type fitted to all the other Norton machines, from the staid 500cc ES2 single to the new twin cylinder models, but for some reason those mufflers were far more effective. Could it be that the sportier OHC machine demanded a less restrictive silencer to allow it to give of its best? Possibly so, but I never found out if this was the case!

Ah, it was a long time ago, but memory was rekindled as soon as the old engine was fired up, because there again was that very fruity exhaust sound, which almost – I say *almost* – overcame the clatter from that noisy engine. There was a large oil stain underneath the bike, the lubricant probably piddling from the primary drive chaincase (which would have been no surprise) but otherwise the bike and its external appearance was really quite clean, even though it had not been touched since its arrival a few months previously.

The first Inter paint finish on tank and frame was a metallic, misty green, or a slivery grey colour, which persisted through the rest of its life, whereas the 1956 model I rode was finished in the less popular black tank with chrome side panels to provide a strong contrast, the frame also finished in gleaming black. The engine continued to employ the traditional, old-fashioned, long stroke 79 x 100mm dimensions from as far back as 1927, the valve gear still unenclosed and with the large and typically unfiltered, steeply downdraught 10TT race carburettor sticking up underneath the tank, its large bell-mouth gaping. Directly beneath the carburettor sat the usual Lucas mag/dyno unit, driven by chain from a sprocket mounted just outboard of the lower bevel gear drive.

Basic though the machine was, with little refinement to the engine in almost 30 years, the bike by now enjoyed a lean and mean look, more than hinting at its very sporty nature. But the International's main problem at that time was that the 500cc model 88 – which was the new designation for the *twin-cylinder* Featherbed model – was every bit as quick, handled at least as well, was far quieter and was very much more civilised, which of course did nothing to help the sluggish sales of the OHC single.

Ah, but you could still take nothing away from the way the International **looked**, because of all the other models fitted with the Featherbed frame, the bike (because of its clear Manx affiliations), clearly enjoyed by far the sportiest appearance, with its 'early Manx' alloy head and barrel and the long vertical shaft-cover which enclosed the bevel gear drive and long shaft which drove the overhead camshaft. Flat handlebars, the shallow 'racy' dual-seat and footrests set towards the rear of the machine allowed an even more sporty appearance once the rider was aboard.

Primary drive was by single-row chain in that *pretend* 'oil-bath' case to a dry clutch, the small amount of oil normally carried within the chaincase intended merely to provide lubrication for the chain, along its lower run. Adjustment to the chain was performed by slackening off the mounting bolts and physically moving the separate gearbox back along its slotted mounting brackets.

The currently accepted unit construction design which sees today's machines employ a one-piece engine/gearbox was not unknown in those days and not always employed on British machines, but one asset of this earlier type of design allowed the gearbox to be totally removed for repairs without disturbing the engine. The clutch and primary drive could be repaired or replaced without (*carefully*) removing anything

The Model 88 Norton 500cc twin, with the original Model 7 power-plant now slotted into the all-conquering 'Featherbed' frame. The International may have used just one of the twin's flat mufflers, which could have been the reason why it endowed the sporty 500cc single with such a 'hearty' exhaust note!

but the outer chaincase cover – and that was better still.

Norton employed a gear-type oil pump and it was the close fit (or otherwise!) of these gears which stopped the oil tank's contents from ultimately finding themselves back in the earth.

Magneto ignition was standard on the Norton (there's no ignition key), while the instrumentation was restricted to a speedometer, ammeter and simple switches for lights and dipper/horn operation. No blinkers and originally no stop light switch either. Mirrors? Forget it, for they were not legally required when the bike was new!

Norton Roadholder front forks and Featherbed frame combine to provide a standard of handling seldom matched by modern motorcycles, while the suspension is on the firm side, with road strips felt through handlebars and seat as the machine is punted along at slower speeds. Such is the price paid in the interests of having the bike go exactly where it was pointed when the chips were down and it was being pushed very hard.

At very high cruising speeds the machine sits firmly on the road with a secure, poised gait, but niggling in the back of the mind there is always the thought that the 'simple' drum brakes

Right hand corners were always a delight, because nothing scraped, with the great Featherbed frame hanging in there perfectly, even in view of an SM rear tyre, a very strange fitment indeed on an out-and-out high-performance sports model like the all-alloy 'Inter'.

might not really be up to the job in modern-day heavy traffic. However, the brakes on the Ryan International proved to be right up to the mark for playing boy racers, just as they proved to be acceptable enough in give-and-take traffic situations.

The bike was at its very best when rushing up to corners then buttoning-off the power and applying the brakes hard while slipping back through the gears. It was boy racer stuff at its best and the height of self-indulgence for which this sports machine was clearly intended.

In a direct comparison to modern motorcycles, its standard appointments are perhaps more fitting to an off-road motorcycle, for it has no electric starter, no blinkers, no mirror (though we had one mounted purely to keep a wary eye on offenders) and an almost total lack of instruments. Regulations in force at the time it was previously registered (in England in 1971) had caught up with the machine and it was (thankfully) fitted with a stoplight.

Two devices fitted to the Inter and seldom seen on modern machines are the valve-lifter (which the SR500 Yamaha used) and a manual spark advance/retard lever (which has now totally disappeared). Both have to be used if first-kick starts are to be the order of the day and then the process is not for the faint-hearted.

The spark control lever is on the left handlebar and it *must* be moved away to retard the ignition timing before that vintage *'long, swinging kick'* is applied. Before this the Amal 10TT racing carburettor has to be 'tickled' – that's another technique you don't see every day – to raise the fuel level in the carburettor.

With no electric starter fitted it makes the old routine of starting the Big Single a ritual which needs to be re-learned in a hurry. Compression ratio on the sports machine was 8.5:1 so the valve lifter would need to be used with some expertise to fire the engine up. The race-bred Amal TT carburettor had no provision for idling, which meant I had to dredge up a 'start-and-idle-reliably' techniques I had not used (or needed) for ages.

From this point, and with petrol piddling

out the carb, the kick-starter is eased over until the piston stops at the compression stroke, then eased over the top using the valve lifter which operates by levering the exhaust valve open and allowing the compressed gas to escape. When that is done, the kick-starter is returned to the top of its swing.

Faint-hearted motorcyclists may then leave the room, for now The Kick is applied, with a long follow-through at least as important as the kick itself. If you have used all your body weight and leant on the starter with reckless abandon, the engine will assuredly fire up and settle down to a series of pops, bangs, grunts, rattles and some distinctly gastric sounds ... then burst into glorious life.

As we have seen, there is no throttle-stop screw and no provision for idling, so the engine must be kept running with the application of some expertise and throttle control in (more-or-less) equal parts.

On the other hand, a light dab at the kick-starter, or no follow-through, will see the thing kick back like a mule, accompanied by an unintentional, ballet-like high kick from the kicker and a whole lot of grinding and other terrifying noises from the motorcycle. It was always an art and it remains an art!

There is some vibration, but the impression generated by the machine at idle is almost entirely of noise. The overhead cam and exposed valve gear rattles alarmingly, there are knocks and groans from the top of the cylinder as the piston rises and is pushed back down again, and the carburettor – unfiltered of course – sucks and slurps rudely through its open bell-mouth.

So, what if it would not meet modern standards? When it was new the International Norton was one of the fastest single-cylinder sports irons available and unquestionably the best handler.

The clutch is dry, with a mushy feel at the lever, but works perfectly well, even when caned mercilessly when changing from a low first gear to a distant second.

Gearbox ratios in the Ryan machine do not appear to be standard, for originally they were very close indeed, with a very 'tall' first gear. To allow for an easy transition from stationary to moving briskly away, the bike has been fitted with what feels to be the standard ES2 roadster first gear, while the close-ratio Manx second, third and top gear are apparently retained.

It means the bike has to be pushed fairly hard in first, then the clutch lever is feathered lightly to slip the clutch when second is selected if forward motion is to be maintained with no drama. So high is second gear in relation to first that a clean change from top whack in the lowest gear will find the engine almost bogging down when the throttle is opened! I would have retained the Inter Norton's slightly higher, closer ratio first gear and perhaps dropped a tooth or two off the engine sprocket in the interests of an easier take off and a much more acceptable change into second gear, had the machine been mine.

But with a touch of clutch slip to keep the engine on the boil it will dig in and pull well to hoist the bike along to more than 60mph on the speedo before selecting third. Second and third gear are quite close and so is top gear, so the very sporty performance of the machine continues with little interruption from the gearbox up until top whack.

Top gear will not dig in and pull well from under an indicated 65mph, though it's a good cruising speed to maintain and the engine is just loafing along at that road speed. The box is so fast that a swift change back to third to overtake is as quick as hand and foot can move, whereupon the bike fairly leaps into the manoeuvre. It's over in a flash, then back into top gear again.

Without extending the nearly 55-year-old motorcycle's engine beyond a reasonable self-imposed limit it was possible to slip along at a cruising speed comfortably beyond the open road Legal Limit on not much over half-throttle and still feel a solid push in the tail if the throttle was opened widely: the word is probably *Magic!*

Unfortunately, vibration can become a real problem. It becomes hand-numbing after a short time from about 55mph to just over 70, where it smooths out again and becomes at least comfortable. But much of one's cruising is done in the lower speed range and it is here that the Norton can become hard work in simply hanging onto it. Norton mounted the handlebars in a rubber clamp to help over-come the problem but it never worked very well. A dim memory does not recall this as a problem when the machine was new. I was a whole lot younger then and many of the big singles could vibrate like pneumatic drills with the Norton no better or worse than its contemporaries.

Brakes are a bit spongy and apparently well-worn, which took some of the enjoyment out of riding in suburban areas; but they were acceptable enough for the purpose, the bike clearly intended for use on the open road with little allowance for heavier traffic situations.

It is almost impossible to pull a gear higher than second in very slow city running and then there must be some use of the clutch if you have to accelerate away otherwise the engine is not happy at all. The problem is the jump from second gear back to first, which is too wide unless the bike is moving quite slowly. It's a bit of a pain, but it can sometimes be a more useful gear than the higher first with which the machines came when new. Again, closing the first gear ratio and possibly fitting that smaller engine sprocket would certainly make quite a difference.

Rushing into slower corners is made rather more difficult if you lose count of the gears because a drop into bottom with the rear brake on comes as an unpleasant surprise – particularly in view of the almost square-section older-pattern Avon SM tyre on the rear wheel, allied to a small steering lock.

Even with some discernible wear in the fork bushes, the bike still corners as if glued to the road surface, but left-handers are spoiled a bit because the prop-stand digs in fairly early, while right-handers are a delight, because only the limitations imposed by the square-section Avon SM rear tyre inhibits cornering speeds. Removing the prop stand entirely and replacing the tyres with other brands exhibiting a better, more rounded profile would result in much more 'urgent' cornering, a pursuit in which the bike clearly shines. Forget the traffic, for this is not where the Norton is at its best. It comes

Left-hand corners were always very exciting, with the prop and centre stands scraping on the deck a little too early, the rear tyre teetering on its knife-edge of rubber. Note the well-rounded front tyre and the near square-section of the Avon SM hoop on the rear. However, the stands grounding so soon may have meant the bike couldn't have been cranked over much further, anyway.

into its own on fast, open highways where its great appeal as a lightweight, bend-swinging road-burner is very hard to beat. The ease with which it sets up its own line through a corner and then sticks to it is almost without precedent, even in view of the slight wear in the bike's fork bushes and rear swing-arm spindles

The Armstrong rear shocks with which this machine was fitted were a touch tired in the damping, but the front forks were very much up to the job and kept the front wheel tracking taut and true. Suspension was generally on the firm side of comfortable, but again allowed the bike to be ridden with some abandon over some pretty grim stretches of tarred 'motocross' surfaces.

Giving hand signals was something I have been called upon to do a bit lately because of this series of Classic test reports and it was pleasing to note that a lane-change could be executed one-handed with ease, regardless of road surfaces.

Unhappily, the dual-seat is covered in an 'early vinyl' material and has become highly polished with time. It hardly makes the ideal surface for serious road-burning for I occasionally found myself sliding about and hanging onto the handlebars firmly over rough road surfaces while cornering enthusiastically.

There is virtually no backlash in the transmission. An engine shock-absorber of the cam-and-spring type is used, with an additional cush-drive in the Norton clutch assembly. You'd expect some slop after the years have taken their toll but the drive is taut and snatch-free. It is hardly *smooth* in the currently accepted manner, but then the speedo has nearly 30,000 miles on it to date and the odometer section wasn't working. The mileage could easily be double this figure!

The Norton International is basically a high-speed sports mount, not acceptable to many modern enthusiasts and comparatively rare even when it was reasonably readily available. It rests quite securely in its niche in the short list of genuine Classic Motorcycles, although its performance might not shock many current machines of a similar capacity. Incidentally and for some odd reason, it leaked very little oil! And, yes, there was plenty of lubricant in the oil tank and more than enough in the primary drive case as well. Wonder what is the answer to that riddle?

It's a good example of an era in which most machines – basic sports models or not – were much less sophisticated than they are today, but the Inter was even then more Spartan than most. And if it does not compare favourably with modern machines in those terms, it must still shine today in areas in which it always shone, well removed now, as then, from machines of similar size and similar disposition.

TECH SPECS

Make: Norton

Model: 30 International

Type:
All-alloy single cylinder, single overhead camshaft design, with bevel gear control via enclosed vertical shaft, with hairpin valve springs, the OHC valve year total unenclosed.

Capacity: 490cc

Bore x Stroke: 79 x 100mm

Carburation:
AMAL TT type race carburettor; 1 5/16" bore.

Compression ratio: 8.5:1

Power @ rpm: 29.5BHP @ 5600rpm

Electrics:
Ignition by Lucas magneto, with the usual Mag-dyno double instrument, generator supplying electrical current for wet, lead/acid battery.

Transmission:
By enclosed ½" x 5/16" primary chain to four-speed gearbox, right-side foot gearchange. One up, three down.

Gear rations:
1st – 10.8:1; 2nd – 6.18:1; 3rd – 5.1:1; 4th – 4.64:1

Frame, wheels, brakes:
Duplex downtube, 'Featherbed' Norton frame, with 'Roadholder', two-way damped front forks and swing-arm rear suspension, originally fitted with Woodhouse/Monroe double-acting spring/damper units. Steel wheel rims front and rear, laced to 8" drum, with wide brake shoes on front wheel and 7" rear brake drum.

Dimensions:
Wheelbase – 1390mm; Saddle Height – 680mm; Weight – 176kg.

Performance: Top speed 155km/h.

Machine loaned by:
BARRY RYAN, Parramatta.

1970 Triumph 'Bandit'

350cc DOHC TWIN PROTOTYPE

It is not often, if at all, that one enjoys the chance of riding a headline-grabbing, extremely rare pre-prototype motorcycle of any kind; much less a very promising motorcycle from a major English manufacturer, a machine which promised much, but which in the end was fated to wither on the vine before it had any chance of being fully developed.

Such a machine was the **1970 twin-cylinder, 350cc double-overhead camshaft Triumph Bandit**, code-named P30, a motorcycle which was clearly intended to provide a serious, 'mid-range' challenge from a British factory to the all-conquering Japanese – in particular Honda – who were dominant in the then-popular 250-500cc mid-range class of commuter and/or sports machines. At that time, the Brits had little or nothing on hand to provide a serious challenge to the Japanese onslaught and so the all-new Bandit stepped up to accept the challenge, which would certainly have been very successful if the fossilised old-fashioned BSA board members had had the vision (and of course the money) to see the machine through its initial teething problems – of which there were many!

We've heard the second-hand horror stories of the original engine's broken crankshafts, overheating (and often seized) engine, exploding contact breaker sets, excessive oil consumption, slipping clutches, faulty gearboxes and a list of other woes which were said to plague the all-new engine. There is nothing new about that, for almost every engine design of any worth has been the victim of initial, serious design faults which resulted in these types of developmental problems, but on almost every occasion those early problems were solved, shelved for the time being, or simply pelted out. Incidentally, it should go on record that this type of information on the often-horrific birth pangs of the development of *any* type of power-plant is rarely, *if ever*, made public and for a raft of very good reasons.

The Bandit power-plant was *initially* designed by the recently retired Edward Turner, who had designed the first 500cc overhead valve vertical-twin Triumph in 1937 and, just as happened with that first 'Speed Twin', which initially had its own share of serious problems, it was up to two of his trusted associates, initially Bert Hopwood and then the brilliant Doug Hele – the latter considered by many to be much the brighter of the two! – to turn the troublesome, poorly designed little Bandit into a viable motorcycle.

They – or at least Hele – descended upon the hapless twin, the final result being that the 'all-new' Bandit employed, in effect, a newly designed engine. Turner's original design was actually thrown out, for the all-new machine differed fundamentally from the original, troublesome Turner-design in almost every area. This included, among other things, the adoption of the 180-degree crankshaft, with pistons rising and falling alternatively. It might be noted that the partners, Hele and Hopwood, were also instrumental in the design and building of the three-cylinder, T150 'Export Only' 750cc Triumph Trident, which preceded Honda's CB750 by only a few weeks in 1968, just two short years before the birth – and premature death – of the prototype 350cc Bandit in 1970.

But why go to the trouble of designing and almost entirely rebuilding a small 350cc twin in the first place, you might very well ask, when a full-sized five-hundred would surely have performed much more impressively, other than to be aware that the three-fifties by 1968 had unaccountably become the world's biggest selling motorcycles, thanks to the high demand from the US.

For some unfathomable reason, the 'medium-weight' 350cc class was a great favourite with major British manufacturers for decades, both before the war and immediately afterwards, with every factory in England – and several others in Europe as well – having at least one machine of that odd capacity in its catalogue. Perhaps this is why the Japanese decided to go down that path?

But for Triumph, the unsuccessful history of that odd engine size was already there, for Triumph had previously made a couple of most unsuccessful three-fifty twins, one of them the ill-fated post-war 3T, which only survived for some five years from 1947 to 1951, having failed to sell in any real numbers as it sat forlornly on showroom floors alongside the much more acceptable *500cc,* and the later, *650cc* overhead valve Triumph twins. In 1957, the overhead valve 350cc Triumph 3TA (Twenty-One), with its neat 'bathtub' rear wheel enclosure and unit-construction engine, was just as unsuccessful as its earlier sibling. It looked very swish indeed and was capable of a reasonable performance, but it remained in that Netherland of odd engine capacities between the 'lightweight' 250cc class and the far more acceptable 500cc higher-performance class; particularly in Australia, where the 350cc machines were never very successful. The little 3TA survived, in slightly modified form, until 1966.

If the evidence was already in place that the smaller capacity vertical twins were not likely to be anywhere near as popular as their larger, more successful brethren, why design an all-new ***350cc*** twin, albeit a modern, double-overhead camshaft design, when the judgement of Triumph's own history was clearly against it? Its success was thus not guaranteed, so we would probably have to put it down to hide-bound tradition and simply let it go at that. But it is true to say that the Bandit machine *was* intended to provide a serious challenge to the OHC CB350 Honda – or even the larger CB450 'Black Bomber' machines, for that matter.

It was also said that the original Bandit's odd frame was not up to the job, either, the original, skimpy telescopic forks 'dangerous' and that the brakes were similarly sub-standard. The original, Turner-designed Bandit frame was also pelted out, the new power-plant cleverly mounted in what was the latest Triumph *twin* frame and running gear, including the large, 200mm front brake.

Naturally, the simpler design parameters of frame and brake assemblies are a very long way

Turner's original Triumph 'Bandit' was a smart-looking machine, but it proved to be very troublesome, so the power-plant was discarded. The frame and front forks were also problematic, and were replaced, which left nothing of the original design. The machine employed a cable-operated disc front brake, a rarity in 1969.

The all-new Bandit, a very exciting, high-performance, mid-range motorcycle which offered much, but which was stifled by the 'stinkin' thinkin' of the fossilised, BSA/Triumph Board. They weren't impressed by full order books from the US, for the new bike had received a great pre-production promo, and was eagerly awaited as a clear threat to Honda's successful CB350.

removed from the design of an all-new *engine*, which could be fraught with all manner of problems because of the many (very fast) moving parts flashing about inside it and the challenges to properly lubricate them. If there may have been a problem with effective lubrication of the brand-new, high-revving twin, then the two engineers overcame this with a double-gear, high-capacity oil pump, which sat vertically below the crankshaft in the base of the inner timing case, the lubricant supplied from a separate tank. The pump fed high-pressure oil through the hollow main-shafts into the big-ends, main bearings and, through a special jet, to the lower cam-chain drive mechanism.

An external oil line to the rear of the cam-drive housing fed the lubricant directly to the inlet camshaft bearings and from a small hole at the base of the cams to lubricate the 'inverted-bucket-type' cam-followers, the oil then running forward under pressure and gravity through special drill-ways into the exhaust camshaft. The oil drained back to the crankcase *via* the camshaft's chain-drive tunnel, oil mist providing extra lubricant to the chain.

Rather than a built-up assembly the new, one-piece, 180-degree crankshaft ended up as a sharp-edged forging which included a substantial central *mass* to ensure rigidity. There was no central main bearing to handle the 'rocking couple' generated by having the cranks disposed at the now-fashionable 180-degrees, but the heavy central mass was clearly intended to overcome this tendency, which it apparently managed to do very successfully. And why not, for Triumph got by very successfully without a central main bearing in their 360-degree twins for decades, the bolted-up crankshaft assembly employing a central flywheel to provide its own rigidity, the assembly supported by a pair of substantial ball bearings.

The short, chunky connecting rods in the new engine were scaled-down versions of the components fitted to the larger twins and were forged from aircraft-quality RR56 aluminium alloy, with detachable end-caps and slipper bearings, their big-end and gudgeon pin centres a mere 120mm apart, the three-ring pistons running a high 9.5:1 compression ratio. The engine main-shafts were 30mm thick, 5mm thicker than the shafts on Triumph's three-cylinder 750cc machines, with *big-end* journals of similarly large diameter – 42mm x 23mm wide – the same size as those on the 750cc Triples. This would ensure sufficient strength for the engine to safely spin at very high speeds and to deliver a high output. Two 27mm Amal carburettors were employed, with air delivered through tiny filters fitted under the dual-seat. The contact breaker sets for the coil ignition system sat under a domed cover sited at the end of the exhaust camshaft.

The design was straight forward enough, but I suggest there were some aspects of the design which might have been better thought out, however. It's clear from the Figure-7 shape of the double-overhead camshaft drive castings that the design originally called for a 'stacked' train of gears from the crankshaft pinion to drive the two camshafts, but it was also clear that the idea was dropped in the final design of the Bandit, during the very early development stages.

That initial design may have meant the engine could be far too expensive to manufacture for a cash-strapped company, but the gear train may have been very noisy as well, unless some form of internal 'sound-deadening' webbing could be cleverly designed, to co-incidentally direct copious amounts of oil into the essential areas as well, for optimum lubrication of bearings and gear teeth. Far simpler, and certainly much cheaper, to replace the train of gears with a trio of small-diameter sprockets and a simple chain, the lower drive sprocket attached to the crankshaft's half-time pinion, which, as we've seen, would then have the chain pursue the tortuous path it has to follow. The usual 'jockey-tensioners' were employed to take care of chain back-lash.

Of course, had there been more money to hand and some more time available, the timing case could have been redesigned – into an inverted, wide-triangular-shape, like the pre-war, three-cylinder, 500cc DOHC Guzzi road racer. This could have been done by employing three slightly larger sprockets to give the chain a much easier life. There is no doubt the ⅜" pitch camshaft drive chain would be capable of assuming its task even at quite high engine revolutions, but at the possible risk of premature wear in the serpentine, 'Figure Seven' configuration. However, if this problem occurred when bench testing the engine at maximum revs for hours at a time, it has not thus-far been recorded; at least not publicly!

The camshafts were retained by a bolt locating the top chain tensioner, which could be removed and the chain slackened to allow the camshafts to be easily removed, should this be necessary. Like the OHC Honda CB350, the large-diameter camshaft bosses at each end of the camshafts ran directly into the

Removing this single bolt – which locates the Weller tensioner to control chain 'lash' – allows the chain to be slackened off and easily removed for replacement or to remove the camshaft(s), should this be necessary. A simple ploy to make owner maintenance all the easier.

alloy material of the cylinder head, the valve clearances adjusted by shims located underneath the cam-followers, which also move in direct contact within the head castings. It has been said that a valve clearance job on the Triumph Bandit could be undertaken in about an hour or so with practice, the clearances checked by removing a pair of close-fitting alloy rocker cover plates.

The Bandit I rode looked very urgent in the flesh and gave a surprisingly good account of itself when put thoroughly through its paces. Early prototype though it was, as evidenced by the Number 3 on the right-hand side panel, the bike performed admirably. That NUMBER 3 on the machine's side panel in fact pointed to the machine as being the *third* pre-production prototype and was one of the very few Triumph/BSA machines *to be fitted with engine internals,* for most of the other twenty or so on display in a variety of locations were later said to have been cobbled together for photographic purposes. There were said to have been a total of just twelve (12) *complete* pre-production Triumph – and BSA – prototypes made and could thus be ridden, but this may be debatable.

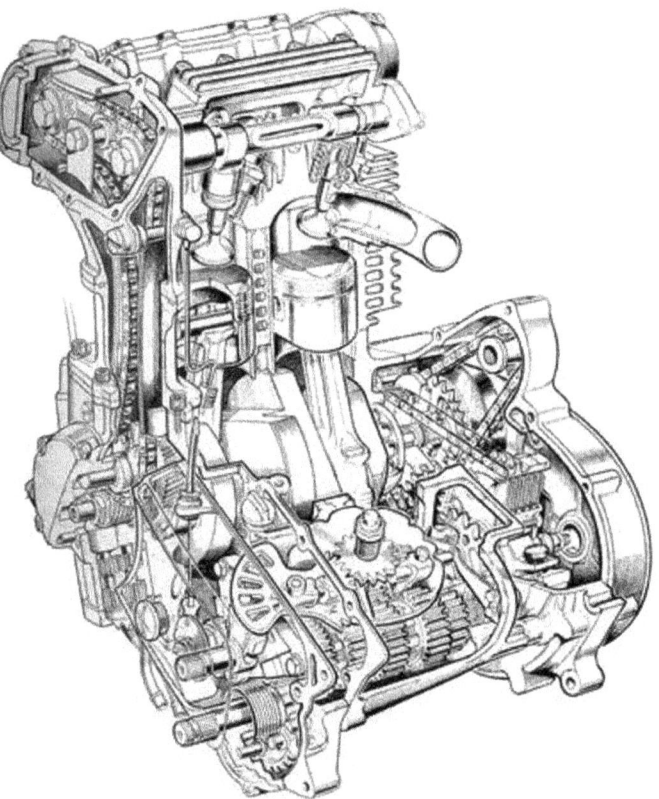

Cutaway drawing of the Bandit's neat power-plant, the engine in unit with the primary transmission and gearbox. Note the projection just above the primary drive on the RH aide, which is where the starter motor – not included – is placed. Note also the tortuous path which the camshaft drive chain on the left is forced to pursue and the tubes on the inlet face for the twin carburettors.

The owner assured me that his machine was fitted with a *hand-built* engine (weren't all engines hand-built in those days?) which was one of only *two* engines to have been very carefully assembled. It has been said that no more than a small handful of Triumph Bandit, and its cloned stable-mate, the **BSA Fury**, were able to be ridden because of the 'display' machines which, as we have noted, consisted of a bunch of engine castings bolted together to give the appearance of completely assembled machines. It's little wonder then, that the rare, early prototype bike I rode carried the proud name *Triumph* on the fuel tank, but with an equally proud **BSA** name on a small, lower engine cover plate!

The T30 Bandit appeared to be little bigger than, say, a 175cc OHC Honda twin, and weighed just on 155kg, which hinted at the possibility of a very spirited performance if the claimed power output was correct. Triumph claimed that the little buzz-box developed some 35BHP at a high 9000rpm, which compared very favourably with the 100mph, 'full-sized' **500cc** Triumph *Tiger 100,* which produced just 30BHP from its overhead *valve* engine and weighed over 35kg more.

The Bandit employed a five-speed gearbox, while the Tiger 100 had just four, with the more fashionable 'over-square' engine dimensions of a 63mm bore (the same bore size as the 500cc twin) with a stroke of only 56mm, the lightweight 350cc machine clearly intended to be driven by a high-revving power-plant.

It was back in 1982 that we found just one of only *five known survivors in the world* of the little Triumph Bandit. The bike was 'discovered' in Melbourne on a trip to Victoria, and I rode that little twin while I was there, emerging from the all-too-brief, two-day test at once very impressed by the little bike's great performance and yet saddened by the model's premature and apparently needless demise.

Turner had seemingly anticipated the entry of Japanese factories other than Honda into the *four-stroke*, twin-cylinder, 350cc overhead camshaft design (Yamaha, Suzuki and Kawasaki were making only *two-stroke* engines at the time) and he was right, for the others entered the mid-range four-stroke field some six years later, fielding machines in that small-capacity class: there was no evidence in 1970 that the other Japanese motorcycles were ever going to appear as four-strokes.

As we shall later discover, Turner may also have anticipated the emergence of other so-called 'Superbikes', which were to follow the 1968 four-cylinder CB750 Honda, with the little 350 twin as the *possible* basis for larger-capacity engines of various configurations. Let's assume a 700cc – or even a one litre – **Vee-4** perhaps; possibly an 'across the frame' transverse four of similar capacity, using the basic Bandit engine as a template for further development?

In fact, had the Triumph/BSA duo of small vertical twins survived in their new form in 1972, they might easily have formed a platform for a whole new industry to develop which could have changed forever the face of motorcycling in England.

You think not? Then read on, and you may be persuaded otherwise. Bear in mind that the duo of Hopwood and Hele had already drafted

It isn't easy to see, but the machine exhibited Triumph upon the fuel tank, and BSA on a lower engine plate. This clearly demonstrates that the machine was very much a 'one-off', as we have remarked, and was certainly a hand-built special; as the 'Number3' on the machine's plastic side-panel also indicates.

designs for *three-cylinder*, overhead camshaft 250 and 350cc *six-speed* Triumph motorcycles, and Hopwood later designed a 'modular' overhead camshaft, 200cc engine which could clearly be 'coupled' into a multi-cylinder power-plant. These were, and remain, little known projects, which could have had far reaching repercussions for the entire motorcycle industry had they been implemented. After all, they already had the fully functioning, high-performance 350cc twin upon which to draw: a template for a multi-cylinder machine... perhaps?

The design of the Bandit engine differed greatly from traditional Triumph (British) practice in many areas. For a start, the cam drive gear was on the machine's *left* side, instead of the traditional right – with a left-mounted gear lever and kick-starter, the primary transmission being on the right-hand side – the engine inclined slightly forward in the frame. Its unique (for Britain) double overhead camshaft and 'oversquare' bore x stroke ratios and 180-degree crankshaft forgings again quite unusual, even if the vertically split crankcases were as old as time. The Japanese were using horizontally split crankcases in the design of their motorcycle engines, which were *said* to provide more ease of entry for repairs but, if major repairs were indeed required, it might not make a whole lot of difference which way the crankcases would need to be separated to get to the engine internals.

Besides that, the unit-construction Triumphs which preceded the Bandit were designed to allow for a complete removal of all the gearbox components without disturbing the engine at all, and the Bandit was similarly designed. This is hard to achieve with horizontally split crankcases. It's called pluses and minuses, swings and roundabouts, or give and take.

To allow for the left-side gear-change lever, the right-hand end of the crankshaft holds the primary drive sprocket, the starter motor sprocket and the Lucas 110W alternator rotor, all carried outboard of the large, main-shaft ball bearing. Primary drive is by $3/8$" x $7/32$" duplex chain (a size employed by BSA on their twins since 1946), with the 23-tooth engine sprocket to the multi-plate clutch and five-speed gearbox. The clutch sprocket had 52 teeth, for a primary reduction of 2.260.

Another sprocket and chain, a single-row of the same $3/8$" x $7/32$" size, runs outside the primary drive to locate the sprocket and epi-cyclic gears on the 'made in India' Lucas starter motor, which sits atop the timing case, directly beneath the twin Amal Concentric carburettors. The alternator rotor sits on the end of the drive-side main-shaft, which means there is a lot of heavy metal out there, and it might have been better to have fitted an extra out-rigger, needle-roller bearing in the outer cover plate – even a large bronze bush might have sufficed. However, it should be noted that a very large roller bearing supports the crankshaft on the drive side, so all is well.

The little Triumph would have been easy to work on, for the right-hand side-cover can be removed to allow full access to the clutch and alternator, while the gearbox internals could be removed entirely by simply detaching the ***left*** side cover's screws and pulling out the bits which may need to be replaced. This is an advantage of the vertically split crankcases, for the replacement of a gear-selector spring or selector plate (not done often, but more frequently than a major overhaul!) could be undertaken by almost any home mechanic, and could be done in a couple of hours. This, as we have noted, could be accomplished without disturbing the engine.

Remembering the ease with which valve clearances could be adjusted – if you could remove the tightly fitted rocker-box covers, which almost fouled the frame rails – the ready accessibility and simplicity of the points assembly, and the almost crudely simple, but entirely efficient, Amal carburettors, and the ease with which side panels could be removed, that Bandit would have been economical to maintain professionally. Routine maintenance would have probably been well within the scope of some private owners.

If the engine was robust and powerful, the frame into which it was fitted was every bit as good, if not a whole lot better. Based upon the

Rob North frame which was originally made for the famous 'Slippery Sam' racing Triumph triple, the 'corporate' Triumph frame was a duplex-downtube, lightweight, full-cradle component, gusseted at stress points round the steering head and swing-arm pivot. The two top frame rails ran from a point behind the steering head to an area just above the in-unit gearbox where the stiffening gusset for the swing-arm rear suspension is fitted.

If that frame was a great deal better than it would need to have been to haul a lightweight 350 twin around, it was all due to the Japanese. Simply put, the Japanese bikes were beginning to sell by the boat-load – particularly in the USA – and it was clear that the once-dead motorcycle industry had enjoyed a long-overdue re-awakening. Triumph's undoubted expertise in frame and running gear design, allied to some new thinking and not a little expertise picked up along the way, spawned a motorcycle which I'm sure would have been capable of easily seeing off many of its competitors, and which added the priceless virtue of nigh-perfect handling and powerful brakes. As we have seen, the little 350 engine was installed into the same running gear as the latest Triumph/BSA twins and triples, including the powerful, 200 mm twin-leading shoe front brake and the 175 mm single-leader rear, with conical hubs and 18" wheels. Turner's original Bandit employed a non-hydraulic, cable-operated disc front brake, a rarity in 1970.

The little bike's lithe shape more than hints at its high performance, while it sits low and lean

Your scribe is just on 1.6 meters in height, or 5'3" on the older Imperial scale, which ably demonstrates the small size of this trim little 350cc machine. Its very pleasing, 100mph-plus performance is thus due to its very good power-to-weight-ratio. Oh, for a full-sized, lightweight five-hundred!

at rest. The riding position is a bit 'upright', with footrests set well forward and handlebars on the high side, while the dual-seat is long, wide and very comfortable. The seat lifts up to disclose the oil tank and much of the electrical ancillaries, again making for easy maintenance when required. Unhappily, the petrol tank is on the small side for Australia, but its 13.5 litre capacity would have allowed it to cover about 275 km before you had to fill it again while waiting for everyone else to finally catch up.

I didn't like the Lucas switchgear fitted to the bike. It was common to the range, as it was to some of the few British machines still being built in 1970, but the switches seemed to be too fragile, were very notchy and not very easy to operate. Each side of the bars is fitted with a switchbox from which sprout flat, paddle-shaped levers which are long and sloppy in operation. The starter-motor button is on the right lever drum, the blinker switch on the left. Oddly, the blinker lever paddle operates up-and-down and it is almost impossible to feel the neutral position.

As usual, the twin Amal carburettors need a touch on the float-ticklers to raise the fuel in the chambers, and a quick stab of the starter button fires the engine in less time than it takes to read all about it. I was frankly surprised to find the all-alloy engine idling very quietly.

It is only when underway that the engine becomes noisy, most of it due to the heavy induction moan which comes from the carbs *via* their miniscule, paper-pack air filters; oiled foam-plastic filters would have been more silent. Induction noise becomes progressively louder as engine revs rise, and it is the only limiting factor in an engine which feels as though it would rev to infinity, and to whatever is beyond that – if anything!

The clutch action is typically light, even though the old cable was a bit on the dry side, but the gear-lever travel is too great, with the result that the left foot has to be removed from the rest to stroke the lever from one upward gear to the next; it was never a Triumph trait, for one of the great joys of the British twins has always been a short-travel and very fast gear change. A quick alteration to the design of selector pawl and/or cam-plate assembly would certainly have followed this pre-production prototype, if the machine was ever to achieve production.

Acceleration is *startling* – for a three-fifty, we must remember – so much so that a wary eye has to be kept on the tacho to avoid sending the needle off the dial in the first three gears, though it begins to level itself out when into fourth and fifth. The bike takes off like a miniature rocket, with little vibration until around the 5500-rpm mark when it begins to tingle the toes through the footrests, to disappear entirely shortly thereafter. All in all, the engine is quite smooth and, apart from the too-loud induction roar, surprisingly quiet mechanically, and it is entirely oil-tight.

A distinct buzzer, the engine will not pull well in top gear until it clears around 4000rpm, which is no surprise when the peak torque figure of 28.4Nm is delivered at a high 7000rpm. The high power output is achieved at 9000rpm – again on the high side, but those engine revs could be reached with no trouble at all. In fact, owner Doug Fraser reckons the engine will still pull strongly – and apparently *safely* – with over 10,500 on the clock and with no end in sight!

I was never going to buzz the engine to anywhere near those astronomically high speeds; my self-imposed limit in top gear was 7000rpm with upward changes made at around 4500-5000 in the lower gears, which was more than enough to blow everything – but everything – sideways everywhere we went.

I might say that once or twice I whanged the throttle wide open for several seconds at my 7000rpm rev limit in fourth gear and the bike responded immediately, leaping away with a renewed vigour I would have sworn could not be there. What could I say about the machine's handling which has not been said on many occasions before when describing something removed from the common herd? The bike couldn't be easily thrown off-line on any of the surfaces over which I rode, but the tail-end felt a bit unstable at times, which was initially surprising. The problem was soon traced to the design of the tyre, which was one of those Avon

SM patterns that appeared many years ago. The pattern is almost square in section, with very little tread wrapped round the sidewalls, so that one corners on little more than a wide knife-edge at speed: was the SM tyre intended for sidecar use, perhaps? It would seem to be so.

I was not too happy with that rear tyre as it took the edge off an otherwise extremely brisk little bike, but it did little to alter the overall feel of a fine, taut machine, with few vices in its overall concept and none I could find in terms of handling, comfort and braking. But the small bike could still be thrown about from one footrest to the other with almost reckless abandon, like very little I can recall before, nor since. I well remember one great, down-hill series of three Ess-bends which I flew down, easily pelting the bike about all over the place, while still firmly ensconced in the saddle – without having to hang off the inside of the bike, all elbows and knees like a badly packed sack of spuds. The bike handled this so brilliantly that I went back and did it all over again, but much quicker this time, if ever mindful of the fact that cornering on that rear tyre's nearly 'square' profile was like cornering hard whilst almost on that rubber knife-edge. It was all great Boy Racer stuff, no question of that, and there should be much more of it, but a rear tyre with a more rounded profile would have transformed the machine's handling beyond recognition, opening up even greater levels of cornering delights. The front brake, which as I've said was fitted to the Bonneville models as well, suffered a little from an elderly cable and it required a firm pull on the lever, but there was no doubting the potency of the brakes at either end of the bike.

The Bandit's owner claims it will easily blow off a hard-ridden DOHC CB450 Honda, which puts it right up there in Triumph Bonneville territory, but I waited in vain for one or another of these two machines to appear and had to content myself with a truly desperate rider mounted on a CB440 Hawk and another on a two-stroke Yamaha RD350 with a set of pong-boxes fitted. We despatched the Honda with no drama, and very easily held off the Yamaha through some great corners until about half-way through fourth gear when it ranged up alongside on a straight section and pulled ahead slightly on the straight to cover us in little black spots as it took off into the distance.

By any standards I know of, that was a very good effort from the little British bike, but I cannot vouch for how much better it might have fared had its owner been in the saddle!

Cutting in from the kerb behind and lining up for a 'late-entry' just after the apex on this tight right-hander. It led to a sweeping series of great, downhill Ess-bends. The bike enjoyed being pelted from one footrest to the other almost as much as I did. Always mindful of the knife-edge of rubber on the square section rear tyre, I went back up and did it all over again, if a little quicker than before. It was all great 'Boy Racer' stuff!

At just under 6000rpm in top gear (just over 110km/h), the bike can be kept in top for most of the time, even up quite steep hills or when pulling out to overtake. It leaps away like a startled gazelle if you drop it a cog and screw the throttle open, but then it peaks again in no time and it has to be slotted back into top again almost before you are past the vehicle in front. Top gear is probably an overdrive, but its performance is quite good; probably better than many other high-revving machines of this capacity.

The engine thrives on really high revs, for it is here that the bike is at its best. It is hard to keep an eye on the twin tacho/speedo heads because they are so small, and both are shrouded to some extent by clutch and brake cables, which makes traffic riding a bit of a chore, but open road riding, where you can concentrate more on where you are going and how the engine *feels* and what it is doing, is much easier.

I mentioned the crankcases earlier, but didn't point out their surprisingly large capacity. The clearance around the cranks is much greater than it needs to be, and I suggest this may be for a very good reason. Clearly, there is room to take a stronger crank with a longer stroke which, combined with a larger bore could, with detail modifications, result in a very high performance 500cc DOHC twin which would easily poke out some 50-plus BHP; more than a DOHC road-race Manx Norton!

Bearing in mind the *power-to-weight ratio* which would then apply, allied to its slimness, powerful brakes and great handling, it's a safe bet that very little with a wheel at each end – if anything! – would have lived with it on the road had it been a full-blown five-hundred, whether in the 1970s or for some years beyond, as the larger capacity Four-cylinder Juggernauts from Japan were beginning to arrive. Was that suggestion from me more than a little starry-eyed? Oh, yes, but I suggest justifiably so.

Of course, for a full-sized five hundred, there would have to be an alteration to the crankcase mouth to allow for con-rod angularity, and larger/longer barrels with different bolt-hole centres would have to be made, but this would not have been beyond the scope of the designers. The makers could have employed a 'square' 68 x 68 mm bore/stroke, or have used the 750 Triumph's 67 x 70 mm bore/stroke and fitted the pistons, con-rods and big-end slippers from this engine; remembering that the big-end journals are the same size on the Bandit as they are on the three-cylinder machine.

If that Bandit was a true rocket-ship (*for its 350cc size, again, be it clearly understood!!*) and enjoyed a standard of performance and handling which could not be matched when it was introduced, then it again flew in the face of the traditional British motorcycle in being entirely oil-tight, with not a sign of a weep, or smear, of lubricant to be seen anywhere on or under the power-plant.

It was **said** that one of the things which wrecked any chance of the bike ever reaching production status was that a batch of several thousand starter motors which had been made cheaply in India simply didn't fit, due, it was further added, to an error in technical drawings. But at least one of them *did* fit – or was *altered* to fit – because the starter motor which came with the Bandit I rode fitted well and functioned perfectly.

The parent company, BSA, had lost some eight million pounds the previous year and was clearly not in a position to pour any more money into the bike, but still managed to build their more popular – if poor-selling at the time – larger-capacity twins.

The poor little Bandit would doubtless have undergone many small revisions to its prototype form to cure the niggling problems I've mentioned, but it was left to quietly wither on the vine, which was a monumental tragedy for Triumph/BSA and, arguably, for motorcycling in general – and, perhaps, world-wide at that!

TECH SPECS

Make: Triumph P30

Model: Pre-Production 'Bandit'

Years of manufacture: 1970-1971

Type:
All-alloy DOHC, vertical-twin-cylinder, the double-overhead camshafts running direct into cylinder head casting, with cams driven by **single-row** $3/8"$ x $7/32"$ chain, cranks disposed at 180 degrees, the engine canted slightly forward in frame, in unit-construction with five-speed gearbox; dry sump. RR56 Alloy conrods, with detachable end-caps and lead/indium/bronze slipper bearings, one-piece forged crankshaft supported on ball and roller main bearings.

Capacity: 349cc

Bore x stroke: 63 x 56mm

Compression ratio: 9.5:1

Power @ rpm: 35BHP @ 9000rpm

Carburation:
Dual 27mm Amal Concentric carburettors, with paper-pack air filters.

Electrics:
Lucas 12-volt, 110-watt alternator, ignition by coil and points, with electric starter motor, blinkers.

Primary drive:
Duplex $3/8"$ x $7/32"$ chain to five-speed gearbox. Primary ratio: 23/52 (2.260:1)

Gear ratios:
1st – 17.1:1; 2nd – 11.48:1; 3rd – 9.03:1; 4th – 7.37:1; 5th – 6.39:1.

Frame, wheels, brakes:
Duplex down-tube, full-cradle tubular-steel frame, with 18" wheels, 350 x 18" tyres front and rear; front ribbed, rear Avon 'SM' block pattern. Front suspension by telescopic, two-way damped forks, rear by swing-arm, with dual, spring/damper units. Front drum brake is twin-leading shoe, 200mm diameter. Rear is drum brake, single-leader, 175mm diameter.

Dimensions:
Length – 198.75cm; Seat height – 75.60cm; Wheelbase – 138.75cm

Weight: 155kg

Fuel capacity: 13.5 litres. Range: Approx. 275km.

Top speed (claimed): 170km/h.

1961 BMW R50S 'Sports'

500cc OHV 'BOXER' TWIN CYLINDER

It was on a long, hard two-day ride into the country with a touring friend of mine in 1961 that I first encountered the near-new, and extremely rare, R50S BMW motorcycle; the genuine sports 500cc machine which enjoyed an all-too brief interlude in the three years from 1960 to 1962. The R50S flat-twin entered Australia in very small numbers indeed, with only a 'suggested' 11 of the machines brought into New South Wales, which would assume not much more than a score of them coming into the country during those three years. If it was a rare machine in Australia, then it was a rare motorcycle everywhere else as well, for there were only 1634 of these sports five-hundreds to have ever been built in Germany during that short period.

There were other models in the small BMW range in the late 1950s to early 1960s, of course, which included the standard R50 (of which, in direct comparison to the 1634 sports R50S, almost 35,000 were built) along with the single-cylinder, 250cc R26, the 600cc sports R69 and later R69S models – of which just under 12,000 were made – and the 600cc R60, which was essentially the more 'softly' tuned sidecar model.

The ever-expanding Japanese onslaught, which resulted in the rebirth of motorcycling world-wide, had begun in Sydney, Australia, just a brief two years earlier, with many of the British factories dramatically curtailing their production runs, ceasing production entirely, or were very soon to do so.

Many factories in Germany, including Horex, NSU, DKW, Hoffman, Adler and Zundapp, were feeling the cold winds of death upon them. BMW alone, itself in financial strife, was left to carry the can for Germany. It was saved by receiving an injection of funds from a German Bank and selling off its aircraft facility, while Zundapp, BMW's strongest competitor at that time, failed to achieve similar funding and managed to hang on by its corporate fingernails for several years thereafter by making a large range of lightweight two-stroke motorcycles, but it was also fated to disappear, for Zundapp was declared bankrupt in 1984.

The machine I rode on that country trip in 1961 was a 'run-of-the-mill', 500cc B33 BSA with cast iron head and barrel, but it had been tuned to a very high standard by being fitting with Gold Star BSA road-race cams and other detailed modifications, including highly polished ports, a huge 2-inch (50mm) inlet valve, higher compression ratio piston, bigger-bore carburettor and tuned exhaust system. The gearbox was fitted with a set of medium-close ratio gears, with a 17-tooth 'sidecar gearing' engine sprocket, which was two teeth lower than standard: it was, in fact, the same engine sprocket as that fitted to the 350cc B31 BSA. The gearing was 'lowered' to pull a sidecar about, the bike all too often little more than the family hack.

The R50S employed BMW's shaft-drive of course, its bore x stroke dimensions 'square' at 68 x 68mm, with a very high – for those days – compression ratio of 9.5:1. Power output was 35BHP at 7650rpm. In view of the extra power of the sporty R50S, the engine employed a more substantial crankshaft assembly, the crank cheeks at 180 degrees to one another, the shaft supported on a large ball bearing at the front, a special 'semi-spherical' roller bearing at the rear. A small outrigger ball bearing on the front end of the crankshaft provided additional stiffness to support the weight of the generator; the camshaft supported upon a pair of similarly sized ball bearings.

The crankshaft was the built-up type with caged roller big-end bearings, but was very different from the standard R50 and the larger-capacity 600cc R60. The R50S could accelerate from 0–100km/hour some ***seven seconds quicker than the 600cc model,*** but it must be said that the heavier flywheels and smaller carburettors fitted to the R60 machine – which was, as I have remarked, the designated sidecar model – would certainly account for that discrepancy.

BMW machines have always been very distinctive in appearance, even in their usual, less-than-spectacular all-black finish, relieved by some white pin-striping and chromed panels. There were several other colour schemes available in other countries, in particular the US, but – with only a handful of exceptions – the machines imported into Australia in those days were very much traditional black. The model we found for this test is no exception, its showroom paintwork and highly burnished chrome plating and alloy castings a tribute to the hard work put into its restoration by its owner, Galvin Marketing's Metzeler tyre importer, the late John Galvin.

It's been said that BMW was embarrassed by the machine, which was not as smooth-running as expected and which was quite noisy mechanically. The exhaust note was more urgent than usual, and even less civilised when really punting hard, but this was part of the charm of the chase and perfectly acceptable to those of us who are into that sort of thing.

A large air filter sat on top of the large gearbox casting, with two chromed tubes leading filtered air to a pair of 26mm Bing carburettors out in the breeze with the horizontal cylinders. The gearbox bolted to the rear of the very large casting which contained the crankshaft and to which the cast-iron cylinders were attached. The alloy cylinder heads were topped by rocker covers which have two distinctive, heavy ribs on the outer faces, very similar to those attached to the 600cc R69 and R69S models, which sets the sports models apart from the standard 500cc machines which have rocker covers with six much less obvious 'fins' on top.

The substantial engine casting has a deep, wet sump which employs its own casting, with another alloy casting bolted towards the front which contains the ignition and other electrical components, while a further alloy casting outside of that rounds out the design and protects the components from the weather.

At the rear of the crankshaft assembly the flywheel and single-plate clutch is bolted, the clutch action controlled by a large diaphragm spring.

The front end of the crank is carried low in the casting, the camshaft on top, driven at half-engine speed by a pair of carefully mated helical gears which were available, even from new, in no fewer than eleven different sizes. The half-time pinion on the end of the crankshaft is steel, the much larger camshaft gear is an aluminium alloy while a small, dished alloy gear beneath the half-time pinion drives the gear-type oil pump which lives in the very bowels of the engine. The wet-sump oiling system is at once force-fed to the crank and big-end bearings, and thence 'splash' fed to just about everything else by special oil slingers on the crankshaft. Pistons are, of course, aluminium alloy, with three rings, the top a specially plated compression ring, the second a chamfered ring, the lower an oil scraper.

Ignition is by magneto, driven at half-engine speed from the front of the camshaft, the magnet integral with the shaft while the stator is fixed to the alloy casting. The bike employs a set of

A huge air filter sits atop large engine castings, clean air conducted to carburettors on either side by neat chrome-plated tubes. Note the kickstarter, which was awkward as it only operated 'sideways'. Being vertically challenged, I couldn't use it until the bike was on its centre stand.

contact points with an auto-advance unit to control ignition timing.

Driven from the end of the crankshaft, the 6-volt generator has an output of 60 watts at 1700rpm and 90W at 2100rpm, with control by voltage regulator, with an 8-Amp/hour lead/acid battery completing the picture. A light in the headlamp shell warns that ignition is switched on, and it announces that current is being generated by simply going out. A neat speedometer is the only other instrument fitted and it, too, sits in the top of the headlamp shell.

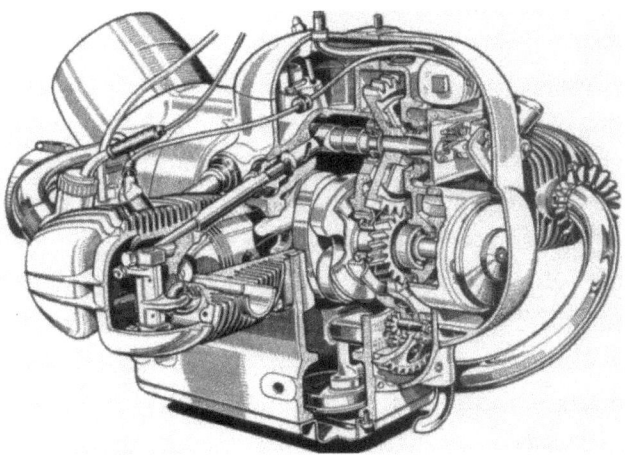

This is the 600cc R69S BMW power-plant. In effect, it is identical to the 500cc R50S (no one was about to draw a cutaway of the rare R50S). It was about as neat and purposeful an engine as one could wish for in the early 1960s, and both engines were well able to deliver the goods.

If the engine is a trim design with no frills, then the final drive shaft is a gem. The drive shaft exits the four-speed gearbox on the right side and is contained within the swinging-fork which controls the rear suspension. A universal joint is attached to the front of the shaft and is supported in needle bearings, the entire unit running in an oil bath. At the rear, the shaft is splined to accept a coupler gear which is free to slide along the splines as wheel movement occurs over bumps.

The shaft gear and large wheel pinions are both spiral bevel gears and are very precisely ground, the drive applied to the centre of the large crown wheel to overcome any possibility of the rear-end rising under heavy acceleration or dipping on the over-run.

The frames fitted to BMW machines from 1955 to 1969 were a great design, and this could also be said of the great suspension system as well, for the German machines of that era had few peers in terms of strength, rigidity and comfort, allied to very fine handling. They had their strange design quirks, and more of that anon, but in terms of overall design and capability they were very nearly out on their own.

In view of the manner in which it was built and the type of material employed in its construction, the BMW frame was beautifully constructed. It was essentially a 'box-section' design, with great torsional rigidity in every plane; it was 'structurally closed', with duplex down-tube and full-cradle support for the power-plant, which fits against a rubber snubber atop the alloy engine castings, and is attached to the frame by two large through-bolts under the engine.

The frame tubes are of multiple section, changing almost imperceptibly from large-diameter oval tubing at the heavily stressed steering head to a more tubular shape of somewhat smaller diameter for the full cradle under the engine. The twin tubes sweep back and curve upwards well behind the rear-wheel suspension pivot-point to meet a single top tube under the fuel tank, changing in section again from round to larger-diameter oval as they go, again to allow for more strength and rigidity at high stress points.

Another tube is interpolated at the juncture of these three tubes, joining a cross-brace just under the steering head and carrying the top engine-fitting with its rubber washers and mounting bolts. Two additional, vertical frame tubes are welded to the mainframe just outside the power take-off from the gearbox, and these provide attachment for the swinging-fork suspension arm. Their position also allows the swing-arm to pivot co-axially with the movement at the universal joint which helps overcome any problems of over-stressing the shaft and attendant bearings.

Far from the usual bronze bushes at the swing-arm pivot, BMW employs fully adjustable 'Timken' tapered roller bearings at this high stress-point, and very large diameter ones at that. To ensure more rigidity, the top mounting points for the rear damper units are welded to braced outriggers and thus are part of the frame. The rear dampers are two-way adjustable for load and hydraulic damping.

The front suspension is by swinging-arm, similar to the rear suspension, and with a similarly sized pair of spring/damper units, the pivoting-fork contained by a pair of tapered roller bearings in much the same way as at the rear, and are of similarly large diameter. These Earles-forks were employed at the time in an on-again/off-again manner by a number of manufacturers both in England and on the Continent, but was a feature of the German twins, and 250cc singles, for 14 years. The BMW frames were fitted with sidecar lugs, the pivot bearing on the front swing-arm able to be moved from its lower mounting point to one directly above to alter the trail angle for easier steering. I must say that any oaf who fitted a chair to a sports mount like this one would deserve to be prosecuted to the full extent of the law.

To round out the features of this great frame, the two sports models, the 500cc R50S and the 600cc R69S, employed hydraulic steering dampers, a very rare fitment indeed in those days, the damper's action controlled by a hand-wheel atop the steering head, in the same manner as the friction dampers on the touring models, if very much more effective.

If there is any one thing – there are two of them, actually! – which I could never come to grips with on those earlier BMW models it was the odd kick-starter. It protruded from the engine's left side, and kicked outwards at that, which meant – at least with my short legs – that starting the device was very difficult, to say the least.

The drill for those with reasonable-length legs is to shove the starter pedal out with the heel of the left foot, but I could never manage that at all. I had to stand on the left footrest, the machine on its centre-stand, and lean on the starter pedal with my right foot. It was much easier if there happened to be a footpath handy, because I could then dispense with the dicey ploy of standing on the footrest, and have most of my weight off the bike as I kicked it over.

But the odd thing which beat me was the technique for starting the bike while facing uphill! The problem lay with the great twin-leading shoe front brake, which is of large diameter and is immensely powerful while going forward, but which simply wouldn't work *at all* going backwards; which naturally happens when you are facing uphill, the bike off its centre stand! You can squeeze that front brake lever as hard as you like and the bike just slips quietly away downhill, and if you are trying to kick the thing over as well you (or at least I) get nowhere fast. Having said that, the BMW brakes are powerful

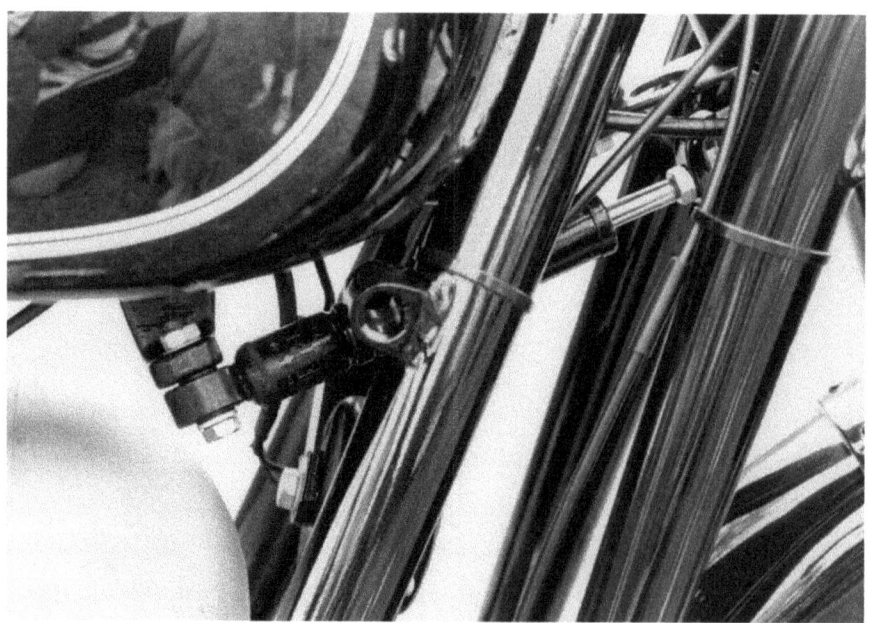

Hydraulic steering damper was a very handy device, and this was probably the first time the neat little damper was fitted to a motorcycle. It worked well and needed little more than a quick flick of the wrist.

Final drive shaft was enclosed within the right-hand swing-arm suspension leg, with a flexible-gaiter over the universal joint at the shaft as it leaves the gearbox. It is probably Neoprene, as a rubber gaiter would have been ruined by mineral oil in no time flat.

and very reliable, the front brake allied to a clever parallelogram linkage to raise the front-end under brakes and thus enjoy the benefits of a built-in, mechanical anti-dive system, but at the expense of some suspension movement. The rear brake requires some thought, particularly on the change back from third to second gear if (perhaps) riding just a little too urgently, because there is some tendency to lock-up the rear wheel if braking hard, and this could be more than a little 'twitchy' if the roads happened to be wet.

The BMW wheels look very robust, to say the least, the large brake drums laced into deeply ribbed aluminium alloy rims. A feature of Earles forks is said to be the lessening of unsprung weight, and here the lighter rims would no doubt help, though this might be negated to a degree by the deep-section, heavily valanced front guard. An even deeper rear guard helps fill in the area above the rear tyre and beneath the dual-seat, heightening the impression of solidity. Tyres are 350 x 18 front and rear: Metzeler, of course, as they were way back when the bike was new.

Weighing in at 198kg, the R50S is not amongst the lightest, but is easy to heave onto the centre-stand because of the roll-on shape of the stand's legs. Oddly, internal gear ratios are the same for all four models in the range and are probably medium/close, differing only in the final drive ratio at the rear wheel.

The R50, R60 and R69S have a final ratio of 3.13:1, the R50S, with one tooth less on the drive shaft, 3.58:1. Overall ratios for the sports 500 are well chosen if you are punting the bike hard, top gear of 5.5:1 allowing just over 160km/h top speed (according to BMW) if you tuck in your elbows, ears and knees and keep your mouth shut.

As I suspected, when I fired the engine up the bike was a bit rough on the idle, though it turned over very reliably, and there was some engine noise as well with more rocking side-to-side than usual with this type of machine; no doubt the quite high compression ratio is responsible for this, allied to the usual longitudinal torque reaction of the flat-twin engine.

Try as I may, first gear engages with a crunch you can hear three houses away, but it was ever thus and there seemed to be no way you could overcome this, but other gear changes on the move are quieter once you know the trick involved. You need to stroke the clutch lever and slip the left-mounted lever up for a higher gear almost before it is fully disengaged, and while engine revs, and noise, are on the way down. There is almost no way you can change back quietly, though sometimes you do and sometimes you don't; that is an art I have simply not yet mastered. I don't get much practice on early BMW machines, so there isn't much chance of getting it totally right any time soon!

Engine running and about to take off. A little (too much) throttle to get underway and the BMW's sudden clutch saw the R50S exit the dirt surface almost side-on. Happily, a firm, sealed surface was just moments away, so no drama – well, at least, not much!

The touring R50 runs out of puff at 5800rpm, with 26HP on hand, the R50S peaks at a very high (for those days!) 7650rpm, with an extra 9HP to call upon, an increase of nearly 40%. If ever a machine needs a tacho fitted it is the R50S, because it is only when you squirt the thing in anger that you really appreciate the incredible difference those extra ponies make.

I've said before that memory is a fickle jade, and it could be a disappointment if one makes mental comparisons between the way things *are* and the way they *were*. I do remember the R50 as a fairly staid performer when ridden as it was intended to be ridden, even though its effortless road manners allowed the miles to be eaten up with ease, simply because the bike was so comfortable and handled choppy surfaces so well. Not so the R50S, which is a true sports mount and has to be treated that way. I speak in terms of the engine's performance, of course, not the machine's handling.

It likes to be ridden much harder than its touring brother, and in fact doesn't really show its best unless being pushed along, with gear changes made much later into the power band. In so doing, you can cleverly make use of the flywheel effect for faster gear changes, the energy stored in the flywheels allowing a real surge into the next gear instead of waiting for it all to happen again.

Because of the weight of the flywheels and the engine-speed clutch, you have to get out of first gear fairly early or the crunch into second would have the Police after you, but from then on, at quite respectable speeds, you can let the engine's power work for you as you wind the bike up through the gears. Third gear is great for most overtaking moves this side of the legal limit, though top gear can be used most of the time unless in heavy traffic or attacking very steep climbs from lower speeds.

Acceleration is quite brisk if you keep the wick turned up, and it's probable – we never had the opportunity, unhappily – the bike could hold its own over give-and-take surfaces with some of the more modern touring irons. It may not be anywhere near as fast, but in terms of many of the other things that matter at least as much in motorcycling, it is still more than equal to the task.

The only real problem with the Earles front forks, because of their pivot point well behind the steering head, is a distinct tendency for the front wheel to follow slightly raised road irregularities – thankfully, tram-lines are no longer the bugbear in Sydney they once were! – and the R50S showed this slight inclination just like all those which went on before. It could sometimes be quite a handful over tram-lines and other raised road irregularities if you didn't treat them with the care they demanded! It just required some thought, and glancing well ahead to see what's coming up, and the drama is lessened. You should do that, anyway, if your priority is for longevity on two wheels.

The long BMW dual-seat, with its combination of long, soft springs and rubber cushioning remains one of the best ever and it nicely augments the supple suspension for which the machine has long been renowned. The R50S handlebars are on the short side and quite flat, which I found suited my shorts stature well, and which enhanced the sports image of the bike. Whether or not the machine needed the hydraulic steering damper I can't be sure, but I nipped it up over rough going at speed on occasion – it needs just a quick flick of the wrist – and eased it off again in light traffic.

The steering damper is apparently quite effective, but you can't ride at very slow speeds with it applied because it isn't nearly as easy to move the handlebars about at those speeds.

As I've said, the brakes are great and very powerful, the front needing little more than a firm squeeze because of the servo-action of the twin-leading shoe design and large diameter drum, the rear needing a touch more pressure, but is equally effective. They are, of course, cable operated but apparently as efficient as the later hydraulic brakes, with none of the bugbears often associated with discs in wet weather.

Clutch action is very light, again cable controlled, but obviously assisted by the very long actuating lever which hangs out of the gearbox for all the world to see.

In many ways the R50S opened up some forgotten vistas in comfort and in handling, the bike pinning itself down well through some quite choppy corners and allowing itself to be flung about from one footrest to the other with just a *little* abandon: it is a rare machine after all, so some caution needs to be taken!

At little more than a brisk trot, the BMW seemed just as happy as it was when it was really on the boil – as long as the special steering damper was slackened off a click, that is!

A quiet rural laneway. The bike steady and fuss-free, but a tightening of that laneway just over the brow — and out of sight — meant swiftly dropping back a cog, and a touch more throttle, cranking it over a tad more and that was all there was to it! Overall, a sweet bike to ride, if sometimes a little temperamental.

You could cry out for things to be the way they used to be, for I contend that BMW made a leap backwards when the Series Five machines appeared in 1969 with their cheaper frame with its bolt-on rear sub-frame to support the seat and rear suspension, and its more 'modern' engine design, but that is merely tossing chaff to the winds.

You could cry out for an electric starter on the R50S, perhaps for an overhead camshaft engine instead of a pushrod-operated overhead valve one; in fact, as with any and every machine, you could cry out for a lot of things.

The facts are that BMW was almost on its last legs when the 1960 models were made, the factory almost broke and only just surviving a take-over bid because of the timely intervention of a friendly bank which took an all-time punt with an injection of funds which allowed the German company to emerged victorious.

History has recorded that the R50S and its stable-mates were made to a standard and not to a price back then, just as BMW motorcycles are today, and those facts are there to be seen by any who wish to judge the machine against its contemporaries. Rare though BMW machines were in Australia in those tough times, they survived the quicksands which swallowed up most of the other motorcycle factories at the time — including virtually all the British *marques* — and set the factory on its way to becoming, today, one of the giants in the European car industry. The fact that BMW still manufactures a range of first-class motorcycles as well as some great cars simply ices a delicious cake for all of us who prefer our motoring to be on just two wheels.

TECH SPECS

Make: BMW

Model: R50S

Type:
Horizontally-opposed twin-cylinder four stroke, with alloy cylinder heads and cast iron barrels. Overhead valves controlled by pushrods. One-piece connecting rods, with caged roller big-end bearings, the crankshaft supported upon plain-roller and spherical-roller bearings. Lubrication by double-gear pump, with oil pressure-fed to main and big-end bearings, aided by oil galleys and oil slingers.

Bore x stroke: 68 x 68mm

Compression ratio: 9.5:1

Power @ rpm: 35BHP @ 7.650rpm

Carburation:
Two 26mm Bing carburettors, with large-capacity mesh air filter.

Electrics:
Magneto ignition, 6-volt Bosch generator to lead/acid battery.

Transmission:
Direct through single-plate dry clutch to four-speed foot-change gearbox and final drive by shaft through bevel gears: 7/25 reduction for 3.58 ratio.

Gear ratios:
(Overall) 1st – 14.7:1; 2nd – 9.77:1; 3rd – 6.94:1; 4th – 5.51:1

Frame, wheels, suspension, brakes:
Double-loop, full cradle frame made from tapered and inserted steel tubing, with heavy reinforcements at steering head, swing arm pivot and rear suspension mounts. Front suspension by Earles-type forks with double-acting, short spring/damper units and hydraulic, hand-adjusted steering damper. Rear by rigidly mounted double-acting spring/damper units, three-way adjustable for tension/damping. Deep-groove alloy 18" rims laced to full-width alloy hubs, 200mm (8") brakes, front twin-leading shoe, with rear brake single leader type. 350 x 18 Metzeler tyres front and rear; ribbed front, block rear.

Dimensions:
Length – 2,125mm; Width – 660mm; Height – 980mm; Wheelbase – 1,415mm

Fuel tank: 17 litres (3.73 Imp gallons)

Fuel consumption: 5.2l/100km (54mpg)

Weight: 198kg (436lb)

Top Speed: 165km/h

Machine loaned by:
JOHN GALVIN, Sydney, NSW.

1950 Series 'C' Vincent 'Rapide'

1000cc, 45BHP OHV VEE-TWIN

1937 motorcycle 'season' saw the introduction of a brand-new Vee-twin into the marketplace in England, the A-series Vincent HRD 'Rapide', a sporty overhead valve twin with its pots disposed at an odd 47.4 degrees, its short pushrods controlled by camshafts carried high in the alloy crankcases

In effect, the engine was 'simply' two of the pre-war 500cc OHV single-cylinder Comet/Meteor cylinders mounted upon a common crankcase, the plot fitted into a slightly lengthened Meteor frame. The machine employed the usual Vincent HRD cantilever rear suspension and girder front forks, but was otherwise not very remarkable at the time. After all, there were a number of other large British Vee-twins about in those days, some of them overhead valve designs, but others were the old-fashioned side-valve type. Royal Enfield had one, so too did AJS and Matchless, in both side valve and overhead valve forms, while BSA had both 750 and 500cc OHV Vee-twins – the latter renowned for chewing up and spitting out its big-end assemblies – and of course there was Coventry Eagle, Zenith, Montgomery, the much-prized OHV Brough Superior and several others.

Some of the manufacturers, like Matchless, BSA and Vincent, employed their own, in-house-designed power-plants, while several others used engines manufactured in England by JAP, Blackburne or British Anzani.

What *was* remarkable about the new twin, though no-one was to know it at the time, is that it was to be the forerunner of the great post war Vincent Rapide, the more sporty Black Shadow we are soon to visit in more depth, the awesome, 70BHP race-worthy Black Lightning, and the later D-series, The latter, those most impressive, all-black streamlined Black Prince and Black Knight machines which were, long after the last of the latter D-series machines had left the factory in 1955, to become the most eagerly sought-after Classic motorcycles of all time.

All this was well into the future of course, the new, pre-war series-A Vincent HRD a result of a happy partnership of two great pioneers, the Englishman Phil Vincent and the Australian Phil Irving, the former a great ideas man, the latter an extremely well-studied but often a somewhat self-taught engineering genius and genuine Aussie larrikin.

The 998cc series 'A' Vincent looked somewhat more agricultural than the much later, post-war machines, and was given the deserved nickname of the *'plumbers' nightmare'* in view of the staggering number of more than ten external oil lines which seemed to run anywhere and everywhere around and about the narrow-angle Vee-twin. The machine's impressive performance was always there, it must be noted, as evidenced by the fact that the heavy-duty Burman BA gearbox with which it was originally equipped was not really up to the job of handling the power of this new motorcycle.

At the end of the WWII hostilities in 1945 the Vincent HRD 'Rapide' re-appeared in the guise of a Series B model, the power-plant very much neater in appearance than the pre-war machine, and, though bearing the same name-plate on tank and engine castings, in many ways an entirely different motorcycle. The Burman gearbox was gone, the new engine now a unit-construction design with integral gearbox.

The name Vincent-HRD still appeared on the machine's petrol tank and on alloy castings here and there, which of course proclaimed its ancestry, but there had been a lot of detail work carried out

Series A, the first Vincent Rapide. It was just one of a raft of other Vee-twins on sale at the time. Note the front downtube, the engine a stressed member of the small frame, which disappeared entirely with the greatly improved, unit-construction, post-WWII series B. The A-series engine developed too much power for the Burman BA gearbox to handle.

The first Series A was always referred to as the 'Plumber's Nightmare' and we can clearly see why this was so. There are ten or more oil lines to be seen on this side, with several more to service the overhead valve gear. Later, pre-war models did away with at least some of these 'offending' oil lines.

internally, the exterior castings much cleaner and less primitive, much more in keeping with the new image the machine was about to generate.

This was due, in no small measure, to an entirely different project than that of the normal evolution which occurs when later versions of an existing motorcycle appear in the market-place. The post-war type-B Vincent engine owed its more acceptable, streamlined appearance (and almost total lack of external oil lines) to a project as far removed from motorcycling as it is possible to be. It was a World War 2 project called 'Picador', which was a War Ministry plan to develop a lightweight 'target drone' aircraft, which was to be sent aloft by radio control and then – hopefully/shockingly – to be shot down by anti-aircraft guns!

What was that, again? To fit a small, target aircraft with a 1000cc Vincent HRD motorcycle engine for the sole purpose of sending the small device into the air, controlling its movements in flight by radio and then have it shot down in flames by some idiot operating a set of anti-aircraft guns? Surely not! Well, that was the plan, believe it or not, and Vincent was said to have made between twenty and thirty highly specialised engines with that object in mind. The new design was much more pleasing to the eye, and bore such improvements from the A-series as a stronger crankshaft assembly, allied to stronger connecting rods, with more substantial caged roller big-ends, larger and more firmly fitted main bearings and most of its internal components hand polished.

The cams were modified as well, and were probably very similar to the famous Mark 2 design as fitted into the post-war Black Lightning racing motorcycles, for **the engine was said to have developed the same 70BHP as the later, rare 'Black Lightning' road racer.** Initially, the Vincent's Picador drone engine was fitted with large-bore carburettors which failed due to terminal fuel surge problems when the small aircraft was blasted from its launching pad with the aid of a set of powerful rockets! A newly designed *fuel-injector system* soon put paid to that nonsense – while the bonus of adding more power – but the machine could not be effectively controlled by radio and thus could never be shot down. The few that made it into the air were said to have plunged into the sea instead, which was at least as sad as being blasted out of the sky.

It's a long, sad story, but in effect this put paid to Vincent's efforts, ate into their meagre finances and may well have helped set the post-war scene for the company's premature demise

The powerful, 73BHP Vincent Picador target drone engine. It was a very much 'cleaned up' Vee-twin, with many oil lines now as internal drillings and oil galleys. It used a double-action oil pump and a Scintilla magneto, with fuel injection. The much cleaner lines were reflected in the first, post-war Vincent B-series twins.

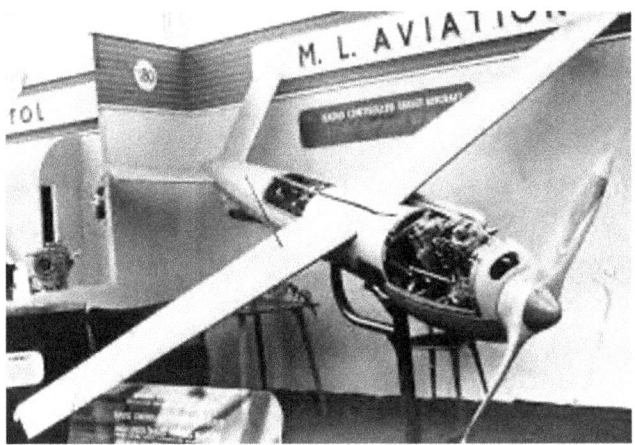

The M.L. Aviation Picador target drone, with the Vincent engine in place. It was said the reason it was so unsuccessful was that the radio control didn't work at all, but some wags suggested that no-one who knew what it was wanted to shoot the thing down! There were said to have been no more than about thirty of the drones built.

juts a decade after WWII was over.

The post-war Vincent HRD engine was still a Vee-twin of 998cc, with the same bore x stroke of 84 x 90mm as the A-series/Picador, the three-ring alloy pistons now a quite low 6.45:1 compression ratio, but the cylinders were now disposed at 50 degrees instead of 47 odd. The engineering principle behind this narrow Vee-angle was initially dismissed by Phil Irving himself, in the interests, so he said, 'of expediency, to allow the engine to be fitted into its 'frame' *(of which there is none, as we have noted later. [My emphasis])* without unduly lengthening the machine's wheelbase.' but the later engine, I suggest, owed much more to the Picador project than it did to anything else.

Irving's much neater, post-war Series B engine remained a high-camshaft design, with overhead valves operated by solid, short steel pushrods, the widely splayed pushrods, unusually, set at the same included angle as the valves they control. Oddly, the valve rockers operated the valves half-way down their stems, beneath the valve springs, using parallel rockers contained within alloy collars which fitted just inside the four large tappet covers. Valve-lash adjustment was by normal screw-and-nut tappets. It employed the pre-war girder forks as well.

Alloy heads and barrels were used, both very heavily finned, the barrels with deep spigots into the crankcases which made them look short, chunky and very robust as they sat atop the enormous crankcase castings. Inside a very large alloy casting sat the timing gears, six in all, including a huge `idler' gear which was driven by the half-time pinion and in turn drove two camshafts, sited at opposite ends of the timing case, thus adding to the overall dimensions of the awe-inspiring engine.

To digress for a moment, the Vincent which is the subject of this report was owned by the Metzler and Belstaff importer, the late John Galvin, and it differs from most other Vincents in one significant area: it must thus be of greater interest to Vincent enthusiasts, and could therefore be even more eagerly sought after.

The Galvin Rapide's cylinder heads have 14mm threaded holes opposite the spark plugs, the holes closed by small alloy bungs. I thought they may have been used to experiment with

As ever, the Vincent steering at low speeds was too heavy for my liking but when the bike was running hard it was a great machine to ride. The suspension was on the firm side but it was well up to the task when pushing hard over uncertain road surfaces. The bike could occasionally wallow a little over a series of uneven ripples but was never thrown off line.

dual-plug ignition at one time, and in fact, one well known English magazine had gone into print many years ago saying just that, but this was apparently not the case. According to Phil Irving himself, a young apprentice was given the task of drilling the holes and tapping the threads for the spark plugs, which of course he duly did – but on the wrong side of the cylinder heads!

Before the lad felt the toe of the considerable Irving boot at his backside, the young chap had drilled fourteen heads, and neatly tapped the threads as well. Rather than melt the alloy heads down or throw them out, with Austerity very much the order of the day, and to save the extra time and expense, the heads were redrilled in the correct place, retapped, and the offending holes closed by the neat alloy bungs I've mentioned. The word was then leaked out to the motorcycle Press that Vincent was experimenting with dual ignition and that just *seven* machines were thus equipped. *Of such stuff are legends made!!*

Cylinders were off-set to allow for better cooling of the rear pot, and also to allow for the two con-rods to sit side-by-side on a common crankpin. The *original* big-end was a three-row, crowded needle-roller design, utilising no fewer than 135 needle rollers of 3 x 5mm.

Later modifications to most machines have seen the adoption of caged roller bearings of somewhat larger diameter: the bike on test, Galvin's Series C Rapide, has had this modification.

Here is the offending bung, with the silhouette of the spark plug in its correct position directly opposite. There would have been just seven Vincents with these bungs in place, which were said to have been part of an experiment in dual ignition(?). Whether or not this would make those very rare machines more valuable remains unknown.

Die-cast 'Specialoid' pistons were pinned to high-tensile steel con-rods located by the crankpin into forged, 40-ton carbon-steel flywheels which were machined on every surface and jig-drilled for perfect balance. The flywheel assembly was supported on no less than four ball and roller main bearings, one of each on either side, the outrigger bearing on the left, drive side, somewhat larger than the outrigger bearing on the timing side.

Hidden away from the gaze of the passing populace, the huge crankcase castings were heavily ribbed internally to add great strength and rigidity, the cases of unit-construction design to incorporate the gearbox and thus assure even more rigidity to the unit. The reason for this immensely strong engine will soon become apparent.

Primary drive to the strange clutch was by a ⅜" x ⁷⁄₃₂" three-row chain, the clutch a servo-assisted design not unlike a spinning brake drum with attendant brake-shoes, with a single, separate clutch plate to allow the machine to be stopped and started up again without stalling. Ignition was by dual magneto which sat directly beneath the front cylinder, the instrument driven from a gear inside the timing case.

One of the oddest features of the Vincent HRD – later to drop the initials and become, simply, Vincent – is the fact that it had no frame, at least not in terms of a motorcycle frame as we know it. As we are now aware, the so-called upper frame member is in fact the **only** frame member, that immensely strong engine forming the greater part of its own frame.

We need not pursue the HRD Rapide roadster much further, for in every other respect it is identical with the Black Shadow sports model we will feature next, but the *Genesis* of all the Vincent machines which were to follow was wrought with the original A-series and reached its final, far more acceptable engine design in that ill-fated Picador project.

Had the Picador project been successful, with – one assumes – the possibility of several thousands of Vincent/Picador drones being built only to be shot down and plunge into the surrounding seas – shock/horror! – Vincent may have enjoyed a large injection of funds, which might then have allowed the small Stevenage factory to be far better placed financially after the cessation of hostilities than was otherwise the case.

What would then have emerged from that small factory and the brilliant pairing of Phil Vincent and the Aussie larrikin Phil Irving, might one think, if a great deal more money had been in the Vincent bank account at war's end? Nobody knowns, and of course nobody ever will.

Had the finances been there, let us dream of a hundred or so Black Lightnings being built instead of just over thirty, even an OHC variation of the Big Twins could have been possible, and the occasional 500cc OHC single variant might also have been on the cards. What if a *four-cylinder* Vincent may have emerged to challenge the 1000cc Square Four, perhaps a raft of small 'bread-and-butter' commuters as well, just to keep the finances healthy?

If the factory had enjoyed more financial stability in the late 1940s might it have almost automatically grown larger and then survived for several more years than it did as Honda was in the process of placing the whole world back on two wheels in the late 1950s/early 1960s? Were that to be the case, could Vincent have been with us to this day? Pure speculation, of course, no more and no less than that, and as such a near-worthless hypothesis. But we can dream, can we not?

The bottom line is this: If only more financial independence and thus greater stability had been possible for the small Vincent factory: what then? Oh, yes, if only!

TECH SPECS

Make: Vincent HRD

Model: 1950 Series C 'Rapide'

Type: Vee-twin, all-alloy, OHV four-stroke, with cylinders disposed at 50 degrees, the two connecting rods attached to a common crankpin, with crowded needle rollers of 3 x 5mm. Crankshaft supported upon four roller and ball bearings, the engine castings forming a unit-construction design, with integral gearbox.

Capacity: 998cc

Bore x stroke: 84 x 90mm

Compression ratio: 6.5:1

Power @ rpm: 45BHP @ 5300rpm

Carburation: Dual Amal 276 Carburettors, 1"-I-16" bore.

Ignition: Lucan Magneto.

Frame, forks, wheels: No frame as such, but strengthened, lengthy oil tank atop engine produces support for the power-plant, which is a 'stressed unit' hung by special brackets attached to base of oil tank and cylinder heads. Steering head is attached to front of tank, to which the unusual 'Girdraulic' front forks are attached, featuring a girder-type fork blade, with central hydraulic damping and two small telescopic forks at rear with internal springs. Cantilever rear suspension is attached to gearbox and is also attached to the rear of the busy oil tank, with dual spring boxes under articulated seat, and a central, hydraulic damper. 'Straight-pull' spokes are laced to steel rims at front, with 300 x 20 ribbed tyre, rear wheel similarly spoked, but with 350 x 19 block pattern Dual, 7-inch (178mm) drum brakes are fitted to front and rear wheels, with 'rocking beam' adjuster atop front guard for the dual front brakes.

Dimensions: Height – 1080mm; Length – 2172 mm; Width – 654mm; Saddle height – 812mm; Ground Clearance – 152mm; Wheelbase – 1435mm; Fuel tank capacity: 17 litres; Weight – 206kg.

Top speed: In excess of 175km/h.

Machine loaned by: JOHN GALVIN, Sydney.

1952 Vincent Series C 'Black Shadow'

1000cc 55 BHP VEE-TWIN

Many people still erroneously maintain that the 'world's first Superbike' was the 1968 CB750 Honda, and to some extent they are arguably correct because it was far and away the biggest, most impressive and apparently best engineered motorcycle which existed *at that time*. The new, over-large, four cylinder overhead-camshaft Honda, with its four fat mufflers and disc front brake was a most impressive looking motorcycle which stood head and shoulders above a swiftly vanishing herd of contemporary motorcycles, many of which were soon to be gone forever. Triumph had its own high-performance road burner at the time, the potent three-cylinder overhead-valve 750cc Trident – along with its BSA Rocket 3 clone – which was in fact slightly quicker than the big Honda and manifestly out-handled and out-braked it as well, but the Triumph looked somewhat pedestrian in comparison to this exciting newcomer from Japan.

But the fact is that – as the CB750 Honda clearly demonstrated – there has *always* been the odd motorcycle whose open road performance, and general appearance, stood it well apart from its fellows. Back in the late 1920s the 1000cc OHV Vee-twin SS100 Brough Superior (which was assuredly one of those extraordinary machines) could be ordered with a written guarantee of a top speed in excess of the pre-metric yardstick of one-hundred miles per hour, but it never rejoiced in the term 'Superbike', although it surely deserved it.

However, the most eagerly sought-after Classic motorcycle of all time – here in Australia, as well as just about anywhere else on earth – is the machine to which the title 'The World's First Superbike' most certainly belongs, for it remains the fastest road-going motorcycle the British have ever built: if we except the latest, twenty-first century machines, of course. It was also assuredly the most impressive in appearance, *at that time*, in spite of its black-on-black paint finish, and it was certainly one of the most unique as well.

It is (dare I say 'of course?') the ***Vincent Black Shadow***, that great 1000cc overhead valve Vee-twin whose initial design first saw the light of day in 1937 as a lightly tuned Vincent HRD Series-A roadster, which in its day produced too much power for its BA Burman clutch and gearbox to be able to handle. The pre-war Rapide's two cylinders were disposed at an odd 47.4 degrees, the short pushrods controlled by camshafts carried high in the alloy crankcases.

Essentially the engine was 'simply' created by having most of the engine internals of two of the 500cc single cylinder 'Meteor' models mounted upon a common crankcase, the plot fitted into a slightly lengthened Meteor frame. The first Rapide was by no means a very remarkable machine, as we have noted in the previous piece on the series-B Vincent Rapide, but it was to become very remarkable in the immediate post-war era.

The brilliant Australian designer of the Vincent motorcycles, Phil Irving, once said that the reason for the odd *47-degree angle* of the original engine was to have it fit closely into a slightly lengthened version of the original frame of the 500cc single-cylinder HRD. He suggested that a wider – say 90-degree? – angle of an all-new Vee-twin would have necessitating a substantially longer frame being built, which might then have resulted in an over-long wheelbase, with the possibility of some 'odd handling'. He also suggested to an Australian audience he was addressing that the 'myth' of that first Vee-twin engine design coming about by accidentally dropping a clear transparency of a drawing of the 500cc single-cylinder engine almost directly on top of a blueprint of the same engine, had **'*more than a grain of truth*'** to it!

The later 1000cc (actually 998cc) *50-degree* Vincent HRD twin, which appeared not long after World War Two, was almost completely redesigned by Irving into a much more smooth-looking unit-construction engine/gearbox power-plant. As we have noted, the engine was actually redesigned *during* the War to provide the motive power for the 'Picador' target drone, then submitting the finished aircraft to the Air Ministry. Several of these small target aircraft were built but, unhappily for us all, were not adopted by

113

the Air Ministry. The motorcycle engine which followed at war's end was a smooth-flowing design very similar to the Picador engine, the necessary oil-ways in the new engine by then mostly contained within the engine castings by internal oil lines, oil galleries and judicious drillings.

The Black shadow engine differed slightly from the post-war Rapide, but it was enough to raise the power generated from a handy 45 BHP to a much more acceptable 55 BHP. All that was necessary to achieve this was to polish the valve gear and connecting-rods, then enlarge and polish the ports a little, raise the compression ration from the Rapide's lowly 6.45 to 1, to a gentle 7.35 to 1 (and above, in many cases!) and fit 1⅛" carburettors in place of the Rapide's 1¹⁄₁₆" instruments. Contrary to popular belief, the cam profiles remained the same, but first gear was raised/ 'lowered' from 9:1 to 7.2 to 1.

The Classic Series-B Vincent HRD Black Shadow pre-dated the Honda 'Superbike' by some 20 years, and the later crop of the so-called 'Mega-bikes' by another ten years; that first Black Shadow, introduced to an awe-struck motorcycling world way back in **mid-1948**! The machine was road tested by the British '*Motor Cycling*' magazine for its 15th July, 1948 issue, the machine recording a top speed of a staggering **122 miles per hour**, a speed entirely unheard of from any road-going motorcycle in 1948, and a speed only just approached by one other motorcycle at that time; the Shadow's sibling, the more-lightly tuned 'Rapide'. The Publicity blurb declared the bike was: *'The Fastest Production Motorcycle in the World'*, which was correctly sub-headed *'This a is a Fact, not a Slogan'*.

The Shadow's elapsed time through the standing-start quarter mile in that first road report was a click under 15 seconds, the bike recording just on 98mph at the end of the run, which were very impressive figures indeed, a speed unequalled by any other motor vehicle on the roads in 1948, whether on two wheels or four. However, that quarter-mile figure could easily have been shaved by a few seconds if the gear-change was up to it, for the earlier Vincent twins refused to be rushed when changing gear, signalling its dislike for this by either selecting a 'false' neutral or refusing to slot into a higher gear *at all*! No matter how hard-ridden an early model Vee-twin Vincent motorcycle may be, a series of 'casual' gear-changes was the only way to be assured that there would be no drama in swapping cogs, whether touring at speed or being involved in some very serious road racing.

The Black Shadow stunned contemporary industry riders when it was road-tested at the time – and later in France when the same machine achieved *127mph* in a published road test report – the Vincent achieving this monumental speed with a very high top gear of 3.5 to 1, the engine loafing along at an easy 5485rpm: little more than a fast idle by modern standards. Cruising at the pre-metric 100mph (which it could do all day long and into the night where possible), the huge, dominating V-twin ohv engine with the jet-black crankcases was *drifting* along at a mere 4500rpm on about three-quarter throttle, with a genuine surge of acceleration left if the

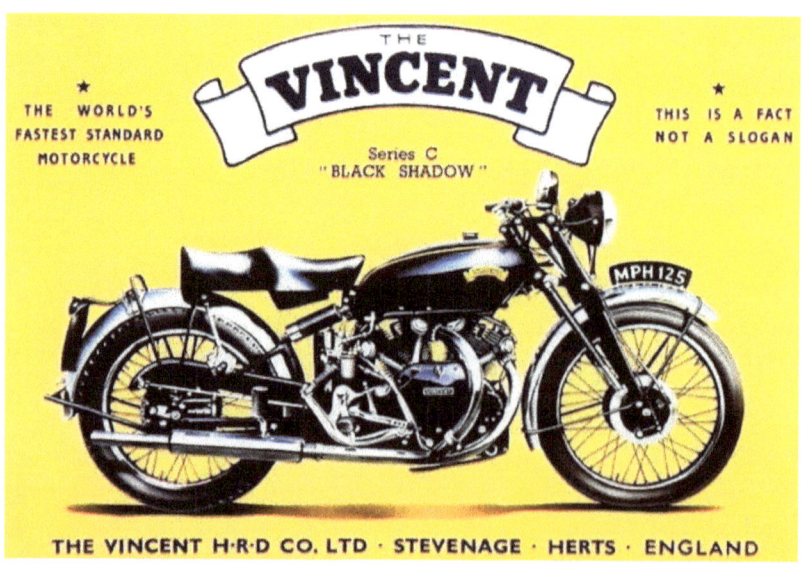

The Vincent brochure proclaims the Black Shadow as 'the world's fastest production motorcycle: this is a fact, not a slogan' which I am here to state is absolutely no exaggeration. Note the 125MPH front number plate.

more adventurous felt like opening the throttle to the stop. Many modern machines would need to have an engine spinning at more than twice that speed to achieve the same open road speeds.

The Vincent Black Lightning, a rare 70BHP road-racing version, of which only 31 were ever built from 1948 to 1952, was delivered to riders with a quoted top speed of 155mph with standard gearing. According to available (reliable?) records, no fewer than *six* Lightnings were imported into Australia from 1949 to 1951, four into Sydney with two more into Adelaide, while two more were brought home to Australia (one by the immortal Tony McAlpine) with – it has been claimed, but cannot be verified – at least two other *engines* arriving as well: these engines were to be used in Cooper, and other, race cars. These rare machines, most of them tuned almost beyond endurance by local experts to produce the best part of 100BHP, were ridden to many wins by such local luminaries as Tony McAlpine, Lloyd Hirst, Sandy McRae, Jack Forrest and Jack Ehret. Ehret enjoyed the distinction of sharing the outright lap record of 1m 42.5 seconds on Sydney's bumpy Mount Druitt circuit with the legendary Geoff Duke, who raced his World Championship-winning 500cc factory Gilera on that fast, 2.4-mile circuit during his visit in 1955.

History was made in 1958 when Sandy McRae made his comeback ride at the great Mount Panorama circuit in Bathurst with the McRae Special; probably the first time anybody in the world had managed to shoe-horn a 1000cc Vincent Vee-twin engine into a Featherbed Manx Norton frame. This was surely the marriage of the century in sidecar racing; as it was with many road-going 'Norvin' motorcycles. The McRae outfit dominated the Mount for five straight years, and then handed the history-making over to another machine of the same make.

The great Victorian sidecar racer Alec Corner scored four times in a row for Vincent, being ousted by Dennis Skinner mounted on yet another Vincent in 1967. McRae came back yet again in 1969 to win the Big One for Vincent for the last time on that same circuit. A monumental achievement for the Vincent engine, whether in its own frame or one belonging to someone else. In fact, the Vincent engine was equally as dominant in sidecar racing on Speedway circuits in Australia and elsewhere.

Vincent's star shone strongly during the years from 1948 to the early 1950s, with little but detail modification to the rear suspension system as the series B and C came and went, but it waned in late 1954 when the conceptually exciting Series D was announced. The new model was the usual trad Vincent all-black, the two machines which came into Australia later in the following year fully enclosed within a series of streamlined fairings which gave them a futuristic air; although some purists were unhappy that the magnificent engine was thus hidden from view.

Smith Sons and Rees were the Sydney agents at the time, and I clearly recall two of the latest models standing on a raised dais on the tiny showroom floor of the Wentworth Avenue store in 1955. The machines were huge and overbearing, exciting more comment than any of their fellows – but they were very expensive, being more than twice the price of other machines which were on hand at the time. Series D Black Knight and Black Prince models were featured with Rapide or Shadow engines, but the high price of the new machine and the depressed condition of the motorcycle market at that time put paid to any chance of them ever achieving satisfactory sales.

I rode some examples of the 1000cc variants in those days, but I couldn't become too enthused over the Vincent Meteor or Comet 500cc singles. Fine machines though they were, they looked exactly like the big twin with the rear pot sawn off and they performed accordingly. There were other five-hundred singles around which performed every bit as well, and these rival machines were far more popular: they were also much less expensive.

Prior to my ride on the original test machine, a very much earlier ride which I enjoyed was on a Series-C Shadow I had traded-in on a brand new R60 BMW way back in 1959, while I was working at a Sydney suburban motorcycle dealership. I rode that bike home on an almost weekly basis for more than *five months* before it was finally sold. Believe it or not, but in 1959, with the industry all but gone to God, **we simply could not find a buyer for the Black Shadow Vincent!** Oh, how I earnestly wish I had bought that machine myself, and kept it for half a century!

And so, when an opportunity to renew my acquaintance with the now-Classic British motorcycle came I couldn't pick the bike up quickly enough! The machine under review was a **1952 Series C Black Shadow**, that veritable rocket-ship of a motorcycle which stood so far removed from the crowd in its day as nothing – but *nothing* – does today. The bike belonged to Sydney's Alan Pride and was in absolutely showroom condition, gleaming in its simply arresting colour finish of black-on-black with much chrome and polished alloy mudguards.

Who says all-black has no beauty; although it has been said that beauty is in the eye of the beholder. Then, behold this gleaming shot of the impressive Black Shadow power-plant, here in all its jet-black glory! An untouched photo with the sun in precisely the correct position.

First impressions, while sometimes misleading, are more often spot-on, and the Vincent lets the world know it is a no-nonsense road-burner of the Old School from the moment you first lay eyes on it. It is long and low, with the 50 degree V-twin engine seeming to fill the machine's frame and bulge out fore and aft. But the engine is really fairly narrow and does not actually hang out of the **frame** at all, for the simple reason that the bike has no frame, at least not as we know the modern motorcycle frame to be.

Instead, the front cylinder head of the big Vincent motor is bolted to a small bracket and is then bolted by its very 'scalp' to a long, box-like semi-triangular, fabricated 'backbone' which is in fact the machine's oil tank, with the top of the rear suspension units bolted to the *rear* of the long, fabricated 'frame'/oil tank, with a rear sub-frame assembly and cantilever rear suspension grafted to the rear of the gearbox. In a similar fashion to the front cylinder head's mounting, the rear cylinder head bolts *via* its own small bracket to the **rear** of the main frame-cum-oil tank at its base and the sub-frame assembly which is stiffened by the gearbox. The tubular sub-frame helps form the base platform for the 'floating' seat and top anchor-point for the modern-looking cantilever rear suspension system.

Three short, fat telescopic units are located under the base of the contoured Feridax dual-seat, which is free-floating and not attached to the rear mudguard, but is supported upon a pair of articulated rods which locate upon the rear sub-frame, their movement controlled to some degree by friction adjusters. Thus, the rear guard is free to move in conjunction with the rear wheel over uneven road surfaces without involving the 'suspended' dual-seat. The two outer, short rear suspension units contain springs which allow rear wheel movement, while the (inner) third unit controls the hydraulic damping.

The Vincent power-plant becomes more than simply a stressed frame member in the most basis sense, for it actually forms the greater part of its own mounting platform and provides its own rigidity. To add to its other duties, the heavy box section oil tank/backbone also has a steering

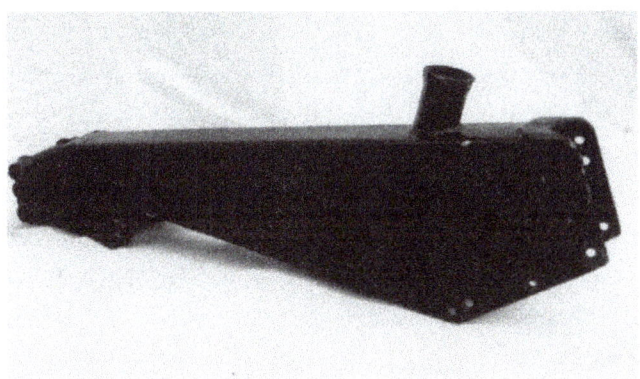

This is the oil tank/frame of the Vincent Vee-twins! Steering head bolts to the front of the tank, to which the front forks are attached, with enclosed springs and damper of the rear suspension attached to the rear. Special brackets attached to the cylinder heads are bolted underneath the tank, and that is almost all there is to it! Almost.

head casting bolted to the front, providing a mounting point for the unusual front forks.

There has yet to be a motorcycle quite as stable in a straight line as the big Vincent, for it literally cannot be thrown off-course by most road surfaces, no matter how much the suspension chatters about, or how busy the wheels. This is mainly because of the unusual Girdraulic front forks, which combine the rigidity of a pair of heavy alloy fork legs with uneven-length pivot arms, aided by a single, centre-mounted damper control allied to a pair of separate spring units housed in short mini-telescopic forks mounted directly behind the thick fork blades. The immensely strong fork blades are moulded from top-grade RR56 aluminium alloy. The rigid fork blades and solid linkages on which they pivot provide a fork assembly vaguely similar to the earlier, pre-war girder-type forks, but they cannot easily be flexed, a situation nearly impossible to achieve with the simple telescopic front fork in universal use today.

An incidental advantage of the uneven linkages is to ensure that little alteration to wheelbase occurs with front fork movement, and a similar situation happens with the rear suspension. Overall, the good inherent stability of

At speed on the Black Shadow from the original, 1979 road test report. This is an unpublished photograph I managed to stumble upon, almost by accident.

Another photo of the long, tapered oil tank atop this 500cc Meteor engine, which is hung by the scruff its neck to the base of the tank, as the twin cylinder Shadow was. Note the rear suspension units bolted to the tank, the suspension controlled by a dual, Vee-shaped rear sub-frame member. Utterly brilliant, with the engine very much a stressed member of the assembly.

the machine is bought about by simply keeping the wheels in line with one another in all planes and maintaining the static wheelbase as closely as possible while the machine is in motion.

The rider is insulated from many of the road shocks upon his 'remote-mounted' seat, and is not as perturbed as he might otherwise be over rough surfaces, but the heavy bike is still something of an odd handler at speed over rippled, fast corners. But this is true of almost everything on two wheels today.

Fast corners on smooth roads can be taken at speeds which would be unheard of with many machines of its era, but the angle of lean seems restricted to a degree by the wide-mounted footrests, which are totally adjustable on their outrigger plates. The left footrest is mounted to the same plate which holds the footbrake lever, which is adjustable at the same time and to the same degree. The footrest and gear change lever on the right-hand side are similarly adjustable.

Steering is quite heavy because of the weight and layout of the front forks and the relative forward mounting of the impressive engine, sufficient for it to be a pain at low speeds or when making tight feet-up turns in narrow areas. The bike requires a wide turning circle and occasionally needs a steadying foot. It's a feature not known on many later machines, though some of the early Japanese heavyweights suffered a similar quirk at low speeds. Perhaps it's no bad thing, for the heavier steering allows the bike to track straight and true at very high touring speeds.

But high-speed cornering on choppy surfaces is not ideal, for the bike tends to wallow if pressed very hard over bumps or heavy ripples. The occasional single bump or pothole has little effect on the machine's stability – though it will shake its head now and again – but a series of uneven surfaces will cause some of its odd meanderings to pose an apparent threat to its stability. Under these circumstances it can at once nod its head and wag its tail, but will still hold a tight line and remain firmly under control: the rider may be a little more unsettled, however!

When pressing on at speed over uneven surfaces, the large clutch dome on the bike's left side can sometimes lightly contact the road surface, but this only occurs when riding far too quickly and cornering much too hard over this type of undulating road surface. The front end can occasionally chatter over a series of deep ripples, though it does not transmit this feeling to the handlebars, and the rear end will kick through the base of the seat on full bump, but

the bike steers to a hairline, while under brakes the front wheel glues itself quite securely to the road surface.

Brakes are extremely good, with the machine fitted from standard with dual drums of 7-inch diameter front and rear. Consider: Brake lining area is nearly as much as it would be if the bike came equipped with *single* 18-inch stoppers at each end! The bike was heavy in its day – but of course not quite so heavy by modern standards – with brakes which would screech the tyres and haul it to a shuddering stop in an almost unbelievable 22 feet 6 inches from 30mph, the rider – or at least me – sliding onto the large fuel tank!

In new-fangled terms that's braking to a trim 6.85 m from 50km/h, and that is almost unheard of in these days of dual hydraulically controlled disc brakes – even with another disc on the back! By comparison, the much-vaunted

This is the complex, front beam which controls the dual, 7-inch front brakes. There was a real trick involved in adjusting the cables, which meant that either the bike could almost stand on its nose if correctly adjusted, or there were almost no brakes if incorrectly adjusted, which happened all too often.

GS1000 Suzuki of the late 1970s (*the time when this Vincent road test was published*) pulled up in 8.2 metres from the same speed, the XS1100 Yamaha took some 8.6 metres, and the Kawasaki Z1-R needed all of 8.8 metres! Did somebody say progress in motorcycle design, with triple-disc brakes by now under hydraulic control? Perhaps, but then again, perhaps not! It has been suggested by some reporters that the Vincent's front brake was very inefficient, particularly at speed, but there is a trick to adjusting the dual brakes at the forward-mounted, horizontal pivoting bracket by which they are controlled. If an adjustment is carried out incorrectly, the front brakes can be quite ineffective or *may not work at all*! Strange, but true.

The bike is also well ahead on points in the fuel consumption stakes, for the original road test report claimed an *overall* average of 51mpg (18km/l) for the big Vincent against about 42mpg (14.8km/l) from the Z1-R Kawasaki and just 36mpg (12.7km/l) from the big Yamaha.

Acceleration is very brisk on the big Vincent, though its standing quarter time is modest enough at 14.8 seconds. But the **top-gear** performance of the old V-twin cannot easily be matched, either way back then or today, for it will pull away with no distress from as low as 50km/h in top gear to its absolute maximum (which we didn't attempt) without recourse to clutch or gear-lever.

It seems to pile on the coals as it goes, compounding its performance in leaps and bounds with little vibration at any stage of engine speed and not much more than the amplified sounds of mechanical action inside a large alloy power-plant. That unique, crackling, and slightly out-of-step exhaust note is music to the ears, and it is unlike any other large-capacity Vee-twin engine.

Top gear acceleration is impressive from about 100km/h onwards, but slip it back to third – which will take the bike to a speed almost twice the legal maximum! – then pop the throttle open and the real dimension of the Vincent is pleasurably evident; the feel of a big, punchy low-revving engine pulling hard and building up the pressure as it goes is truly awe-inspiring

The open road is really the Black Shadow's territory, for it suffers heavy traffic badly: at least it did in the hands of this short-statured rider. It is not an easy bike to ride at very slow speeds when traffic is heavy, in part because of the inherent heaviness of the steering at low speeds, but also due to the high gearing and a clutch which can be too sudden in operation for that type of work.

It is a strange clutch, in effect two separate components which work in conjunction; a single-plate pilot clutch of similar design to a normal unit, and a servo-clutch with drum and shoes (rather like a small internal expanding brake)

Thirty-four long years after the original road test report was published, the new photo shoot saw another Shadow put through its paces. Flat-out in second gear and coming onto the apex of this one-way traffic road, the Vincent could be pinned down to hold a very tight line, even over the occasional rippled surface. Photographer Bill Forsythe was perched precariously upon a large boulder directly above.

which comes into operation when the engine is running at higher speeds. The servo action does not come into effect fully until the engine is running at reasonable speeds and the road speed is about 75km/h. Phil Irving, the Australian designer of the machine, reckons the clutch was designed to withstand 140 BHP, and was first intended to run in oil. Apparently, it didn't work as well as it should, and was adopted on road machines as a dry clutch. It doesn't always work too well dry either, particularly if you don't know how to adjust the thing! The Vincent clutch, in a word, could sometimes be a real challenge.

The gearbox also suffered in the hands of those with little mechanical sympathy, for the change is very notchy and, as I mentioned earlier, quite slow. There is no way a fast gear-change can be made either up or down, simply because the selector cam-plate design won't let it happen.

Jack Carruthers, one of the all-time greats of Australian speedway sidecar racing, and one of the best riders of the Vincent marque ever, carried out some non-standard modifications to the gear cam-plate in the interests of quicker and more positive gear-changes, and with marked success, but the standard box remains slow. However, there was a factory modification to the cam-plate design on the later Vincents, which was quite successful in markedly speeding up the gear-change.

The bike is fitted with the standard Amal carburettors and Vokes air filters, the latter able to stop pigeons and small rocks entering the works but allowing free entry to sparrows and small gravel chips. The higher ratio 8.5:1 pistons are augmented by magneto ignition from the rare bronze-bodied Lucas TT mag fitted to a mere 20 of the better-known 70 BHP 'Lightning' racers, and to very, very few roadsters.

Even though the magneto throws a purple spark of monumental proportions the bike is still hard to start, though fitted as standard with the world's longest kick-starter. It was once stated by an enthusiast that starting the Vincent engine was like 'kicking over two 500cc Venom Velocettes at once' and this, let me assure you, is no exaggeration!

It won't fire on the 'short dwell' of the first compression on the front cylinder simply because you come across the second compression before you are into the swing of the first, and the 'long dwell' is damn near as hard. A clutch lever-sized valve-lifter on the left handlebar makes the job a lot easier as you ease the piston over compression on the slow dwell, but it requires all the strength you can muster to swing the engine over so it will fire first-up next time round. Starting a Vincent Black Shadow can be hard work unless the correct drill is followed to the letter, and even then, it isn't easy.

The engine is dead smooth at all speeds, with the two-into-one exhaust system throwing a crackle through the single muffler which an enthusiast would walk uphill backwards and barefoot over broken glass for miles to hear. It is a great sound, but unhappily much of it is lost on the rider, for all he can hear is the wind whistling above his helmet as he clings onto the machine.

The bike differs in many ways from many of its fellows, with many a technically innovative feature which sets it even more apart. Consider the 'simple' rear chain adjusters. They need no spanners, but instead employ large alloy hand-wheels, with spring-loaded balls which slip into indents in the adjuster body, the wheels loosened off by stout Tommy-bars, again with no spanners needed. Another example is the construction of

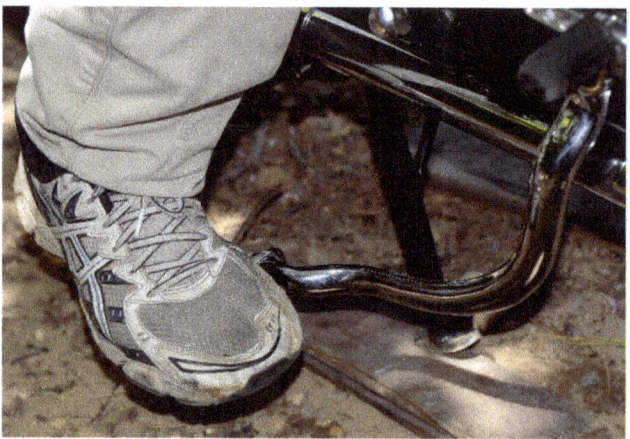

This is the world's longest kickstarter, and we needed every last inch of its travel in firing he engine up. There is a new, electric starter which can be fitted, and one could argue it ought to have been standard ware from Day One, for the big Vincent was never an easy machine to boot into life.

the wheels, with their 'straight pull' spokes laced to the inside of the dual drums on a spool hub, and which were tested and found to be far and away the strongest ever made, which of course meant they were almost totally free of the flexing which can have an adverse effect on handling.

It is said that the tommy-bar fitted axles can be removed without the aid of spanners simply by grabbing the short bars and screwing them, but I have yet to meet the person who can do it! I tried it manfully with my miniature wrists and all they (my wrists!) did was to go snap, crackle and pop; nothing happened to the axles at all, and the tommy bars remained unbroken and unbent.

The long list of advanced features which adorn the old Mega-bike would bore us all and fill this entire piece, but the most interesting aspect of the bike is at once the overbearing engine's apparent strength and its excellent power-to-weight ratio.

It remains an 'old fashioned' overhead valve design with the high camshafts carried in the centre of the shallow-angle V with the short-looking cylinders deeply spigotted into the crankcase. Massive main bearings are of the roller type, and the big-ends are also roller bearings. A huge bronze gear served as a timing gear inside the cases, though alloy and even steel replacements have been forthcoming on some machines. Primary drive is by triple-row chain.

The Black Shadow has triple valve springs and an odd, forked rocker arm to control the valve movement, the short pushrods are solid stainless steel, with the usual tappet 'screw-and-nut' adjustment. As I've indicated, the Vincent was a very high-performance motorcycle in its day and could stand a very good chance of heading a bunch of hard-charging desperates even now.

There were more than 14,000 Vincent twins made overall, and there were said to by just under 1,700 Black Shadows, and all of them were effectively hand-built. It is not everybody's bike and it never was, and in fact could be a real pain to any of the newer riders who are more attuned to the undoubted luxury of the more sophisticated modern motorcycle, with their electric starter motors (there is French-made starter motor which can be fitted to Vincents, which might be handy), high-performance engines and other 'essential' goodies. But the Vincent Black Shadow remains a deeply revered, true Classic machine which has endured the test of time as no other motorcycle will ever achieve.

NB: While it was Alan Pride's 1952 Black Shadow I rode for the test report which was originally published in *Two Wheels* magazine in 1979, I could only find one or two original photos, but with the help of Vincent Owner's Club of NSW Secretary, **Alyn Vincent,** I was kindly loaned a slightly modified 1950 Shadow in 2013 for me to ride, and for **Bill Forsyth** to photograph. Forsyth's later photos of the Vincent were taken some *34 years after the first report was published!!* The 1950 model was loaned to us for the photo session by its owner **Rob Paton,** and I thank him most sincerely for the privilege – and, more importantly, his trust, for he had never met me before I presented myself at his doorstep!

On 19 January 1953, Jack Ehret rode his 70BHP, 1951 'Black Lightning' Vincent – the race version of the Black Shadow – to a speed of 147mph, a new record for Australian motorcycles. The bike, one of only 30-odd ever built, was to sell dented, bruised and covered in baked-on engine oil and grease, for a massive $A1.1 million in 2018. Ehret had previously owned the machine for almost 50 years and raced it very many times in the earlier years.

TECH SPECS

Make: Vincent

Model: Black Shadow Series 'C'

Year of manufacture: 1952

Type:
All-alloy overhead valve Vee-twin four-stroke, using high camshafts and short stainless steel pushrods. Cylinders set at 50 degrees, with slight offset to the right allowing side-by-side connecting rods on common crankpin. Built-up crank carried on ball and roller bearings, triple row needle rollers in big-end assembly. All ports, con-rods and most other reciprocating parts highly polished, the engine essentially hand-built. Dry sump lubrication from frame-carried oil supply to reciprocating, plunger-type pump with pressure feed to main and big-end bearings, valve train and large gears in timing case.

Bore x stroke: 84 x 90mm.

Capacity: 998cc

Compression ratio: 8.5:1

Power @ rpm: 55BHP @ 5500rpm

Ignition: Lucas racing Magneto.

Carburation: Dual 1⅛" (32mm) Amal 289 Type, with Vokes air filters.

Transmission:
Primary drive by triple-row chain to four-speed foot change gearbox, carried in unit with engine, through dry, self-servo clutch assembly. Primary chain adjustment by spring-blade tensioner from outside gearbox, with chain carried in full oil-bath alloy chain-case.

Gear ratios:
(Overall) 1st – 7.25:1; 2nd – 5.5:1; 3rd – 4.2:1; 4th – 3.5:1. Right foot change, one up, three down pattern.

Frame and suspension:
No frame as such, but fabricated steel *backbone/oil tank* mounted by special brackets to cylinder heads. Rear of engine/backbone section carries mounts for rear suspension. Front forks mounted to steering head which is bolted to the front of the welded steel 'backbone.' The engine essentially forms its own rigid frame assembly. Front suspension is by patented 'Girdraulics', using combined girder/telescopic forks with heavy, aircraft-quality RR56 fork blades and short, rear-set telescopic units, with centrally mounted single hydraulic damper. Rear suspension is by light-gauge, heavily triangulated cantilever arms, with two spring units under nose of the seat, controlled by a single, hydraulic damper sited between them. The Feridax dual-seatis suspended upon articulated arms attached to rear sub-frame, with friction adjustment.

Wheels, brakes, tyres:
Spool hubs front and rear, with straight spokes laced to steel rims, dual cast-iron brake drums with external cooling fins bolted to hubs. Dual internal expanding brakes of 175mm (7") fitted to front wheel, with cable control to front brakes by high-leverage, transverse beam, infinitely adjustable. Rear wheel also fitted with dual 175mm (7") drum brakes operated by dual rods.

Front tyre:
325 x 19" ribbed (standard on this model, others with 300 x 20"), with 400 x 18 block pattern on rear. Metzeler tyres on test machine.

Dimensions:
Length – 2135mm; Width – 635mm; Saddle Height – 735mm; Ground clearance – 140mm; Weight – 208kg; Wheelbase – 1400mm; Fuel capacity – 18 litres.

Performance:
(*From original road test report, 15 July 1948*): Top speed, 205km/h; Standing quarter, 14.8 sec; Braking from 50km/h, 6.85m; Fuel consumption: 18km/l.

Machine(s) loaned by:
ALAN PRIDE, and ROB PATON.

1939 SB500T DKW

500cc TWIN CYLINDER TWO-STROKE

It is at best little known to modern-day motorcyclists and at worst not known *at all*, but the once-proud DKW motorcycle factory was the largest in the world in the late 1920s, producing a prodigious number of two-stroke motorcycles over the many years since its inception in 1919, and a great many cars as well. In many ways the company was an industrial giant in its time, for the factory was busily involved in building many thousands of small motorcycle and aircraft engines – and *occasionally* planes as well – the development of early forms of plastics, and input into the design of front-wheel drive for cars and lightweight, three-wheeled trucks, as well as designing and building a range of stationary and industrial engines. At one time, in the 1930s, DKW supplied its motorcycle engines to more than 50 small manufacturers in Germany alone, as well as to factories in several other countries.

But in all that time, with the glaring exception of one or two models of a single-cylinder side-valve motorcycle the company built in 1930 (after it had recently purchased the fairly large, if now little known, Schuttoff motorcycle factory and used one of that company's power-plants) DKWs entire output, both in motorcycles and four-wheeled vehicles, including Army vehicles built well after WWII, were fitted with two-stroke engines. In fact, the last medium sized saloon/sports car manufactured by DKW left the factory gates in 1966, and it was, like every car which preceded it – *powered by a two-stroke engine!*

In saying this we much except the fearsome, all-conquering, V12 *overhead camshaft* **Auto Union** race cars of the 1930s, whose monstrous engines were designed and built by the *Horch* factory, which had joined with Audi, Wanderer and DKW (the overall owners of the group at the time) to form the four rings which are now to be seen only on Audi motor cars.

A glance at the DKW *motorcycle* tank badge might cause some to query what the four **'AUDI'** circles are doing attached to the initials – sometimes *above* the DKW initials, sometimes *below them* – for surely those four rings belong to the luxury German car? Yes, as we have pointed out, they do, but DKW was so powerful that in 1928 the company bought-out the ailing *Audi* brand, and teamed up with Wanderer in 1933 (another by-now little-known German car and early motorcycle manufacturer, which was later sold to NSU) and Horch, yet another large car factory which was well-known at the time, but little known today, to form the '***AUTO UNION***' group denoted by the four rings which, many years later, was obtained by the huge Volkswagen corporation.

Fuel tank and knee-pad logos of all DKW motorcycles in the 1930s, the four rings of the AUTO UNION clearly visible. DKW was so big at the time they bought out Audi, Horst and Wanderer adding these marques to DKW to become the Auto Union. It was purchased by Volkswagen many years later, the original four rings now adorning all Audi cars, which are the luxury mode of VW.

As an example of the almost incestuous relationship which existed in the conglomerate in those days, some of the larger Wanderer vehicles had their car bodies manufactured by the coach-building side of Horch, while Audi and some magnificent Horch cars employed Wanderer power-plants!

A faintly similar situation exists to this day, and this is the reason why the large VW Passat is, in effect, a thinly disguised AUDI, albeit a lower-cost, less luxurious version, the Passat mounted upon the same rolling chassis and utilising the same power-plants. This also applies to the smaller VW and Audi cars.

No company on earth has ever committed itself so devotedly to the design and implementation of two-stroke technology in motorcycles, which culminated in DKW *split-single* (twin) cylinder machines winning the 250cc World Championship in 1938, followed by winning both 250 and 350cc Championships in 1939 with similarly odd engine designs. And during those years of developing the high-performance two-stroke engine, DKW was all but unbeatable in European road race events, in all capacities from 250, and 350cc right up to the viciously swift, ear-splitting, **six-piston**, 500cc 'supercharged' split-twin (four) cylinder machine! This came about by the DKW factory working with the German company Zoller in 1931 to design and implement a type of piston-controlled crankcase 'supercharging' into its factory racing motorcycles. The Zoller company was famous at that time for their very efficient superchargers, which were fitted to many top-class race cars.

The DKW company started innocently enough when its founder, an engineer from Denmark named Jorgen Rassmussen, whose factory had been manufacturing parts for early steam engines since 1902, attempted to build a small steam powered car in 1906 which he called the '*Dampf-Kraft-Wagen*' (Steam Driven Car) which was on the far side of unsuccessful. In 1919 he built a small, 18cc two-stroke engine as a toy, which he called '*Des Knaben Wunsch*' (A Boy's Dream). Shortly thereafter, and probably by accident, he established the tiny **DKW** company by slotting the slightly enlarged 25cc two-stroke engine into a small pushbike frame, the new 'motorcycle' then allotted the nickname '*Das Kleiner Wunder*', or 'The Small Wonder', by the buying public.

You may pick whichever one of those titles you wish in describing the huge German motorcycle manufacturer which was shortly to evolve, because each and every one of them has been credited at different times with supplying the DKW initials, even though no-one is really sure which one to blame. The Steam Driven Car was clearly the first, but it was unsuccessful and was very soon forgotten, and most people plump for '*The Small Wonder*', but in the end it really doesn't matter; except perhaps as a Pub argument in Germany, or anywhere else on earth for that matter. That is assuming one can find anyone who remembers what those initials stood for, much less their origins.

DKW built a staggering variety of two-stroke motorcycles over the decades, including the world's most copied motorcycle design, the 1936 RT125, a small 125cc single-cylinder, rigid-frame commuter with girder front forks. The drawings, jigs, dies, moulds and patterns for the little RT125 were stolen by the Allies as 'War Reparations' when they over-ran Germany at the end of the Second World War, the design then declared 'void' and the filched material gleefully handed out to the British, American, Russian and French victors. The RT125 was made until 1955 after the war by DKW, but its 'clones' had previously been seen as the crude Harley-Davidson *Hummer*, the East German *IFA* and *MZ*, the Russian *Voskhod*, the Polish *WSK*, the Italian MiVal as well as – of all people! – Maserati, and the most famous one of all, England's *BSA Bantam*.

There were several other copies of the German lightweight made in Poland, France and Norway, among other countries, and they were of course almost identical, the only major difference between any of them being the BSA Bantam, which had its gear and kick-starter levers mounted on the 'British' right-hand side. There were slight differences in electrical components and some carburettors, of course, but otherwise they were virtually identical to the poor little DKW RT125.

This is the 1954 RT125 three-speed DKW, which has nothing to do with the SB500. It is of interest simply because its 1936 design was stolen by the Allies when they overcame Germany after WWII. They handed out all the info on this commuter bike, which was then copied by 42 other factories, including five of them in Russia.

Even the Japanese got into the act, if some years later. Here is an almost identical clone of the RT125, Yamaha's first ever motorcycle, the 1955 YA1. The differences were the Yamaha's four-speed gearbox, the smaller, 5-inch front brake and the 'fishtail' muffler. Even the simple, rear brake pedal was identical to the RT125.

This is the British copy of the RT125, the 1948 BSA Bantam, again almost identical to the original German machine, except for the right-hand side kickstarter and gearchange pedals. Oh, and the God-awful Wico-Pacy ignition/lighting system!

Hard to believe though it may be, but even the American Harley Davidson company unaccountably built this very ordinary copy of the RT125 DKW. This Harley Hummer has been absolutely ignored by other Harley owners, who have clearly been embarrassed by this all-but forgotten commuter machine.

The final copy of the long-suffering RT125 was made by the Japanese in 1955, in the form of **Yamaha**'s first ever motorcycle, the YA1, which was virtually a carbon-copy of the *then-current*, 1954 DKW, right down to pinching the design of the German machine's telescopic front forks with their rubber gaiters, along with the too-strikingly similar, 'double-action' plunger rear suspension and the German machine's cantilever-hung single saddle. There were some differences, however, for the Yamaha employed another gear, giving it as four-speed gearbox, while the primary drive to the gearbox was by a pair of gears, instead of the usual primary chain.

Obviously, there must have been few bits left over and a bunch of DKW instruction books on building an RT125 hidden away somewhere in Germany during the war, for the immediate post-war, rigid-framed DKW motorcycle faithfully adhered to the blueprint of the pre-war German machine; and why not, for the little 125cc gem must have been quite some motor cycle, even as a 'humble' ultra-lightweight machine. The later, plunger-frame, telescopic forked DKW was made from 1954 to 1957, the Yamaha copy from 1955 to 1958 – so they overlapped for a few years, while the Japanese factory was even then developing a new 250cc *twin* two-stroke, which was introduced to America towards the end of 1959, the bike copied (again?) from the German Adler company's trim little 250cc sportster, which had gone down the gurgler with almost everyone – and everything – else a year or earlier.

Before the war the DKW factory's range of road-going motorcycles included a 500cc two-stroke twin; a comparatively high-performance machine with three-speed, wide-ratio, hand-change gearbox and *electric starter*. There were a surprising number of DKW machines imported into Australia both before and after WWII, with a few of the large pre-war five-hundred twins still kicking about here and there. One of them, a **1939 SB500T DKW**, is the tidy unit owned and restored by arch-enthusiast Vin Minogue, the man responsible for several machines which I have featured in other test reports published in a variety of popular motorcycle magazines, as well as in this book.

The 500 Deek is not very remarkable in appearance but sufficiently rare to excite comment when the casual observer becomes aware of what it is and even more so when the marque's long history is quietly related.

The machine I rode is a trim-looking, if lumpy, machine and is, as one would expect from the restorer of more than a few of these Vintage machines, finished with a high level of expertise and great attention to detail. Typically, the colour scheme is black-on-black, with chrome-work confined to tank panels, the deep metal dish over the crankshaft's electrical system and some fiddly parts like hand levers and headlamp rim, with the plating work very tastefully done, while the black baked enamel is unmarked on frame, mudguards and tank. There are no oil leaks to be seen anywhere.

If the finish is great, then the bike looks like a simple, black motorcycle not far removed from a host of other machines of similar vintage, but it is very different in many areas which are not quite so apparent; some of them historically, some of them internally, some of them in a very practical way and none of them obvious.

The 500cc twin DKW was very much a surprise packet, for its 'lowly' 18.5 BHP imbued the bike with a very exciting performance, with such great torque from low engine speeds that it could pull top gear almost everywhere it went; uphill, downhill or at high touring speeds along the flat.

Across the range, including of course the racing machines, DKW adopted the Schnuerle 'reverse-loop' scavenge system and flat-top pistons in 1929, just three years after the German engineer Adolph Schnuerle invented the system and some ten years prior to the machine under review. The all-new design did away with the oddly shaped deflector-type pistons and semi-'squish' combustion chambers which were in use with two-stroke engines at the time. This new system was very rarely used – or understood – when it was first introduced, although it is in almost universal use today in two-stroke engines, from out-and-out racers to simple lawnmowers, but DKW adopted the system wholeheartedly and made it universal to all its road-going motorcycles.

Racing DKWs used disc-valves, reed valves, superchargers, 'pumper' pistons, split-singles, split-twins and a host of other odd designs, but it's true to say that DKW in effect pioneered the introduction of the loop scavenger system, although they by no means invented it.

Amazingly, there are several American two-stroke outboard motors which still use the thoroughly antiquated, inefficient, 'cross flow' scavenger system, with its now-quaint deflector-piston design, which begs the question of why they continue to do so.

Simply put, the Schnuerle system allows the inlet mixture which is transferred from the crankcase to be directed towards the *rear* of the cylinder wall by carefully angled passages, or 'ports', which are situated on the sides of the cylinder walls between the inlet and exhaust ports, the inlet charge arising from the crankcase to displace the burnt gases which are rushing out of the exhaust port(s). Thus, the piston-controlled 'transfer' ports can be sited very accurately to take maximum advantage of the two different gas streams with their attendant pressure pulses.

It is much more efficient than the older three-port system, which usually had its transfer ports directly *opposite* the exhaust, but employing a deflector piston with a large, near-vertical 'lump' on top of it to help direct the swirling gases into their various trajectories, the inlet charge directed upwards and thus away from the exhaust, the exhaust gas making its exit across the top of the piston on its steeply sloped crown. With a cool inlet charge coming onto one side of the piston crown and the hot gas escaping across the other, the three-port system invariably led to local heat and distortion, and this – allied to low compression ratios forced by the design – always limited the power available. By the way, the dramatic collapse of a lumpy piston's deflector crown was by no means unknown in those days, particularly if the fuel-air ratio was a little on the lean side!

The English 'Scott' engine was water-cooled, which helped, but the factory still used deflector pistons until the late 1950s and even Villiers – the engine manufacturers who supplied millions of power units to factories in England, Europe and Australia – used the three-port design with deflector pistons until 1949. That's odd when you realise Villiers introduced its first *loop scavenge* engine with *flat-top pistons* way back in 1934, a scant five years after DKW adopted it as standard!

If DKW was a step ahead of most contemporaries in engine design, it was also ahead of the herd with its electric starter – almost unheard of in the pre-war era, but standard ware on the big SB500.

The device was, in fact, a SIBA 'Dynastart', which was attached to the crankshaft's right side and, of course, it was spinning at engine speed. Left alone the component was a very large generator, but a touch of the starter button earthed the generator which then became an equally large electric **motor**, which would spin the engine with ease until it could fire up and run all by itself. Once the starter button was released, the 'starter' then reverted to its role as a generator, and a large-capacity one at that. All of 120-watt, the six-volt Dynastart is far and away the heaviest component on the machine, with literally miles of tightly wound copper wire in its flywheel-cum-generator armature.

The DKW features coil-ignition with automatic advance and an odd double-coil in a large Bakelite box above and to the right of the engine, with its back to a large battery box on the machine's left side. A simple button on the outside of the coil's box is depressed to earth the generator and fire the engine. Carried inside the battery box is the voltage regulator and cut-

Just behind the carburettor sits this Bakelite box, containing the machine's twin coils, with the battery on the opposite side. Note the small button on the side of the case, which is pressed to 'earth' the generator and engage the starter motor. Note also the bar under the single saddle, upon which the unique <u>horizontal</u> saddle springs are sited.

The enormous final-drive sprocket is almost half the diameter of the rear wheel sprocket, which, in company with the wide-ratio, three-speed gearbox, provides a clue to the wide spread of usable power generated by the lazy 500cc twin cylinder engine. Note the clever adjustment screw under the saddle, for differing rider weights.

out for the generator, a clever ploy which keeps all the electrics in one neat container, with the battery close by.

Contact points hide behind a small plate in the deep dished cover over the large generator 'flywheel', and are driven, of course, from the end of the crankshaft. They are accessible by unclipping a spring-arm over the small metal cover-plate and simply lifting it off.

A single carburettor is used, either a Bing or an Amal, with medium-sized bore which has its air-filter hidden between battery and coil. The mixture feeds through a single manifold which branches into two almost from the point at which the carburettor is clamped on, the very short induction allowing for typically good throttle response over a wide range of engine speeds.

Small detachable 'windows' over the transfer ports allow easy access if one wants to fiddle with shapes and sizes, but this was always a feature of these machines and was intended to help in the manufacturing process, rather than as a tuning aid.

Cylinder heads are well-finned alloy with pleasing radial fins, but the cast-iron barrels are quite lightly finned – which indicates a mild state of tune – and the engine thus appears to be no bigger than a 250; in fact, it surprises most people who enquire about the machine and are told the engine is of 500cc capacity.

Bore and stroke dimensions are square at 68x68mm, the compression ratio a quite mild 6:1, the engine producing a modest 18.5bhp at around 4500rpm – which is very mild by today's standards.

There is no oil pump, the engine making do perfectly well with the time-honoured 'petroil' lubrication, the oil mixed with standard grade fuel at a 24:1 ratio.

Primary drive is by straight-cut gears to a multi-plate, 'oil bath' clutch on the left side, with the unit-construction gearbox containing no more than three gears with wide ratios. The engine gear sports 29 teeth, while the clutch housing employs 65 teeth, for a primary reduction of 2.24:1: the engine, of course, runs 'backwards' in relation to the road wheels. Gear change is by hand, with a very neat gear lever attached to the right side of the tank, the lever travelling in a small 'gate' which ensures a positive gear selection. The crankcases are tiny, dominated on one side by the Dynastart and its cover and on the other by the primary drive cases.

Clutch operation is by worm-and-shaft, the mechanism directly under the primary case oil filler cap. Oddly, but typical of many German motorcycles of the period, there is an auxiliary, heel-operated pedal on the clutch shaft which can also operate the clutch withdrawal mechanism and thus over-ride the normal handlebar lever; it probably serves as a fail-safe in the event of a broken clutch cable, but I suspect its main purpose would be to employ much quicker gear changes in the event of a challenge being thrown out by someone!

You can roll the throttle off, disengage the clutch with your left heel and reach across the tank to shove the gear lever into a higher gear with your free left hand if you must and, awkward though it looks – and is! – the gear change is many seconds quicker. I tried it a few times just for fun, but the bike is not easy to control one-handed over rough surfaces when you are applying these forces in different directions, so it is hardly worthwhile to attempt to do this. But with practice comes ease!

An equally strange device is the *heel-operated* rear brake pedal, which is sited well above the right footrest, and needs quite a stretch to operate, with the rider's foot removed from its footrest. It's a bugger of a thing – Vin did not agree! – because you *can't use the awkwardly placed pedal with anything like the finesse you would have if it was toe-operated, particularly if you happen to be riding over bumpy surfaces.*

How's this for a scenario? You have accepted the challenge from another motorcyclist and you are diving very late into a corner, your left hand across the fuel tank for a swift downward gear change, your right heel on the rear brake pedal, your left heel on the clutch pedal, three fingers round the front brake lever, and your right hand blipping the throttle at the same time. I have no idea when, how – or indeed *if* – you could execute a swift hand signal or rude gesture while thus engaged, but I reckon that, if you were to try this exercise as well, you would then be too busy picking yourself up from the roadway and rubbing all your sore spots to bother about hand signals of any kind. Other than perhaps shaking your fist at your highly amused, rapidly disappearing challenger.

This is not to say the DKW handles badly – it doesn't – it's just that in these modern days we are used to keeping both hands firmly on the handlebars and executing these movements with a great deal more subtlety and much less drama: and much more quickly, it should be noted.

Front forks are fabricated from steel pressings and are immensely strong in all planes, the centrally mounted, single spring is well controlled by a hydraulic, friction-damping device contained within a large metal boss atop the steering head. The forks are attached to the frame by spindles and brackets, which was normal practice with girder type forks. The heavy-duty frame continues the pressed-metal theme and there is no rear suspension. However, rear suspension is handled very ably indeed by a large and well contoured single saddle which is hung by its nose upon a neat, infinitely adjustable cantilever suspension system which employs a pair of short, horizontally positioned coil springs which are un-damped. The springs are well contained by being wrapped around a convenient frame tube.

A hand-wheel adjustment underneath the saddle allows for a large measure of infinite variations, although it might well be too embarrassing to be used when viewed by the general public. If you use it in traffic, it looks as though you are leaning forward and picking your backside as you ride along, and is better done in private.

Under normal circumstances you hardly miss the non-existent rear wheel suspension, for that sprung saddle is so very effective, but the bike can become very twitchy when braking heavily over uneven surfaces, thanks in part to that awful rear brake pedal, but also in some measure to the large movement of the saddle; a mixed blessing if ever I saw one. On a couple of occasions, I rode that bike over rough tram-lines in Melbourne with both feet eased off the footrests and all my weight then resting upon the saddle, and I was frankly very surprised at the ease with which the seat soaked up even the worst of road irregularities.

There is, however, a catch. As I've said, there is no damping, and thus the springs have a tendency to snap back into position after being wound up. It seems okay in potholes, but ripples and bumps will see the seat absorb the initial energy but then fly back to its neutral position and nearly jerk your backside well out of the saddle. It took a while to learn the drill of easing your weight off the seat a touch when this happens, with the result that you stay more securely in the seat and thus enjoy a surprisingly good ride, and with quite acceptable handling.

Typically, the girder forks allow the bike to flop into corners with some gusto, and it can be a problem because of the low-slung frame and fat mufflers, which inhibit cornering clearances. The bike corners well, but not too sportily because of these limiting factors.

The engine fires with the touch of the button, but that big Dynastart is pretty noisy as it goes about its business. There are some alarming clunks and grinds to be heard before the engine suddenly decides to chime in, but it then idles quietly and very reliably at a speed which would put your little lawnmower to shame.

Clutch action is smooth and the slow gear-change even more so, the gear ratios very widely separated to take advantage of the engine's extremely wide torque band. I've never felt a two-stroke with such low-speed grunt, with **a clue to its** performance provided by the huge final-drive sprocket and the *comparatively small one on the rear wheel: the two runs of the rear drive chain all but parallel to one another.*

The bike pulls like a train from almost a slow idle and its top gear performance is a revelation – even more so in light of the powerful but extremely peaky two-strokes which are so much the norm today. Peak power is a handy 18.5bhp at only 4500rpm, an engine speed at which most modern two-strokes are only just clearing their lungs, and long before they are at their best.

There is only a little time lost with that slow gear-change, even though you have to back off the throttle and change gears with the same hand, because the engine's great spread of power allows it to dig in again and pull away with renewed vigour.

The exhaust is a bit fruity and doesn't fall far short of breaking windows, and that's a bit of a worry, while the engine's tendency to four-stroke (even to eight-stroke) with the throttle closed on the over-run is really unpleasant.

There is an in-built shock-absorber mechanism on the engine main-shaft gear, made obvious by a lump on front of the primary drive casting, but I found it none too efficient because the bike tended to lurch along badly with the throttle closed, its rider nodding his head in time to the machine's lurches, whether he liked it or not. The exhaust's deep, booming '*Plooong-da-Ploooong, Plooong, Ploong*' on the over-run was actually louder than the exhaust under power, and attracted some attention as I nodded along.

The front brake tended to squeal a bit, although it worked very well indeed, but I found it hard to come to terms with the rear brake pedal, particularly when my knees were flexing as well over rough going. I found it hard to control rear wheel braking with any finesse when lifting my foot off its footrest and then 'finding' the powerful rear brake. I was not happy about that.

Acceleration is deceptively fast, if only because of the engine's apparently relaxed performance, but the occasional (experimental) large handful of throttle in top gear would see the bike leap away with an amazing turn of speed. It belied the low power output of the lightly stressed engine, for the bike is hardly a lightweight at 400lb (160kg) dry. Of course, these 'horses' are 18.5 tough-as-teak Clydesdales, not the under-nourished Shetland ponies which power many of the latter-day, high-revving, more highly tuned two-strokes.

Once in top gear, the big Deek behaved as though its transmission was automatic, for it only needed a touch more or less of throttle to keep up with traffic or to blow most of it absolutely sideways. It could storm main road hills in top gear with great enthusiasm, with never the need to change down unless baulked by heavy or slower traffic.

The bike was very relaxing at speed, but again there was a disturbing tendency for the unsprung tail to hop about under rear-wheel braking on bumpy surfaces, and to pivot about the steering head on bumpy, fast sweepers whenever the wheel was clear of the ground. But you could pin it down to the pegs through any type of corner on dead smooth roads if you were driving under power, and it would zip round with absolute sure-footedness.

Front forks were a bit noisy, though quieter than some other girders, the lack of rear wheel suspension more than compensated for by the great saddle suspension already noted.

There is no doubt the hearty German motorcycle was intended as an open-road, mile-eating '*Gran Tourer*', the sort of machine not often seen today this side of the later Cruiser motorcycles.

Using the 'Imperial' figures of the day, the Deek was good for an indicated 40mph in first gear, a handy 66mph in second and would sit all day on its top whack, Minogue assures me, of around 80mph, uphill or down. On the open road, the engine bopped along very easily in top gear at a gentle 4050rpm while showing 70mph on the speedo – the machine's only instrument.

DKW also claims – get this – fuel consumption figures of 80/76mpg depending on how hard you want to ride, with oil consumed at 1872mpg in the process. Can you imagine any other 500cc two-stroke twin cruising at 70mph on the open road and returning 76mpg at the same time? I suggest these figures would be totally unknown today, but were hardly remarkable in the immediate pre-WWII era.

Unlike many of its contemporaries, the wheels are not interchangeable, though the rear wheel is quickly detachable without disturbing the chain, sprocket or brake drum.

This, then, is the 1939 SB500T DKW, well and truly alive and kicking more than three-quarters of a century after it left the world's largest motorcycle factory virtually at the outbreak of war. It was a proud old steed and it did its job as well as its designers had intended it to.

It's trite but true to say that the road-going DKW was a simple and straight-forward design from a factory which was turning out some very, very exciting racing two-strokes at the time. You could call it boring in comparison to modern-day high performance two-strokes, you could say ordinary in fact, and you 'sort-of' might be right, but I suggest you would swiftly change your mind once you had ridden the punchy, low-revving SB500T DKW for a few days.

TECH SPECS

Make: DKW

Model: SB500T

Years of manufacture: 1934–1939

Type:
Twin-cylinder 500cc two-stroke, with cast iron cylinder barrels, alloy heads. Built-up crank, with caged roller big-ends and ball main bearings.

Capacity (actual): 493.90cc

Bore x Stroke: 68 x 68mm x 2.

Compression ratio: 5.8:1

Power @ rpm: 18.5BHP @ 4500rpm

Carburation: Single, 24mm Bing (or Amal) Carburettor, with wire-mesh air filter.

Ignition: Battery, contact points, dual coil.

Electrics:
6-volt Siba 'Dynastart'; a combination of 120-watt generator/starter motor/external flywheel, w. voltage regulator, 8-inch electric head, smaller tail-light. No blinkers or stoplight switch.

Transmission:
Straight-cut gear primary drive with 2.24:1 reduction, through oil-bath, multi-plate clutch to three-speed hand-change gearbox, with final drive by chain; the engine revolving 'backwards' in relation to road wheels. Gearbox *internal* ratios: 1st – 2:64; 2nd – 1.48; top – 1:1. Overall (final drive) ratio is 1.75:1
Suggested overall ratios: 1st – 10.34:1; 2nd – 7.29:1; 3rd – 4.52:1.

Frame, suspension, wheels:
Full cradle, tubular and pressed metal frame, fabricated pressed-steel girder front forks, with central spring and friction/hydraulic damper control. No rear suspension, cantilever sprung single saddle, with adjustable spring rate. Steel rims are 19", with 350 x 19" tyres front and rear. Large, 8-inch (200mm) internal expanding drum brakes front and rear; with quickly detachable rear wheel.

Dimensions:
Length – 2125mm; Width – 920mm; Height – 675mm; Wheelbase – 1385mm; Ground Clearance – 115mm; Saddle Height – 675mm; Weight – 190kg; Fuel tank – 14 litres; Approx. 300km range.

Performance: First gear: 70km/h; Second gear: 110km/h; Top Gear: 130-135km/h.

Fuel consumption: approx. 4.5L/100km.

Bike loaned by:
VIN MINOGUE, Melbourne, Australia.

1975 Munch 1300TTSIE Mammoth

1300cc OHC FOUR CYLINDER
110 (DIN) BHP: 125 (SAE) BHP

When people speak of highly specialised, serious motorcycles which are 'bespoke', 'distinctive', 'unique', 'hand-built', 'one-off specials', or any one of a dozen or more appellations, we automatically think of something really special which might emerge from a major motorcycle manufacturer; a rare, high-performance machine perhaps, which may have been either a prototype design, or a highly secret, pre-production machine of some type, possibly one which had never – could never – reach the production stage. We would usually expect such a machine to be something well removed from the norm, and probably made in a well-established, modern, highly computerised factory either in Japan, Germany, Italy, England or even America, and for the most part we would be correct in that assumption.

The Munch Mammut (Mammoth) was one of these very special, if not quite one-off, machines which were hand-built in very limited numbers, and it was made in Germany. But the small number of these rare, fantastic machines were manufactured in a very small factory by an arch-enthusiast called Friedel Munch, who began his skilled career in the late 1940s as a young mechanic, racer and engine tuner, specialising in OHC Horex roadsters and, later, with the DOHC road racing machines. The plump, gnome-like Munch built around 360 of his own monstrous Mammut motorcycles (as he so accurately called them), with a small group of highly skilled engineers, and was involved in the manufacture of nearly 480 machines all told, even after he was forced to relinquish control of his small operation. The Mammoth name provides the perfect description of these huge Autobahn Blasters, for they were monstrous motorcycles which would never fit into any pigeon-hole, even though his motorcycles were, without question, some of the most amazing, 'one-off', 'unique' and clearly distinct motorcycles ever to have been constructed anywhere.

Rest assured, however, that the Mammoths which Munch built, monstrous and intimidating as they were in their day, were entirely rideable (but not easily, and then usually only by equally large people!) and were much more powerful than most motor vehicles on earth had any right to be in the 1970s, whether on two wheels or four. This includes serious road racing machinery: again, on two wheels or four! In fact, a Mammoth's daunting road performance could not properly, or safely, be recorded on anything but the very fastest of road racing circuits, because the top speed of even the lowliest of them could not safely be attained anywhere on the open road. Anywhere, that is, except for the high-speed German Autobahns, which were, or should be, the bike's natural habitat.

Munch had previously fitted highly tuned, 500cc twin-cylinder DOHC Horex road race engines into his own frames and running gear, the machines by then being built in one of the Horex marque's small factories, which he was able to purchase, along with a large inventory of spare parts and complete engines, after the German motorcycle manufacturer closed its operations early in 1958.

But his first effort at fitting the large car engine he used so often in his later machines occurred in 1966, when he shoe-horned an air-cooled, OHC 68 BHP 1000cc, four-cylinder NSU 'Prinz' engine into a 'Featherbed' Norton frame and running gear. The single overhead camshaft was driven by chain, the transverse four-cylinders set across the frame. Because of its good power-to-weight ratio, it was something of a success, but the large and heavy engine was simply too much for the lightweight Norton frame – and brakes! – to cope with, so Munch set about building his own frames and running gear from then on, the frame based upon the legendary Featherbed Norton, thereby 'inventing' the series of Mammoth motorcycles which were to follow for some years thereafter.

After fitting what he claimed was the ideal engine into his own frame, Munch proudly showed the first of his specially built Mammoth motorcycles to the NSU people, who were very impressed by the marriage of their NSU Prinz engine into his substantial frame and running gear, which included a specially designed, magnesium alloy rear wheel, and a huge twin-leading shoe front brake, the latter developed some years earlier for his road racing Horex machines. NSU had dropped out of the motorcycle market by then as they followed Horex to the grave, along with almost all of the world's motorcycles factories, be they large or small – so the car company was not too interested in building bikes again, but they were clearly quite happy to sell brand-new NSU Prinz engines to Munch.

By 1967 some 30 Munch Mammoths had been built, each one ridden and fine-tuned by Munch himself, the enormous, twin-leading-shoe front brake by now some 250mm – that's all of 10 inches! – in diameter, the special mag-alloy rear wheel, with its 'paddle-wheel' vanes fitted in place of the more standard spoke-wheel because it was claimed that no 'ordinary' motorcycle could hope to handle the power – and the weight – of the huge motorcycle. As it happened, several spokes, with nipples still attached, were pulled right out of a Mammoth's wheel rim within 500 Kilometres while on a road test report, which certainly proved the point!

Later Prinz engines were 1100 and 1200cc versions, the latter poking out a very respectable 85 BHP, making the 1967 Mammoth motorcycles the most powerful road irons in the world; the huge motorcycle capable of achieving the Imperial 100 miles an hour (160km/h) in just under 10 seconds, up there with GP race car times, with the 'classic' 0-100km/hour time achieved in just over six seconds. In 1970 Munch took a specially tuned 'lightweight', all-alloy, 1370cc NSU-engined 'Daytona Bombe' to the steeply banked American oval in an attempt to break Mike Hailwood's one-hour record of 154mph, which the British rider had set with his 500cc MV road race machine in 1965. Within the first three laps of the track the 125 (DIN) BHP Munch was

Huge 250mm (10-inch) twin-leading front brake, with its long lever and wide brake shoes, adorns the giant Mammoth. It proved to be powerful in the extreme, needing just a couple of fingers squeezing the handlebar lever to elicit a yelp from the Metzeler front tyre, and this happened at almost any speed. Over-braked and needing some care, but still very handy.

After one or two practice laps, this over-bored, 1300cc Daytona 'Bombe' was lapping the high-speed oval in America at an astonishing 178mph average speed, but the 400 x 18 rear tyre called it quits after just on four laps: it was completely shredded! Tyre technology in 1970 was nothing like the technology which exists in 2022, be well assured of that fact.

well ahead of the record, being timed (it has been officially recorded) at an *astonishing* **178mph** (285km/h) average, but the 400 x 18" rear tyre could not hope to withstand the immense power of the engine or the weight of the bike, much less the track's ragged surface, which was as rough as a wood rasp. At just on four laps the tyre was shredded, and the attempt was called off.

Clearly, tyre technology at the time was nothing like the science it is today, so one can only wonder as to what might have happened to that one-hour record had the 1970 Mammoth been outfitted with one of the far wider rear wheel rims and fat, bald tyres used on today's GP racing motorcycles.

In the early spring of 1974, just four years after the failed record attempt, two Munch Mammoths were imported into Melbourne by the businessman Max Redlich. One of the monsters was the road-going 1200cc TTS 'Tourer' with its impressive, fire-engine-red paint finish, its dual, 43mm twin-throat Dell O'rto carburettors, and its twin NSU headlights; the other Munch, *the subject of this report,* was the fuel-injected, all-black, **1974 1300TTSIE, Super Sports** road-going version of the Daytona Bombe, which was an out and out rocket ship of the highest possible order! It retained the later, 1200cc air-cooled overhead camshaft NSU engine, as indicated on the overhead cam-chain cover, but, like the Daytona machine, the engine had been enlarged to 1300cc, by over-boring each cylinder by 3.5mm, and had also been very heavily 'breathed upon' by Munch and his small band.

The NSU engine required an enormous amount of work before it could be used in a motorcycle, of course, even though Munch only purchased the cylinder block, cylinder head and engine internals, because he had to manufacture special castings for an all-new primary drive, wet sump, oil pan and gearbox – the latter using gearbox internals from the Horex, which were modified by Porsche. A special, sintered-bronze, multi-plate clutch had to be designed by Munch to handle the enormous power, while all the special castings were made from Elektron, a very strong, ultra-lightweight magnesium alloy. The cycle components and running gear remained a constant, including Munch's large-diameter, almost box-section, full-cradle frames, but the rear section of the later Munch motorcycles were radically different to the original machine. They were to remain almost unaltered from 1967 to 1978; and beyond, even after Friedel Munch was no longer intimately involved in the manufacture of his huge motorcycle, having twice (in 1971 and again in 1973) being declared bankrupt. He was forced to sell much of his controlling interests in the business, but the Mammoth name was still maintained for some time afterwards, with Munch continuing in the business as an expert, 'hands-on' consultant.

The brutish-looking Mammoth employs a large, one-piece Elektron mag-alloy casting which bolts firmly to the rear of the box-section frame at four points, immediately behind the fuel tank and at the rear of the gearbox, to incorporate the rear mudguard, a substantial base for the long dual-seat, and the top mounting points for the heavy-duty, double-action Koni rear spring/damper units. The extremely lightweight casting was naturally reinforced at the points where the rear suspension was mounted, along with other strengthening gussets at high stress points. The huge casting also contains two pannier-style 'pockets' in which are located most of the Bosch electrical components, including two very large

The NSU engine would arrive at the Munch factory very much 'naked' as this earlier, rare NSU engine has done. A few odd parts of the casting would need to have been sawn off, but otherwise it was all there. Note the overhead camshaft drive chain, with its Weller chain tensioner in place.

Very many components of the Mammoth were cast in lightweight magnesium alloy, including this large casting, which bolted to the rear of the gearbox and upper frame rails. It consisted of the dualseat base, the mount for silencers, rear Koni spring/damper units, footrests and many other components. Note the mag-alloy rear wheel with its 10-inch brake and coupled, strengthening vanes.

NB: *The Dutch expert on Munch motorcycles, Erik Meesters, who is compiling a book on these exclusive machines, told me in 2016 – more than forty years after this in-depth road report was originally published – he doesn't know of a duplex chain being fitted to the final drive of any Mammoth he has seen, or heard of, but the importer and original owner of the machine assured me the highly powered Super-Sports 1300cc Rocket-ship was thus outfitted, so I took their word for it at the time, even though – because of the fully enclosed, oil-bath rear chain – I couldn't easily check this out for myself. But I do suggest that, with the enormous power this Juggernaut generates, which was more than twice as much as the most powerful factory racer in 1974 produced, a somewhat heavier-duty chain might have been a very good idea, both for reliability and longevity.*

12-volt batteries – the most impressive mag-alloy 'bath tub' casting topped by a long, neatly sculpted two-level dual-seat.

A one-piece swing-arm and chain-case assembly contains what was said to be a duplex 5/8" x 3/8" final drive chain on the machine's left side allowing a totally enclosed and fully sealed oil bath, ensuring a relatively long and trouble-free life for this highly stressed component.

Again, and clearly in the interests of saving weight, the huge rear swing-arm suspension assembly is moulded in the same light magnesium alloy and is attached firmly to the lower half of the boxed frame by a huge spindle, which allows the swing-arm assembly to pivot on a pair of large, fully sealed ball bearings, an upper section of the chain-case providing the lower mounting point for the rear suspension unit on that side. A large mag-alloy plate on the opposite side provides the mounting point for the spring/damper unit on the right side. A Jockey-tensioner is contained within the oil-bath chain-case, allowing the chain to be adjusted in seconds without disturbing the rear wheel and without altering the machine's wheelbase. Rear wheel removal is accomplished by simply removing the axle and dropping the wheel out – without moving the chain or rear brake drum assembly, or losing a drop of oil. Other manufacturers might well copy these two latter features with advantage!

The beautifully finished alloy rear wheel was the first of its type to be fitted to any motorcycle, embodying extreme lightness with immense strength, the hub fitted with another huge Munch twin-leader drum brake of no less than 10" (250mm) diameter. Of course, the brake backing plate and the wide brake shoes themselves are also lightweight Elektron castings, the brake plate fully ventilated and heavily ribbed for additional strength.

Polished outrigger plates – also mag-alloy castings – bolted to each side of the rear of the machine provide mounting points for rider and pillion footrests, rear brake pedal, gear lever linkages and other essential items.

Elektron castings are used very extensively on this huge 660lb (295kg) machine; the alloy has also been adopted for gearbox, transmission cases, front brake assembly, the huge, ribbed wet-sump case and front fork yolks. The front brake is a heavily ventilated 10" twin-leading shoe component again, as we have noted, of Munch design and manufacture, the front wheel secured to the frame by massive Rickman motocross forks containing thick chrome-moly stanchions and special Munch springs. Few of these highly expensive, hand-built Munch roadsters have graced the world's freeways; fewer still have found their way to Australia. However, as we've noted, an Australian distributor for Munch did exist, if only for a short time. The Melbourne-based firm Maxaco Industries, through their motorcycle enthusiast director, Max Redlich, imported the two machines in 1974 and exhibited them at that year's Melbourne International Motorcycle Show.

Though basically similar – it's been said no two Mammoths were ever quite alike – the two Munch machines differed radically in appearance and specification. The scarlet, dual-headlamp tourer fitted with gigantic humpback tank was listed at $A5500 complete with full instrumentation, twin, dual-throat Weber carburettors, 95DIN BHP motor and (dare we mention it?) crash bars! Its stable-mate – listed at around a cool $A7000, which was almost three times the price of a brand-new R90S BMW motorcycle in 1974 – was the sports variant I mentioned earlier, the machine finished in gleaming black with a single 8" quartz halogen headlamp and four-intake Kugelfischer-fuel-injection.

It's worth noting that magnesium/aluminium alloys – which are often about 80% magnesium, 18% aluminium and the rest zinc – are very prone to early corrosion, the material needing to be well coated to keep the elements at bay, as well as the effects of oxygen in oxidising the material, so it was heartening to note that this had been attended to on both machines. The coating, which can be applied either as 'diffusion coatings' in a sulphur bath or by heavily anodising the material, could clearly be seen on the numerous mag-alloy castings, in particular on the smoother surfaces. It appeared to have been applied as a form of anodising (which we usually come across as coatings on aluminium mugs and cups, often seen in a variety of colours) and was very

Here, in all its glory, is the four-trumpet, unfiltered electronic fuel injection system. These injectors certainly played their part in added to the very high power output of the reliable - in fact, nigh bullet-proof - 1300cc NSU OHC car engine.

smooth to the touch.

The importer quite happily made the latter Sports model available to me for a full day's testing, a day which, sadly, passed all too quickly. He seemed to have no reservations about loaning the world's most expensive motorcycle to a short and somewhat imperfect stranger – indeed, he needed little prompting – but he did remark on the distinct possibility of the thing being dropped, and warned that 'everyone else has managed to do so'. I found that blithe statement more than a little unsettling, to say the least!

*NB: Many years after this test report was published, I read, in a publication called 'The Munch Story', that 'the machine could only be ridden by person **of at least 1.8 metres in height, and preferably taller**'. I am just on **1.6 metres in height,** so make of that what you will!!*

The Sports model which I rode is fitted with the over-bored 1300cc engine – yes, the ID badge does say Munch 1200 – and includes such goodies as high-compression, 11:1 pistons, Schleicher high-spec sports camshaft, University of Heidelberg computer-designed exhaust system and the most impressive four-trumpet Kugelfischer mechanical fuel injection system! Perhaps we could also mention the re-worked ports, which had been opened up somewhat and then highly polished, the hand-built and carefully balanced internals ... let it suffice to say that

It was a long reach to the handlebars on the Munch, with arms at pretty near full stretch. So much so, that my jacket tore off its buttons at the top of my jeans and crept up my back, which had never happened before this, nor at any time afterwards. But wind pressure at very high speeds took much of the weight off my wrists. Thankfully!

the NSU engine in Sports trim delivered no less than 110 **DIN** BHP at a very high 8000rpm!

We shall remark here that the Continental DIN horsepower figure refers to the power available to a vehicle's driven wheel and is measured (generally) at the final engine-drive to the rear wheel itself. Japanese horsepower ratings are invariably calculated on the American SAE (Society of Automotive Engineers) standard with power measured in the vicinity of the spark plug leads. If one mentally adds 15% to the DIN rating to allow for this discrepancy, one arrives at the typically more optimistic American figure, so read 125 BHP (**SAE**) for this engine, compared to 82 BHP (SAE) for the most powerful Japanese motorcycle built **at that time** – a power bonus for the huge Munch of some 40%. WOW!!

Okay, back in 1974 how does one with very short legs approach an un-streamlined $7000 German masterpiece weighing over 600lbs, fitted with a high wide and handsome engine developing enough power to easily top 150mph in the old money? Well, the device has a wheel on each end just like any other, and a set of handlebars with standard control layout – and a proud importer who starts it up and helps you aboard – but, in a word, one still approaches such a vehicle a mite gingerly, to say the least, if only in view of its rareness and price! The fact that it is also far too big for the rider is really of little consequence, particularly when such a large and enthusiastic audience is on hand to witness (some of) the road test.

When started the big, all-alloy engine ran with very little mechanical noise, which was a surprise, and proved to be velvet smooth throughout its entire speed range and, when upright, the Munch gives little hint of its immense weight. *That surprise is yet to come!*

One's first impression is of sitting inside the machine rather than on top of the thing, for one is surrounded on three sides by masses of metal. Low, flat bars force my arms forward till my chest rests not uncomfortably almost atop the high-back tank, my jacket unhappily creeping up my back, while the two-level dual-seat(beautifully contoured and extremely comfortable) bumps up at the back to hold the rider securely in position; rest assured, it needs to do that!

The air-cooled engine looks to be almost a metre wide and it seems to burst from the confines of the impeccably finished fame, hanging well outside the rider's legs. As indicated, the Munch's bulk, including its height, is not apparent when mounted or mobile, but it is a very different story when the big-iron is stationary and one has to clamber aboard: a set of retractable wheels as an optional extra would have been very handy indeed for most owners, regardless of the person's shape and size. No problems are experienced in placing the behemoth on its prop stand and jumping to the ground, or indeed in wheeling the device cautiously about (?), although it is a slow process and fraught with problems, even for people of more 'normal' – that is average, or better – size.

But extreme caution must be exercised when one has to remount after a stop. As soon as weight is lifted the bike's prop stand flicks up, leaving the machine with no support and a great deal of weight over the centre line if it is not entirely vertical at the time. The resultant crunch as the device falls over is most upsetting. It happened to me twice. The first time, I had the presence of mind to avoid damage to the Monster by being trapped underneath it, and the second time it happened the bike subsided all on its own when I had to stop for a tram to allow its passengers to clamber on or off the confounded thing. Happily, the machine never fails to attract an admiring throng wherever it stops, so there was no shortage of eager helpers to provide assistance in setting the bike upright again and helping me back in to the saddle. But I did not need to be advised by everybody who stood me up again that the bike was much too big for a man of my small stature; I already knew all about that!

The drill is soon learned, of course. First, you lift the bike off the prop stand while standing alongside it and press the electric starter button on the right handlebar. Next, slip quickly into the saddle so you can pop it into gear and dart off suddenly if it threatens to fall over.

Gear engagement in the 4-speed gearbox is light, silent and dead positive. Munch uses a much-strengthened gearbox designed by Porsche's research team, with the special, 12-plate, sintered bronze clutch driven by matched helical gears. Extreme rigidity is ensured for the output shaft, as it is mounted in three huge bearings. Power delivery through this transmission system is smooth and predictable, with the clutch action incredibly light and drama-free.

I was surprised to discover that my short undercarriage could be retracted immediately the Super-Megabike begins to move; in fact, both feet are on the footrests long before the clutch is fully home. Low speed handling in Melbourne peak-hour traffic can often be more than a little off-putting, but the big Munch showed little signs of the heavy steering I felt certain would be in evidence by virtue of the high mounted, tall engine, which imbued the machine with what was clearly a very high centre of gravity. I was impressed with the fact that the extremely high 'top hamper' – as it used to be called – seemed to have no effect whatsoever on the bike. Clearly the steering geometry and weight distribution were spot-on, which perhaps should have been no surprise at all.

Though by no means distressed, the highly tuned engine did not feel particularly happy trickling at a slow idle in traffic, but throttle response with the fuel injection system was incredible; I had only to think the throttle open and the engine wound up instantaneously. I have never experienced such dramatic response, even on the best-carburetted sports or racing machines I have ridden. This was all the more remarkable in view of the precision-ground racing camshaft and high-compression pistons fitted to the test model, which should have made the bike more than a little 'lumpy' to ride at these pedantic speeds.

In spite of the importer's assertion that one needs only the first two gears in city use, I found upward gear changes could be made at just on 2600rpm without distress to engine or rider, and a comfortable, easy gait of an indicated 60mph

The 'offending' handlebars, designed more for high speed than for comfort, at least fell readily to hand. The twelve-plate, sintered bronze clutch was surprisingly light, the potent front brake – as I have noted – a little too touchy for my liking, but still very necessary on a true road-burner like this machine was.

in top gear was possible at the same very low engine revs. However, if the bike was given its head somewhat as we changed into third gear, the bike really began to come into its own, flashing off with the feeling that the engine would much prefer to be wound out a bit more if it was to give of its best.

On the move, the big German 4 can be flung about from one footrest to the other with a nigh-reckless abandon known to very few machines – and to none within a bull's roar of its bulk. The thick Rickman front forks traverse even the bumpiest, most pot-holed roads without transmitting any noticeable degree of shock to the rider. They are perfectly well suited to the character of the machine, and are admirably complemented by the two-way damped, three-way adjustable Koni rear suspension spring/damper units.

There is little discernible pitching even when cornered hard and there is no sign of frame flexing or rear wheel hop even when injudicious amounts of power are applied at the wrong times: like halfway through a medium-paced corner, *just to see what might happen!* Handling and comfort proved to be as near perfect and makes little difference over the varying road surfaces on which the tests were conducted, even when cornering at high speeds over some bumpy road surfaces. However, the heavy bike can sometimes become a little twitchy if ridden much too quickly over the mid-corner ripples which can suddenly appear on even the smoothest road surfaces.

Brakes are powerful yet progressive and eminently controllable. The front brake is very light in operation but will elicit a yelp from the Metzeler ribbed rubber when applied hard, while the rear brake – though deliberately spongy in view of its similar design – helps haul the heavyweight to a no-drama straight ahead stop in the best 'giant-hand' tradition.

The invisible giant hand is also very much in evidence in getting the machine mobile again, for it pushes hard and sustained when the throttle is opened briskly at almost any speed in almost any gear. Acceleration is at once neck-snapping, arm-wrenching and mind-boggling as we pile on the coals, and yet it still seemed oddly restrained, with little but a sudden surge of unleashed power as speed builds up. There also seemed to be no limit to the Munch in terms of sheer speed, but wind pressure with a very high performance, un-streamlined motorcycle such as this one becomes much too much to handle at some of the very high speeds we attained, so its uppermost speeds remained, at least for me, to be of somewhat academic interest; besides I was not really dressed for extremely high-speed pursuits anyway. Oh, for a trim fairing which would make riding at those ridiculous speeds so much easier, while adding much more to the top speed as a bonus!!

I stress that time was at a premium when the tests were conducted and all times are therefore unofficial, but 60mph still came up in a timed 4.5 seconds, still in second gear be it known, while we carefully calculated that a quarter-mile could be covered from a standstill in about 11 seconds, a fantastic elapsed time for a large, *registered, naked,* road-going motorcycle back in the early 1970s.

I cannot imagine the times a serious quarter-mile specialist could attain in an officially controlled series, particularly if the machine was fitted with the streamlined fairing it so urgently required, but an elapsed time of nicely under 10 seconds would seem to be entirely achievable: very fast indeed for a road-going(?) motorcycle in 1974!

I soon became used to the feel of the Munch, and realisation dawns that a well-sprung, heavy machine enjoys the distinct advantage of being almost imperturbable over just about any type of terrain; perhaps the large mass resists sudden road shocks and tricky cambers?

Nor does the added weight of a pillion passenger exert any noticeable influence on the machine. One of our photographers, Ray Ryan, bummed a lift home – he claimed there was no transport for him, even though three other motorcycles, and two cars, were present. I noted the fact that his presence made no discernible difference to the 'feel' of the machine's handling or cornering speeds, even when the machine was flung with some abandon through some very swift Kew Boulevard corners on the (long) way back to our original meeting place. Within the limitations imposed by local traffic, straight-line performance of the projectile also seemed remarkably unimpaired.

Comparisons are ever odious and quite pointless without something physically present to provide a comparison, but I venture to say that no motorcycle burning up the world's road surfaces in 1974 could have lived with this utterly amazing motorcycle in terms of acceleration or sheer speed. The bike will top 100mph in second gear if pushed, and will top that speed quite happily in third while still accelerating viciously. Top speed is quoted as 147mph, a speed I do not doubt for a moment; un-streamlined though it is! I never attempted to find out if this was true!

Perhaps some of the fleeter lightweight twins could shade the Munch slightly through a slower corner, but it would need to be ridden very hard to do so. On fast, bumpy corners the German machine would leave Metzeler tyre marks over any adversary, you may be well assured of that! Top-gear performance places the mammoth machine in the large, 'family automatic' car category. It needs no disc brake, for the spongy-feeling 10" twin-leaders haul the beast to an eyes-out-on-springs stop with ho-hum ease every time and with no sign of brake fade.

What a Monster! Weighing all of 670 pounds in the old scale and built for someone very much bigger than me, it was a very imposing sight when it was first presented to me. But I had to ride it, and ride it I did, for probably the greatest buzz I have ever enjoyed on two wheels; and that is really saying something. The great power of this Mammoth had to be experienced to be believed, you may be well assured of that fact!!

The quartz-halogen headlamp stabs the gloom ahead of the rider like a great death-ray; fizzing and crackling for what seems like a mile ahead, it allows unheard-of cruising speeds after dark. Everything about the machine is robust and shrieks power – particularly the dual horns, which mount, facing forward, just under the headlamp.

Despite the long list of plus points the Munch enjoys, I found one minus point more than a little annoying. The engine is air-cooled, with twin oil coolers assisting the large engine to keep its cool. And yet, though the engine showed no sign of overheating, it bathed my shin bones with a furnace-like breath. I was wearing short boots at the time so it became very uncomfortable and it was almost a relief to climb down now and then to allow the bright red, steaming skin to cool off. A minor point which I feel would present no problems to a rider attired in more suitable, full-length boots.

The rider to whom such a machine is apparently directed would have had so much fun gobbling up his contemporary Superbikes and spitting them out that this minor annoyance would probably pass unnoticed. The lucky fellow who could afford to own a Munch would have owned the most expensive commercially produced motorcycle in its day, far-and-away the most powerful machine available at the time, and even today the finest example of one-upmanship ever perpetrated.

It also happens to be one of the best engineered examples of hand-finished craftsmanship around. Sure, it has that cobbled, one-off look about it – the huge, domineering engine-room would always see to that – but you could always be sure of owning the only one on the block. I owe a vote of thanks to Max Redlich, and the bike's owner, for it isn't every day something like a Munch Mammoth comes along, and I shall be forever grateful to the machine's owner for allowing me to take his pride and joy for a solid workout.

As a footnote, I apologised to the Mammoth's owner when I reluctantly handed the bike back, because there was a dent in a plated metal cover on the machine's left side caused, I thought, at the time when I dropped the bike at the tram stop. 'Oh, don't worry about that,' he replied. 'I did that myself when I dropped it. It tries to fall over every time I stop somewhere. I've dropped it about ten times already.' That man, it should be noted, was somewhat solidly built and stood just above average height of 1.8 meters, so I felt somewhat heartened to hear about that!

TECH SPECS

Make: Munch

Model: Mammoth TTSIE 1300

Year of manufacture: 1974

Type:
Transverse, air-cooled four-cylinder chain-driven OHC NSU engine, with alloy cylinder head, cast-iron barrel. Steel connecting rods with detachable end-caps and slipper big-end bearings, three-ring alloy pistons. One-piece steel crankshaft supported upon large diameter, slipper main bearings. Later type 'thin-shell' bearings by Munch in lead/indium/bronze. Lubricant supplied from immersed gear-type oil pump, to crankshaft and big-end, main slipper bearings, thence by oil lines, oil ways and oil galleys to overhead camshaft and its drive chain.

Bore x stroke:
78.5:1 x 66.6mm x 4 (over-bored from original 75mm in 1200cc engine)

Capacity: 1289cc

Compression ratio: 11:1

Power @ rpm: 110 (DIN) BHP @ 8000rpm

Induction: Four-inlet 'Kugelfischer' fuel injection.

Transmission:
From engine via specially designed, matched helical-cut primary drive gears through 12-plate sintered bronze wet clutch, to Porsche-modified Horex four-speed foot-change gearbox and double-row 5/8" x 3/8" rear chain drive in fully sealed oil-bath chain-case.

Gear ratios: The ratios varied from model to model, so the ratios on the rare 1300TTSIE (as on the 1200cc machine) are a 'guesstimate'. But Holland's Munch expert, Erik Meesters had supplied me with a variety of ratios, with the information that 'no two Mammuts were ever quite the same'.

Gearbox internal ratios:
1st – 2.53:1; 2nd – 1.55:1; 3rd – 1.14:1; 4th – 1.01:1, with the final drive sprocket either 13 or 14 teeth, with the rear wheel sprocket either 33, 34 or 35 teeth.

Electrics:
Bosch 6-volt, 400-watt generator to twin, lead/acid batteries. Starter motor, electronic ignition.

Frame:
Reinforced duplex-downtube full-cradle tubular steel, with Magnesium alloy castings at stress points under long seat, at swing arm and steering head and other areas.

Suspension, wheels, brakes:
Front suspension is by special Rickman Brothers heavy duty two-way damped telescopic front forks, with swing-arm rear suspension controlled by a pair of two-way damped, multi-adjustable Koni spring/damper units.

Front wheel:
19" alloy rim, laced to 250mm (10") twin-leading shoe drum brake, with 350 x 19" Metzeler ribbed tyre. Rear wheel: 'Vaned' magnesium alloy casting, laced to 250mm (10") Twin leading shoe drum brake, with 400 x 18" Metzeler block tread tyre.

Dimensions:
Wheelbase – 1388mm; Weight – 295kg (660lbs); Fuel tank capacity – 20 litres (5.5 gallons).

Top speed
Unknown, but said to be 'in excess of 147mph'.

Machine loaned by:
MAXACO INDUSTRIES (Unidentified owner) Melbourne, Vic.

1953 Sunbeam 'S7'

500cc OHC TWIN CYLINDER
– SHAFT DRIVE

The **1946 'Luxury Tourer', 500cc S7 Sunbeam** motorcycle was one of Britain's most innovative – indeed fascinating – motorcycles, and certainly one of the most unique motorcycles the then-giant BSA factory ever made. It was said of the very unusual machine, in the publicity blurb out of England, that here was *'The Machine Which Will Be Modern 10 Years Hence'* but unfortunately the machine was 'Dead Within 10 Years', because it didn't really click with enthusiasts either in England or in any of the many overseas countries in which it was marketed, and it was deleted from the BSA/Sunbeam catalogue after just seven short years. In fact, the first batch of early examples of the Sunbeam S7 which were despatched to South Africa were hastily recalled due, it was said, to problems with heavy engine vibration and poor handling.

There was no word of any other problems with the machine, although there was said to be a serious problem with the rear shaft drive components failing completely on earlier models, or at least wearing out much too quickly.

One would expect that its specifications should have made the later, more mainstream-looking Sunbeam S8 far more acceptable than the obese S7, at least on paper, because it was the same all-alloy, air-cooled, 500cc vertical twin engine, with an overhead camshaft driven by chain, and it employed shaft-drive which, along with the OHC design, was a rarity at the time in Britain. Only the odd, 150cc water-cooled *side-valve* LE Velocette, which appeared a few years later, employed shaft final drive. The Sunbeam S7 had fat, 'balloon' tyres – as they were called – short, thick spokes laced into wide, car-like wheel rims for strength and freedom from flexing over bumps, solid-looking front telescopic forks – which were Sunbeam's own, owing nothing to BSA – large and substantial brakes, and the then-fashionable, plunger rear suspension.

But to many motorcyclists the engine looked *odd*, for its in-line vertical-twin design was quite different from anything the Brits had made before, and the bike looked to be bulbous and somewhat unwieldy in comparison to the slimmer and much more-sporty (looking) motorcycles which were to be seen everywhere. This, of course, was quite deliberate, because the original Sunbeam S7 was never intended to be a sports machine, for it always belonged to that fairly exclusive class of the 'Gentlemen's Luxury Tourer', a class to which very few British motorcycles in the early 1940s belonged; a class of motorcycle which was never popular just about anywhere on earth. This may well have been one good reason why the S7 proved to be so unsuccessful, and was probably the reason why the more 'sporting' S8 Sunbeam was launched.

The 'all-new' S8 was more in keeping with current designs, the original engine and transmission power-plant (still with shaft drive, of course) retained, but now benefitting from slightly higher compression ratio pistons, the lot by then fitted into a more 'standard' – if modified - BSA frame with its correspondingly slimmer BSA front forks, and BSA's slimmer wheels and brake assemblies, making the machine some 22lb lighter, and thus slightly more powerful, its more nubile appearance hinting at a more spirited performance. The 'new' machine came equipped with a quaint, oddly-shaped, almost 'Art Deco', cast aluminium muffler to replace the longer, fatter muffler fitted to the over-weight S7.

Unhappily the S8 Sunbeam was no sports machine either, and was not much more successful than its obese older brother. In fact, the

The S8 Sunbeam was, in essence, the OHC engine and shaft drive slotted into the modified BSA frame, which saved almost 11kg (25lb) in weight. Note the BSA forks, much thinner tyres, and 'Art-Deco' alloy muffler. Sadly, the S8 was no more successful than the big, beefy S7.

slightly higher power developed by the lighter machine's engine proved to be too much for the worm-and-worm-wheel shaft drive assembly in the rear hub, which (again) either stripped itself entirely or wore out far too quickly for anyone's liking. The Sunbeam engine was slightly detuned to overcome the problem, but the shaft-drive's serious issues persisted if the machine was subjected to rough treatment.

The Sunbeam final-drive train was very similar to the worm-and-worm-wheel type used on Peugeot motor cars at the time, but was never within a bull's roar of the successful French car's bronze-and-steel drive gear; the latter requiring a *vegetable-based oil* for its effective lubrication; which should perhaps have been specified for the Sunbeam as well. It has been argued – and rightly so? - that the far superior *bevel gear* final-drive system fitted to BMW motorcycles would have been a safer alternative, both in terms of longevity and power delivery – a fact which the German machines apparently proved, because their crown-wheel-and-pinion shaft-drive assemblies were (and still are) virtually trouble free.

Oddly, the early, **prototype** S7 machines employed the superior crown-wheel and pinion design long used by BMW and other makes, including the Danish Nimbus, which begs the question of why this type of shaft drive design was not adopted for the Sunbeam when it was finally launched. The weak point of worm and worm-wheel design is said to be the 'wiping action' of the contact area of an elongated drive worm - which is usually made from phosphor-bronze – and is far 'coarser' in pitch, so the wiping action is greater than that which would occur in a crown-wheel-and-pinion drive, which could result in a higher rate of wear. Hence, the apparent need for a vegetable-based oil for lubrication, which was recommended for the Peugeot car's worm and worm wheel final drive, which was fitted to the 202 models at that time.

Clearly, BSA was well aware of this, because the later **S10** model, which existed only in prototype form, was redesigned in 1957 to again employ shaft drive, this time by a set of BMW like *bevel-gears,* allied to the completely redesigned, far more efficient **cross-flow** cylinder head, the carburettor on one side the exhaust on the other' where, arguably, it should always have been. This design would have resulted in a far more acceptable performance, with – we would expect – a longer life for the crown wheel and pinion shaft-drive components. Regretfully, BSA, in its wisdom (?), decided not to proceed with the new S10 model.

If the Sunbeam's twin cylinder power-plant looked odd to the eyes of most motorcyclists, then it assuredly 'borrowed' much of its basic design from many of the four-cylinder car engines which abounded just after the war. The two cylinders were in-line astern, looking like a short *car* engine which had had two of its in-line cylinders chopped off, the impressive, one-piece aluminium alloy casting which formed most of the engine a marvellous work of art. The large aluminium alloy casting combined the cylinder block, crankcase and the upper attachment for a deep, alloy sump casting, to which the oil pan was bolted, and it included the large bell housing onto which the clutch compartment and gearbox were attached, forming, in essence, a lightweight unit-construction design. The huge, one-piece alloy casting was very heavily ribbed externally right down to the sump plate, both in the interests of effective air-cooling, and additional strength and rigidity.

A cast-iron alloy called '*Bravidium*' (a special nodular cast iron similar to '*Meehanite*' which is used in many engine components, including crankshafts and motorcycle flywheels) was used in the lipped cylinder sleeves which were pressed into the large casting, the sleeves similar to those used in 'wet-sleeve' engines like the Standard Vanguard and Citroen fours. The sleeves were locked securely in place when the high-silicon content Y-alloy cylinder head was bolted in place.

The alloy cylinder head contained a single overhead camshaft which was chain-driven from the rear of the cylinder block, with the chain lash controlled by a Weller tensioner, while the valves were parallel to one another and sited at an unusual angle. The car-type rockers were similarly at an odd angle, the camshaft actually sited slightly *below* the valves, while a large alloy plate sat atop the assembly, allowing easy access for inspection and valve clearance adjustment. The small, two-lobe distributor for the coil ignition system took its half-engine-speed drive from the rear of the overhead camshaft. At the base of the cam-chain drive a crankshaft-mounted intermediate gear meshed with another which drove a similar gear to finally drive the oil pump, which was situated deep within the oil pan of the wet sump engine. Externally, the engine castings were very clean, because there were no external oil lines.

The unusual in-line OHC twin bared for closer study. Note the overhead camshaft design, driven by chain from above the gearbox, the bulky crankshaft and the large, one-piece alloy casting – with the bellhousing for the clutch assembly and attached gearbox. This is an early model, for a much deeper oil sump was fitted to later models, thus allowing for more oil capacity and somewhat cooler running.

Again, following most automotive designs, the engine's combustion chamber was not the usual 'cross flow' design applied to other motorcycle engines, but was of the more old-fashioned (some say less efficient, which is not always the case) design which had the single Amal carburettor - with its attendant, chrome-plated air filter – attached to the right-hand side of the cylinder head, with the two exhausts emerging from angled headers on the same side, framing the carburettor. This would seem to be an inefficient method of supplying a fresh charge of inlet gas, because the blast of heat from the exhaust ports in such close proximity to the carburettor might be expected to have an adverse effect upon volumetric efficiency by heating the inlet charge. The two exhaust header pipes sweep down and curve to join into one pipe just ahead of a small section of flexible pipe ahead of the long, tapering muffler. The small piece of flexible pipe was interpolated to allow for the engine to move about under normal vibration, as the engine was flexibly mounted on a series of 'Silentbloc' sleeved-rubber 'snubbers' which fitted the large power-plant into its solid, all-embracing, duplex down-tube frame.

The substantial, chunky crankshaft is Meehanite cast iron, similar to the high nodular, ultra-close-grained material as the cylinder sleeves, the crank supported at the front upon a substantial, deep-groove ball bearing, and on the rear by a large, white metal bush contained within a cast iron 'spider' casting. The large white metal main bearing of course runs much quieter than a ball or roller bearing might, and the cam-chain is similarly much quieter when running than would be a cam drive by either a series of power-sapping 'stacked' gears or a bevel and vertical shaft. This seems to have been done because any engine noises which could otherwise be present might have been greatly amplified by the resonance created within the huge, alloy engine/crankcase casting. However, the front main bearing needed to be a substantial ball type, the better to handle high thrust loads generated when the large, 7" diameter clutch – with its six strong, perimeter springs – would be disengaged.

The large front main bearing also helps to support the pancake-type 6-Volt generator which is attached to the front of the crankshaft and hangs outside in the breeze, where it is enclosed within a neat, chrome-plated dome.

The short, nuggetty connecting rods employed in the 'over-square' engine, which features bore x stroke dimensions 70 x 63.5mm, for an engine capacity of just 487cc, are forged in the ideal RR56 aluminium alloy, the big-end bearings thin-shell, lead-indium-bronze material, while the 6.8:1 low compression pistons (which employ an unusual 'squish' crown) are of the four piston ring type, with the two scraper and oil control rings above the gudgeon pin, the lower oil ring almost at the base of the long-skirt pistons; again a feature long used in car engines, as well as in some European motorcycles.

The final drive shaft is taken from an offset shaft which emerges from the rear of the large gearbox, the offset allowing the exposed drive shaft to run directly to the enclosed worm-and-worm wheel drive within the rear hub. A normal Hardie-Spicer universal joint is at the rear of the shaft, with a rubber/metal joint at the front. The centres are exactly 292mm (11.5 inches) between the two flexible joints, a length the designer considered to be 'ideal'.

From every point of view the Sunbeam OHC engine was, and remains, an odd engine design for a motorcycle, but it was always intended to be very much the last word in luxury machines, with a standard of smoothness and comfort without precedent. The frame featured the typically un-damped plunger rear suspension, which of course limited the rear wheel movement to about 75mm, but the ubiquitous single saddle was hung from a pivot behind the fuel tank by its nose, its own cantilever movement allowing an extra degree of comfort. In practice it worked fairly well.

Arguably, the spring-base single saddle was abandoned at some compromise to the motorcyclist's comfort, for the dual-seats which followed were not sprung, and were all too often very firm. Very few dual-seats of any make were fitted with springs, though the German Denfeld or Beier examples fitted to BMW, NSU and early Zundapp motorcycles were very notable exceptions and were comfortable in the extreme. Clearly, a softly-padded, single seat which is embracing but will in itself move through some 65 mm or more of 'suspension' travel adds immeasurably to the comfort of a machine - no matter how well sprung the bike itself may be.

If a motorcycle is *plunger* sprung (or, even worse, with no rear suspension at all) a single, sprung saddle is darn near a life-saver! A solo-seated Sunbeam's pillion passenger could only be carried on one of those bullet-proof rubber pads bolted to the rear guard, or the occasional short, sprung Lycettes saddle, which might allow even the hardiest of pillion riders to make rude remarks about the efficiency or otherwise of contemporary plunger rear suspension, whether Sunbeam or not.

The Sunbeam made a great compromise to rider comfort by the adoption of a pair of fat 450 x 16 balloon tyres fitted to wide, car-type wheel rims, and surmounted them with huge, deeply-valanced mudguards which had no peer for sheer bulk – even the large Harley-Davidson 'fenders' shrank by comparison.

The whole machine shrieked of luxury in its long low-slung silhouette and distinctly overweight appearance. Sunbeam's S7 was very much a long-distance touring rider's machine, with an easy, smooth gait and a measure of comfort which was not always in evidence back in the 1950's, although the rear cylinder may tend to overheat during a hard squirt into the bush on an Australian summer's day. A colder-running spark plug (a KLG FE100 in the rear, say, against a 'hotter' KLG FE70 up front) was said to be helpful.

Sunbeams were never very much in evidence in Australia during their short lifespan of 1948-1956, and they are even fewer today. But there are some examples of the marque alive and well, and all seem to be in fairly good condition. There is supposedly a very handy supply of spare parts available in England to service the 10,000 or so machines which are supposed to be still in existence, which – if true - is really quite remarkable for a low volume machine like this one.

The subject of this report is an excellent **1953 S7 Sunbeam** model, still finished in the original 'mist green' which alternated with trad black or metallic grey as the standard colour scheme, and it is as close to bog standard as could reasonably be expected after many decades. The bike has been fitted with a set of small fibreglass saddlebags, with some quite out-of-place yellow pin-striping to relieve the basic green paint job and it now sports even fatter 500 x 16 tyres, but is otherwise almost in original condition.

And so it should be, for the speedo shows only 13,000 miles, which the machine's owner, Ivan Casson of Emu Plains, an outer Sydney suburb, claims to be original. From a distance, the bike looks as though it just left the showroom floor, though there are some inevitable pock-marks here and there under paintwork, and some of the chrome has been pitted in a few places.

Luxury specifications of the Sunbeam S7 do not extend to an electric starter, which was never standard ware on many motorcycles of that era, anyway, so the rotund machine must be kicked over just like its lesser contemporaries. There is some slight resistance felt because of the unusual layout of the starter (it couldn't be the piddling 6.8:1 compression ratio!) but the engine will fire up in one or two kicks if the right drill is used.

Even though the car-type engine's crankshaft is set in-line with the frame and revolves at 90 degrees to the road wheels, to compensate for the shaft layout there is clearly a mechanical advantage in the design of the gearbox in view of the ease with which the engine can be turned over with the kickstarter, and the ease with which it starts.

Naturally the tiny carburettor must be tickled to raise the fuel level in the float-bowl and it is then better to kick the engine over a couple of times before turning on the coil ignition. Once this is done the engine will fire up easily and idle reliably; if a little on the 'lumpy' side. The idle speed is set on the low side and the engine thus tends to rock about in the frame a little, jumping sideways in its soft rubber mounts. The muffler is rigidly mounted at the rear of the plunger suspension, and this is where that short section of flexible exhaust piping just behind the two-into-one exhaust pipes comes into its own to compensate for the flexible mounting of the engine.

Typically, there is a small fracture in the flexible section, with some loss of exhaust gas and the inevitable mumbling through the single muffler when the throttle is backed off; there is also an occasional back-fire on long descents, particularly if the throttle is snapped off quickly, but the power delivery remains crisp overall.

The exhaust is currently on the loud side due to the loss of the packing material in the muffler. Originally an absorption-type muffler with few 'baffles', the straight-through pipe should be packed with a sound-absorbing material like fibreglass between its perforations and the muffler shell, but much of the material is clearly long gone, and a noisy exhaust naturally results. It must be said that the 'fruity' exhaust note is not really in keeping with the image of the relaxed tourer.

The front forks need some attention for the oil seals are not too good and most of the miniscule damping medium is long gone. Even from new, because of the almost un-damped front spring action, the forks tended to oscillate, which makes the front-end float along as the front wheel patters in harmony with the lightly-controlled springs.

The huge tyres are a bit squashy by modern standards, though there seems little doubt of their effectiveness in ironing out many of the roadways' small irregularities. They flex perceptibly and certainly absorb the initial road shock before the suspension comes into play, but they also move about alarmingly if the bike is pressed hard, a thing one assumes the gentlemanly Sunbeam rider would never stoop to do! The prop stand will dig in through left hand corners, the muffler on the right handers, but that is as far as one would want to go anyway, because the tyres are so soft and squashy that the bike simply does not like being pushed too hard into corners. The sports variant was fitted with the more 'standard'-sized BSA wheels and tyres for the rider who wanted the luxury of shaft drive but still wanted to ride the bike with some enthusiasm: those modifications to the S8 assuredly allowed for more spirited cornering.

It must be said, however, that handling is quite acceptable over most surfaces, including dirt, but the machine still feels a bit like a great green marshmallow. There is never a problem in pointing the bike where you want it to go and having it go there, but it feels soft and squashy

The fat, too-flexible tyres did not like to be treated this way, the bike cranked over so hard the prop stand was on the deck, the left footrest not far behind. When ridden with such enthusiasm, the tyres behaved like giant, black marshmallows, which badly affected handling. But most S7 owners would usually ride their machines in a much more 'civilised' manner.

as it does so. You could never say it handled in that taut, secure manner which was so typical of British motorcycles of the period, but again this would probably not concern the average Sunbeam owner.

Clutch action is light, and the usual Shaft Drive Principle applies when changing gear if the dreaded crunch is to be avoided, the engine-speed clutch taking its time to fully disengage. Changes are more leisurely than usual, but can be made quickly enough in view of the fact that it is, after all, a Luxury Tourer and not a sports model.

In spite of the choppy, un-damped plunger rear suspension with its limited movement, the machine is extremely comfortable over reasonable surfaces, and it takes most shallow pot-holes and bumps in its stride. The plunger suspension can be heard rather than felt, but the softly-sprung single saddle works beautifully to iron out whatever road shocks the tail-end allows to be transmitted to the frame. Single bumps are merely floated over, but a series of ripples or corrugations will cause the back of the machine to leap about, which is a little off-putting. In fact, if the machine is not absolutely square-on to the direction of travel, the whole bike can pivot around the steering head when the rear wheel clears the ground. Very exciting, and good fun sometimes, but not really up to scratch in modern terms and probably a little hazardous in heavy traffic.

Rear wheel hop on rough surfaces is a problem under very heavy braking, even though the large brakes are not particularly good, and there's sometimes an inevitable loud screeching from a rear tyre in torment. With reasonable care this does not occur, but emergency braking over rough road surfaces certainly renders the horn superfluous as an early warning device – a fat tyre in torment lets the whole world know all about it!

Perhaps the only serious criticism which could be levelled at the cantilever-sprung Sunbeam saddle is the fact that it has no control over the soft spring which provides this most comfortable ride. If the bike leaves the ground over a particularly savage bump the saddle spring takes up all the shock, but the bike returns to earth with a thump and pops the saddle back to the start of its travel and lifts the rider out of the seat. Over a series of slight corrugations, the saddle movement is a continuous series of dips and rises, dips and rises, which adds to the general impression of 'squishiness' in overall handling. It is quite acceptable, but strange nonetheless.

The engine is turbine-smooth at every speed above a fast idle, and has few peers in modern motorcycles – thanks, of course, to the rubber-mounted engine. Norton tried it on the 'Commando' models and couldn't get it to work effectively, but it is perfect on the Sunbeam and needs no attention.

There is no vibration to be felt anywhere from footrest to handlebar, or through the spring saddle, but a heel placed against the engine as the bike is being ridden shows that there is generous movement. The engine jumps about vigorously within its rubber restraints when the power is applied from rest and it moves about again when the throttle is backed off, which is probably the reason for the leak in the flexible section of exhaust pipe, and may do no favours to the worm drive assembly in the rear hub as well, but none of this is felt by the rider.

There is no trace of transmission snatch at any speed either, with no slack to be taken up and no loud clanks or grinds from engine or transmission, even if the throttle is backed off and suddenly opened up again.

The combination of smooth engine and very soft, comfortable springing makes for totally effortless long-distance touring, the job for which the bike was originally designed. Cruising speed seems best at around 100 km/h or a little above and it will run without effort to the occasional 115, but I naturally bowed to its advanced age and let it lope along completely fuss-free for most of the time on open roads. Acceleration is far better than I expected; indeed, it is fairly brisk, particularly in view of the reasonable power output of 28 BHP, which was quite on the pace for a full-size 500cc vertical twin back in the late 1940s/early 1950s. The fast Triumph T100 twin of the same era produced 30BHP, which hints at a similar power output from the Sunbeam had it been a full-sized five hundred.

The frame copes very well with the suspension limitations I've already outlined and the bike remains amongst the most stable machines ever on smooth highways. Perhaps it was the doughnut tyres, or the very low centre of gravity from the low-slung engine, but the bike tracks dead true and in fact does not want to go round corners on its own. It must be physically dropped into a corner and actually held down, for it gives the impression that it wants to stand up again.

Instrumentation is simple and confined

The ignition switch (with key in-situ) was placed out of sight on the side of the battery box, the ammeter in close attendance. It seemed an odd thing to do, but clearly would have worked well enough. Note the unenclosed drive shaft, and its universal joint, emerging from the gearbox to drive the worm-and-worm-wheel assembly contained within the base of the wheel hub.

to a speedo in the headlamp shell, with a red generator warning light and a green oil pressure light, with the main light switch and ammeter carried out of a rider's forward vision, on the outside of the large battery cover.

The Sunbeam is an oddity with its unusual engine sprouting a distributor where the carburettor would normally be, its twin exhausts exiting the side of the head one behind the other with the carburettor sandwiched between them, and its unusually low-slung engine. Its general air of obesity is such that one would guess its age as closer to a machine built in the 1930s, rather than one built some 15 years later.

But it remains an honest machine, with a very low-stressed engine and a standard of ease and comfort which is hard to fault even by the standards of modern frames and modern – for 'modern' read 'infinitely better' - suspension systems.

The Sunbeam engine was a design which *would* have been 'Modern 10 Years Hence' had it survived, and it just *might* have been modern even today; particularly had the S10 survived, with its much better, longer-lived bevel gear final drive and more powerful, cross-flow cylinder head design. Thankfully, there are still a very surprisingly large number of Sunbeam S7 and S8 machines in existence, with a large range of spare parts said to be readily available from specialist suppliers in England. This means that the Sunbeam shows many modern enthusiasts that there were some odd machines about in the post-war period and that not all progress is for the better, or to reinforce the thought that those that went on before laid many a foundation stone for those machines which were to inevitably follow, often more than half a century later.

This S8 Sunbeam employed the S7 OHC power-plant, with its shaft final drive, fitted into a duplex downtube frame and wheels from the twin-cylinder BSA models. It used the BSA telescopic front fork, with more 'normal'-sized tyres. It weighed some 15KG less than the S7, had a cast-alloy 'Art Deco' muffler — for better cornering clearance — and slightly higher compression ratio pistons. The bike was expected to be more 'acceptable' to more sporting riders, but this was not to be. It was a later iteration, for it appeared in 1949, just three years after the 'fat' S7 was launched.

TECH SPECS

Make: Sunbeam

Model: S7

Year of manufacture: 1953

Type:
All-alloy overhead camshaft in-line vertical twin, camshaft driven by chain, which is controlled by 'Weller' tensioner. Camshaft located slightly beneath the parallel, angled valves, with an off-set 'squish' combustion chamber, and semi-domed, four-ring pistons. One-piece 'Meehanite' cast-iron crankshaft is employed, with detachable-end RR56 alloy connecting rods fitted with thin-shell, indium/lead/bronze, steel-backed big-end slippers. The crankshaft supported on deep-groove ball main bearing at the front and large white-metal bush at the rear. Wet sump lubrication.

Bore x stroke: 70 x 63.6mm

Capacity: 487cc

Compression ratio: 6.8:1

Power @ rpm: 26BHP @ 5800rpm

Carburation:
Single Amal 276 carburettor, with wire mesh air filter.

Electrics:
Ignition is by Lucas coil, points and distributor; electrical generation by Lucas 60-watt 'pancake' generator, driven off the front of crankshaft.

Transmission:
Direct drive from crankshaft through flywheel-mounted, 7-inch, 6-spring single-plate clutch to an 'in-unit' four speed gearbox bolted to the large bell housing, with right foot change, one up, three down pattern. Final drive by exposed shaft to worm-and-worm wheel transmission in rear hub.

Gear ratios:
1st – 14.5:1; 2nd – 9.00:1;
3rd – 6.5:1; 4th – 5.3:1.

Frame, wheel, brakes, suspension:
Tubular steel frame, brazed into cast and forged lugs, with full-cradle engine support. To absorb any 'sideways' vibrations the engine is bolted to the frame at three points, the lower mounts contained within 'Silentbloc rubber snubbers, an upper mount at the rear of the engine is 'spring-mounted' to the top frame rail. Telescopic front forks are Sunbeam pattern, with one-way damping. Plunger-type, short-travel rear suspension. Single saddle hung by its nose with cantilever suspension medium. Rims are 16" diameter, laced by short spokes to 8" brakes front and rear, the wheels shod by 500 x 16 tyres, with ribbed front, block pattern rear.

Dimensions:
Length – 2180mm; Width – 790mm; Wheelbase – 1440mm; Ground Clearance – 110mm; Fuel tank capacity – 15.5 litres; Weight – 196kg.

Top speed (suggested): 130km/h.

Machine loaned by:
IVAN CASSON, Emu Plains, Sydney.

1938 Indian 'Chief'/ Yeats Sidecar

1200cc SIDE-VALVE VEE-TWIN

'Big oaks from little acorns grow' is a boring old saw, if an often entirely accurate one. This applies absolutely to many an enterprise, including many of the largest and most respected motorcycle factories on earth, many beginning their lives with a whimper from the humblest of beginnings. Some whimpers developed into a roar, others might have soldiered on for a while only to quietly disappear after a couple of years' hard graft, often through no fault of their own, while others became, for a time, minor manufacturers. In passing, it must be said that most of those smaller manufacturers were entirely happy with that, for they often wished for nothing more: simple economics, no doubt?

As I have mentioned many a time and oft, some of today's most fondly remembered motorcycles were the descendants of crude machines initially built in someone's garden shed, small engineering workshop, motor garage, or occasionally in the blacksmith's shop; often by earnest amateurs rather than highly skilled engineers.

The Indian motorcycle company in America provides a prime example of one of those early pioneers, from its inception way back in 1901, when its first machine was built, which looked like a strengthened bicycle frame into which a small, under-powered engine had been fitted, and the following year when just on 143 machines were built, to its sad and lingering departure in the mid-1950s — and apparently forever thereafter, for its name kept cropping up from the early 1950s to 1955 with the frightful British Brockhouse/Indian 250cc side-valve 'Scout', and a small Indian 'Papoose'. The latter was nothing more than a bright red Corgi fold-up ultra-lightweight bike which was a later copy of the tiny fold-up, un-sprung, 98cc two-stroke, one-gear 'Welbike' originally dropped by parachute during WWII to provide a crude form of mobility to paratroopers.

There are many who suggested that little Corgi disaster with the Indian 'Papoose' name on its small tank should have died at birth, or shortly thereafter. There was also a large crop the tiny mini-bikes which featured the Indian name on miniscule fuel tanks of machines built in Taiwan, Outer Mongolia, West Woop Woop and other unusual countries. In a further — if vain — bid to keep the name alive, there were also a number of 'Indian' motorcycles built in Italy by Italjet which were powered by 750cc twin-cylinder (British) Royal Enfield engines, or 500cc single-cylinder engines gleefully supplied by an ailing Velocette factory.

But it is a joy to see that the nonsense is now over and done with, because once more the proud old Indian name has risen from the ashes after being more or less dormant since 1953, when the last of the genuine Indian Chief motorcycles was made. Sixty years later, when the all-new machines reappeared, they were by now bigger, flasher and certainly better than ever, with all-new livery and lashings of heavy chrome plate. By the good graces of the Almighty, and the demands made by the later owners of the proud old name, who made their feeling about the design and overall appearance of the new machines known to Polaris Industries — who are the new owners — the small range of all-new motorcycles are instantly recognisable (even from a distance) as genuine Indian motorcycles.

If the latest Indian motorcycles appear to be ahead of the game, then there is nothing new about that, because the Indian marque was always in pioneering mode. For example, Indian improved upon the American Sylvester Roper's basic 'twist-grip' device — the entire handlebar revolved! — which Roper employed for his steam-powered two-wheeler in 1869. This was followed by Gottlieb Daimler's 1885 crude idea for a 'roll-on' front brake control on his odd wooden two-wheeler, along with the crude left-handlebar twist-grip on the little-known 1900 Singer 'Motorwheel'.

Indian upstaged them all when it adopted (if not actually *invented*) a much more worthy twist-grip *throttle* control in 1904. This device is, of course, in universal use on all motorcycles and motor scooters to this day. Indian later employed another twist-grip on the opposite handlebar to control the manual advance/retard ignition timing. Other manufacturers used the lawnmower-like throttle control levers for many years thereafter until, inevitably, they *all* converted to twist-grip throttle control, while retaining the little levers to control the ignition timing before auto-advance designs appeared. Indian might thus be able to stretch a point and be able to claim the credit for 'almost inventing' the motorcycle twist-grip.

Again, it was way back in 1914 that the Indian Electric brilliantly employed the first-ever electric starter, the device functioning as a 6-volt generator when the engine was running, but when the generator was 'earthed' by pressing a little button it would then revolve and function as a 12-volt electric motor to turn the engine over and fire it up. The machine also employed full springing, which was by no means standard practice in those days, with front and rear suspension by quarter-elliptic leaf-springs, the front by trailing link, the rear by an early type of swing-arm, while the spindly board track and dirt track Indian OHV racing machines which were campaigned in the early history of the marque were often fitted with *four-valve* cylinder heads – in particular the 1000cc overhead valve Vee-twins. While by no means the first to adopt multi-valve cylinder heads and/or overheard valves, Indian was again well ahead of the game.

To push the point even further, when nearly all of the fledging motorcycle manufacturers were using crude leather, or rubber and canvas, belt-drive from late in the 19th century until almost into the 1920s (mostly to the rear wheel, but more than one odd machine driving the *front* wheel!) the Indian factory adopted chain-drive from its miniscule power-plant to the rear wheel from not long after its earlier models did from Day One in 1901, which was certainly a logical step for a manufacturer of bicycles, but an advanced feature nonetheless. The other American giant, Harley-Davidson, was one of the many people who employed belt drive to power its first machine, which was built in 1904. While Indian was always a force to be reckoned with in domestic races in the very early days, Indian also won the 500cc Senior event on the Isle of Man in 1911, in fact filling the first three places, and won many, many events on the bumpy Brooklands banked circuit, including Bert le Vack's string of victories in 1921. Among a string of great finishes in other international events, Indian also took out the Belgian GP in 1923 with its 500cc side-valve single, the great Freddie Dixon in the saddle.

From 1927 until the early 1940s the factory manufactured the four-cylinder Ace motorcycle, incorporating the design into its own range as the *Indian* Ace in the early 1930s, the low-slung machine with its four in-line cylinders owing much to the Henderson in-line four which appeared some 15 years before the ACE design. Slightly earlier, in the years just prior to – and just after – World War I, Indian had become one of the largest motorcycle manufacturers in the world.

My first job in the motorcycle trade just after I had left school in the late 1940s was to unpack hundreds of crates of an enormous number of

The 1914, eight-valve 1000cc Indian Vee-twin dirt track racer. It featured no suspension, no gearbox and no brakes. The bike needed pedals to start the engine, the rider perched upon an unyielding, bullet-proof single saddle. Whether the riders of these machines were exceedingly brave or terminally dumb has thus far never been recorded.

Typical belt drive motorcycle, this is the 1910 Harley-Davidson single, built just four years after the first H-D machine was made. The long lever on the fuel tank was used to lower the small pulley on the drive belt, allowing the engine pulley to revolve without transmitting power to the belt. A simple type of 'clutch', perhaps, if a bit hard on the belt?

genuine Indian spare parts which the Sydney agents had acquired at auction, and I became very familiar indeed with the internals of these very substantial Vee-twin engines, even before I became fully aware of what the various parts actually were, where they went and what they actually *did*. Indian motorcycles had seen service as the 7/9HP machine in large numbers during WWI, while there were two quite successful models employed during WWII.

The smaller 741B Indian 'Scout' was a popular solo mount, in both 500cc and the rarer 750cc capacities it might be noted, while the much larger 344 model, the 1200c 'Chief' – introduced from 1922 as a *1000cc* machine, to be enlarged to its full 1200cc capacity in 1924 – was a great sidecar machine which saw duty after WWII as a police transport machine in New South Wales, until the sprung-hub Triumph, and later swing-arm BSA outfits, took over this job in the mid-1950s. Unhappily, they in turn were phased-out when the dreaded Morris Mini-Minor appeared on the scene a scant five years later, to almost destroy the entire motorcycle industry worldwide.

I owned one of those WWII Indian outfits for some three years when the police decided to unload them in favour of the later British vertical twins, the bike having had only two previous owners: the army and the police! I've had a soft spot for these big motorcycles ever since, for that punchy outfit served as a great family transport on a daily basis, took me to the Bathurst motorcycle road races at Easter three times and went on many, many an excursion to favourite beaches or family picnics into the scrub.

Little wonder that I jumped at the chance to ride Wal Maynard's **1938 1200cc, 340 Indian Chief** outfit when the opportunity presented itself and I enjoyed every (all too-brief) moment of it.

The Indian Chief was usually listed in its standard colour of bright red, perhaps in deference to the Native Red Indian, but one could specify any one of *seven* colours or combinations to special order in Dupont's nitrocellulose duco at the time. Among them was the very fetching Navajo Blue, with all-over black yet another variation on the 'standard' Indian Red. Wal's outfit is finished in the rarest colour of them all, a kind of No-Nonsense White, and it looks an absolute gem, the white paint finish well-offset by frame and some cycle parts in jet black.

Specifications of the Indian Chief twins hardly varied from that original 1922 model, with the later machines merely providing variations on the theme, with some regard to a more up-to-date appearance and more flowing lines. For example, the rear brake arm and exhaust system were contained *within* the confines of the early machine's heavy frame in the 1920s, but some 10 years later, pre-war models employed these systems *outside* the frame rails. There was probably a good reason for this simple modification (which may have applied initially for the so-

Impressive, narrow angle 1200cc Vee-twin, with oil pump outside the timing case, the oil fed from the tank directly above, as a small compartment in the front of the near-side fuel tank. The descending chromed rod is from the un-gated gearchange lever on the bike's right-hand side. It was mounted there because the Indian used a confusing, left-hand twist-grip.

called 'Civilian' plunger-sprung machines) but no one seems to know what it is.

The engine is a large, side-valve Vee-twin, its cast-iron cylinders disposed at 42 degrees with the large inlet and exhaust valves carried on the right-hand side of the cylinders, the valve heads uppermost in typical side-valve fashion. The exhaust valves are cleverly mounted well away from the cylinder bore to help overcome local distortion, with the exhaust ports very heavily finned in that area from 1940 onwards to provide optimum cooling for the 'army' models. The front exhaust port faces forward, the exhaust towards the rear, the two exhaust pipes converging just underneath the machine's large footboards, leading from there into a slim, noisy 'silencer'. Inlet valves are fitted as close to the cylinder bores as possible in the interest of a more ideal, if still tortuous, gas flow. Cylinder heads, with their heart-shaped combustion chambers, are very heavily finned and cast in light alloy.

Essentially a long-stroke design, with bore x stroke dimensions of 82.5 x 113mm, the lumpy-looking engine pokes out a handy 35BHP (26Kw) at a gentle 4000rpm, with an engine capacity of 1208cc. A single T-shaped inlet manifold is screwed in place between the two cylinders and has a 35mm Schebler carburettor bolted to it, facing directly outwards and carrying a simple air filter. This carburation had remained unaltered from 1932 to 1948, so could be said to have been efficient and entirely reliable. A major change to the army 344B models in WWII was to have a very large, heavily oiled air filter fitted.

Ignition is by Delco-Remy, well known to owners of early Holden cars. In fact, the Indian points assembly will fit early-model Holden cars without modification (and vice versa of course), the 6-volt coil-and-points system employing a neat two-lobe distributor, which sits atop an outer cast-iron casting containing the oil pump, the two units driven almost as one. The oil pump was redesigned for the 1938 season, the new double-plunger pump increasing the output by a staggering 100%, with new drillings to allow more lubricant to be supplied under high pressure to the big-end and main bearing assemblies and the cam-ground piston skirts. The smaller, 500cc and 750cc Scout models continued to employ the 1937 oil pump.

The distributor/oil pump housing is bolted directly to the alloy timing case, with oil taken from an in-built compartment at the front of the right-side fuel tank, the engine thus a dry sump design, the large-diameter oil feed and return pipes emerging from the base of the timing case, directly underneath the oil tank. Incidentally, the fuel tank is in two pieces, and can be detached separately. The chrome-plated instrument panel, which contains the ignition switch, ammeter and a large speedometer, was bolted to the top frame tube from 1938 on, so the panel remained in place if the two fuel tanks had to be removed for some odd reason. The speedometer is driven via a thick cable which is controlled from a small gear-case attached to the rear wheel hub.

The bolted-up big-end assembly is very wide, with the two long, spindly, one-piece connecting rods the so-called 'fork-and-blade' type like interlocking fingers and sharing a common crankpin, unlike many modern machines whose con-rods are side-by-side. The substantial big-end bearing is a multi-row caged roller type, very similar to the caged roller main bearings which support the engine's mainshafts, the latter being separate, detachable shafts which are screwed in and locked firmly in place in the centre of the massive flywheels.

Primary drive is via a four-row chain to a huge 15-plate clutch, with no fewer than 16 springs to keep it functioning for many trouble-free years with little attention, the top row of chain at the rear driving a small sprocket attached to an external pulley to drive the high-capacity 6-volt Autolite generator by a vee-belt. Might it look a little old-fashioned? Perhaps it might, but again it is very efficient, undoubtedly long-lived and trouble-free.

The entire clutch and primary drive assembly is contained within its own alloy chain case, with its own oil supply. The gearbox is a three-speed unit, with hand gear change by an un-gated lever on the right side of the fuel tank, the solo gearing ratios somewhat on the wide side from 10.955 to 1 for first gear, 6.238 to 1 second gear and top gear of 4.437 to 1. Sidecar gearing was not much lower, from 11.5 to 1 in first gear, 6.54 to 1 in second gear and 4.65 to 1 in top. The gear lever was moved forward for lower gears and back again to change into the higher ratios. Some idea of the machine's great pulling power may be gleaned from the sidecar's high top gear ratio, the large 450 x 18" tyres and machine's dry weight of 220kg solo. The overall weight with the large sidecar attached would raise that weight quite considerably.

I can personally vouch for the grunt of an Indian Chief engine with my bike sometimes carrying a bunch of picnic gear, two people in the sidecar and myself on the bike, because we covered many hundreds of miles on my old 344 outfit from late 1954 to 1956-odd, while it flew over the cuntryside, uphill and downhill, with consummate ease. Vibrated a bit, I might say, and was more than a little noisy, but it exhibited low-speed pulling power like you wouldn't believe!

The wheels are interchangeable, which is handier than you might think, but the large brakes always seemed to be more ornamental than functional and hark back to a time when there was plenty of time to stop and/or space in which to manoeuvre. They work well enough for most situations, and in fact can be locked if you try hard enough: I suggest the bike's weight may well be a contributing factor to its longer-than-normal stopping distances.

My outfit had plunger rear suspension which allowed for about 70mm of rear wheel movement, with front suspension handled by leading-link forks with a multi-leaf quarter-elliptic spring carried horizontally over the top of the front mudguard. That very unusual front fork was the type used by Indian for more than 40 years. Plunger rear suspension was originally listed for 'civilian' use from 1940 until the last Chief was built in 1953 and was supplied in particular to the 'Australia Only' **344** outfits which were intended for army use. Incidentally, the similar, **340B** model Indian was built initially for the French markets, to have the sidecar fitted onto the right-hand side.

Maynard's 1938 Chief has no rear suspension but, like my later Indian, employed a large pan-saddle which pivoted from its nose, with a single, spring-loaded pillar supporting it to provide more than a (personally measured) 110mm of movement to the saddle, and with it a surprisingly smooth and comfortable ride, and over almost every surface. Of course, it employed the same type of leaf-sprung, leading-link front forks as the ex-army 344.

I had converted the throttle and ignition timing cables on my Indian to allow for the

With both feet off the ground, 600cc per cylinder and no valve lifter – plus the 'short dwell' and 'long dwell' of the narrow-angle Vee cylinders – it took every bit of weight I had to fire the engine up. My passenger is assisting with the left-hand twist-grip. Naturally, I had retarded the ignition timing by rolling off the right-hand twist-grip control.

throttle control to be on the (correct) right-hand side of the handlebars, with the advance-retard control on the left, because the original Indian throttle control was on the left handlebar. It was there, it has been said, to allow a police pursuit rider to hod the throttle open with his left hand, so he could fire his revolver at the miscreant in front with his right hand!

Maynard's 1938 model still had the twist-grip throttle control on the left side, which of course carried with it some considerable inconvenience, to say the least! That was bad enough, but the foot-operated clutch had also been altered by someone so that it worked as the Harley-Davidson did, i.e. to engage the clutch you would move the heel-toe pedal forwards and rock it back to disengage the clutch again. Wal's was of course exactly the reverse!

Oh, it's easy enough to alter the controls, for the wires controlling the carburettor and manual spark advance were both piano wire and could be detached and swapped around in about 10 minutes flat. The worm clutch release arm was vertical in the one o'clock position on one machine and five o'clock on the other – the Indian at one o'clock – so that was just as easy to alter.

What I found strange, and it amazes me to this day, is that I hadn't ridden an Indian outfit since mine was pinched more than 50 years before and I was riding Wal's machine as if it was my own but with the major controls exactly the wrong way around! It was bad enough rolling the throttle off to be greeted with bangs and back-fires from a suddenly retarded ignition timing, but even worse to shudder to a stop with the clutch still engaged while the toes on my left foot pointed to the ceiling.

Wal didn't say much but he looked at me a bit sideways now and again. He was firmly ensconced in the sidecar for some time and he wasn't about to go anywhere without me. Or vice versa, and I don't blame him for that. I didn't have any trouble with the gear change, which was still (thankfully!) forward for first, then back for second and top, because my outfit had the gear lever on the right side as well, which had meant changing gears across the tank if in a hurry or casually buttoning-off and using the one hand for both jobs if the traffic was heavy. Unlike the Harley-Davidson gear-change, which is on the other side – and, happily, employs a right-hand twist-grip – there is no gear-gate on the Indian, but there is never any question about missed gear-changes. Unless you take your time and are careful over selecting gear, up or down, everyone within earshot knows all about it!

It was much more manageable with both hands on the tiller, unless giving hand signals or changing gear. If you were so inclined you could look down at the forks working, which they did quite well, but there was no damping of any kind – either friction or hydraulic – so the leaf spring was a bit firm and needed a fair nudge before it would perform its natural office.

The lack of rear suspension only became noticeable when braking over choppy surfaces, because the sprung saddle absorbed bumps and other irregularities with remarkable ease. Not perhaps as infinitely variable as a good swing-arm with hydraulic or gas-controlled spring units, but still better than some which had suspension a bit on the firm side and topped by a too-firm dual-seat.

As we have noted, the sidecar ratios are slightly

different from the solo ratios quoted but not by very much, the lower ratio 11.5:1, with top gear still high at 4.65:1. The bike pulled this without the slightest fuss, with the usual tendency to drive the bike round the chair with the power on, and the other way around when you buttoned-off again. There's nothing new about that.

It's a rare Yeates sidecar, with long leaf springs to allow the body to float on its own suspension, while the sidecar wheel is sprung independent of the sidecar body's suspension upon the Yeates patented C-spring to help overcome the transmission of road shocks from the sidecar wheel to the bike. Or, more specifically, the handlebars! One reason for handlebar 'shimmy' is simply because sidecar wheel shock moves the bike from the vertical plane, this movement and the accompanying leverage resulting in the handlebars moving about to compensate almost automatically.

For all that, the bike handles quite well in a lumpy sort of way, the sidecar trail angle allowing for quite light steering effort. Ideally, the sidecar was mounted to the bike at four points: two at the rear, one in the centre and one on the front, all with heavy-duty bolts and nuts and all with rubber bushes to absorb road shock and provide the necessary flexibility for cornering.

As usual, the engine isn't terribly smooth and the exhaust is a bit hearty, but there has always been something about the feel of a big punchy Vee-twin which is endearing in a rough-and-tumble way ... a very good reason for the great success of Vee-twins from very nearly the turn of the century. Ask any owner of a Harley, Ducati, Moto-Guzzi, Moto Morini or other Classic – and not-so-classic – Vee-twin and they will very quickly tell you all about it.

The sidecar is more comfortable than it looks, the long leaf springs which support the body and the C-spring for the sidecar wheel soaking up the worst of road shocks surprisingly well. There is no attempt at either hydraulic or gas damping for the suspension on the sidecar – or the bike as well, for that matter – and it all looks rather crude by modern standards, but the ride, either as driver or passenger, is great and a thrill a minute!

True, it's more than a little draughty in

Away at last, after finally coming to grips with the 'wrong-way' clutch operation and the left-hand twist-grip. Happily, I had explained it all to the owner – sitting in the sidecar with eyes closed and shaking his head slowly – but I had road-tested a couple of his machines prior to this, so I trust he was happy enough.

the chair and you'd be beyond the pale if you couldn't hear the thumpy old engine at work, but it's great fun to take a spin in the sidecar for a change. I don't know that I liked it all that much, for one zips along without much control over what's happening to the vehicle, and that was never my idea of having a good time on a motorcycle.

However, I did have a good time on Wal's Indian Chief, though it would have been better, and less dramatic, if the throttle control was on the right-hand side of the handlebar, and the foot clutch control the other way around!

Incidentally, the sidecar has a large compartment sticking rudely from the rear of the body, and of course I wanted to know what it was there for. Wal informs me it was there to carry a small scale used by mounted traffic inspectors, who would whip it out at roadside checks and place it under a truck wheel to check its laden weight. Apparently, the sidecars were in very heavy use at the time, and this was a special-order sidecar body designed for local government. You can understand a motorcycle surviving for some 50 years, but a locally made sidecar is something else again, particularly a very rare one like this.

As we've seen, the year 1953 saw the end of the Indian as we knew it, the name bought by the British Brockhouse corporation, who proceeded to launch their single-cylinder side-valve-engine 250cc Indian Brave in 1953 to celebrate the fact. I was still working at Sydney's Indian distributorship at the time and was forced to ride one to the registry office for some ill-advised customer who thought the name still meant something. As we have noted, Royal Enfield was yet another engine fitted to the so-called Indian, as the Velocette was, and the machines all employed modern swing-arm frames and telescopic forks, but the mystique of the Big Indian Chief had unhappily vanished.

The reason for these odd engines being employed as 'Indian' motorcycles was that the former race-car driver, journalist and publisher Floyd Clymer tried to resurrect the name by fitting the Royal Enfield or Velocette engines into a modern frame and applying an Indian transfer to the petrol tank. This pleased neither the Royal Enfield, Velocette nor Indian fanciers, so the bikes were not successful. Let us not mention again the last rash of 'Indian' (ugh!) motorcycles, the rash of mini-bikes which came from Taiwan with the once-proud name on their minuscule tanks, except to say what a pity that all was.

There are many examples of the proud old Indian warrior to be seen here and there, which should please us all, if only to show a new breed of motorcyclists just how one of the other big, brash and – in its time – unbeatable American motorcycles was built.

The new Indian machines now seem certain to awaken a whole new breed of motorcyclists to what the great and proud Indian name was all about when Indian was King all those long, long years ago.

TECH SPECS

Make: Indian

Model: Chief

Year of manufacture: 1938

Type:
Side-valve 42-degree Vee-twin. Cast iron cylinders, with specially sited inlet and exhaust ports. Detachable aluminium alloy cylinder heads. Bolted-up crank and I-section connecting rods, with 'fork-and-blade' configuration, caged roller big end and caged roller main bearings. Dry sump lubrication, with oil contained in a right-side compartment of fuel tank.

Bore x stroke: 82.5mm x 114.30mm

Capacity: 1208cc

Power @ rpm:
35BHP (23Kw) @ 4000rpm

Carburation:
Through $1^{3}/_{8}$" bore Schebler carburettor, via small oil-and-mesh air filter, to T-shaped inlet manifold screwed into ports between Vee-cylinders.

Primary transmission:
By four-row roller chain through 15-plate heavy-duty clutch in oil-bath, within cast-alloy chaincase, to three-speed hand-change gearbox operated by 'un-gated' hand lever on right side of fuel tank. Forward for first gear, then rearwards for others.

Gear ratios (solo):
1st – 10.955:1; 2nd – 6.238:1; 3rd – 4.437:1.

Gear ratios (sidecar):
1st – 11.5:1; 2nd – 6.54:1; 3rd – 4.65:1.

Electrics:
Delco-Remy ignition by distributor, coil and points. Separate, heavy-duty Autolite 6-volt generator, driven by single-row internal gear from primary chain attached to pulley and v-belt.

Frame, suspension, wheels, brakes:
Heavy gauge tubular-steel frame, with full cradle engine support. Front suspension by leading-link, quarter-elliptic leaf spring, no rear suspension, but large pan-saddle supported upon a sprung pillar, with 110mm movement. Interchangeable 18" wheels, with 450 x 18 block pattern tyres front and rear: 8" drum brakes front and rear.

Weight (solo): 218kg (480lb)

Sidecar: Australian-built 'Yeates' all-steel sidecar, the body mounted on two full-length leaf springs, with patented 'C-spring', long-travel sidecar-wheel suspension.

Machine loaned by:
WAL MAYNARD, Melbourne, Australia.

1953 BSA A10 'Golden Flash'

650cc OHV VERTICAL TWIN

The 650cc overhead valve vertical twin **A10 BSA 'Golden Flash'** – or Golden Flush as some owners of other machines so rudely called it – was not so much a Classic Motorcycle as a Classic example of the type of twin-cylinder motorcycle which was one of the bread-and-butter machines which kept the industry afloat in the immediate post-war years, and into the 1970s as well. The BSA twin was by no means the first of its type, for vertical twin motorcycle engines existed in Belgium and France just prior to the 1914–1918 war – the 1920, 500cc side-valve vertical twin French Bleriot, with disc wheels, a crude type of telescopic front forks and some with rear suspension, for example – but it was typical of the models which the eager motorcyclist of the first 20 years after WWII wanted, indeed demanded. The A10 BSA was at once sturdy and reliable, with an open road, 100mph performance which was far more than many a rider would ever need, particularly in view of the fairly simple plunger-type rear suspension system it initially employed, allied to limited cornering clearance and tyres which, we were to learn some years later, certainly left a lot to be desired.

Bert Hopwood, one of the two men who helped Edward Turner turn the sow's ear that was the *prototype* 1937 Speed Twin Triumph into a genuine silk purse, is credited with designing much of the 'new' 650cc BSA twin, which was a greatly re-worked version of the 500cc A7 twin introduced a few years earlier. But the vertical-twin BSA designs had their Genesis as far back as 1933, when the great British motorcycle designer Val Page introduced the first 650cc, 6/1 model Triumph to the market-place. That first vertical-twin **Triumph** employed a *semi*-wet sump (the oil was carried in a special compartment within the crankcase castings) and exposed overhead valve gear, the primary drive by helical gears, which meant that the engine actually revolved backwards in relation to the road wheels, with the rearward-placed camshaft driven by gear at the base of the cast iron cylinder barrel. The Triumph had its hand-change gearbox bolted directly to the flat face at the rear of the crankcase castings, the geared primary drive of course needing no adjustment.

The post-war 650cc BSA twin's cast-iron cylinder barrel and head looked very similar to the 6/1 Triumph, although the overhead valve gear was, of course, fully enclosed within a large, one-piece alloy cover, while the BSA's single camshaft was in the same position as the Triumph 6/1 machine; at the rear of the base of the barrel. The BSA gearbox was bolted directly to the flat surface of the alloy crankcase casting in the same manner as the earlier Triumph, but the BSA primary drive differed radically from

In 1909 Louis Bleriot became the first man to fly an aircraft across the channel from France to England, but he remains almost totally unknown for the motorcycles he made. This is a 500cc side-valve vertical twin, with two-speed gearbox and belt drive, first thought of in 1909 and built from 1920–23. It produced 8BHP and was capable of a speed of 80km/h. Of the several hundred which were built, there are said to be just 12 survivors.

the earlier machine in employing a duplex ⅜" x ⁷⁄₃₂" chain, with a slipper tensioner fitted beneath the alloy primary-drive cover to allow for simple primary chain adjustment. There were other similarities to the earlier twin-cylinder *Triumph* engine, including the 650cc BSA twin employing the same 70 x 84mm bore stroke as the earlier 6/1 Triumph. Perhaps this should come as no surprise because Hopwood's boss in the design office in 1946 at BSA, when the first *500cc* twin was designed, and later when the all-new 650cc A10 was being developed, was a quiet, shy gentleman called *Val Page!*

Clearly, there can't be much doubt that Page had more than a little input into the design of the new 650cc twin. Incidentally, the men knew one another well from a much earlier time, because Page was also Hopwood's boss with Ariel in the 1920s, and in the 1930s with the Triumph *marque*.

The vertical twin BSA grew to 650cc in late 1950, probably in answer to the dowdy-looking Battleship Grey 650cc 'American Market' Triumph Thunderbird, which arrived in Australia earlier in the same year and had become immediately popular. The new 650cc BSA machine bore an external appearance not unlike the earlier 500cc machine, but it was in fact a very different engine; and not only in its engine capacity. The all-new BSA vertical twin was to retain the same engine size through some subtle design evolutions which saw both Sports and Super Sports variants and ended with the viciously fast 'Rocket Gold Star' twin (the highly tuned engine slotting into the single-cylinder *Gold Star* frame) until finally a smoother-profiled, all-new unit-construction model – the A65 – arrived in 1963. The later design allowed the engine to be built in one piece with its primary transmission and gearbox, which was less expensive to make, vibrated less, was freer of oil leaks and also allowed for the bonus of a somewhat higher performance.

Prior to the new A65, the 650cc A10 power-plant remained entirely recognisable, even after the more modern swing-arm rear suspension was adopted very late in 1953, the so-called BSA Golden Flash – some were finished in gleaming chrome and black but were still referred to as Gold Flash – the machine used by the New South Wales Police as a sometime solo mount and a frequent sidecar combination. In fact, it was only the introduction of the Mini-Minor which prompted the local police to abandon the BSA and locally built *Murphy*, or *Dusting*, sidecar for station-to-station transport: just for the record, that little roller-skate of a car helped to ring the death knell for motorcycling almost everywhere on earth in the late 1950s and early 1960s.

The BSA Golden Flash motorcycle provides a prime example of the type of twin-cylinder machine which flourished in those years after WWII. Like many of the similar, twin-cylinder machines which flashed about the Nation's roads in those days, this model is still to be seen on every nation's roads to this day, while the much earlier post-war motorcycle, which are still to be seen, are usually kept in near-showroom condition.

The subject of this test, a **1953 A10/BSA** belonging to Col Brenchley, is all that and more. In fact, thanks to the more modern stove enamelling and plating techniques, the overall finish of the sparkling old Beeza is probably better than it was when it was brand new! Understandably, the gleaming, chrome-bright machine has won many local awards.

Typical of its era, the Golden Flash is powered by the 70 x 84mm, long-stroke, pushrod-operated overhead-valve engine we have already noted, with the primary drive by its duplex chain to a separate four-speed gearbox. The chain is enclosed within an oil-tight, polished aluminium chaincase on the machine's left side, with the lower run of chain only just immersed in oil. As usual with British bikes of that era, the clutch is contained within the same case but is essentially a dry component, although *damp* might be a better word. This could easily be proven by an incautious owner who would bring about instant, calamitous clutch slip if the chain-case was over-filled during normal service.

The BSA engine was referred to as a *semi-unit construction type* because the gearbox was bolted rigidly to the flat face at the rear of the crankcase castings – as we noted with Page's 6/1 Triumph – instead of being mounted separately on special brackets behind the engine, like most of its contemporaries. Two additional bolts lock the gearbox to the frame as well, the essential primary chain adjustment made to the slipper tensioner by an external grubscrew under the chaincase which brought pressure to bear upon a slightly curved, spring-loaded tensioner.

Naturally, unlike most current designs, the gearbox carries its own oil supply, as does the primary case. In the design of the dry sump engine – again unlike modern motorcycles – the oil is carried in a separate container attached to the frame just underneath and at the back of the fuel tank. The single camshaft at the base of the barrel is gear-driven inside an 'inner' timing case, which drives another gear for the magneto. The highly polished outer timing case contains a tiny, 8mm x 3mm chain which drives the forward-mounted 6-volt generator, which supplies current to the lead/acid battery.

The Gold Flash cylinder head is cast iron, with an integral inlet manifold, unlike the earlier, 500cc A7's detachable, aluminium-alloy inlet manifold. A single AMAL carburettor is used; the pre-Monobloc type with a fuel-raising 'tickler' on the separate float bowl. Sometimes an 'induction bias' occurred with 650cc BSA twins, which resulted in a slightly greater charge being fed into one or the other of the two cylinders – probably due to an un-square mounting face which pointed the carburettor ever-so-slightly more towards one pot than the other. Strangely, there was a BSA parts-listed, slightly tapered 'anti-bias' gasket available which could be fitted to overcome this problem!

Apart from this quirk (which never manifested itself with any of the other British vertical twins) this staunch power-plant provided a solid and reliable power delivery which could see a BSA twin cover prodigious distances at high average speeds without much more than the simplest of routine maintenance.

The bottom half of the engine was very sturdy, with a special high carbon/nickel forged steel crankshaft employing a bolted-on central flywheel with additional bob-weights and split, RR56 alloy connecting rods with detachable end-caps and steel-backed lead/bronze/indium slipper bearings. The unusual, concave-topped, three-ring alloy pistons fitted to the earlier examples bore a surprisingly low compression of just 6.5:1, which was raised in later models to 7.2:1 but were still quite low by modern standards. A large roller bearing was mounted on the drive side, while the more lightly stressed timing side crankshaft was supported upon a large, metal backed, white-metal bush in similar fashion to the earlier A7. This large bush was quite long lived, but needed to be replaced on occasion, even though it was fed the first breath of fresh, clean oil from the gear-driven, high-capacity pump mounted right alongside it.

An advantage of the semi-unit construction design, and the basically simple overhead valve layout, lies in the ease with which any reasonable owner can carry out servicing and most repair jobs without removing the engine from the frame – an advantage not always enjoyed by owners of more complex, modern motorcycles.

The power-plant was bolted into a full duplex-down-tube frame with telescopic front forks and the dated plunger rear suspension which, on this particular model, was almost at the end of its run. The A10 BSA employed telescopic front forks which appeared to be identical to the smaller A7 model, but in fact they allowed an extra 1 inch (25mm) of travel. The new swing-arm rear suspension, in such universal use today, was first adopted on the Golden Flash in late 1953 as a precursor to what was left of the model's production run. The earlier, two-way damped front forks with their slightly longer travel remained and they well augmented the infinitely better rear suspension adopted on later models.

A very neat nacelle on the test machine contains the simple Smiths speedo, light-switch/ammeter combination which was all one ever had – or needed! – on machines of that era. Blinkers were not used, of course, though their great boon to safety is currently unarguable, and most riders could manage to find neutral gear without the aid of a little green light in those days of yore!

The short-travel plunger rear suspension was used on several British machines from the immediate pre-war era to the early 1950s, even though some makes – notably Royal Enfield, AJS and Matchless – adopted swing-arm rear suspension on some models from as early as 1949: Royal Enfield was the first roadster motorcycle to adopt this now-universal rear suspension system, its 350cc (and later 500cc) Bullet singles and vertical-twins employing the system from late in 1948. The major advantage of the short-travel, un-damped plunger suspension lies in keeping the drive chain in an almost constant tension. Unless the pivot-point for the later swing-arm (or pivoting-fork, as it is sometimes called) rear suspension is co-axial with the rear drive sprocket – achieved by mounting the pivot directly opposite the centre of the sprocket – the

This is the BSA plunger rear suspension, very popular for many machines in the early 1950s, even though such machines as Royal Enfield and the AJS/Matchless duo had adopted the superior swing-arm rear suspension. It allowed about 75mm of undamped movement, and was easier on rear chains, for it followed virtually no arc as it moved and made it much easier to adjust the drive chain correctly.

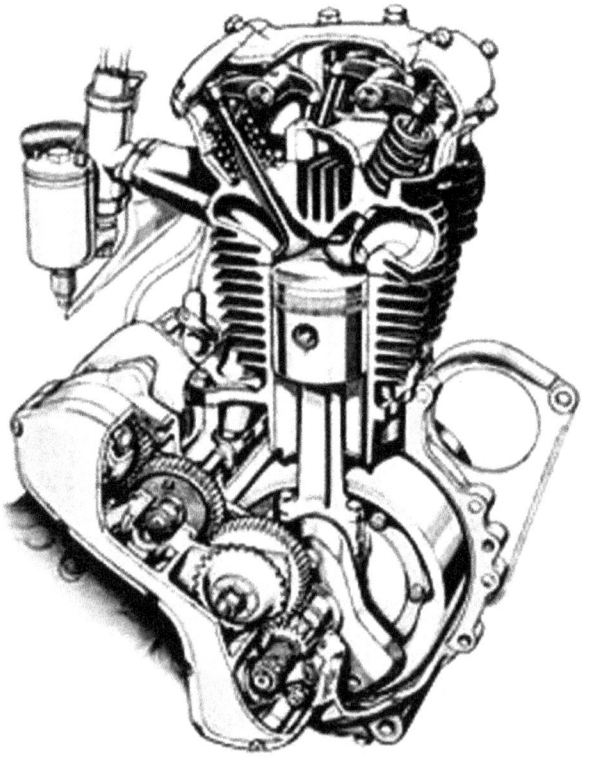

Cutaway drawing of the BSA power-plant. Note the oil pump's worm drive on the end of the shaft supporting the crank's half-time pinion, which in turn drives an intermediate gear. This gear drives the camshaft gear which, in turn, drives the magneto gear. The bracket on the front of the crankcase supports the 6-volt generator, which is driven by a small 8mm x 5mm chain, itself driven by the narrow sprocket attached to the face of the intermediate gear.

rear wheel travel naturally follows an arc, with a subsequent dramatic variation in chain tension throughout its travel. This almost inevitably results in a slightly shorter chain life.

In comparison, little more than straight up-and-down movement of about 75mm is allowed with the older plunger system, so the rear chain tension remains reasonably constant, although the bonus in the later, more efficient swing-arm rear suspension allows for almost 110mm of rear wheel travel, with much better comfort and far better handling than the plunger rear suspension could ever provide.

On smooth road surfaces the Golden Flash handles well and is comfortable enough, but the limited travel of the rear suspension on uneven surfaces can all too often make for a choppy ride because of the un-damped springs and a too-firm, unyielding dual-seat; initially, most plunger rear suspension systems were at their best when augmented by the nigh-universal, much softer spring-mounted single saddle to take the edge off bumps and potholes.

However, the machine does not handle well by modern standards when ridden briskly over rough surfaces – and again this is due almost entirely to the grease-lubricated rear suspension. The rear axle is located by a pair of springs which are enclosed within smart steel sleeves, and are located above and below each side of the axle, where they can sometimes allow the rear wheel to get out of kilter with the front end as it moves through its near-75mm of travel. This happens because the spring tensions or frictional loadings may not be a 'constant', which could then cause one side of the plunger system to move slightly further than the other, cocking the wheel to one side and altering its 'geometry' in relation to the front wheel.

The bike will drop readily into corners, though the BSA centre-stand does not allow it to be dropped over too far, even when there is plenty of daylight under the footrests. It will track very securely, although a dip in the road or an unexpected hole will catch the rear wheel on full bump, sometimes resulting in a sharp tug at the handlebars, with a resultant 'weaving'. It can be a bit unsettling, but is not a dangerous trait once a rider knows of this and gets used to its effects on handling. Nipping up the friction-controlled steering damper when riding at speed could help the situation, but it could be ever-present on rough, undulating roads when riding at high speeds.

I must say I had almost forgotten this trick and it is only by making this sort of comparison that one can see how much better the swing-arm rear set-up really is – it is not yet perfect, but the pivoting-fork suspension in current use is far more acceptable and allows safer handling at most speeds this side of the ridiculous. By contrast, the A10's long, slow-travel BSA front forks proved to be first-rate in ironing out most road shocks, and are certainly on a par with the best in current use, but the old twin-cylinder BSA trait of heaviness at the steering head is still evident. It's hardly serious, but the bike tends to teeter on the centre of the tyre tread when upright and at speed, which is a mite disconcerting. Somebody once referred to this as the 'invisible cannonball syndrome', as though a couple of these unseen projectiles were attached by ropes to the steering head where they flop about willy-nilly. Oddly, it is also noticeable at slow speeds in heavy traffic. In other words, the A10's steering was always 'heavier' than most.

But this syndrome is by no means unknown on some of today's much vaunted motorcycles, in particular the first Z1R Kawasaki models and the pre-1975 BMW short-wheelbase, flat-twin 750s, so it may not qualify as a serious fault – at least not by direct comparison with machines which should not continue to suffer from this near century-old quirk!

Speaking of comparisons between the old and new, for those of you who may find something faintly familiar about the A10/BSA, might I draw your attention to the first of the vertical-twin Kawasaki W1 machines? Here is an engine (indeed, one could argue, almost an entire motorcycle!) which is a dead-ringer for the pre-unit BSA, right down to similar, external oil lines from overhead valve rocker gear and the separate gearbox, with the earlier model's gear lever still on the (British) right side, the rear brake pedal of course on the left. It was, in fact, a copy of the later Road Rocket sports model. At least they had the decency to wait until BSA's new unit construction engine appeared in 1963 – but little attempt was made to disguise the origins of the model. Though the engine differed in the bottom-end (notably by the adoption of a ball bearing on the timing side crankshaft, where the BSA employed the steel-backed white metal bush) and a more bulbous timing case, the castings were almost identical, if not, at the very least, remarkably similar. As just two examples, it has been suggested that the A10/Road Rocket BSA rocker box gaskets and the small cover-plate gasket on the BSA gearbox will fit the later Kawasaki machine perfectly!

The later model A10, with swing-arm rear suspension. It was a neat and trim machine and out-handled the plunger-sprung models. But some of the longer travel and greater comfort of this superior rear suspension system was often negated by fitting a too-firm dual-seat.

This, obviously, is the Japanese Kawasaki 650, which was clearly outwardly almost identical to the BSA. While we can't see the different bore/stroke ratios, a major difference is the wider base of the timing case, for the Japanese bike employed a small ball bearing on the timing side mainshaft, replacing the BSAs small white metal bush

As a matter of interest, the Japanese factory tried for a time to deny that the Kawasaki was a direct pinch from the later, swing-arm BSA twins, but it doesn't take a very sharp eye to see that they are (almost) like two peas in a pod. In fact, the Kawasaki W1 was originally a **Meguro** X650, the smaller Japanese manufacturer swallowed up by Kawasaki Aircraft Corporation in around 1960 when Meguro was in financial difficulties. The Kawasaki W1 bore x stroke measurements differed from the BSA for they were 74 x 72mm, whereas the BSA 650 – as we have seen -- was a long stroke engine of 70 x 84mm dimensions, but the two power-plants – both engine and gearbox – remained *outwardly* almost identical, so the parentage cannot readily be denied.

It is interesting to note, however, that Meguro had been *legally* building 500cc vertical twin BSA A7 clones since 1954 after the company was granted a (very) limited licence by the British factory to make the machines in Japan, and in 1957 the engines were increased in capacity to 650cc, so perhaps – just perhaps – Kawasaki could be excused for claiming the W1 as a Kawasaki motorcycle in its own right??

The Kawasaki machines were fairly popular in their day, the Police force in Victoria using a fleet of 650cc W1 Kawasaki motorcycles for daily traffic control and as early pursuit motorcycles for some years before they adopted the all-white CB750 Honda Highway Patrol motorcycles not long after the big CB750 was introduced in 1968.

The city Council also used the Kawasaki W1 for some years thereafter, often as traffic control as well as checking for parking infringements and the like.

But to return to BSA after that brief (and hopefully historical) diversion, the A10s acceleration is reasonably brisk, even though the single carb is small and the 35 BHP power output very modest by today's standards. The bike can be punted along in top gear from as low as an indicated 25 mph without sign of distress. This is a pointer to the fact that the essentially 'old-fashioned', long-stroke, low-revving engine is very lightly stressed; a fact proved by the very high mileages between simple servicing and the infrequency of major overhauls. Once in top gear the engine is happy to pull like a train, but it will only do so on small throttle openings. Open the throttle with anything like reckless abandon at low engine speeds and you get some induction roar with hissing accompaniment (that's because of the lack of air filtration) and some loud, unhappy pinking sounds from an engine clearly in distress.

But the gearbox is, as ever with British motorcycles, light in action and very fast. There's no excuse for not changing to a lower gear when necessary. Clutch action is also very light, again a feature of the old Brits, and this makes changing up or down a joy, so there is little excuse for not using the gearbox as it should be used.

Like many models before it as well as a great many today, the box grates into first gear, but the only resistance felt on all other changes is from the selector springs and the movement of the gear selector cam-plate. Unlike modern machines, neutral must be selected before the engine can be kicked over, and of course no starter motor is fitted.

Mirrors were not required by law when this machine was new, and neither were stoplights – or blinker lights – and the lack of them makes riding in traffic a pretty nervous business. You can't tell who is breathing down your neck, and you can't tell where they are, or if they are in (too) close attendance! But rear vision mirrors and after-market stop-light switches were always available to owners of those earlier machines as 'after-market' accessories, so a prudent owner was usually well-advised to fit both of those essential safety aids: most of them did just that!

Starting the bike took me back to years ago, for the old Amal carburettor, with its separate float bowl and fuel-raising 'tickler', needed to be flooded to provide juice for the long kick, and 325cc of each cylinder is not as easy to punt over as it once was. Perhaps the Golden Flash BSA is getting a bit old for that sort of thing. But then, aren't we all!

The donk needed several kicks to bring it to life, and it then idled in the typically lumpy way of that period. Coming onto the carburettor needle as we moved off at about one third throttle made for some transmission snatch, but this could be easily tuned out by carefully adjusting the idle mixture screw (which I did) if it proved to be an annoyance; again, reminiscent of the simple type of carburettor which was used at that time.

Even with the simple 'head steady' nipped up – a device, which was a flattened, metal strap bolted from the cylinder head to the front down-tube – vibration was, of course, part of the engine design, as it always was in vertical twins at the time. There is no way it could be described as unpleasant; rather was it a sign of an honest engine working at its task, the essential changes of engine masses inevitably resulting in the transferring of some minor shock loads to frame and rider. There were some machines which made a feature of heavy vibration, but the BSA twin, at its best, was not one of these. A latter-day, weighted, contra-rotating shaft would have easily overcome that problem. Some modern motorcycle designers go to great pains to mask the inherent vibration by building those counter-weighted shafts which revolve in odd directions, but the initial vibrations are still there, masked by other vibrations which are *said* to cancel them out (?).

Perhaps it would have been nice to have enjoyed this feature on the early British twins but it was apparently deemed unnecessary. Or perhaps they simply didn't think of it?

Incidentally, a simple investigation of the efficacy of that BSA/A10 head-steady in transmitting engine vibrations to the machine's frame could easily be attained by removing the device and riding the bike without it. In no time at all one would soon come to understand just what engine vibration truly was!

The Flash BSA is a perfect example of a mid-1950s large-capacity British vertical twin, the type of machine which is often much-maligned by modern riders who have perhaps never seen one of them, and would certainly never have ridden one.

It would be a surprise to many modern-day riders to find out that the drum brakes are brilliant; the alloy-back plate, 8-inch (200mm) front brake in particular. The wide shoes, quick-opening cam and long fulcrum lever certainly help, and so too does the bike's comparative light weight. All-up, the 650cc BSA weighs in at an acceptable 408lb, or just on 185.5kg. That front anchor is very powerful and progressive in action, with little hand pressure required. The 175 mm rear drum is equally efficient, and both brakes enjoy the priceless boon of being just as effective in the rain as they are in the dry, which is not always the case with 'modern' disc brakes.

The virtues of the BSA twin have been spelled out and so too have its vices, but it remains a prime example to be stacked up against the later twin-cylinder models from Japan with similar engine capacities, and of course against England's 'Great Survivors' … the latter-day DOHC Triumph vertical twins.

It shows up reasonably well in direct comparison, quite apart from its comparatively leisurely performance; though it was quick enough in its day, with a top speed of 102mph recorded in 1950 by the British Motorcycling magazine's detailed road test. It was dead reliable, its handling and comfort were not remarkable, but were certainly acceptable enough at the time, and its fuel consumption was better then – though we hardly knew it at the time – than many a high-performance 250cc motorcycle today.

As a point of interest, the test model leaked not a single drop of oil on test, and remained in showroom condition throughout.

With the accent very much on fuel consumption as we head along in the twenty-first century one can't help but wonder whether the simple, medium-weight vertical twins might once again appear with low compression pistons, single carburettor, 'soft' camshafts, small (overhead) valves and modest power outputs.

And if they did, how well would a latter-day, 'old fashioned' 650cc twin like the A10 BSA stack up against its modern counterparts? The latest offering of the exciting 650cc Royal Enfield twin from India generates the feeling that it just might come into its own again very well – very well indeed!

TECH SPECS

Make: BSA

Model: A10

Year of manufacture: 1953

Type:
Air-cooled, overhead valve vertical twin, with camshaft and operating pushrods carried under the rear of large cast-iron cylinder barrel. Forged, 70-ton high carbon/nickel steel crankshaft, with bob-weights and bolted-on central flywheel. Low-compression, three-ring pistons disposed at 360 degrees, alloy connecting rods, with detachable end-caps and lead/bronze/indium slipper big-end bearings. Crankshaft supported by large roller bearing on the drive side, and a large, steel-backed white metal bush on the timing side. Lubrication is by gear-type, high-capacity pump. Oil is contained within a separate oil tank.

Bore x stroke: 70 x 80mm

Capacity: 646cc

Power @ rpm: 35BHP @ 5500rpm

Compression ratio: 6.6:1

Carburation:
Single 1 –1/16" Amal carburettor; no air filtration

Electrics:
Lucas Magneto ignition, with auto-advance. Lucas 6-volt, 60-watt chain-driven generator, with current to lead/acid battery

Transmission:
By double-row ⅜" x 7/32" primary chain to separate gearbox bolted to rear of crankcase casting, with chain adjustment by grub-screw to slipper tensioner. Final drive by 5/8" x 3/8" chain

Gear ratios:
1st – 11.41:1; 2nd – 7.77:1; 3rd – 5.35:1; 4th – 4.42:1

Frame, suspension, brakes, wheels:
Duplex, tubular-steel frame, tubes brazed into cast/forged lugs, reinforced at steering head and gearbox. Front suspension by long-travel, BSA telescopic forks, with plunger type rear suspension. Dual-seat fitted. Front brake is 8" drum, 7" drum brake at rear. Steel, 19" wheel rims, with 325 x 19" ribbed front tyre, 350 x 19" block pattern at rear.

Dimensions:
Length – 2100mm; Height – 1010mm; Wheelbase – 1375mm; Ground clearance – 110mm; Seat height – 750mm; Weight – 165kg; Fuel tank – 17 litres.
Top speed – 165km/h.

Machine loaned by:
COL BRENCHLEY, Sydney.

1935 Matchless Model-B 'Silver Hawk'

600cc OHC VEE-FOUR

It has been said that the period between the two major World Wars of 1914-18 and 1939-45 was one of the golden eras in motorcycle engineering, because some of the finest examples of advanced motorcycle design we have ever seen appeared during those turbulent years. Unhappily, times were tough in those days, not only because of the tragic aftermath of World War I, but because of the Great Depression of the 1920s and 30s when many of these very advanced machines were designed and built but often failed because of the grim economic times which prevailed. It's true that many of these fine machines look more than a little 'agricultural' when viewed in direct comparison with late twenty and early-21st century motorcycles, but it must be remembered that they were highly advanced products *at that time* and, as such, deserve to be viewed from that point of view.

Many of those once great and famous names have long gone, but happily their memory lives on, not only in the hearts and minds of many a fossilised enthusiast, or somebody discovering them anew, but because there are several great examples of these noteworthy motorcycles which are still with us, and which are often to be seen on Classic and Vintage days, or Club outings, always ridden with great enthusiasm by their proud owners.

In fact, it might come as a surprise to many a modern-day enthusiast to learn that virtually every 'advance' in the design of latter-day motorcycles had already been ridden upon the world's roads more than **90** years ago. Such things as positive, oil-pumped lubrication of high-performance two-stroke engines, multi-cylinder, overhead camshaft engines, four-valve cylinder heads, cantilever rear suspension, coupled brakes, and over-the-Imperial-100mph-performance was the stuff of legend when a newcomer's doddering old grandfather was still in short pants. **The 1930 Silver Hawk Matchless** was just such a machine. A remarkable motorcycle arguably more than half a century ahead of its time, it was designed by Bert Collier (one of the three Collier brothers involved in the Matchless motorcycle empire), and it appeared at the Olympia Motorcycle Show, London, in November 1930, with the last example made in 1935 – a scant six-year production run in which this very desirable machine evoked some great interest, but unhappily very few sales. In fact, just 550 of these exciting machines were ever sold, and only around 60 are so far known to have survived. The reason for the machine's lack of success is as clear as it is two-fold; the bike was introduced in the middle of the world-wide depression, where its luxury appointments and subsequent high price was stacked against any real hope of lasting success, and it was up against yet another four-cylinder motorcycle; the first, 500cc OHC Square Four Ariel, which was introduced co-incidentally at the same Olympia Show. The Ariel was entirely successful, pressing on with several detail changes, some of them major, others cosmetic, until 1959: the much more 'masculine-looking' Matchless for just those six short years.

An exciting machine, did I say, and one which stood head and shoulders over most of its contemporaries all those long years ago? Yes, it was, if one cares to note its advanced specifications, which might almost have been lifted from the catalogue of a motorcycle made in the 21st century, rather than the one designed and built 20 years prior to the middle of the **20th** century.

Consider this: The Matchless Silver Hawk was an overhead camshaft Vee-Four of 600cc capacity, with its cranks disposed at 180 degrees. It used an odd four-into-two-into-one exhaust system, had cantilever rear suspension, complete instrumentation, coupled brakes and a marvellous top gear performance which must have put many of its contemporaries in its shade. In this regard, it differs dramatically from modern multi-cylinder, high performance motorcycles because the engine's wide spread of power has no peer amongst modern machines, including the next 'series production' Vee-Four, the 1982 V45 'Sabre' Honda OHC Vee-Four, which was built some *50 long years after the Matchless Silver Hawk!* As we have noted, that stolid old Matchless was well ahead of its time in 1930.

177

The Silver Hawk's extremely low saddle height is ably demonstrated by the vertically challenged rider. Normally seated, with feet firmly planted on the ground, I am pointing out to the low-slung machine's tall owner that there is a well discernible kink at my knee joint! However, cornering clearance at speed was not compromised.

Having said that, the older machine could not hope to compete with today's great road-burners in terms of *outright* speed or acceleration, but the top-gear performance of the punchy, slower-revving Matchless engine, with its much wider spread of usable power, is unknown today.

Though it was a Vee-Four configuration, the four pots were contained within a *single* monobloc casting and were at a very narrow angle of just 18 degrees – a somewhat narrow angle to be sure, but clearly ideal for a single, cast-iron cylinder block to be cast as this one was, which incidentally allowed for a *one-piece* cylinder head to be employed, a rarity indeed on a Vee-Four engine. The cylinder head was also made from cast iron, which was the material in wide use for that application in motorcycle design at the time. The cylinder head was attached to the barrel by 12 studs and lock nuts, with two separate, figure-eight shaped copper/asbestos head gaskets interpolated. The cylinder block casting was small enough to give the impression that it belonged to a more 'ordinary', large capacity twin-cylinder machine, and one might have been forgiven for thinking this was the case, for there was no hint that the block contained four separate cylinders.

Prior to the Silver Hawk's design, another brother, Charles Collier, had designed the faintly similar 400cc Vee-twin *side-valve* Silver Arrow two years earlier, which had its cylinders spaced at the same 18 degrees, and the Hawk was clearly a follow-on to this more 'ordinary' machine, but with its pots very slightly further apart, and at a greater angle to each other, almost certainly with the view to better cooling of the rear cylinders in this higher performance engine.

There is still some argument that the Silver Hawk cylinders were also spaced at 18 degrees, as in the Arrow's design, and this is so, while some argue the angle was actually 26 degrees, and this is also true – or nearly so! The Matchless literature from the factory always stated that the cylinders were disposed at 18 degrees to each other, but that the 'firing angle' – *which is the distance the pistons are apart at the top of the stroke* – was then 26 degrees. Hopefully, this should clear up any further arguments!

Clearly, the Hawk employed a much sportier design than the more plodding two-cylinder side-valve machine, the Arrow managing to be more popular (in view of its much lower price, among other things) with some 1,600 Arrows being purchased during its short production run.

An inspection of the Silver Hawk motor uncovers several near unique design features, some of which are in use in modern machinery, and some more typical of the age in which it first appeared.

The single overhead camshaft lies parallel to the crankshaft and sits directly between the two banks of cylinders, contained within a large, alloy housing which bolts direct to the cast-iron cylinder head. The eight-lobe camshaft is driven by a very impressive, vertical shaft on the engine's right side via two pairs of bevel gears, the upper gears, with a two-to-one reduction ratio, situated beneath a large, circular cover plate, the plate proudly emblazoned with the machine's name. The eight valves are vertical and parallel, each operated by slightly curved rocker-arms with the usual screw-and-nut tappet adjusters. The inlet valves are the inner four. Large inspection plates atop the valve train can be quickly removed to provide easy access for simple servicing.

Fuel is supplied to the inlet valves through a cast-in single manifold directly underneath the camshaft. This manifold branches into four in a cruciform shape to provide as close-to-equal length for each short inlet port as possible, but almost certainly at the expense of some volumetric efficiency lost through heating of the inlet tract, which was bound to occur. A single, surprisingly small bore, carburettor is attached to the end of the manifold and peeps out from the left side of the engine, with the incoming air filtered by a small, mesh air-filter.

In this design the four exhaust ports are naturally on the outside of the head casting, with the rear cylinder ports facing rearwards. The four-into-one exhaust system is achieved by a pair of heavily finned cast-iron manifolds which bolt across the front and rear exhausts, which direct exhaust gas to a pair of outlets on the right-hand side into which a pair of large-diameter exhaust pipes are inserted, adding to the false impression of a large-capacity vertical twin. These pipes are joined just under the right footrest, the exhaust gas then conducted through a single silencer which is flattened and fishtailed at the end in the fashion so typical of the 1930s. Spark plugs are located at an angle of 45 degrees just inboard of the exhaust ports, and again are very readily accessible.

A skew-gear from the camshaft drive just above the lower bevel connects via another shaft to the rearward-mounted generator/ignition system. Interpolated between the drive and 6-volt generator, with its attendant ignition coil and a car type distributor, is a shock absorbing rubber 'doughnut', which would doubtless also allow for any slight misalignment of the electrical components upon their solid mounting platform.

These components sit directly atop the four-speed, hand-change Sturmey-Archer gearbox, the ignition coil mounted above the generator, while the four-lobe distributor, almost identical to the type fitted to the Austin Seven car of the same period, sits near-vertically inboard of the rear exhaust pipe, worm-driven from the start of the generator drive shaft. That shaft is driven by a skew-gear from the base of the camshaft's vertical shaft.

The crankshaft is a built-up unit and comprises two pairs of pear-shaped counterweights into which the two crankpins are bolted, with a thick centre shaft to lock the assembly together – the cranks being at 180 degrees to one another, while there is no central flywheel. Connecting-rods are long and very spindly and employ huge gudgeon pin holes, with each crankpin accepting a pair

One-piece cast-iron barrel and vertical camshaft drive dominates the Silver Hawk engine. Note the camshaft's bevel gear cover plate with its proud emblem; the right foot rear brake lever; hand gear change and the rubber 'doughnut' drive to the generator and distributor. Also note the four-into-two-into-one exhaust system.

of rods side-by-side, mounted on crowded roller big-end bearings. The crankshaft is supported on its outer ends by two large, well-lubricated, phosphor-bronze bushes, with (unusually) a centre main bearing as well; the latter a caged roller located in a large steel plate which is secured in place by the long bolts which pass through it and lock the vertically split crankcase halves together.

While later British vertical twins like Triumph and BSA employed a large centre flywheel, and thus no centre main bearing, the later Matchless and AJS vertical twins of the 1950s also used a Silver Hawk-type centre main bearing, which was not altogether a success, for there could occasionally be small oil leaks present in that area.

On the Vee-Four timing side, the short mainshaft has a worm-drive machined halfway along its length to provide the drive for a vertical plunger which in turn drives the double-action plunger and reciprocating oil pump. At the other end of the crankshaft, on the machine's left side, the mainshaft is tapered and keyed to accept the engine sprocket. The latter provides an oil-bath primary drive to a multi-plate clutch by a duplex 3/8"x 5/32" chain.

The primary drive is contained within an unusual cast aluminium alloy oil-bath, the chain tension very cleverly rendered automatic by a pair of spring-steel blades locked in position on the upper and lower chain-runs and tensioned by a long spring which runs round the front of the inner chaincase. The rear of the two tensioners is located in special grooves machined in the inner chaincase half.

One of the main features of the Silver Hawk engine is its excellent dry-sump lubrication system, which draws its supply from a six-pint container bolted to the front of the crankcase. Located where it is, the oil tank needs very few external lines to connect it to the gear-driven oil pump, and thus allows for a neat and tidy external appearance.

Oil is fed to the two main bearing bushes under pressure, then through the mainshafts to the big-end bearings, while the cylinders enjoy their own direct oil feed. The lower set of bevel gears run completely submerged in oil, which seems just as well for the vertical-shaft teeth are so shallow as to resemble splines rather than the heavier gear teeth usually employed in this highly stressed area: the upper bevel gears are much more heavily defined.

An odd-looking separate oil line runs from the engine to the fuel tank/handlebar-mounted instrument panel where it operates the oil pressure 'warning' device, and from where it is re-routed directly to the camshaft and rocker areas, before draining back to the crankcase via small grooves machined vertically into the upper bevel-gear drive's phosphor-bronze bearing.

It was fashionable at the time to run long-stroke engines, and the Matchless, with bore and stroke dimensions of 50.8 x 73mm, is no exception. The 6.1:1, low compression alloy pistons are quite long, this model equipped with just two compression rings, the lower one with an undercut in the ring-land to control oil consumption by trapping oil and 'squeezing' it through holes in the ring groove and into the vast interior of the crankcases. It has been said that later model Hawks were fitted with three-ring pistons and these types of pistons have appeared in some machines which have been extensively restored in recent times. In the form of oil mist, any oil which would be scavenged from the inside of pistons would no doubt add its own lubricating quality to various bearing surfaces before dropping into the base of the crankcases and then being scavenged back to the oil tank.

Lubrication is thus complete and very thorough, so it is no wonder these low-stressed engines survived a great many years in quite good condition, even after many years sitting idle in fowl-houses or damp garages! Perhaps the old power-plant may have had it fair share of design faults, including – it has been said - the occasional blown head gasket, but lack of longevity is surely not amongst them. The first models were said to suffer from high oil consumption, but minor modifications to the oiling system and the addition of oil scraper rings in the pistons of later machines apparently overcame this problem.

If the Silver Hawk Matchless engine was

remarkable for its day, and remains so, then the frame was no less exciting, for it too was removed from many of its contemporaries. The Matchless featured a triangulated, cantilever rear suspension – and not for the first time in motorcycling, it must be noted, for both Vincent and Moto-Guzzi, among others, employed this suspension system – the Matchless pivots mounted in Silentbloc rubber bushes behind the gearbox and just under the single saddle, operating upon a pair of barrel-shaped compression springs carried almost horizontally underneath the single sprung saddle. Their movement is controlled by friction dampers adjusted for load by a pair of hand-wheels either side of the frame, just underneath the rider's single saddle.

Strongly triangulated, the modern-looking pivoted fork allows a quite long travel and a remarkably comfortable ride; that sprung saddle, as usual, taking the edge off any bumps which may not have been soaked up by the suspension. For the record, rear suspension was looked upon with some suspicion in those far-off days, the Matchless in fact being the only four-cylinder machine in the world so equipped at that time.

Front suspension is well served by a girder fork with large centre spring and, again, a friction damper mechanism with hand-wheel control. At the time when this bike was new, this type of front fork was fitted to just about everything on two wheels (as telescopic forks are today) with the forks attached to the steering head at two points by four long spindles and their attendant linkages.

The frame, which is essentially the same frame in which the Arrow's engine resided, is very solidly built, and consists of a heavy-gauge single down-tube which splays into a duplex engine mount, and a similar large-diameter frame rail running back from the steering head to meet a vertical tube from the back of the gearbox at a point under the saddle. This latter tube is of large-diameter and heavy gauge, for it takes much of the brunt of the rear suspension. The massive engine thus forms a substantial part of a very strong and rigid frame. Some of the more lightly stressed auxiliary tubing, including the triangulated rear suspension sub-frame, is much thinner and a lighter-gauge steel.

I have always been fascinated by the Silver Hawk Matchless, ever since I heard of its existence sometime in the late Forties as a kid, but I thought there was little chance I would ever see, much less actually *ride*, one of them. To my utter surprise I found a Silver Hawk quite by chance when in Melbourne some years ago, and I could hardly wait to get my hands - and, hopefully, my backside – on it!

The bike is longer in the flesh than photos would indicate, but the real surprise is the ultra-low saddle, so low, in fact, that your scribe – who possesses a pair of the shortest legs in motorcycling – could place both feet firmly on the ground when seated and still have a discernible bend at the knee! What a pleasant change *that* makes.

Ken Hall, a highly skilled diesel engineer, owns the bike, and with it a spare engine awaiting re-conditioning, which allowed us to take a peek at the internals and take some photos of the various components. The bike was in a pretty grim state when Ken found it, but its appearance now is of a brand-new machine, just delivered from the showroom floor.

The four-speed, grease-lubricated gearbox sports a hand gear-change, with the gear-gate on the right-hand side of the petrol tank, which was in nigh-universal practice at the time, and the operation of this, along with the brakes, is the only adverse feature of this particular example. The petrol tank has some movement under the action of changing gear and Ken's home-made gear-gate is not, as he says, 'notched' in precisely the right places. This means that the occasional gear is sometimes missed because each of the four gears, and of course neutral, are in slightly different positions each time you change gears. The problem, as often happens, disappears almost entirely with practice as you learn to make the right allowances. It is helped by being able to 'feel' the gears being engaged.

Originally the large brakes were coupled, with a long front brake cable coming from a bell-crank operated by an auxiliary rod from the rear brake pedal – mounted, quite unusually, on the machine's *right* side – with a separate handbrake cable, but on Ken's machine the brakes are (thankfully!) operated independently. Coupled brakes were in fashion for a very short time in the 1930s, but have thankfully been long dispensed with; except, for some unaccountable reason, the re-appearance of the linked-brake system on many modern scooter designs. The rear brake was a bit spongy but worked well enough, and the front, though very effective, tended to shudder and moan under pressure. Both brakes are quite large, being all of 8 inches in diameter, and were quite effective.

These small things apart, the Matchless was almost pure bliss to ride.

The tiny carburettor, which sticks out the left side of the cylinder head, just under the tank, needed a quick tickle to raise the fuel level, then a light dab on the kick-starter – no 'long, swinging kick' to fire this one up! – had the motor burbling away almost as soon as I leant on the pedal. The motor can actually be kicked over by hand just as easily, assisted no doubt by the low 6.1:1 compression ratio. The engine idles very reliably, with just a touch of lumpiness and the exhaust, though muted, sounds deep-throated, quite masculine, and entirely delightful. Had either Mozart or Beethoven composed an 'Exhaust Symphony' they could hardly have bettered the sounds of the four-cylinder Silver Hawk at work.

On the other hand, the rest of the power-plant was noisier than I thought it would be, with some alarming clunks and grinding sounds coming from somewhere in the interior. The noise increased and a roadside conference with the bike's owner plumped for a loose clutch assembly.

Half an hour later a couple of errant clutch springs and their attendant sleeve-nuts had been found swimming in the primary chain-case oil and were swiftly retrieved and nipped into place again. Virtually all of the odd noises then disappeared, the engine running very much smoother, and all was well with the world. As a bonus, when the large alloy primary chain-case casting was removed we were able to see the

Alloy primary chain-case contains duplex-chain-driven large, multi-plate, six-spring clutch. The spring loaded 'jockey' chain tensioners are sited upon the upper and lower runs of chain, while rounded-off ends of the tensioners are located in 'cast-in' notches just behind the leading teeth of the clutch sprocket.

entire primary drive mechanism in close detail.

The 600cc four delivers a claimed 26BHP (20 kW) at 5200 rpm, but this modest performance still allows for a fairly brisk acceleration and a good cruising speed of around 100 km/h. The miles-per-hour speedo – on Ken's bike equipped with a slightly skittish needle - shares the quite large and imposing instrument panel on the handlebars with the ignition switch, an ignition warning light, a little oil pressure warning light, an ammeter, the headlamp switch and a steering damper adjusting knob. It was surely amongst the best-equipped instrument panels on any machine of its era, many of which had very few instruments of any kind; many 1930s motorcycles, in fact, listed a speedometer, or horn, or indeed lights, as optional extras! All these 'essentials' were standard on the Sliver Hawk, that impressive instrument panel sporting no fewer than seven (7) separate instruments and/or switches.

A collar like a mini twist-grip drum on the left side of the 'bars controls the headlamp dip while a shy little button sprouts from the right side, almost unannounced alongside the front brake lever, to control the asthmatic horn.

Top gear performance is a revelation, the bike happily pulling from a speed just above a brisk trot to a maximum the owner claimed was just over the metric 140 km/h. I was not about to hammer this bike at anything like those high speeds – quite apart from due deference to its advanced age I couldn't see how I could have stopped the thing quickly – but it ran very happily at an indicated (Imperial) 65 mph and there was still a fistful of throttle left if needed.

As I've said, acceleration is quite good, though some forward momentum is lost when changing gear by hand on the throttle side, particularly when running up steep hills from a slow approach, but the engine's impressive low-speed grunt overcomes this time lapse easily enough. Ah, yes, it was a more leisurely age all those long years ago, with engines designed to pull well from slower speeds – as well as lower engine revs – and with less recourse to the gear lever.

By their very design, with all their working parts naked and thus out in the breeze, girder forks tend to be noisy and they chatter a bit over choppy going, the noise augmented by a similarly noisy rear-end on the Matchless, but the Silver hawk was a very comfortable machine and it handled almost to a hairline, whether on sealed surfaces or over dust-covered corrugations on unsealed dirt roads. Once again, I mourn the passing of the sprung saddle, which takes the last edge off the worst of the bumps and potholes as a dual-seat never can, simply because the well-designed, more flexible saddle employs its own 'supplementary suspension' system.

The mechanical action of the friction dampers, with their brake-pad like friction disc material

Dipper switch 'collar' is odd, but effective at dipping the entire reflector. Headlamp bulb is single-filament type.

Tiny horn button is almost invisible, and hard to find with heavy gloves. The croaking horn is somewhat asthmatic.

Full instrumentation was rare on machines of this vintage, but the Silver Hawk has seven dials, switches and 'tell-tale' lights. Note the steering damper knob, which dominates the centre of the large panel.

and spring-controlled plates would seem crude compared with modern hydraulics, and indeed they are, but the dampers are infinitely adjustable simply by nipping the hand-wheels up a bit tighter if you happen to be heavyweight – or vice-versa – and they always work well.

It's enough to say that the Silver Hawk's suspension soaks up bumps and ripples surprisingly well and there is no sign of wallowing or 'pogo-sticking' as it does so; seemingly regardless of road surface. You can change line when and/or if necessary through a bend on the old steed with little effort and the occasional corrugation – on dirt surfaces as well as sealed roads – elicits little more than an assortment of rattles and bangs from the suspension as it goes about its business. The tail end will step out a little sometimes when cornering at high speeds over really rough going, and there is the occasional thump on the wrists and a twitch at the handlebars, the latter controlled easily by yet another friction damper via the ubiquitous steering damper knob, but the bike point blank refuses to be thrown off-line no matter what the various road surfaces tried to dictate.

The Silver Hawk Matchless I rode is a 1935 model, the last of the line, the machine still fitted with hand gear-change, although at the time (for the princely sum of an additional thirty shillings – which is all of three dollars) it could be ordered with the more modern, and infinitely more preferable, positive-stop foot gear-change. The motorcycle remains a fine example of one of the most advanced designs of its era. In fact, were the same basic design to appear today on a bike with a Japanese name on the tank, it would be accepted as just another first-rate example of the modern-day Superbike. Of course, it would have an all-alloy engine with a bigger bore size, for a capacity closer to one litre, possibly be water-cooled to give the rear pots an easier life and probably employ a wet-sump, have revised internals to handle the extra power, be fitted with an extensive electrical system, electric starter, use hydraulically controlled suspension both ends, be hung with disc brakes, have a much higher centre of gravity, weight at least 40kg more ...

Let's forget it, and leave the old bike alone, to bask in the glory of days gone by, to enjoy its exclusiveness – there are only four of them in Australia, as far as is known – to point with no little pride at its proven longevity and to let others know it had all happened before Honda built its first overhead camshaft Vee-Four some 50 years later, to be followed just a year later by Yamaha's V-Max rocket ship.

The Silver Hawk should shine like a beacon on today's marketplace to demonstrate to the world that this machine was one built many, many years before its time, as it should show a new generation of motorcyclists yet another example of a great design which was new when their grandfathers were pedalling pushbikes about.

Unhappily, it was not well enough known for that, but perhaps this new look at a very old machine – some could say a technological masterpiece – may bring it into the modern-day spotlight as it has never been spotlighted before.

Note: *In passing, Collier designed another overhead camshaft Vee-Four in 1935 – the very year that the Silver Hawk was withdrawn – a machine even lesser known than the Silver Hawk. It was a 50-degree 500cc four with cast-iron cylinders and a pair of light-alloy heads, with its overhead camshafts driven by chains. Unenclosed hairpin valve springs were employed, the machine wearing the AJS nameplate, the ailing A.J. Stevens company purchased in 1931 by the Collier Brothers. The AJS name continued to be employed, alongside the Matchless marque, for half a century thereafter.*

The AJS four was only a prototype motorcycle, for the exciting new four-cylinder machine never made it to the production line. Of course, it would have been a very expensive machine to produce, and thus not very popular, but a later 500cc AJS was campaigned as a factory road racer in air-cooled form. Finally, it was supercharged and water-cooled and, producing a handy 60BHP, it was the first motorcycle on earth to have lapped a Grand Prix circuit – at Ulster in Ireland in 1939 - at an average speed of over 100mph, with Walter Rusk in the saddle. The bike failed to finish because of a front suspension-linkage problem, but that lap record is now part of history.

It seems clear that the Matchless Silver Hawk failed to survive because it was introduced in the middle of the Depression when money was very tight, and its price of 75 Pounds, which was about two or three times the price of many other machines in the marketplace, slotted it into the luxury class. Besides which, people are often suspicious of a new model, usually waiting for later models to be improved after the bugs – if any - were ironed out. The bike never had a chance, but one can only imagine how it stood proudly above the common herd as few others of its era ever did.

1935 MATCHLESS MODEL-B

'Now let me see; according to this map, we have about another 50 or so to go.' There is no doubt the Silver Hawk Matchless must have been a very fine touring iron in its day. With no one but our photographer about, and on a near-private, traffic-free road in the bush, your rider is attired in the garb so synonymous of the era in the early to mid-1930s, when this machine, rare though it was even then, was very probably King of the Highway.

Although it was a little noisy in its operation, and is surely 'agricultural' to modern eyes, the un-damped front suspension, which was well augmented by the rear-end's cantilever suspension, proved to be comfortable over corrugated dirt surfaces. The sprung saddle took the edge off any hidden potholes with which this road surface was pock-marked. The suspension movement was well controlled by 'hand-wheel,' adjustments on the front fork's pivot point and directly under the rider's saddle.

At much more 'serious' speeds on tar-sealed surfaces, some of which were broken up in several places, the bike remained even more comfortable and could be steered almost to a hairline. The rear-end of the bike stepped out a little over heavy bumps, the suspension sometimes crashing into deep potholes. However, both suspension systems seemed to be tuned well enough, as it was infinitely adjustable with more — or less — tightening of the friction discs by the hand-wheel adjustments.

It must be said that Harry Collier, of the three Colliers brothers, Harry, Charlie and the later, younger brother Bert, was nothing if not very daring indeed in his approach to the design of their various machines. The **Silver Hawk** was very much Charlie's idea, for which he took most of the credit, but it was said to be designed by 'young' Bert, who had apparently studied draftsmanship, for he continued to design the range of Matchless and AJS motorcycles right up until WWII.

The brothers had been manufacturing Matchless motorcycles since 1901, and had purchased the AJS (A. J. Stevens) name from the Stevens factory in 1931. As it happens, Stevens motorcycles were later being built and sold in England and elsewhere, including Australia, which may well have surprised the Collier brothers.

As the Silver Hawk was slowly, if very surely, sliding down the gurgler in 1935, an all-new, 50-degree, vee-4 **500cc** overhead camshaft AJS was created by Bert Collier. The engine was like two separate Vee-twins, the camshaft driven by chain, which came up between the two separate twin cylinder engines. Fork and blade con-rods were adopted, with two carburettors feeding each of the twin cylinders. The hairpin valve springs were exposed. The machine was exhibited at the 1935 Olympia Show, but disappeared shortly thereafter, never to be seen again. There are just two, somewhat grainy photographs of the machine, and here is the better of the two, if still grainy.

But the V4 five-hundred was to appear again as an out-and-out, supercharged road racer which appeared, in air-cooled form, in 1936. It was beset with many problems, including overheating, but was still being raced in this form through 1938. But Matt White, who had designed motorcycles for New Imperial, was approached to re-design the Vee-Four, which he did, using the original as a template. The latest, 1939 machine was water-cooled, the valve springs by now enclosed, the bike still supercharged, by now producing a 'suggested' 80BHP at a high 7.200rpm.

One of its most impressive performances was in the 1939 Ulster GP in Ireland, where Irishman Walter Rusk established a new record – on the opening lap! – of 100.03mph, the first ever 100mph lap record in England, and probably just about everywhere else. He led the race for several laps before one of the lower mounting brackets which locked the Web girder forks to the steering head snapped, the bike by then entirely un-rideable.

The great Jock West, the company' Sales Manager, rode the bike to victory in Belgium in 1946, but supercharging was banned shortly thereafter and the V4 AJS was reluctantly retired.

This is one of only two photographs which have been seen of the 1935 500cc Vee-Four OHC AJS, which was to follow the 600cc Silver Hawk as it faded from the scene in that year. It was shown at the 1935 Olympia Motorcycle Show, but disappeared shortly thereafter and was never seen again, except for...

...the air-cooled, supercharged, road racing version of the road-going machine, which appeared in 1936, but suffered from many teething problems, including overheating. Constant improvements saw this newly developed road racer from 1939, by now fitted with enclosed valve springs, plunger rear suspension, water-cooling and still supercharged. The 500cc engine was by now producing a 'suggested' 80BHP!

TECH SPECS

Make: Matchless

Model: Model B 'Silver Hawk'

Years of manufacture: 1930–35

Type:
18/26-degree cast-iron head-and-barrel 'Mono-bloc' Vee-Four, overhead camshaft, with eight vertical valves. Overhead camshaft drive is on engine's right side by vertical shaft and bevel gears. Bolted-up crankshaft, with pairs of connecting-rods sharing a common crankpin, located upon crowded-roller big-end bearings, and pistons spaced at 180 degrees. Centre main bearing caged roller type, while main bearings are a pair of large bronze bushes. Dry sump, with 6-pint oil tank bolted to front of large crankcase castings.

Bore x stroke: 50.8 x 73mm

Capacity: 594cc

Compression ratio: 6.1:1

Power @ rpm: 26BHP (20Kw) @ 5200rpm

Carburation:
Single 1" Amal, with separate float-bowl, metal mesh air filter.

Electrics, ignition:
Lucas 6-volt generator, with wet lead/acid battery. Ignition is by coil and points, with four-lobe distributor. Full instrumentation, with 7 switches/dials.

Transmission:
By duplex 3/8" x 5/32" primary chain in full oil bath, to multi-plate clutch and four-speed, hand-change Sturmey-Archer gearbox. Final drive is by 5/8" x 3/8" roller chain.

Gear ratios:
1st – 17:1; 2nd – 12.4:1; 3rd – 6.9:1; 4th – 5.7:1.

Tank capacities:
Fuel – 11.3 litres (2 ½ gallons).
Oil – 3.46 litres (6 pints), with fabric oil filter.

Frame, wheels, suspension:
All-tube frame, brazed into cast lugs at steering head and other stress points, and full-cradle engine support. Front Forks are girder type with single central spring, controlled by friction dampers. Rear Suspension is 'cantilever' type, with triangulated sub-frame, via Silentbloc pivots at gearbox and under seat, with two barrel-shaped compression springs controlled by a pair of friction-damping adjusters. Wheels are 19" rims, laced to 8" brakes – originally coupled – front and rear, with 325 x 19" tyres, ribbed front, block pattern rear (400 x 19" tyres optional extra).

Dimensions:
Wheelbase: 1230mm; Ground clearance – 120mm; Saddle height – 612mm.

Weight: 172kg (380lb).

Fuel consumption (est.):
4.8l/100km; approx. 280km range.

Top speed: 140km/h.

Machine loaned by:
KEN HALL, Kilmore, Victoria.

1942 Zundapp 'Wehrmacht'

KS750 OHV 'FLAT-TWIN' OUTFIT

The Crimean and Boer Wars were campaigned much too early in history to have had motor vehicles pressed into service, while mules, donkeys and horses were to be seen humping supplies about and also providing mobility for a large number of soldiers, from senior officers hidden away in the safety of their various headquarters, to some of the front-line infantryman, and the much more serious Mounted Lancers.

The First World War was somewhat different, because it saw the first application of a wide variety of motor vehicles deployed in an equally wide variety of theatres of war.

The Second World War was different again, for this time there was an even wider variety of motor vehicles, and they came to this monumental conflict from almost every nation on earth. In fact, the desert floor in Africa – among many other places – saw a huge number of some of the oddest vehicles this world is ever likely to see in one place, even in comparison to some of the largest Motor Museums in the world, many of the latter displaying a staggering variety of machines on two, three, four and many more wheels.

On the burning sands of Africa there were tanks of many types, from the American Sherman and Grant, to the Allied forces' Matilda, Centurion and the pneumatic-tyred Staghound, while the German Panzers were to be seen scatted about all over the desert floor. 'Blitz Wagons' from General Motors and Ford were rugged and very strongly built, but otherwise looked bulky and thus very ordinary, but they were offset by the odd-looking German half-track personnel carriers which were like mechanical Centaurs with the front ends of motorcycles attached randomly to tank-tracks at the rear. There were Bren gun carriers which could stop a sniper's bullet but which were open at the top to the fierce desert winds and the machinations of marauding enemy aircraft.

There were also handy little four-wheel-drive lightweight transport vehicles nipping about which were – according to the American Army Ordinance sheets – officially called *'Trucks: quarter-ton, 4 x 4, GPW'*, which were usually called GPs ... or just plain **'Jeep'** for short.

There were Armoured Personnel Carriers (APC for short, which was *not* a headache remedy!), gun carriers, staff cars, scout cars, appropriated ex-civilian vehicles ... and then, of course, there were *the motorcycles.*

Ah, yes, the motorcycles. They came in a bewildering array of makes and models from the American 750cc side-valve WLA Harleys, the 500cc and 750cc Vee-twin Indian solo bikes, and their stable-mate, the huge 1200cc Indian 'Chief' which was used as a sidecar machine. The British had their 500cc Norton solos and the 600cc outfits, the latter used mostly for transporting arms and ammunition about, while the famous WD/BSA 500cc side-valve solo was probably the most numerous. The Poms rounding out their two-wheelers by more than a few overhead valve, 350cc G3L Matchless machines, the occasional Ariel, the even more occasional 350cc OHV Triumph and the rare Royal Enfield and Velocette singles.

There were several other marques from England, including a few very small two-stroke machines as well from James and Royal Enfield, but the German machines were, as usual, streets ahead of everyone else! They used NSU, DKW, BMW and Zundapp machines for the most part, as well as the odd Horex, but by far the most numerous of these were the highly specialised machines with horizontally opposed engines and, of course, shaft final drive, which were supplied by BMW and Zundapp, both for solo and sidecar use. The Germans used motorcycles in far greater numbers than any other of the armed forces, the machines used in many different pursuits; they even enlisted an entire *Battalion* of motorcyclists, which none of the other armed forces seemed to contemplate. In effect, these outfits were the German equivalent of the American Jeep, and they were every bit as versatile, if not more so!

The BMW flat-twins included side-valve and overhead valve engines of between 500, 600 and 750cc, while the Zundapp employed four distinct models; a 500 or 600cc side-valve twin, the rare, side-valve 800cc flat-*four* and the subject of this test report, the 750cc overhead valve horizontally opposed twin cylinder **1942 Zundapp KS750** combination, which was probably the most numerous of the lot. Available records show that there were 18,630 Zundapp outfits supplied to the war effort, against 16,510 BMWs. There is little photographic evidence of the Zundapp 500 or 600cc *twins*, but there were just over 500 of the 800cc flat-four outfits, while the smaller-capacity flat-twins, according to some authorities, were mostly ridden as solos. It would thus appear that motorcycles built by Zundapp, a company founded before BMW, may have out-numbered the BMW machines campaigned in WWII by about two-to-one.

The KS750 Zundapp which almost by accident fell into my twitching hands is a near-perfect, well-restored model owned by veteran and vintage enthusiast Vin Minogue, of Melbourne. The bike is very original and finished in 'Desert Campaign Yellow', and sports several authentic insignias, an Afrika Korps insignia on the tank, with the 'D' motif of the 21st Panzer Division of North Africa in the Western Desert, and the round insignia of the Motorised Infantry. There were other insignia, a mounting for a light machine gun, pannier boxes, 'Jerry-cans' and a spare wheel.

The tough KS750 outfit looks rugged enough to do the job well, glorifying in a heavy-gauge frame of odd shape, with thick front fork legs and distinctly agricultural sidecar mounts. Heavy-gauge wide wheel rims are laced with sturdy spokes and covered by deep, wide and suitably heavy-gauge mud, sand and (possibly) bullet-proof guards, the wheels shod by fat tyres. The heavy guards were designed to be well clear of the tyres, to allow for the build-up of mud which might occur on unsealed roads in other areas, or for chains to be fitted, for the machines were also used in campaigns in Europe against Russia and other nations during snow-bound, icy winter offensives. Naturally, the incidentals like footrests and handlebars are also suitably sturdy.

The outfit looks absolutely authentic, right down to the sidecar and its fittings, and it comes as a shock to discover that its owner bought the bike from an English Zundapp fancier back in 1972, and he picked up a *Russian* sidecar and chassis which bolted straight on! The much later sidecar body was made by using the *original* Zundapp pressings, and the sidecar chassis was similarly 'stolen' from the Germans. The cheapest part of the entire restoration, the sidecar and chassis, were bought, with spare wheel, for just $300, with another $120 for freight. The sidecar was designed to be fitted to the right-hand side of a motorcycle, in typical European fashion, and it was built in the Ural factory in Russia especially for the factory's post-war 'Cossack' and other 650cc flat-twins.

But the sidecar suspension system is not original, having been fabricated by the new owner, with the help of George Hempenstal, a great buddy from Twin-G sidecars in Melbourne. Short, quarter-elliptic springs provide the suspension for the sidecar body in similar fashion to the R75 BMW. Originally, the Zundapp sidecar wheel was sprung by a combination of torsion bars and cranked levers – a much better system – but the essential parts were simply not available during the restoration and proved to be virtually impossible to fabricate. It is hard to carp at this however, for it's a safe bet that many an odd part was substituted in time of war and it's possible that an elated advance, or a swift, blubbering retreat, would see Zundapp outfits festooned with purloined BMW bits, and vice versa.

It might be noted that part of the rival BMW's brief when it submitted its design for approval was that 70% of its engine/gearbox parts, along with its ancillaries and accessories, should be interchangeable with its rival, the Zundapp KS750 – which the German Government considered to be vastly superior to BMW – because of the emergency repairs which would need to be carried out often, and probably under extreme conditions. Cannibalisation of damaged machines, of whatever make, would surely have been almost a routine exercise made much easier by this 'standardisation'.

The KS750's extremely strong image is never more evident than in the design of its odd-looking frame, which is made from a number of welded and riveted steel pressings and substantial steel tubing, very strongly gusseted at the steering head; the latter enclosed within a hugely braced, square section shroud. Carefully welded, the fabricated frame is a fully duplex, box-section design, the 'squared-oval' pressings tapering in diameter from the steering head to a much smaller diameter at the rear wheel, without a discernible change in section. The immensely strong frame is well-braced to eliminate side-thrust loads encountered when used with a sidecar. For extra strength, two stamped plates are welded to the bottom of the frame, one beneath the gearbox, the other under the driver's seat, midway along the frame.

It was not a frame specially made for the Wehrmacht outfit, however, for a similar design was used for some years before the war by many other Zundapp models, in particular the flat-four 800 and flat-twin 600cc models. The frame design was originally an English patent, designed and built by the then-famous Coventry 'Eagle' company in the 1920s and built by Zundapp – and others – under licence to the British firm. It's probable the Wehrmacht outfits were manufactured without reference to the English company's patents during the war, much less to the Coventry Eagle licencing conditions!

The front forks are also fabricated from welded, heavy-gauge steel pressings and include the best features of the older girders and the more modern telescopic forks in their clever design. The long, rigid fork legs contain short, heavy springs sited in the top section, just above the position of the lower triple-clamps, with the heavy fork assembly attached to the steering head by four thick bolts and parallelogram linkages: clearly, unlike the BMW machine, there are no telescopic 'fork sliders'.

Inside the top of each fork leg, both of which are covered by a dust-proof 'dome', is a large rocker-arm, similar to an engine-valve rocker (though very much larger) which bears upon the fork springs under the action of the movement of the fork's top linkage. This occurs as the non-telescopic, rigid fork legs move up or down.

The transverse, horizontal pivot-pin to which the upper linkages are mounted employs a small gear pinion midway which meshes with a near-vertical rack attached to a small piston in an hydraulic reservoir; the 'rack-and-pinion' action of fork movement applying hydraulic damping to control the spring action. The linkage pivot pins rotate within hardened, needle roller bearings.

Simple but brilliantly executed, the design results in a set of forks with immense strength and resistance to flexing and side-thrust loads. The rival R75 BMW telescopic forks were said to be 'vastly inferior' to the stronger KS750, were prone to problems with side-thrust loads and were often beset with oil leakage problems.

Heavy 'rocker arms' attached to front transverse bar operate 'backwards' on springs to provide a very effective front suspension, aided by centrally mounted, two-way hydraulic damping.

There is no rear suspension, but a well-fitted and comfortable rubber single saddle with a pair of coil springs underneath it helps iron out bumps from the rear of the sturdy outfit. However, I know from personal experience that only one day spent on that small saddle while sliding about on sandy surfaces or leaping over bumps and crashing into potholes might see many a Zundapp KS750 rider hastily eating his dinner off the mantelpiece at headquarters … or off the top of that very same saddle while crouching alongside the bike!

The Zundapp power unit is similar to the BMW with which we are all so familiar, the horizontally opposed, 750cc air-cooled twin adopting the efficient overhead valve operation. But it is not a 180-degree horizontally opposed twin as it first appears, for the two of the pots are at 170 degrees to each other, having been angled lightly upwards at 5 degrees on each side for extra ground clearance. The engine is well over-square with bore/stroke dimensions of 85 x 75mm, delivering just 26BHP (19kW) at a low 4000rpm. This is clearly a very low power output from a rugged, over-engineered engine of this high capacity, but it would have been more than enough for the conditions which might prevail under combat, with the engine clearly tuned to provide the necessary high torque at lower engine speeds.

The crankshaft is a one-piece forging, with the heavy steel connecting rods split at the big ends and fitted with Zundapp's almost unique split-cage needle roller assembly. Usually, connecting rods with detachable end-caps like these employ plain metal bearings, but Zundapp has used the split, caged-roller big-end bearings for years on many models, including it two-stroke engines. Similar split-cage big-end bearings have been used by Moto Guzzi singles as well.

However, the owner has had a conversion set of plain-metal big-end slippers fitted: quite acceptable, without compromising the engine's design or its inherent strength, for there is a very good supply of high-pressure lubrication to the highly stressed big-end assemblies.

Under a large alloy cover in front of the engine sits the 6-volt crankshaft-mounted generator, with its attendant voltage-regulator directly above it. Behind the generator is a set of radially cut gears, one on the end of the crankshaft, the other driving the camshaft which is located directly above the crankshaft. Valves are controlled by cam followers and long pushrods.

A large alloy casting atop the main engine castings conceals a twin magneto, which is driven by straight-cut gear from a similar gear on the camshaft, and a squat, single 30mm Solex carburettor, accompanied by a large 'Neuman' centrifugal air-filter which is mounted at the rear of the casting, its gas mixture conducted to the cylinders by a pair of curved, tubular inlet manifolds. Again, the design is similar to BMW, but Zundapp had been making this type of gas-induction system for many years.

Wet-sump lubrication is employed, the small, plunger pump driven from the base of the crankshaft gear by its own helical gear. The crankshaft is supported on a large roller bearing at the front, with a caged needle roller as an outrigger bearing to support the longer shaft on which the generator spins, while a large, double-row ball bearing at the gearbox end supports the short, chunky shaft upon which the two-plate dry clutch is a taper-and-key fitting.

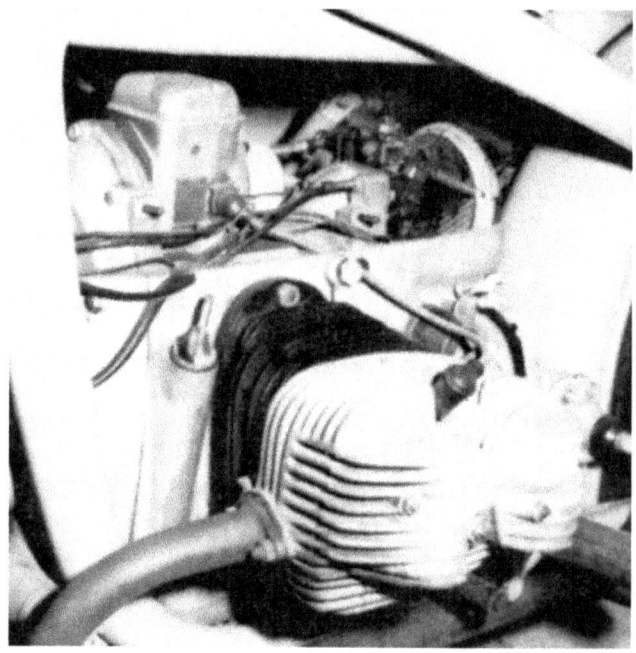

Removal of the alloy casting atop the engine allows the magneto and carburettor to be readily accessed

Inner hand-change lever with black knob selects four speeds for road, outer lever selects off-road and reverse gears, while lever under rider's saddle engages sidecar-wheel drive

Unlike most Zundapp motorcycles which fitted the odd chain-and-sprocket 'gear' boxes, the KS750 has a set of square-cut gear-cluster internals in its four-speed gearbox, probably a government requirement for the arduous job ahead of it, plus of course the more 'universal' use if parts needed to be swapped around. Final drive is by unenclosed shaft.

The gearbox employs no fewer than four gear levers! In the fail-safe method so typical of German design in the early 1940s, the KS750 has both hand and foot gear-change levers, the former in a gear-gate on the right side of the frame at the fuel tank, the latter in the normal position, controlled by left foot. Gear pattern is one back from neutral, three forward by hand or one down, three up by foot. But there are in fact two hand gear levers on the side of the fuel tank, one alongside the other; a shorter lever is employed to select low range for desert use, or to select a higher range for the highway. We couldn't find a hill steep enough to try it out on, but the Germans claim the Zundapp could climb a one-in-two slope in low/low, while the Bee-Emm could manage only – only? – a one in two-and-a-half! On exceedingly rough, or deep sandy surfaces, the speed of a K750 outfit was 'governed' by its low/low-ratio gear to some 3 miles per hour, in the interests of not running over any foot soldiers who may happen to be struggling along in front of it!

And what is the purpose of the *fourth* gear-lever? Ah, that is a small, knobbed lever just ahead of the power take-off at the rear hub – the knob just under the right side of the rider's saddle – which is used to engage *the sidecar-wheel drive* if and when necessary. The ratio of power to the rear wheel in relation to the sidecar-wheel drive is 70/30, intended to be used *only* in heavy going off-road. The right-hand side of the tank also employs a small switch to cut-out the engine by earthing the magneto; it isn't really an ignition switch as such, for these only apply when coil-ignition is used, which would require the complication of a lead/acid battery.

To make climbing steep sand hills safer the Zundapp has a front axle which extends nearly 100mm each side of the fork legs which could allow a passenger to leap off and run round the front and stand on the axle-cum-footrests to stop the outfit from flipping over backwards! It's a hard statement to believe, I know, for the longer axle was probably meant for towing a damaged motorcycle about, but in view of the steepness of some of the sand dunes the outfit would be likely to encounter, that statement about a machine flipping over on very steep, soft surfaces would seem to make very good sense! (Photo overleaf clearly demonstrates this!)

Although the engine crankshaft revolves across-the-frame, the KS750 kick-starter (unlike BMW) operates in the normal way, though fitted on the bike's left side. A skew-gear takes care of this. The bike never failed to start in about half-a-kick and proved a surprise by idling smoothly and with a very, very quiet exhaust; this was

probably to allow the bike to creep up on (or away from) an unsuspecting enemy.

The exhaust consists of a large collector box which fills the area beneath the engine and gearbox, to emerge into a fat, tear-drop shaped muffler which runs behind the frame on the machine's left side and is covered by a triangular, fluted cover. A single pipe emerges from the cover to expel the gases, the whole unit matt-black and almost totally invisible. But if the engine is quiet, then the exhaust is a great deal more so, the engine running very smoothly to make for an overall impression of Silent Teutonic Strength.

A large-diameter, car-type clutch could be expected to be very heavy at the lever, but the KS750 clutch frees very well with a very soft, almost vague feel. Foot gear-change lever travel is short, but the gear-change might best be described as 'alarming' in view of the grim clunks and grinding noises which emerge from the rear of the box. It may well be due to the heavy, straight-cut gears, or some back-lash in the sidecar take-off point, but it was difficult to make a gear-change without letting most of the neighbourhood know all about it. Fast or slow, high revs or low, it made no difference – that gear change is noisy, which seems to negate – to some extent – the over-silent exhaust system!

One odd feature of the gear-change was to see, out of the corner of the eye, that hand gear lever moving ghost-like from gear to gear. I tried the hand-change as well, and it worked very well, but with no discernible difference in clunks or grinds.

But there was a surprise in store when I tried the low range on occasion. First time I tried it I was surprised to find how low the gear was, and to note it only seemed to work on first gear, which was not the case for the machine appeared to employ four ratios, but the second time I popped the little lever a little further into low range I opened the throttle briskly to find myself taking off at a rate of knots *backwards!* To add another dimension to that tricky gearbox, *it had a reverse gear as well!*

Brakes were excellent, in no small measure due to the hydraulic rear and sidecar-wheel brakes and the very large diameter drum brake on the front. We did most of the test in the sand, which is a natural brake in its own right, but braking on the street on our way to and from the test site was equally as impressive, in terms of both smoothness and progression.

Though a heavy and certainly a no-nonsense machine, the KS750 is a very good handler, and really quite comfortable. There is no sign of flex in those rigid fork legs and the handlebars are well-shaped for pelting a sidecar about, even if the sidecar is fitted on the 'wrong' side of the bike!

I've ridden many outfits over very many years, but in Australia they all had the sidecar attached to the 'correct' (left-hand) side, and there is certainly an art in learning to ride one. But when you are called upon to ride an outfit with the sidecar on the 'wrong' (right-hand) side, it is a whole new ballgame. A few hard laps of a rough, sandy basin with a firm base, large humps and the occasional tussock of grass soon overcomes the odd feeling, and from then on berm-bashing the old Zundapp or waving the sidecar-wheel about in the air, was great fun.

The WWII German sidecar would steer very precisely, regardless of the type of terrain and how bumpy it became, but there was a great deal of sidecar wheel feed-back to the handlebars with no one in the chair, while the sidecar spent some of its time well off the ground. In duty, the KS750 was required to carry a crew of three, augmented at times by a small trailer, so the unusual front suspension is set up for a very heavy load. It was a bit on the firm side but the forks would soak up rough bumps easily, even when hit sideways, with little deviation from the straight and narrow.

The front wheel will wash-out in serious understeer if cornering very briskly through left-hand corners on unsealed surfaces – and even more so, I have been told, if the sidecar wheel is being driven as well! – but a quick easing-off of power allows the wheel to dig in again under the influence of sudden weight transfer as the back steps out, and a few degrees of opposite lock with the power full-on again will see the outfit corner almost on rails. On right-handers this allows the sidecar wheel to remain clear of the ground – and the bumps – while most left-handers are a pure joy, with the driver hanging into the corner, with as much weight over the front-end as possible to overcome the possibility of often-dangerous, terminal understeer.

Top speed on the Zundapp is around 110 km/h on the straight and narrow, or as quick as you are brave enough on the rough, the bike's all-up weight (with passenger) of 400kg gluing its wheels to the road. The bike can haul an allowed 840kg (that's 1,850lbs) with its three-man crew and all armaments including a spare wheel, fuel can, six pannier bags and machine gun. It is set up to tow a small trailer as well, the strength of the heavy-spoke, wide wheel rims and fat 450 x 16 tyres probably being the only limiting factor.

Handlebar control levers are the once-fashionable, straight-pull 'reverse' type, with pivots inside the handlebars and the levers themselves sprouting from within. They look a bit odd by modern standards but were very

popular when the bike was built and were said to allow for longer cable life.

As I've said, everything about the Zundapp KS750 shrieks strength, even to the size of the power take-off point at the rear-drive hub, where a huge alloy collar locks the torque-tube for the sidecar-wheel in place. The tube would contain a long, splined shaft to take the power under the sidecar body and into a secondary differential inside the sidecar-wheel hub. Though almost original, the Minogue Zundapp has yet to be finished, for Vin has only just managed to secure a set of sidecar-wheel drive gears, after literally searching the world for them.

The sidecar-wheel hub had been sitting in the dirt for some time, with the result that the gears had been chewed away by rust. It was a relatively simple matter to replace the sidecar-wheel braking system (after all, it is easy to modify, or adapt, an existing hydraulic system) but KS750 Zundapp sidecar-wheel differentials would have to be a scarce commodity at any time … and nigh-impossible all these years after the bike was first made, even in those vast quantities.

In fact, many of the parts which went to make this unique outfit had to be fabricated by Vin and his equally enthusiastic veteran and vintage enthusiast mates, from the handlebar levers, which were cast from patterns made by Vin and George Hempenstall, to some of the small alloy engine covers.

When the bike arrived from England the machine was in a badly decomposed state because there was no headlight and no saddle springs, with numerous oil leaks from the engine and gearbox. The restoration was total; from

the basic mechanicals like the big-end bearing replacement to the hand-manufacture of odd gaskets, alloy castings and control cables.

N.B: My original test report was published in 1982, with parts hard to obtain at the time, but today there is a thriving spare parts replacement/restoration company in Germany operated by Hans Peter – Homme, where almost everything for both KS750 Zundapp and K75 BMW machines is claimed to be fairly readily available – or can be fabricated – including major engine parts, gaskets and, it has been said, sidecar-wheel drive components.

The bike, as we now see it, is so well restored that it looks as though it might have been recently supplied to the Wehrmacht to be put through its paces. Of course, it has no chrome – nor should it – and its paint finish is the correct matt yellow, but it looks and feels great, the perfect example of what a great deal of enthusiasm, hard work and skill can wring out of a bike which could just as easily have ended up on the scrap heap somewhere, just as many thousands of its mates must have done.

During their war-time career, the Wehrmacht BMW and Zundapp outfits were used almost as the Allies used the ubiquitous Jeep for, as we have noted, these machines were produced in their tens of thousands and they would assuredly have been used to great effect.

A wartime photo of a couple of WWII Zundapp KS750 outfits in action as they climb this steep, dirt hill somewhere on the Continent, with the so-called 'passengers' hanging out to keep the sidecar wheel on the deck, or as close to that as possible. In this guise, either as a sidecar work horse or in some other pursuit, the nearly 35,000 sidecar mounts from Zundapp and BMW were at least as busy as the American Jeep, for they were called upon to assume pretty much the same duties. Arguably, they were equally as effective as the Jeep, and possibly even more so in an exercise such as this one.

These machines were also designed to be capable of hauling about a small, specially-designed trailer in which could be carried supplies, ammunition or – in the event of a swift retreat – a bunch of soldiers hanging on for their very lives. Or, should it come to that, perhaps a high-ranking officer in the well-sprung sidecar, with his assistant perched upon the single saddle as a 'kind of' pillion passenger. One assumes the pillion passenger would be ever-ready to leap across and attempt to keep the bike on an even keel over rough going, or to rush forward and jump onto the wide front axle to keep the outfit from flipping over on very steep climbs!

TECH SPECS

Make: Zundapp

Model: 1942 KS750 'Wehrmacht' outfit.

Type:
Air-cooled, 170-degree horizontally opposed twin-cylinder four-stroke. Overhead valves controlled by pushrods, with camshaft carried above crankshaft. One-piece crank, with steel conrods employing detachable end-caps to accept split-cage needle rollers in big-end, connected to four-ring alloy pistons. Short, rigid crankshaft supported upon one double-row ball, one large roller and one 'outrigger' needle roller bearing. Wet sump lubrication; oil supplied through worm-driven piston/plunger pump via a sump-mounted filter.

Bore x Stroke: 85 x 75mm

Capacity: 751cc

Compression ratio: 6.2:1

Power:
26BHP (19.3Kw) @ 4000rpm; Torque: 38 Ft/Lb (51.5 Nm) @ 2650rpm

Carburation:
30mm car-type Solex carburettor, with 'cyclonic' centrifugal air-filter

Electrics:
Noris 6-volt DS50/70 generator. Ignition by Bosch twin magneto

Transmission:
Direct-drive through two-plate automotive-type dry clutch to four-speed gearbox and final shaft drive to rear wheel, with power take off in rear hub for sidecar-wheel differential. Gearbox includes hand and foot gear-change mechanism, with reverse gear and dual range for off-road and highway use. Separate hand-lever for rear hub allows sidecar drive to be connected at will. Gear positions are foot-change on left, one down, three up; hand-change, one back, three forward.

Gear ratios (overall):
High range: 1st – 27.9:1; 2nd – 13.23:1; 3rd – 8.26:1; 4th – 5.78:1.

Low range (overall): 1st – 35.89:1; 2nd – 17.01:1; 3rd – 10.6:1; 4th – 7.43:1.

Differential ratio: 5.78:1.

Suspension, wheels, tyres, brakes:
Fabricated, one-piece, pivoting front fork legs, with 'rocker-arm' control of short fork springs and two-way hydraulic damping. No rear suspension. Interchangeable wheels with steel rims laced to conical hubs, fitted with 450 x 16 balloon tyres. Drum brakes; 200mm front and rear. Front brake is cable operated, with hydraulic control to rear and sidecar.

Dimensions:
Length – 2,385mm; Width – 1,650mm; Height – 1,010mm; Wheelbase – 1,410mm; Saddle height – 785mm; Ground clearance (laden) – 460mm; Weight (all-up) – 400kg; Weight allowed (with full crew and armaments) – 840kg.

Fuel tank capacity:
23 litres. Oil capacity: Engine, 2.25 litres; gearbox, 1.25 litres; rear diff, 4 litres; sidecar diff, 2 litres.

Performance:
Top speed – 110km/h – but with three-man crew – 85km/h. Fuel consumption – 11.5km/l; fuel range – 300–325km. Minimum speed – 3.5km/h. Turning circle (left) – 5.6 metres; (right) – 4 metres.

Machine loaned by:
VIN MINOGUE, Melbourne, Victoria.

1939 Rudge 'Special'

500cc OHV SINGLE CYLINDER
(FOUR VALVE)

Motorcycles designed with four-valve cylinder heads might be old hat in the 21st century, because just about everybody seems to be making them, but riders new to motorcycling may not be aware that there is really nothing new about multi-valve cylinder heads; either in single-cylinder motorcycles or those with multi cylinders. As long ago as 1911, highly specialised Vee-twin Indian motorcycles with four-valve heads (called '8-valvers' in those days) were being raced at very high speeds on the dangerous board and dirt tracks in America, with Harley-Davidson in close competition with similar designs not long afterwards. In 1912 Peugeot manufactured their 7-litre L76 GP race car with overhead camshafts and multiple valve gear, while the Peugeot 500cc double overhead camshaft twin-cylinder road race **motorcycle** was similarly endowed with its own four-valve cylinder heads, and double overhead camshafts, from way back in 1909!

It might not have reached the consciousness of most British manufacturers prior to that time, but Sir Harry Ricardo just might have heard of it, because he designed and built a special, four-valve 500cc single-cylinder engine for Triumph in 1921, the OHV design continuing until 1928. The occasional Ricardo Triumph was raced, but met with only limited success, its most impressive performance being the setting of the one-hour record of 76.74mph set on the bumpy Brooklands track in England. This was a rare event indeed for the British factory, which had commissioned the 'new' design. The all-new four-valve cylinder head and barrel took the place of an ailing 500cc side-valve model, but the bike was never intended to be raced, even though it was to prove to be a capable performer on a variety of circuits. The machine was, in fact, considered to be a 'one-off' special by most enthusiasts at the time.

The Triumph factory had never evinced much interest in racing at any time; as evidenced by the immediate post-WWII 500cc all-alloy *overhead valve* GP Triumph twin which was to be raced for only a few years thereafter. The GP Triumph was a reasonable performer at club level but could never have been considered a really serious road race motorcycle. Its production run was only for a couple of years, and it was raced with somewhat limited success. This was simply because the factory, under the instructions of its chief designer Edward Turner, showed no interest at all in developing any of its engines to be used in any form of racing. True, there was a complete racing kit for the Tiger 100C, post-1951 500cc all-alloy twins, and more than one American rider (besides the great Gary Nixon) rode Triumph motorcycles to many victories in AMA flat-track events in America, as a great many riders did in races throughout Australia as well, on tar-sealed as well as dirt tracks, but the Triumph factory itself remained disinterested.

But Ricardo's Triumph must have struck a chord with the Rudge–Whitworth factory, because nearly all of its roadsters and its road race machines – along with some replicas – were fitted with four-valve cylinder heads from 1924

The rare, 1921 500cc Triumph four-valve single, designed by Sir Harry Ricardo, may well have persuaded Rudge to abandon their outmoded, inefficient 'inlet-over-exhaust valve' layout. Rudge adopted the far superior four-valve design for all their 250, 350 and 500cc machines, including their very successful racing models.

This is a drawing of the busy Rudge 'Ulster' cylinder head and barrel, almost identical to the 'Special' except for the placement of the radial exhaust valves. Note heavier, shaded central 'slave' rocker which opens the exhaust valves. A rocker pushes down the right side of the slave rocker, which opens the right-hand exhaust valve, while the slave contacts another rocker-arm which in turn pushes down to open the left exhaust valve at the same time. **Note:** *also the long head bolts which come up from the base of the barrel to cinch the cylinder head down.*

on, when its first multi-valve engine, the smart-looking 350cc single, was fitted with four valves, all of them out in the breeze, for the overhead valve gear was not enclosed and was thus exposed to the elements. Previous Rudge engines had adopted the old-fashioned, inefficient 'inlet-over-exhaust' design.

One year later, the first of the larger, 500cc Rudge motorcycles appeared with four-valve cylinder heads, and a similar, four-valve head was also incorporated into the swift little 250cc single several years later, the small machine manufactured by Rudge from 1931 to 1936. That little Rudge was a very successful road-racer in the 250cc 'Lightweight' class, but with only a few more wins and major places to its credit than its 500cc siblings, the 250 filling three of the first four places in the Isle of Man Lightweight TT in its introductory year of 1931, with the first three places taken out again in 1934.

Although multi-valve cylinder heads were virtually universal in aircraft engines for many, many years from pre-WWI onwards, Rudge was actually unique at one time, for all its single-cylinder motorcycles employed four-valve heads for decades. Royal Enfield tried the multi-valve design in the 1930s, as did Ariel, Excelsior, New Imperial and one or two other British factories for a time, but they were mostly abandoned within a couple of years. Only Rudge (*'Rudge it, don't Trudge it'* was their business motto) pressed on with the four-valve design with their 500cc single-cylinder machines right through until the marque's sad demise in 1940, their once-naked overhead valve gear fully enclosed on the punchy 500cc singles by a large alloy rocker-box casting from 1937 onwards.

Though available for many years as a roadster or sports model in 250, 350 and 500cc capacities, it is as a 500 single that the Rudge is perhaps best known to enthusiasts, in either 'Special' or 'Ulster' guises: differing from one another very little cosmetically, though with some essential detail changes in engine specifications – particularly the four-valve heads fitted to the two models. The Special is Rudge's 25bhp tourer, the Ulster, with slightly higher compression ratio, bigger carburettor and more sporting cam profiles, produces a very handy 30bhp, the sports version capable of a top speed of just under 100mph.

There are a small number of Rudge motorcycles being ridden to Rallies and Club Day outings in Australia, and the odd one can occasionally be seen in almost daily use, while there are some which are perfectly preserved show-stoppers. One machine which fits both categories is the **1939 Rudge Special** owned and restored by ex-Speedway rider Neville Hutton of Chadstone, a suburb of Melbourne.

Hutton's Rudge Special is in absolutely showroom condition, with eye-popping chrome plate and dazzling black, relieved by gleaming gold pin-striping, the lot well augmented by aluminium castings buffed and polished to a mirror-like finish. You'd think a motorcycle with an all-black paint finish would be somewhat undistinguished, but the stove-enamelled Rudge glows like a black opal, the gold pin-striping adding the finishing touch to this gleaming, almost opalescent paint finish, while the very large, complex alloy castings with which the Rudge is blessed are gleaming with nary a fingerprint to be seen anywhere. It's a sight to behold; the machine in better than showroom condition.

Engine specifications would seem pretty basic, with bore and stroke dimensions of 84.5 x 88mm and pushrod–operated overhead valves, but Rudge had a trick or two up its sleeve, for the sports versions were amongst the fastest single-cylinder roadsters in their day. Back in 1928, a highly modified 500cc Rudge could be purchased – on 'Special Order', and at a somewhat higher cost – with a written guarantee of 100mph top speed, while an 'ordinary' Ulster model was road-tested by *Motorcycling* magazine in 1939 with a top speed of 92mph in full road-trim, the engine running at a brisk 5250rpm with a top-gear ratio of a high 4.53:1. This was very fast for an over-the-counter pre-World War Two 500 single, and the performance stacks up quite well against today's (by now quite rare) Honda and Yamaha road-going 500cc singles.

Part of the secret of the Rudge's high performance lay in the machine's four-valve cylinder head, which, as we've seen, became unique to the entire range after its adoption on both of the 500cc models from 1924 until 1940.

If the four-valve cylinder head wasn't designed by the Japanese – and there are some out there who still believe, in fact claim, it was – then, as we have already stated, it wasn't designed by Rudge either, though it was adopted from the time the older machine's inlet-over-exhaust design was dropped by the factory and, as we have noted, for some years the smaller-capacity 250 and 350cc models featured the four-valve head as well.

A single, tubular pushrod tower on the engine's right side and the large rocker-box cover make the Rudge Special look like an overhead cam design, and this impression is heightened by the twin exhaust ports and the large, alloy rocker-box cover, but an overhead camshaft design was not contemplated by the factory; Rudge was apparently well content with the simpler overhead valve design, controlled by pushrods, and they had every reason to be happy with the decision.

The Rudge Special cylinder head has the inlet and exhaust valves parallel to one another like a vertical twin, the valve angles allowing an efficient pent-roof combustion chamber, with the spark plug mounted centrally on the left side of the head. The pair of very long, steel pushrods operate the four valves through two rockers, with a single arm for each pushrod and double arms to operate each pair of valves. In comparison, the sportier Ulster model employed the more efficient radial design, where the two exhaust valves were displaced towards the extreme outside of the cylinder head, where they in essence formed part of a sphere. Rudge claimed the Special's exhaust ports were radial (which they were) but the inlet and exhaust valves themselves remained parallel to each other, while the sports Ulster machine employed a different valve layout.

The Rudge Ulster was named after Graham Walker's spirited win in the 1928 Ulster GP at the astonishing *average* speed for the race of **just over 80mph!** It was claimed that the 1928 Ulster GP was the first road race on record to have achieved an average race speed of over 80mph, a great achievement at the time. Walker was to become the Rudge company's Sales Manager in 1929 and was later to become a renowned BBC road race broadcaster and Editor of the famous British *Motorcycling* magazine.

The Special's inlet port is very smoothly

bifurcated from the single carburettor to the two valves, the changes in the one-inch (25mm) port sections allowing for a very large area and therefore a very easy passage of combustible mixture. On the other hand, the two exhaust ports are splayed out towards the outer area of the cylinder head. This allows for a series of deep, vertical fins between the exhaust ports to be a feature of the cast iron cylinder head, and it also allows for maximum air-cooling of this otherwise vulnerable and very hot area.

Close proximity of the two inlet valves overcomes the need for a tortuous inlet tract or twin carburettors (as fitted to the Excelsior 'Mechanical Marvel' 250 single of 1933), while the widely splayed exhaust ports allow for the adoption of a well-balanced and aesthetically pleasing twin exhaust layout. In passing, Rudge developed several four-valve heads with the more efficient, if also more complex, *four* full radially disposed valves employed at times over the years, particularly in their very successful racing engines, throughout the range from 250, 350 and 500cc models. The 1939 Ulster sports model was fitted with an aluminium/bronze alloy head for the first time, its parallel inlet and radial exhaust valves controlled by no fewer than four rocker arms in a most ingenious manner.

Today the four-valve head is back in vogue, and for several very good reasons. In this design the valve and port areas are greater in area than could usually be achieved with a single large valve, and heat dissipation is easier to achieve; the valve gear is usually lighter and thus more reliable, particularly at high engine speeds. A pair of smaller inlet ports allow for higher gas velocities at lower engine speeds than a single, larger port would, while the large inlet ports area (as distinct from size) does not restrict gas flow at peak engine speeds.

If the Rudge four-valve head was quite efficient and a little unusual in its day, then the rest of the engine is fairly straightforward. The cylinder head on Hutton's Special is cast iron and so is the cylinder barrel, the base of the barrel very thick and held to the crankcases by a row of stout little studs. The head is attached by studs which screw into it from below; clearly a necessity because there isn't much room inside the head for holding-down bolts with the long valve rockers and all that valve gear jumping about.

An unusual feature of the Rudge engine is the pressure-fed and 'flood' lubricated rocker gear, which receives some 12 pints of lubricant an hour at 5000rpm, almost as much as the caged-roller big-end's 13-pints per hour at the same engine speed. Usually, a single-cylinder 500cc would have its rocker gear lubricated from a by-pass line in a junction on the oil return pipe, while in some cases the necessary oiling of these often-forgotten parts would be by oil mist which wends its way up the pushrod tubes. In the 1930s, many machines, Vee-twins as well as singles, had exposed valve-gear which was lubricated by oil can, rain water, fog, or the occasional tall dog.

Valve guides are chilled cast iron, the tops chamfered to act as oil scrapers to overcome the possibility of high-pressure lubricant running down the valve stems and being sucked into the combustion chamber.

Ignition is by BTH magneto which sits – as it does on most British 500 singles – directly under the single AMAL carburettor. It is driven by a single-row chain, the drive sprocket attached

The long lever which actuates the centre stand tucks away neatly, well clear of the rear brake pedal, but is still very close to hand when needed.

to the end of the short camshaft. Beneath the camshaft, the simple, but clearly very effective, oil pump is driven by a small worm-wheel which is attached to the end of the crankshaft's half-time pinion.

Rudge always used drop-forged steel flywheels, which were by no means universal at the time, and this allowed the drive-side main-shaft to be serrated with very thin splines to carry the engine sprocket and its cam-and-spring shock absorber. The special high-carbon steel was assured of great strength in this highly stressed area, even though the main-shaft was of quite a small diameter. The connecting rod is similarly drop forged, but its section is smoother and more of a dumb-bell shape than the more usual H-section: the 'RSJ' (roof-supporting joist) used domestically and in heavy industry, is another example of the strong H-section. However, this 'dumb-bell' section is said to provide for more reliability from this very highly stressed component, which has been proven to be the case, for conrod failure has rarely – if ever – occurred with Rudge racing motorcycles.

The big-end is a three-row caged-roller component, the engine main-shafts supported on roller and ball main bearings on the drive side, a single roller bearing on the more lightly stressed timing side. The close-fitting, Y-alloy, slipper-type piston has just two rings, somewhat wider than fitted to modern machines, the gudgeon-pin located by brass end pads which can lightly bear against the cast iron cylinder walls.

Primary drive to the multi-plate 'damp' clutch and separate gearbox is by chain, the drive assembly carried in a huge alloy casting which dominates the machine's left side. It is a beautiful casting, which also encloses the drive to the front-mounted 6-volt Miller generator, and it has been buffed to a near-chrome-plated finish on the Hutton Special, the flat, outer face of the huge cover relieved by large domes to cover the engine sprocket shock absorber and the large clutch assembly.

Outboard of the large casting is a long lever which is used to haul the bike onto its centre-stand – very handy indeed, but not really necessary on a machine of this size. It could,

The lever can be used while normally seated and it takes little effort to haul the machine onto its centre stand. It is even easier to use when raising the stand again before riding off. What a handy lever that could be – or a button if electronic – if fitted to any one of the heavyweight Japanese four-cylinder machines!

however, be a very, very handy fitting on modern heavyweights, because that simple handle whips the bike on and off its stand with consummate ease.

The Rudge looks a gem, and there is more to it than skin-deep beauty because the engine fires up with a touch of effort and idles reliably… if a little on the noisy side.

As part of the starting 'drill' you have to back off the manual ignition timing, then flood the carburettor with its little 'tickler', find the correct position of the piston, ease the engine over its compression stroke with the valve lifter lever on the left handlebar, and then swing through with all your weight on the kick-starter.

It's a surprise when the old engine fires up about half-way through the kick and plonks away wooffily until you open the ignition timing to full advance again with the small handlebar-mounted lever. Exhaust note through the large-bore twin pipes and long mufflers with the 1930s tailfins is then a bit 'hearty' and there are some rattles from the engine room, but the bike has an eager feel about it, almost like a dog which has seen you open the front door and wave its leash about.

For some reason it lets you know when you are selecting first gear by crunching loudly and I found the clutch action a bit heavy, but all was forgiven when the clutch was home as the throttle was tweaked open.

The Rudge felt very secure, its girder front forks and rigid rear-end noisy in operation but comfortable enough – thanks to that oft-mentioned sprung saddle – and handling typical of a pre-World War Two British single. It's a fairly straightforward frame, but it employs the added rigidity of full-cradle support for the power-plant and this is reflected in the tight handling and eager responsiveness through medium-paced corners, even over rough surfaces.

Brakes are coupled, the rear pedal operating the front brake at the same time through a long cable, and I confess I wasn't too happy with this layout. The front brake is operated by its own lever, but you could not apply the rear brake without bringing the front one on as well and that was a bit disconcerting. I must say I had no trouble with it, but I rode a friend's pre-1940s Panther many times as a kid and it had coupled brakes as well. It often tried to pelt me up the road when braking hard and peeling over for corners, and once or twice it was successful.

I have no idea how the Panther's brakes were adjusted (my mate had no idea, either!) but I must confess the Rudge behaved itself very well under heavy braking, though it did bring some memories flooding back!

It has been said by some that the gearbox is the Rudge's Achilles' heel, but I am not certain why. It has been pointed out that the lower casing of the gearbox shell is very close to the lay-shaft gears and there is no room to allow for, say, a broken gear tooth or piece of selector spring to sit on the bottom of the box without being drawn into the spinning gears. But this may have been a rumour spread about by riders of rival machines which had to eat the dust of hard-ridden Rudges, for it might be reasonable to suggest that broken gear teeth and/or busted gear-change springs would be so rare as to be the stuff of legend!

Be that as it may, the gear-change was quick and easy – if sometimes noisy on downward changes, particularly into second gear, which couldn't be hurried – the ratios well suited to the engine's performance. The Rudge enjoyed that wide spread of power so much the hallmark of large-capacity British singles, but it liked to be buzzed a bit in the intermediate gears as well where its 'four-valve' deep breathing could clearly be felt. The engine isn't really a buzz-box, but the four-valve head still made for a spirited performance if you wanted to squirt the bike in second or third gear before giving the bike its head in top.

It pulled well and could be plodded along in top gear at quite low speeds, with surprisingly very good acceleration, or it could be wound out through the gears to the higher engine revs very quickly, depending on one's personal preferences, while there was some vibration as is usual with this type of machine. It was not the hand-numbing, backside-tingling vibration you

The Rudge 'Special' was a very capable performer, which could be easily thrown about from one footrest to the other, even in view of a rigid rear-end. Again, that simple, sprung saddle did a great job in ironing out many an uneven road surface.

experience with some of the old singles for it wasn't really all that intrusive, but you knew it was there.

Though the mufflers appear to be low-slung there is plenty of cornering clearance – in fact there is daylight under the footrests with the mufflers still clear when cornering briskly, and it's then only a question of how well the rigid rear-end hangs on as to how much further you want to punt it. The bike was rare enough to be treated with due respect, so we didn't explore the outer limits of its performance as we might have done with something similar – and of course very much *newer.*

It was all good fun nonetheless, providing us with more than a glimpse of how the best of single-cylinder motorcycles were built before the Second World War. It's a great engine and it has a proud past, with many, many wins in International road-race competition to its credit and a long list of accomplishments in competition off-road as well.

There are some limitations in the design of pre-WWII rigid frames and girder front-ends, which are apparent when thumping over uneven surfaces at speed, but the Rudge would run straight and true on a chosen line even if its rider was sometimes more than a little unsettled.

It's only of academic interest, but Rudge obviously had the formula right with its modern-as-tomorrow cylinder head, and you can't help wondering what the potential would be of a Rudge engine being fitted into a Norton Featherbed frame. I know the earnest brigade of dedicated Rudge fanciers out there would be horrified at such a suggestion but I can't help that.

The machine we have under review, the fine 1939 Rudge Special, was virtually the last of a long line of great motorcycles, for the marque disappeared the following year in quite unusual circumstances.

Rudge was apparently in financial strife for most of its life even though the company augmented its income by supplying its engines to many European manufacturers, as well as local competitors, under the *'Python'* brand name.

After the company's founder died in 1936, the company was sold to the most unlikely EMI group (owner of the HMV gramophone record label, among other things). The last few machines to be built – some of them bright red! – were made by the HMV factory from 1938 till 1940, when a war contract to supply radio equipment to the Allies saw manpower withdrawn from motorcycle manufacture and the marque quietly died.

A great shame, but there are many enthusiasts out there who have been trumpeting the imminent return to the marketplace of an all-new Rudge five-hundred, or are dreaming of the day when this may happen; we have heard this before, but it simply won't go away! A latter-day resurrection, naturally with all the modern *accoutrements*, were it ever to occur, would assuredly result in a very acceptable machine indeed. In the meantime, however, there is little to complain about; except, I must say, having to hand back this old gem, the gleaming 1939 Rudge 'Special.'

Not all Rudge machines were painted black-on-black, and it goes well back to the earlier machines, as evidenced by this 1930, 350cc model, with its hand-gear change attached to the right-hand side of the fuel tank, and original Rudge-Whitworth name. It was finished in a maroon colour, but there were many over the following years which were painted in a lighter shade of red, which was maintained by the final owners, EMI, for many of the very latest Rudge motorcycles were finished in a genuine Fire Engine Red.

There was never a blue Rudge, nor was there a green, mean Rudge machine, but the almost-traditional black finish, relieved, as we are aware, by large, heavily buffed alloy castings and chrome plate, remained far and away the most favoured 'colour' by the factory as well as by Rudge enthusiasts.

TECH SPECS

Make: Rudge

Model: Special

Year of manufacture: 1939

Type:
500cc Single-cylinder, four-valve engine, with cast iron head and cylinder barrel. The two inlet valves parallel, the exhaust valves 'semi-radial', with splayed exhaust ports and dual exhaust pipes. Separate oil tank, with dry sump lubrication, high pressure oil feed to caged-roller big-end, ball/roller main bearings and high-pressure feed to complex overhead valve gear.

Bore x stroke: 84.5 x 88mm

Carburation:
Amal 6-type, 1" carburettor, no air filter

Compression ratio: 6.8:1

Power @ rpm: 25BHP @ 5600rpm

Transmission:
By fully enclosed, 'oil-bath', ½" x 5/16" primary chain through four-speed Rudge gearbox, with right foot gear-change, one up, three down pattern. Final drive is by 5/8 x 3/8" chain.

Gear ratios:
1st – 13.28:1; 2nd – 7.36:1; 3rd – 5.62:1; 4th – 4.53:1.

Electrics:
Ignition by BTH magneto, electricity by 6-volt Miller generator, to wet lead/acid battery; large, 8" headlamp, and small, circular Miller tail-lamp.

Frame, suspension:
Tubular steel inserted and brazed into cast or forged lugs, with 'full cradle' engine support. Front forks are Webb-pattern girders with single compression spring, friction damper control. No rear suspension, with sprung saddle supported on short compression springs.

Wheels, brakes:
Steel 19" rims, laced with unusual 'offset' spoke pattern. 350 x 19" ribbed front tyre, 350x 19" block pattern on rear. Large, 8" front brake, 7" on rear, initially 'coupled'.

Dimensions:
Length – 210cm; Wheelbase – 135cm; Ground clearance – 12cm; Saddle height – 120cm; Weight – 131kg.

Top speed (suggested): 145km/h.

Machine loaned by:
NEVILLE HUTTON, Melbourne.

1970 (Dodkin) Velocette 'Thruxton'

500cc OHV SINGLE-CYLINDER SPORTSTER

Perhaps it was the smallest motorcycle factory in England – or one of the smallest – but the prodigious output of Birmingham's Veloce Limited facility must have made many of the much larger manufacturers green with envy, for the output of this first-class, family-owned factory was astonishing.

It all began, as most factories did, with a couple of impecunious men, one of them a Johannes Gutgemann, who later changed his name to become John Goodman, cobbling together a trim little motorcycle in 1905, the machine fitted with a four-stroke single-cylinder, 300cc proprietary engine designed by the brilliant Belgian Paul Kelecom. Kelecom became justifiably famous for his neat little engines, which were later used as the basis for his first four-cylinder power-plant, these very, very early multiple-cylinder engines fitted into the frame and cycle gear of the once-famous shaft-drive FN machines, which were initially made back in 1904.

In 1913, even as war clouds threatened, Veloce built a small, two-stroke machine it called the *'Velocette'* – for small Veloce – which was introduced in 1915, the new name so catchy it was to be used from then on for every other machine which was to be made in that small, tightly controlled, family-owned factory. It was a fairly successful machine and it led to one of the company's better-known lightweight machines, the 1930, 250cc GTP two-stroke. The new machine was well ahead of its time, the bike fitted with an impressive looking engine which employed dual, large diameter exhaust pipes and a fat, external flywheel which gave it a much more Macho image than many of the two-strokes which were on hand at the time.

The Velocette two-stroke engine was positively lubricated by a unique, throttle-controlled oil pump from 1932, which *augmented* the new 'positive-stop' foot gear-change mechanism, Velocette being the first motorcycle manufacturer in the world to adopt this positive-oiling system for two-strokes, as it did with the now-ubiquitous, positive-stop, foot gear change, originally adopted on its road race OHC singles from 1929. This forever moved the marque from the traditional hand gear change which was then in universal use. The neat GTP seemed to disappear during WWII – along with the single-cylinder 500cc OHV MSS model – but re-appeared after hostilities had finished. Then it ended its days when the last of them was made in 1946.

The 250cc GTP two-stroke was a very capable performer, even in view of its 'old-fashioned' deflector-type piston design. Performance was helped greatly by the large, external flywheel. The GTP was the earliest two-stroke to be fitted with a throttle-controlled oiling system to enable perfect lubrication, the oil carried in a separate container.

The positive-stop foot change mechanism was first employed by the factory for its highly successful KTT-series road racers in 1929 and was, of course, adopted across the range. The later, 1938 350cc overhead cam – and later double-overhead camshaft – Mark VIII KTT racers reached the pinnacle of success after the war, culminated in winning the 350cc World Championships in 1949 and in 1950. Not a bad effort for a factory of this modest size! The very rare **500cc** KTT racers were not nearly as successful, only a small handful having been built.

In 1939 the unfortunate Harold Willis (who died at a too-early age from meningitis) designed and built the one-off prototype 500cc OHC twin-cylinder 'Roarer', a supercharged road racer, which was not able to be fully developed, while a road-going overhead valve, shaft-drive version – another prototype called the Model 'O' – was built by a certain Phil Irving, who was even then becoming internationally famous as the designer of the exciting range of Vincent Vee-twin motorcycles. In those immediate pre-war years, the busy Phil Irving seemed to be cropping up everywhere in the motorcycle scene in England.

There were other machines built in the late 1920s to early 1930s which were somewhat more successful, in particular the bevel-driven, overhead camshaft 350cc KSS Sportster and the KTS 'Touring Sports' versions of the KTT racer, but these were essentially labour intensive and were thus not very profitable. The K-series roadsters were designed by Percy Goodman, a son of the founder, and were constantly developed from 1925 until the last one was made in 1948.

It was decided in 1933 that a trim little single-cylinder 250cc overhead valve, 68 x 68mm bore/stroke MOV model would round out the Velocette range, the machine very successful and quite rapid for its day, being capable of a genuine 70mph, which was faster than some of the more plodding five-hundreds, while a longer-stroke version, the 350cc MAC, was also listed. Just

This is the twin-cylinder, OHV, three-speed, shaft-drive, rear sprung 600cc Velocette Model O, and it is the only one of its type ever made: the onset of WWII saw to that! It was designed and built by the seemingly inevitable Phil Irving. Even if the jigs, patterns, dies, moulds, tech drawings and notes may still be in existence (somewhere?) it's a safe bet there is no way another Model O will ever be built. How sad!
Photo by permission of Dennis Quinlan (The Velolbanjogent)

two years later, a 500cc overhead valve model, the well-revered MSS, entered the catalogue, to finally take its place against a host of other 500cc OHV British singles. It became one of the factory's best sellers because of its spirited performance, which was due in no little measure to the later introduction of the justifiably famous '17/2' sports camshaft.

As we have noted, the first Velocette machines to be built just after the war were the GTP two-stroke, the KSS OHC sportster, the little 250cc MOV and the 350cc MAC, the MSS model, for some unaccountable reason, having vanished during hostilities. After the KSS and GTP models were phased out in the late 1940s, the strange little LE plodder appeared, a 150cc – later 200cc – water-cooled, shaft drive side-valve machine. The LE became something of a success but was never able to make a profit due to its very heavy 'start-up' and manufacturing costs.

It is not generally known, but the near-silent LE became a fairly successful farm bike for a few years in New South Wales and elsewhere, mainly because it was so comfortable, was shaft-driven and was able to be ridden up very close to sheep and cattle without spooking them because it was almost as quiet as a sewing machine – and just about as powerful!

In 1951 the little MAC received a much-needed tarting-up with the adoption of an all-alloy head and barrel, the smoothing out of its 'Map of Africa' timing case, and the cleaning up of its agricultural-looking external gear-change mechanism, which had remained mostly unaltered since 1929. In 1953 the smart-looking three-fifty achieved near perfection with the adoption of a full swing-arm rear suspension system, to augment Velocette's own, recently designed telescopic front forks. The company's front forks, which had taken the place of the spindly 'air-sprung' Dowty 'Oleomatic' telescopic forks, were allied to the adjustable, swing-arm rear suspension and dual spring-damper units, imbuing the new 1953 model with a very comfortable ride and first-class handling.

But what of the 500cc MSS; where was it? Most Velocette enthusiasts wanted to know what had become of the 'big' five-hundred, and it wasn't only the Australian riders who shouted long and loud for the larger machine to re-appear, for the Americans, who had 'discovered' the little 350, were clamouring for something bigger as well.

Suddenly the all-new 500cc MSS arrived on the scene in 1954, appearing to be almost identical to the smaller 350, while sharing the same frame and suspension, but of course fitted with an enlarged alloy head and barrel and the new 'square' bore x stroke dimensions of 86 x 86mm. The cylinder barrels on both machines were lined with a cast-iron sleeve moulded as one with the alloy barrel in Wellworthy's 'Al-Fin' process. It was a bit late in the game for the new five-hundred to be re-introduced, however, because even then the sales of motorcycles were beginning to slide down the gurgler world-wide. But the new five-hundred was reasonably successful, the factory fearlessly emboldened the following year to introduce re-designed engines for the more-sporty 350cc Viper and 500cc Venom models.

The 'standard' MSS pushed out a respectable 23BHP at just on 5000rpm, while the higher-spec **Venom** (which continued Velocette's basic overhead valve design in employing a high camshaft and short pushrods, but featuring some improvements to the cam profiles, porting and a stronger bottom half) produced a very handy 34BHP at 6200rpm. This was an impressive performance increase which was very acceptable indeed to Velocette fanciers. Sales began to pick up anew, to be further enhanced in 1961 when a highly tuned Venom achieved a 12-hour record on the steeply banked, badly lit, pot-holed and bumpy Montlhery circuit in France at 104.66mph, with a remarkable 24-hour record of just over 100mph to follow! Not bad for a 'simple', single-cylinder overhead valve British motorcycle, highly tuned though it may have been.

This great average speed included time lost when a large French rider fell off the machine at night – bending the gear-change lever, which took more than a half-hour to remove,

Grainy shot of Velocette managing director Bertie Goodman trying (unsuccessfully) to tuck his bulk inside the bike's trim fairing. A group of jockey-sized riders might have raised the record even higher, but it still remains a most impressive performance, which has never been equalled.

straighten and re-fit – while the distinctly lumpy Bertie Goodman, grandson of the company's founder and its current managing director, also found it almost impossible to get his bulk inside the machine's trim full fairing! The track was illuminated at night by the headlights of several cars, their 'strobe' effect making riding in the dark very dangerous, while the light fog which drifted across the area during the night added to the drama.

Had jockey-sized riders been employed, with no accidents and the bumpy track better illuminated at night... and with no fog?? To date, no motorcycle of any engine capacity, or from any country, has ever been able to achieve these remarkable figures, much less better them.

By now well-established, the Venom received its last hoist to glory in 1964 when the exciting Thruxton model was introduced. A thinly disguised racer in road-going trim, it was named after the well-known aerodrome circuit which played host to one of Britain's best-known long-distance races.

The Thruxton was essentially hand built, and it may lay claim to being the world's first single-cylinder Superbike; *if we may exclude the immortal 500cc DBD34 Gold Star BSA, of course!* The Thruxton featured a race-bred Amal GP carburettor with 1³⁄₈" bore, a huge 50mm (2-inch) inlet valve and a modified version of the famous MSS 17/2 sports camshaft. The compression ratio was a daunting 10.8:1, and the engine had a claimed output of 41 BHP at *'only'* (and isn't it low by modern standards?) 6700rpm!

Fitted with alloy rims, BTH race magneto and twin leading shoe front brake carried in full-width alloy hub and a similar hub on the rear, the bike weighed only 390 pounds (177kg).

By comparison, the much later Kawasaki Z1-R Superbike produced 90 hp at 8000rpm but weighed 540lbs (245kg); some 150lbs (68kg) more. In terms of BHP per litre the Velocette enjoyed a slight advantage – and at some 1300rpm lower – but the big Kwaka enjoyed an edge in the power/weight ratio. However, the Japanese machine was manifestly out-handled, out-braked – and often thoroughly out-performed on the open road – by the much smaller Velocette.

Quite apart from the 1961 24-hour record,

the Velocettes 500's proudest moment came in 1967 during the Production race at the Isle of Man, when two Thruxton models scored a one-two in the 500 class. Pulling its highest top gear of 3.5:1 and sporting a megaphone exhaust, the Thruxton was said to have bettered over 130mph on one of the fastest straights, which would put it on the very short list of the fastest overhead valve, push-rod singles ever made.

Sadly, Velocette went into liquidation in 1971, but not before a number of the latter-day Thruxton models had reached Australia some years earlier. And that includes the machine under review; the last of the single-cylinder Superbikes, the **1970 Dodkin Velocette Thruxton**, owed by arch-enthusiast Alan Morris, to whom I am not related. The bike carries the Dodkin prefix simply because one-time specialist Geoff Dodkin bought a supply of parts from the Hall Green firm just before it went down the drain and built a series of specials with many of his own parts fitted.

The Thruxton under test carried a cast-alloy Dodkin top fork bridge-piece, an Amal 30mm Concentric in place of the temperamental race-bred Amal GP fitted to the earlier models, and several smaller non-standard parts.

That 1970 model still bore more than a passing resemblance to the machine which spawned it 35 years before. The 'square' 86 x 86mm alloy cylinder barrel and alloy head remained as they were when the bike had re-appeared in 1954. The timing case was slightly more rounded but still similar to the 'Africa' shape of the pre-war model, while the generator still sat ahead of the base of the cylinder barrel, driven by a belt from the engine sprocket. At least it was better than earlier examples which used the same flat belt as the one fitted to the Austin 7 car, for later machines used different pulleys and a V-belt.

Thankfully, the later models all sported the Velo redesigned Brooklands-pattern fishtail muffler which made the machine sound so very distinctive and set it apart from most of the other post-war British singles; the notable exception being the 1947 International Norton, which also fitted a fishtail muffler which passed for a *genuine 'Brooklands Can'*.

It was not only in the muffler that the Velocette differed from its fellows. Though essentially similar to other five-hundred singles in basic design, Velocettes were possessed of as

Calling back to base in this original 1979 shot, after a very vigorous, hard squirt along some very swift roads. The Thruxton clearly enjoyed the experience every bit as much as I did. Note the black, dished cover over the belt drive to the forward-mounted generator, remembering that the most expensive motor vehicles on earth still employ belt drives to many of their electrical components!

many different characteristics as there were models. Just as the 1000cc Fours which spring from the major Japanese manufacturers are similar in design philosophy but poles apart in behaviour, so too are the punchy old British singles of yesteryear.

The Dodkin Velocette features most of the allure of the Thruxton while adding a few refinements of its own. The riding position is not amongst the most comfortable you'd find, for it features the rear-set footrests and low handlebars which were so much the rage with this type of 'Cafe Racer' machine nearly a decade earlier. It means that most of the rider's weight is on wrists and reproductive organs until it is offset with high wind pressure generated at peak touring speeds. It also means gear-changing is not the easiest of tasks until the 'feel' of the machine is mastered.

This applies to the rear brake in particular, which has the lever positioned to allow maximum pressure to be applied when the rider is well back on the humped-back seat; a riding position which does not work very well at lower speeds. The suspension works well and the long dual-seat is soft enough, so the bike is not really uncomfortable, but it does take some time to become accustomed to the way it 'feels' when punting it along with some urgency.

Many people argue that a Big Single cannot be effectively balanced – and that heavy vibration is therefore a standard feature with this type of design. These people have not ridden a single-cylinder Velocette, for one of the most remarkable features of the model was its uncanny smoothness at almost any engine speed. A slight and narrow vibration period sets in at around 4800rpm but that's all. The machine is quite free of *any* major hassles from vibration.

No doubt the short, rigid crankpin, the comparatively narrow flywheels and the tapered main bearings on which the assembly sits are responsible for much of the engine's smoothness, but I clearly recall an old 500 OHV Ariel single (the green-tank VG model) I once owned, which is still amongst the smoothest-running engines I have ever fired up and squirted in anger.

The reason for Velocette's smooth running lies in an inherently well-balanced engine, which in Velocette's case is contained within a low, lean and distinctly hungry-looking frame. The bike appears smaller than many a modern-day 500 – in fact not much bigger than a modern-day 250 – while the obvious sports design turns many heads at race meetings and traffic-lights.

Primary drive to the decidedly strange clutch is by chain in the pressed-metal chaincase so typical of the period, with the clutch essentially dry and the primary chain immersed in oil.

The very narrow crankcases allow the primary drive to be kept well inboard of the frame rails, with the clutch tucked well inside the general lines of the engine and the generator drive and final-drive counter-shaft sprocket carried well outside the primary chaincase.

A small, pressed-metal case covers the vintage-like belt drive to the forward-mounted generator, while another complementary case covers the

The tacho/speedo instruments are boldly placed and hard to ignore, unless riding at the speed in which the bike is often ridden. It is then a whole lot safer to watch where one is swiftly moving than to be watching a pair of grinning faces.

Several things: note the huge carburettor, and too-short kickstarter. Also, the rear-set footrests and large muffler, which was tucked so closely to the frame that it very rarely scraped. Rear spring/damper units employed no pre-load but are attended to by adjusting the angle of the units, moving them back or forth in the unique, slotted upper mountings.

final drive sprocket for the rear wheel. The unusual design allows the final-drive sprocket to be replaced with ease, or a tossed chain to be threaded back again in a few moments, but it makes for a peculiar clutch design and it takes some time to come to grips with adjustments when the need arises.

If there was a weak point in the Velocette clutch design then it was always the thrust bearing, which was supposed to be loaded only when the clutch was withdrawn. This was fine provided the Velo owner merely slipped the lever to the bars when making gear changes, but it was murder if he was unwise enough to sit at lights and still in gear with the clutch lever held to the handlebars. You aren't supposed to do that anyway – but it was doubly dicey with the Velo!

Owners of the marque will doubtless argue that there was no real trick to adjusting the clutch – which should not be adjusted by merely nipping up the cable adjuster – but it was not amongst the easiest chores and was always fraught with the risk that a maladjustment would cause pressure to be placed on the thrust bearing even when the clutch was not freed. Among other makes, I used to sell Velocette spare parts many, many years ago, and there was always a fair call on complete clutch thrust bearings.

The trick to adjust the clutch was to insert a pin through a convenient hole in the final-drive sprocket and wheel the bike back and/or forwards until the correct amount of free-play was noted at the handlebar lever. The pin slipped into a groove on the outside of a large screw-in lock ring which held a series of 16 short, strong clutch springs in place and which in turn bore against a plate which actuated the clutch release and which made contact with the aforementioned thrust bearing and – as I said – it was an odd clutch assembly. Happily, the Dodkin Thruxton on test gave no trouble at all in this department – or any other for that matter!

The clutch came in for its fair share of work, let it be known, for the Thruxton is very high-geared and not about to move away from the mark unless coaxed to do so with some throttle and a little more clutch. Once it begins to bite the clutch works beautifully, taking up the power with ease and smoothness. The exhaust note is typical Velocette: once heard, never mistaken. It's a deep *'woofy'* sound, resonant and hinting at the power of a well-tuned engine, but in no way offensive. The muffler appears to be too low-slung to be fitted to an unashamed sports mount which should be pelted through corners with abandon, but the extremely narrow crankcases allows the muffler to be tucked in very close to the side of the machine, and it will only touch a road surface on bumpy corners while at the most absurd lean angles.

Typically, the Velocette feels light at the steering head and makes heavy, armoured tanks of some latter-day machinery. It takes some time to grasp the fact that one does not have to heave the machine down and hold it there if one wishes to corner like someone who should be led quietly away and sat upon 'til the police come.

But the riding position is something else again. Low speed riding results in too much weight on the wrists and that makes riding to the city limits before a long blast into the country a bit daunting. Oddly, these odd thumps and nudges have much more effect on the rider than they do on the machine – arguably better than having it the other way round. At high speeds where wind pressure asserts itself by lifting the rider's body slightly, the problem virtually disappears.

The Thruxton is a total delight to fling about from footrest to footrest through a series of fast, sweeping Ess-bends. The twin-leader Dodkin brake on the front of our test bike is a beauty and slams the Velo to a tyre-yelping stop in short order and with no sweat at all, seemingly in perfect harmony with the rear anchor. Drum brakes are standard ware on the Velocette, but disc brakes were neither specified nor needed, for there is no way a machine like this one would need to be heaved to a stop any quicker.

Nor is there any need to buzz the engine to get it to come to the boil quickly. Upward gear changes can be made at no more than 4000rpm, even when pressed. Allowing third to run out to 5000rpm before slipping into top sees a cruising speed well above the legally acceptable come onto the clock – and then left far behind!

It is only at these road speeds that the semi-prone riding position comes into its own and the Velocette sings its song of joy, freed from the fettles of suburbia and allowed to have the free reign it so obviously demands. Cruising speeds are simply a matter of rider skill and road surface, for there seems to be no upward limit as far as the motorcycle itself is concerned.

Open, sweeping bends are attacked with great confidence, with the muffler occasionally zinging lightly on the deck when the suspension goes to full bump on the right, or the footrest lightly kissing the tar on the left, very slightly ahead of the prop stand. Again, these seem to be the only limiting factors to cornering speeds, for it is the usual application of some common sense which really dictates top cruising speeds.

One medium-paced corner was attacked on the Thruxton with some enthusiasm, elbows and knees tucked in, the bike leaping out of a hollow approaching this tightening-radius corner while attacking it full-stick in second gear. It cracked round pulling hard, and the change to third was made just as the bike was being lifted up again, the engine pulling beautifully and that familiar Velo thump on perfect pitch. It was really Magic Stuff, let there be no doubt about it, and there should be a whole lot more of it!

Why is it that an old-fashioned, single-cylinder British motorcycle backed with a great racing history, but with its fair share of oil leaks and old-fashioned design, can stir anyone to make these sorts of noises?

Believe me, it is only after having ridden a motorcycle which goes precisely where it is pointed and which does most of your own work for you, that you realise how great that little motorcycle really is.

But who is going to put up with an outmoded machine like the Velocette anyway when one can fire an engine up by simply pressing a button and when one can light the way home with even more safety by merely flicking a blinker switch instead of holding a hand out at arm's length to let some twit know what one plans on doing – and then finding that the person has no idea what that old-fashioned hand signal means, anyway!

But as an exercise in building simple, well-engineered and potent roadsters which had the most exemplary manners – minor oil leaks, 6-volt lights and all – and which could be ridden at very high speeds with a high margin of safety, the British had the game well and truly sewn-up.

When I said 'lighting my way home with

In 2020, just over 40 years after the original report was published in 'Two Wheels' magazine, and by now well into my 80s, I couldn't resist a couple of swift laps round the block on the Thruxton. Others were looking for an ideal 'photo shoot' location at the time.   Photo credit: Lyn Morris (wife)

safety' it might have sounded like a crack at the Velocette's electrics. This is not quite right for the Velo came on strong in the lighting department, thanks to owner Alan Morris fitting the headlamp shell with a Cibie QI light unit of Death Ray potential. He also fitted a *Japanese battery!*

There was one hassle with the machine, but that was soon overcome with practice. As I said, the Velocette was not fitted with an electric starter and it was never amongst the easiest of machines to start simply because of the low-geared kick-starter and comparatively light flywheels. But it could be done: with enough practice.

That ultra-short kick-starter *must* be in precisely the correct position relative to the piston, and it must also be in sync with the manually adjusted ignition setting if the bike is to fire up in one kick whether hot or cold.

Well, I'd lost the knack somewhere over the years, because it took several kicks and some alarming sounds from the Velocette engine – and some alarming sounds from owner Alan Morris (and myself) as well, I might add! – before I could get the engine to come to the party.

Being equipped with the shortest legs in

motorcycling didn't help either, but the problem was soon cured when I employed the cunning ploy of standing with my left leg on the footpath and leaning on the kick-starter with a bit more muscle. Following-through with the last few inches of travel provided the oomph needed to fire it up in one kick. Or no more than two kicks with practice, even when the engine was stone-cold.

The Thruxton is a highly tuned beast and it has some claim to temperamental behaviour I suppose, and such are the quirks the modern-day rider would probably not accept – unless of course the essential, exhaust valve-lifter was dispensed with and a starter button was fitted to the right handlebar!

The fact is that the first of the SR500 Yamaha singles – with its smaller, lighter flywheels – was also a very difficult machine to start unless you had the knack, so it's at least one quirk which cannot be levelled at the older design alone.

Would that the Velo had some of the great refinements which the overhead camshaft SR500 Yamaha enjoyed …

Would that the Yamaha had some of the priceless assets the Velocette took with it into history!

This last model of a great marque was built in limited numbers by a man who tried, along with several other British stalwarts, to save the name even after Veloce Ltd went to the wall. It is still said in Velocette enthusiast circles that the jigs, patterns and dies are still in existence, with spare parts still easy to source internationally.

The Thruxton Velocette remains an example of one of the finest Classic single-cylinder motorcycles ever built: in Britain, or elsewhere. We may never again see a Big Single which so well combined the elements of an enduring, reliable and extremely potent road-burner, and which, with little coaxing, could blow most highly touted rivals into the roadside verges – with the possible exception (again!) of the well-revered Gold Star BSA, some might say? Well perhaps that is so, but as many a long-term, serious Velocette owner would argue … perhaps not!

TECH SPECS

Make: Velocette

Model: Thruxton

Year of manufacture: 1970

Type:
All-alloy, single-cylinder overhead valve four-stroke, with camshaft carried high in timing case and valve control by short pushrods and hairpin valve springs. Built-up crank, with short crankpin, narrow flywheels and shafts supported on tapered roller bearings; one-piece connecting rod with caged roller big-end. Dry sump, with separate oil tank

Bore x stroke: 86 x 86mm

Capacity: 499cc

Compression ratio: 9:1 (many available)

Power @ rpm: 41BHP at 6200rpm

Carburation:
Amal 30mm Concentric, no air filter fitted.

Ignition:
BTH racing magneto, manual advance and retard.

Electrics:
Belt-driven Miller generator, 6-volt, 18-amp/hr battery.

Transmission:
By enclosed roller chain to multi-plate 'damp' clutch and separate four-speed constant-mesh gearbox, with right foot change. One up, three down pattern.

Gear ratios (Overall):
1st – 10.1:1; 2nd – 6.97:1; 3rd – 5.30:1; 4th – 4.4:1. Many different internal ratios originally available, with top ratio varying from 3.5 to 4.7:1

Frame, suspension:
Single down-tube, splaying into full-cradle type, welded steel with special cast lugs at steering head and swing arm points.
Front forks: Velocette make, with coil springs and two-way hydraulic damping, telescopic design.
Rear: swing arm with Woodhead-Monroe units with adjustable top mount position. The spring/damper units are not themselves adjustable for spring tension or damping.

Wheels, tyres and brakes:
Front alloy rim laced to full-width hub containing twin leading-shoe internal expanding drum brake. Rear alloy rim laced to full-width alloy hub containing single-leader drum brake inboard of rear sprocket. Dunlop K81 tyres fitted to test machine, 325 x 19 ribbed front, 350 x 19 block pattern on rear.

Dimensions:
Length – 2013mm;
Wheelbase – 1345mm;
Seat height – 775mm;
Ground clearance – 150mm;
Weight – 179kg;
Tank capacity – 22.5 litres.

Performance:
Top speed, 175 km/h; Standing quarter, 15.1 sec.

Machine loaned by:
ALAN MORRIS.

1938 500cc Scott Squirrel

TWIN-CYLINDER TWO-STROKE

Way back in 1905 when most 'motorcycles' were little more than lightly powered pushbikes and were still fitted with pedals to assist in climbing hills, the brilliant, innovative and assuredly eccentric inventor Alfred Angas Scott introduced into the small marketplace his marvellous two-cylinder, 333cc water-cooled two-stroke motorcycle which shone like a beacon for others to follow. Just six of the machines were built in England for Scott by the fledgling Jowett Car Company before he began to build his own shortly thereafter, the Jowett Brothers' vehicles becoming much better-known (and reasonably popular) just after World War Two as the horizontally opposed, four-cylinder, 'Javelin' saloon and 'Jupiter' sports/tourer motorcars. He had made several earlier models, but this machine was the first to be made in any real numbers. It was to be the first of many thousands of future machines, right up to the early 1960s.

The new Scott motorcycle was a very advanced design, employing a triangular, 'open' frame like a girls' bike which allowed women to ride it with ease (and quite a few did!) while it was probably the first machine ever to be fitted with a kick-starter. It also employed a simple, if fairly effective, early example of telescopic front forks, and its specifications also included a rare two-speed transmission, which was controlled by a small heel-and-toe lever on the machine's right side which engaged – or disengaged – a pair of sliding 'dogs' which were in-built into its chain-driven primary drive transmission. In the days when almost all of the crude two-wheelers which were puttering about employed belt drive, and most of them had no primary transmission at all, the machine was advanced enough to use chain drive to the rear wheel as well. It was thus rightfully claimed to be an 'all chain drive'.

The fuel tank was wrapped around the bike's upright seat post and was thus sited between the rider's knees, while the original 'telescopic' forks remained in place with little but minor modifications until 1931, when the machine seemingly took a step backwards in replacing this advanced design with a set of girder forks of a type used by almost all of its contemporaries. But the engine's basic design was so brilliant that, apart from the essentials of modern, cosmetic changes, including the adoption of the more efficient 'loop scavenging', flat-top pistons in some machines in 1958 (where, going full-circle, again just six motorcycles were built), it remained pretty much as it was for all of *50 years*.

That's all of 50 years; and arguably 20 years longer, because a fellow called George Silk resurrected a 'kind of' Scott motorcycle in the mid-1970s. If not in name, the first Silk/Scott (he used Scott transfers on the tank of his first machines, along with his name) it was at least Scott in substance, for his original machines used rebuilt Scott engines before he began to build his own, still based upon the older Scott design – including, it must be noted, a return to the 'old-fashioned' deflector pistons – in an instantly recognisable, if much more modern-looking roadster.

To publicise his new machine, Alfred Scott entered one of his new machines in the Isle-of-Man Senior event in 1910, where it was the

Three years after the first-ever Scott was built, here is the 1908 machine, said to be designed for women to ride. It's rudimentary, of course, but still far ahead of almost all competitors, particularly in its comparatively high performance. It could have used a front brake to advantage!

The 1970s Silk 700S was a high-performance motorcycle, thanks to its large-capacity, two-stroke engine. Silk initially used rebuilt Scott engines, but finally began to make his own, still using Scott's design as a template.

first-ever two-stroke to be campaigned, and it astounded everyone the following year by setting a new lap record – over some pretty grim unsealed road surfaces, be it known – of more than 50 miles per hour average! It won the 500cc Senior event in 1912 and again in 1913, where it showed it was by far the fastest machine on the long circuit – and everywhere else! – so much so that it was thenceforth 'handicapped' (or *penalised* if you like) by having its 500cc engine capacity multiplied by a factor of 1.32 whenever it competed against the rash of 'inferior' four-strokes. Unfair perhaps, but it provided some great publicity for the Flying Scott, which did no harm at all to sales.

Scott built several sidecar machine-gun carriers which he hoped would be used during the First World War, and immediately afterwards designed a strange contraption he called the Scott 'Sociable' which looked not unlike a sidecar machine over which somebody had draped an oddly shaped car body. It, too, was hoped to be adopted by the armed forces, but it looked not unlike a car which had had its left front wheel stolen, so it's probably no surprise that it was rejected. It had two wheels in line like a motorcycle, with a third wheel carried on the left side like an outrigger, the machine powered by the larger 600cc Scott motorcycle engine, which was available in the roadster bikes along with the 'standard' five-hundred. The strange Sociable looked to be very unwieldy and was in fact dangerous if driven into left-hand corners too quickly, and may well have been a disaster if driven at *any* pace over rough country.

However, Scott decided to press on with the device and initially offered it to the public in 1919, at the same time as he left the company he founded and to which, for some unaccountable reason, *he was never to return*. The Sociable was finally manufactured in 1921, where some 200 of the vehicles were said to be built during the next six years. Unhappily, Alfred Scott, that inimitable genius, passed away in 1923 from the onset of pneumonia which he contracted after driving home in his open Sociable in wet and chilly weather. He had already been ill, and had compounded this by wearing clothes which were still soaking wet from a recent foray into a large, damp cave he was exploring. 'Pot-holing' – as it is still called – was said to be a passion of his.

If the Scott Sociable remains an oddity and by no means a successful one, then the Scott motorcycle remains secure in its niche as one of the most revered Classic motorcycles ever built, in fact it is (perhaps rightly?) considered by many Scott enthusiasts to be the greatest two-stroke machine of all time, its only modern counterparts, the post-war 500cc twin-cylinder two-stroke Suzuki Titan twin from the 1970s, and the rare Ossa five-hundred twins said to be not in the same league as the Scott machines. Of course, DKW built their own 500cc twin-cylinder two-stroke motorcycles before WWII, and they appeared to have been every bit as popular as the Scott of similar – or larger – capacity.

Scott always claimed his machine was years

ahead of its time and in many ways he was right. The machine I rode for this test report – a **1938 500cc Scott 'Squirrel'** – was extremely basic in terms of its rudimentary suspension (or lack thereof) and its poor brakes, but there was nothing plebeian about the design of the engine unit itself.

Essentially, a twin-cylinder two-stroke is a 'modular' design which consists of two entirely separate engines coupled to a common crankshaft, for the essentials of crankcase compression and the efficient transfer of gases from crankcase to combustion chamber require separate crankcase chambers for each set of cranks and separate ports for each of the two cylinders.

In the Scott design this requirement is carried to the extremes of providing the primary drive from the *centre* of the two separate crankshafts and carrying the two connecting rods outboard of the two separate crank chambers on overhung cranks. Thus, there is no 'outer' engine mainshaft and thus no main bearings in the outer 'cases'.

Because there is no outer crank-cheek into which the big end's crank-pin is inserted and no supporting mainshaft, plus the two cranks disposed at 180 degrees, with its resultant, in-built 'rocking couple', serious crankshaft (that is, *centre mainshaft*) flexing would be expected to occur in this design, but the thick and stubby centre shafts of each crank are firmly supported on gas-sealed, large roller bearings in the flywheel's centre, the assembly key-locked on tapers as they fit closely into the middle of the large, centrally mounted flywheel. A long bolt passes through the hollow centre of the left half-shaft locks into its mating shaft on the right side, locating the whole assembly firmly against the main bearings and into the carefully machined tapered centres of the two bosses and the flywheel itself. Extremely accurate machining would be necessary to be sure the entire crank assembly would be 'true' in every plane as it is tightened.

The assembly is extremely rigid, with gas sealing assured by spring-loaded gland seals on the two half-shafts which butt into the flywheel as they enter the large crankcase, while the outer face of the overhung cranks – located in their individual crank chambers outboard of the main cases – are equipped with additional flat, face-type sealing plates. The big-ends employ crowded rollers bearings which – along with the conrods – are well contained by special plates which are located at the face of the rods by small screws which engage with threaded holes drilled into the ends of the overhung crankpins. The two 'Pilgrim' oil pumps – essentially the same as the 'total-loss' oil pumps fitted to Speedway motorcycles and some early roadsters – are driven from small 'pins' on the outside plates' locating screw, which drives another plate through an annular groove, the latter plate's central shaft having a small slot in its end which locates against the oil pumps' central drive spindles.

The left side oil pump provides most of the lubrication, and is 'timed' to coincide with the end of each transfer phase, so that oil is not only

The strange-looking 600cc Scott 'Sociable' looks as though someone (a) threw a metal bedspread over a motorcycle/sidecar and added a windscreen, or (b) had stolen the left front wheel from somebody's sports car. It would have been a shocker through left-hand corners without a passenger to keep the third wheel on the ground!

pumped, but 'sucked' into the mini-vacuum inside the separate crank chambers, where it feeds the main and big-end bearings. The other pump supplies a much smaller amount of oil through small-diameter pipes and oil galleys to the skirts of the long pistons.

If the lower half of the engine pursues the 'separate motors' theme as far as it can, the barrel, pistons and single carburettor are apparently at odds with this premise. Employing very deep spigots, the one-piece, two-cylinder barrel appears to be very short when it is secured on the crank chambers. It has a series of massive inlet, transfer and exhaust ports carefully machined into three faces of the deep spigots and has 16 studs with which to attach the alloy head. The barrel itself is attached to the cases by just four bolts.

The transfer ports have detachable covers (the reason for this is simply that half the transfer ports are located beneath the top lip of the crankcase castings when the barrel is inserted) with the ports running from the crank chambers to the barrel on the same face as the single carburettor, and of course directly opposite the exhaust ports. It's another unusual arrangement by current standards, for the more modern, 'loop-scavenged' two-stroke engines have these carefully sited transfer ports running up the sides of the barrels between the carburettor and exhaust ports.

The major difference in the much later two-stroke design, with the 'Schneurl' loop-scavenging system and flat-top pistons, is that the Scott engine (and many of its contemporaries) used the three-port system which had the exhaust and transfer ports directly opposite, and thus facing, one another. In this design, both sets of ports are open together, with the transfer gases controlled by the so-called 'deflector' piston, which has a large hump-like, near-vertical deflector on the crown to direct the incoming gas up the side of the cylinder walls away from the hot exhaust gas which is being expelled ahead of it. The exit of the exhaust gas is then controlled by the side of the piston **opposite** the transfer port by a more steeply sloped, curved shape facing the exhaust outlet and is thus designed to keep the two gas streams as far removed from each other as possible.

Good low-speed pulling power was a feature of this type of design, because the ports could be accurately machined and very, very large without losing structural strength – the deeply spigotted barrel and high-lipped crankcase would see to that – but the main drawback was the low compression ratio forced upon the designers by the 'hunch-back' deflector pistons.

Simply put, the engine is not a high-revving design, nor was it ever intended to be. The overhung cranks, no matter how strong and perfectly aligned, might not allow for overly high revs anyway, simply because, as we have noted, they were supported on the one (central) side only, and the in-built 'rocking couple' of the 180-degree action may further restrict this. It was nonetheless an utterly brilliant design by Mr Scott, and it has clearly stood the test of time as others of its era have too often failed to do.

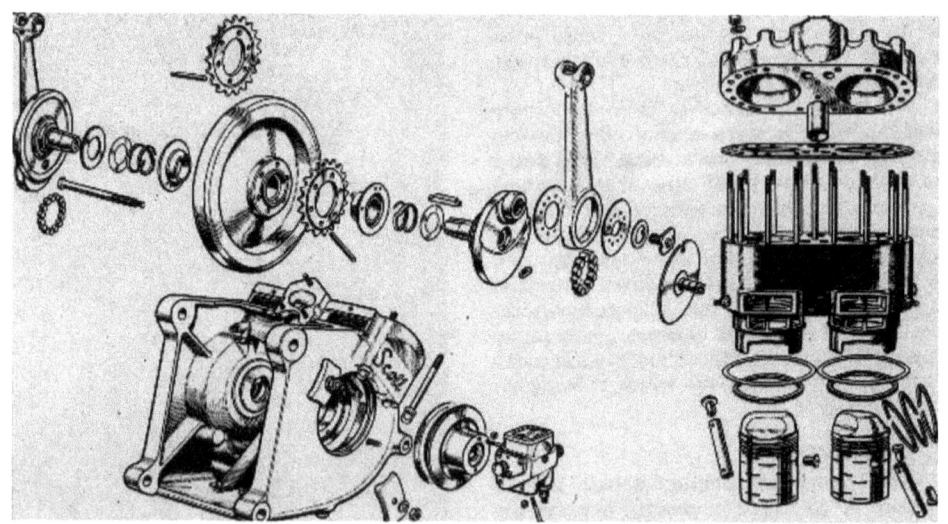

Drawing of the Scott engine. Note the 'overhung' cranks, with single mainshafts which go into the centre of the flywheel, the two hollow shafts nipped up on tapers by a long through-bolt. Note the drive pinion to the R.H 'Pilgrim' oil pump and the 'deflector' type pistons.

But, 'old-fashioned' though the engine design may have been, the bike's performance was by no means docile!

Positive lubrication is a great feature of the design, with a separate oil supply from a compartment in the petrol tank, the lubricant metered to the engine through the dual-supply, 'total loss' Pilgrim oil pumps, mounted externally and driven, as we have seen, from the ends of the overhung cranks.

The chain primary drive is taken from the flywheel, with the drive sprocket riveted direct to the left face of the large flywheel; a smaller sprocket attached to the opposite side of the component providing the drive for a Lucas Mag-Dyno, that once-common dual instrument which supplied spark for ignition and current for lights and battery.

The semi-close-ratio gearbox has just three gears – and very tall gears at that, with plenty of clutch and a generous handful of throttle needed if you want to get off the mark very sharply. It makes a mockery of the modern, multi-speed gearboxes fitted to latter-day, high-performance two-stroke machines, for the wide spread of power and good low-speed torque developed by the Scott engine makes the use of a five or six-speed gearbox unnecessary.

This is just as well, for the Scott gear-change – probably because of the ravages of time – is somewhat uncertain until you learn to 'pre-load' the gear lever before selecting the gear you are fumbling about for. Some Scott motorcycles were fitted with four-speed gearboxes, but they proved to be more nuisance than they were worth, because it was said of them that 'there are four gears to choose from, but about 16 false-neutrals as well'. It has been said that much later modifications to the (redesigned?) four-speed Scott gearbox entirely eliminated this serious problem.

Water-cooling is taken care of by the thermo-syphon system as no water pump is fitted. A rubber hose from the rear of the cylinder head carries the rising hot water to the radiator header tank, while the cooler water in the bottom of the radiator circulates to the front of the head at the hotter exhaust ports. A simple system, which relies on convection currents, it is nonetheless quite effective. On one occasion during this day-long test, however, some steam escaped from the radiator overflow pipe in heavy traffic and took some of the coolant with it. The trouble never occurred while on the move, and it was a fearfully hot couple of summer days.

First gear will carry the Scott to an indicated 75km/h without distress, and probably higher if I had ignored the age of the old steed, while second carries the bike comfortably beyond the legal limit. Top gear is a gem, and will pull from a brisk canter to an indicated speed of about 135km/h. According to the original road-test report the bike could exceed this speed without trouble, but the thought kept impinging on my mind that the bike was a rare one, and would probably not be an easy one to replace! It would probably have taken an age to stop the bike from high speeds as well, for the brakes were not very effective. However, if the worst had come to the worst, there is apparently no shortage of newly made Scott spare parts available overseas, if one knows where to find them.

Starting was never easy, even though the time-honoured drill was used. With fuel on, one would tickle the carburettor to raise the fuel level till the Amal carburettor was flooded, then kick hell out of the thing with the throttle less than about one-quarter open.

Suddenly and without warning, the engine would leap into life and shatter the silence with that once-famous and revered Scott yowl, before it settled down to a lumpy idle. If the throttle was closed off too much the engine would stall and – even though running well at the time – would then need to be re-tickled and kicked as heartily as before. If the engine had stopped in traffic … ?

The engine pulls very smoothly, and with acceleration which is very surprising. The exhaust header pipes are very large diameter, and the bike differs from other two-strokes in having a two-into-one exhaust system. This 'Siamesed' system has always imbued four-stroke engines with good mid-range pulling power, and it has apparently helped the big two-stroke in this area as well.

As I've said, the old two-stroke accelerates well – in fact it blew off the traffic at every set of lights with no trouble – and this is helped by the take-off drill forced by the tall first gear. It needs a generous handful of throttle and a touch of clutch slip (in that order, might I add!) to get underway, and the exhaust sound is Pure Magic! It scurries off the mark with a howl like a monster from a horror movie, but it takes some hanging onto if you are to go along with it.

Unhappily, the saddle position is probably the worst I have ever come across; to say it is uncomfortable is to understate the situation very seriously! The frame design is unusual, even by modern standards, and is of the fully triangulated type. It makes for a very rigid assembly (very handy if the suspension – or lack of it – is not up to scratch), with the steering head well braced and the large engine acting as a structural member of the frame.

This triangulated design sees a pair of tubes sweep down from the steering head to the base of the crankcases, with a similar, shorter set fixed to the top of the cases above the gearbox. These tubes then sweep up to a point under the single saddle then rearwards to carry the rear wheel.

Therein lies the problem, for the seat is mounted on a small post atop the point where all the road shocks are forced to converge, and the seat on this machine cannot be effectively sprung of itself. Usually, a spring saddle was hung by its nose and pivoted to allow the springs to take much of the shock, but in this case the seat is mounted on the frame protrusion as if on a bicycle, and the large saddle springs simply do not work effectively.

Riding the bike at brisk speeds over indifferent surfaces was for all the world like being forced to run along while touching your toes and being booted up the behind every two or three metres by an enthusiastic, obese wharf-labourer wearing a size-10 worker's boot equipped with a steel-toecap!! I remain convinced this cannot be the original saddle.

There was a 1938 600cc Scott 'Clubman' which was available for a short time with a simple, plunger-type rear suspension, allowing about 70mm of rear wheel movement to knock the edge off poor roads surfaces. The suspension system was enhanced by a far better, more normally mounted sprung saddle: oh, how I earnestly wished that rear suspension had been attached to the Scott Squirrel I was riding, for it was an absolute shocker!

Oddly enough, the bike handles beautifully and can be pinned down to some very dramatic angles of lean with plenty of confidence; that is, of course, if the road happens to be billiard table smooth. On some occasions the tail stepped out pretty smartly over really choppy corners when the wick was turned well up, but it still hung on without complaint. Naturally, this had the effect of tightening the bike's line in a corner, and this combined well with the girder fork's usual tendency to allow the bike to flop into a corner. The modern tyres with which the bike has

The shocking non-standard saddle. The original seat bolted to the same single tube, but had a small pivot at the seat's front, which allowed the long springs under the saddle, and the two springs supporting it, to work well over bumps. It is something this awful seat could never have done! Ouch!

On a very smooth stretch of road, halfway through cranking the Scott onto its right footrest, the bike behaved itself almost perfectly. A huge handful of throttle on straightening up, however, saw the bike leap away like a startled gazelle. The rider was equally startled!

recently been fitted allowed cornering speeds on smooth surfaces to be very definitely above and beyond the norm!

The old bike has got its act together as far as the essentials of steering geometry are concerned, for it tracks beautifully over most road surfaces (though much of the enjoyment is lost in just hanging onto the thing, if the road was bumpy) but it isn't quite so hot in other areas.

Gear-changing can be a hit-and-miss affair even though it is the positive-stop gearbox other makers were beginning to adopt at the time, but this may be due, at least to some degree, to honest wear-and-tear. It will select first gear readily enough, but you have to play a tune on the gear-lever to get it ready for the change into second; happily, it winds out long enough to allow you to do this, and the same applies to selecting top gear from second.

But changing back is a bit of a lucky dip for the pedal tends to stay where it rests and has to be sawed back and forth to preload it for a drop back to the lowest gear. This can be a monumental pain, particularly if the road surface is bumpy and you are concentrating hard at what is going on ahead of – and around – you.

It's compounded by the spongy brakes, effective enough if you have the room but would not really be up to the job in 'panic stops', situations which might manifest themselves while you are trundling rapidly along while fiddling with a heavy clutch action at the same time as sorting out a gearbox which could be full of false neutrals as well!

If there was no attempt at rear suspension, then the front-end was at least reasonably well – 'controlled' by girder forks with the single, undamped coil spring which was in very wide use on many pre-war motorcycles. Allied to the oddly mounted saddle, the rigid ride makes a daunting task out of a swift lurch round the block – much less a long squirt into the country.

I recall riding many a rigid-framed motorcycle as a beardless youth, and the thought occurred many times on this test that we were either heroes of a very high order way back when – or there was something sadly awry with our mental processes.

For all that, the Scott is a very endearing machine in many ways.

Its performance is perfectly acceptable even by modern standards, its throaty exhaust note something a true enthusiast would run a long way to hear, even if over rivulets or rocky outcrops (and bare-foot), its handling on smooth roads something to wonder at, its odd marriage of advanced features and old-fashioned engineering something not often seen then or now.

It could be said its lack of sophistication is part of its charm, for it is at the very least an example of a large-capacity two-stroke motorcycle whose engine defied convention – or comparison – when compared to its contemporaries, but it is not as pleasant a machine to ride as it should/ could have been. Oh, for a modern-day Scott/ Silk.

The general lines of the engine, with its very short, un-finned cylinder barrel and dominating radiator, the external oil pump and odd bolted-on bits and pieces stamp it as an oddity – yet it existed in largely unmodified form for some 70 years after it first fired up! It is truly a tribute to the genius of Alfred Scott, let there be no doubt about that.

It is unusual to find a modern machine which will do most of its work in top gear once it is underway, which is at odds with its high gearing and reluctance to pull hard from rest unless high engine speeds are used.

Overtaking is a breeze, with the bike very happy to cruise at just over 100km/h and plenty left for more urgent riding. It was a bit embarrassing to pull out and flash past a car only to find the driver screw up his face at the raucous exhaust note and wind his window up to escape. We never needed the electric horn, the Scott and I, for we could be easily heard long before we were seen!

Wide throttle openings compounded the felony as induction roar through the unfiltered carburettor was almost as noisy as the exhaust.

This test was conducted over mostly short journeys, simply because the Scott proved to be too uncomfortable to ride very far at any one time. But it sure turned heads everywhere it went, and its open road performance left many modern motorists gasping in its two-stroke smoke. The exhaust note is deeper than any other two-stroke while it sounds like nothing that has ever gone before it, and certainly nothing which has ever followed.

So, the Scott Squirrel remains an enigma; very much a product of its era, and yet something of a rarity, its unique and advanced engine powering a machine exceptionally uncomfortable to ride. Yet a few modern motorcyclists with sufficiently deep pockets made the acquaintance of the first Scott to appear just after war, still with no rear suspension, but equipped with *Dowty 'Oleomatic'* telescopic front forks, and the latter-day version in the 1958 'limited-production', fully sprung, dual-seat equipped 500cc Scott which employed flat-topped pistons, of which only six were ever built. They were clearly still recognisable as a Scott.

Later, as we have discussed, there was the 1980s Scott 'alter ego', the 700cc Silk, perhaps best described as a latter-day version of the machine with which Scott would have been most impressed, and still entirely recognisable as basically a Scott motorcycle.

When it's all boiled down to basics, any bike whose fundamental design remained almost unaltered for some 70 years (except for a somewhat more modern look, a far more acceptable suspension and more effective brakes.

'I do love to be beside the seaside'. Listening to the once-famous Scott 'yowl' is like listening to some giant robot tearing in half a sheet of corrugated iron, across the corrugations, naturally! It is a sound not enjoyed by everybody, particularly non-motorcyclists.

TECH SPECS

Make: Scott

Model: Squirrel

Year of manufacture: 1939

Type:
Water-cooled vertical-twin two-stroke, with detachable alloy head and one-piece, water-jacketed barrel, employing deflector-type pistons with cross-flow three-port system. Built-up crankshaft with overhung cranks and riveted-on central flywheel primary drive, locked with tapered shafts and centre bolt. Roller big-end bearings carried outboard of centre chamber, special gland sealing for crank chambers against flywheel cheeks. Roller main bearings.

Bore x stroke: 56.6 x 71.4mm

Capacity: 498cc

Power @ rpm: 24BHP @ 5000rpm

Ignition:
Magneto ignition by Lucas Magdyno, 6-volt generation to wet lead/acid battery

Carburation:
Single 6-type Amal, with separate float bowl. No air filter.

Lubrication:
By duplex-feed Pilgrim total-loss pumps driven from end of both crankpins, with positive feed to centre main bearings, big-ends then by oil galleys and mist to cylinder walls and pistons, rings. Oil tank combined with petrol tank. Positive, separate oil supply to both transmission chains.

Transmission:
From sprocket riveted to central flywheel to multi-plate clutch and separate three-speed gearbox with semi-positive-stop right foot-change, one-up, two-down pattern. Final drive is by chain.

Gear ratios (overall):
1st – 9.90:1; 2nd – 6.316:1; 3rd – 4.62:1.

Frame and suspension:
Triangulated, duplex down-tube design in welded tubular steel, with no rear suspension and single spring saddle, pillar-mounted in centre of assembly. Webb-pattern girder front forks with single central spring and dual friction dampers.

Wheels, tyres, brakes:
Steel rims front and rear, hubs containing 175mm internal expanding drum brakes. 325 x 19 ribbed tyre front, 325 x 19 block pattern tyre rear.

Dimensions:
Wheelbase – 1390mm; Ground clearance – 125mm; Weight (wet) – 177kg; Fuel tank capacity – 19 litres (2 litres of oil in separate compartment).

Performance:
Top speed (suggested) 135km/h; Acceleration, machine still in second gear at 120km/h at end of 400m (no time); Braking from 50km/h, 11.8 m; Consumption, 13km/l.

Machine loaned by:
COL BRENCHLY, Sylvania Waters, NSW.

1933 Zundapp K800 'Flat Four'

800cc SIDE-VALVE FOUR-CYLINDER SHAFT DRIVE

The **1933 K800 shaft-drive, 'flat-four' Zündapp,** was not the first machine to use an engine of this type, because the first flat-four (which was only a sort of four because of the double-ended pistons which were enclosed within just two long cylinders) was designed in England by a Colonel Holden for his odd-looking motorcycle way back in 1897. However, the German Zundapp factory was one of the very few serious motorcycle manufacturers to employ this type of engine design in any real numbers: the only other manufacturer of a flat-four engine at that time – the mid-1930s – was the Austrian Puch company, its P800, coincidentally an 800cc side-valve flat-four which was very, very similar to the Zundapp.

The number of Puch flat-fours to be made at that time is unknown but, in all, there were around 1000 of the side-valve, horizontally opposed Zundapp 787cc K800 motorcycles built from 1933 until the beginning of the Second World War in 1939, with an additional, unspecified number of them supplied thereafter to the Wehrmacht for use as solo or sidecar machines up until 1940. It was the first of their all-new overhead valve 750cc flat-twins, which appeared in the early 1940s, which allowed the 'flat-four' 800 to be quietly discontinued.

Not only was the K800 a rare machine, but its horizontally opposed engine configuration was – and remains – just as rare today, at least in motorcycle applications, for that engine configuration was only adopted again more than 45 long years later by the Japanese in 1974, when the first-ever GL1000 Honda Gold Wing, a shaft-drive overhead camshaft 1000cc monster, appeared. In fact, this type of engine design has been adopted by only five or six marques since Holden's first machine lurched uncertainly about the countryside; the final drive from the Holden engine's long, long connecting rods bolted directly (with no primary drive to clutch or gearbox) to bell-cranks at each side of the rear axle!

The 1939 prototype Brough Superior 'Golden Dream' was also a flat-four, and so too was the Wooler, which appeared in the late 1940s, both of them very exciting British designs, but neither machine ever made it into any form of mass production, for only the occasional prototype of these machines were ever built: there were only five, 500cc Wooler motorcycles made and they were quite remarkable, for it was said only two open-ended spanners were needed to entirely dis-assemble the entire machine. There was no mention made of a screwdriver, much less a pair of pliers!

The most famous 'flat-four' engine is, of course the Volkswagen 'Beetle'– and air-cooled at that – which has been manufactured in the millions since the first VW was originally built by NSU (which, incidentally, was a well-known *motorcycle* manufacturer at the time) in 1934, while the small Citroen 1100 from France, the

Colonel Holden's shocker from 1897. It was said to be the first four-cylinder motorcycle; but this is debatable, for it employed just two long cylinders and double-ended pistons, with a surface carburettor and coil ignition. The connecting rods were coupled directly to a pair of bell-cranks on the rear axle! It must have been a disaster to ride, with pedals causing the front wheel to shimmer, the rear wheel wagging its tail in concert. Not for me, thank you, Sir!

Italian Lancia, Japan's Subaru, and indeed the British Jowett motorcars also adopted the rare flat-four design many years later.

Rare on the ground though the flat-four engine may be in motorcycle designs, there is at least one of them alive and very well indeed in Melbourne, Australia, a rare motorcycle in the hands of its eager restorer, Vin Minogue, who once had a veritable garage full of unusual motorcycles, and equally unusual power tools, numerous bins jam-packed with a staggering variety of odd motorcycle spare parts, and a couple of happy dogs. Minogue's machine which, as we have noted, is one of the few horizontally opposed designs in the history of motorcycling, is a prime example of the 1937 Zundapp K800 referred to earlier. As we've seen, the first of the K800s was built in 1933, and survived for just those eight years, until it was supplanted by the KS750 flat-twin, the all-new 750cc machine pressed into service by the Germans in WWII during the Afrika Korps campaign in the Middle East as well as in heavy snow on the Western Front.

Because of its side-valve configuration, with no valve gear contained within the cylinder heads, Zundapp's 'boxer' four is a very squat engine, which allows for a similarly squat, low-slung frame and a very long wheelbase, while the low saddle height means that even the shortest of legs (which include my own) can be comfortably bent at the knee while normally seated and with both feet firmly planted upon the ground. Even then, a reasonable amount of clearance under the footrests and the shallow, exposed cylinder heads, allows for some very enthusiastic cornering at fairly high speeds on smooth roads with a touch of daylight still visible between the ground and the boot-soles. The very low centre of gravity engendered by the engine design also helps enormously, of course, for the 800's C of G is probably almost underground!

The Minogue K800 doesn't exhibit that 'hands off' showroom finish quite so much as it does an honest and neat appearance, with strict attention to detail where attention is needed, and a neat restoration with no trace of oil leaks or dodgy workmanship. The bike is clearly ridden often, as it should be, and I'm sure most people would agree with the owner's avowed philosophy that these old irons are meant to be ridden as often as possible after being restored, rather than being gaped at in a glass trophy case somewhere.

I must say it comes as a surprise to be told that the engine was by no means complete when the Minogue Zundapp was first unearthed, with several of the major alloy engine castings either missing, or chewed away by corrosion; the 'reverse' handlebar levers — which sprout from inside the ends of the handlebars — were also missing. New castings were designed and made from scratch, of course, for there was nothing available at the time from the factory, because Zundapp was involved in the later years in the manufacture of small two-stroke commuter machines and, of all things, sewing machines.

Working from photographs and some shredded bits of aluminium, Vin made the top engine cases and a set of alloy lever blades with the help of George Hempenstal, the fellow Vintage enthusiast who moonlighted from his panel-beating business by making Twin-G sidecars in Melbourne. As you'd expect, the new castings are absolutely first-class and they fit as though they were recently supplied from the Zundapp parts bin.

The old-fashioned side-valve design was a type very popular in the 1930s but now obsolete except for some four-stroke lawn mowers and the occasional small industrial engine. The valves are located in the cast-iron cylinder barrels with their heads uppermost and their stems pointing downwards and parallel to the cylinder bores — their movement controlled by cam followers with the camshaft carried on top of the crankshaft. Tappet adjusters are reached by removing detachable plates at the base of the cylinder barrels.

Because of the side-valve design, the inlet ports are cast into the area at the mouth of the crankcase where the barrels are bolted on, the single ports then branching into two separate tracts to feed the inlet valves which run in close proximity. Of course, this means that the exhausts exit from the top of the cylinder barrels, the rear exhaust facing rearwards. Each cast-iron cylinder casting contains two cylinders, one behind the other, each of the flat-faced light-alloy heads attaching with no fewer than 13 short head studs. Pistons are aluminium alloy and feature three rings, while the four conrods are steel forgings with detachable end-caps.

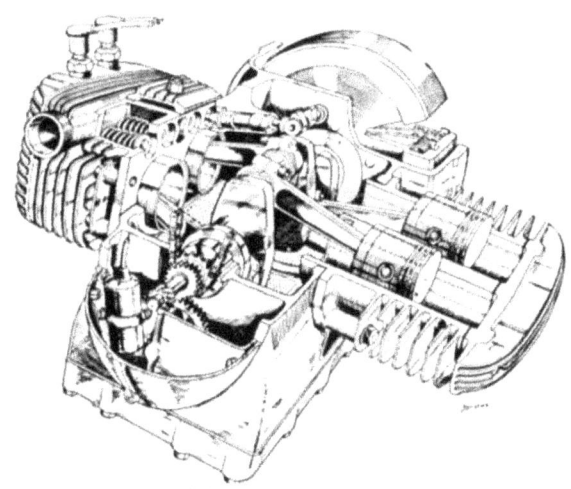

Cutaway drawing of the 800cc, four-cylinder side-valve engine, minus gearbox, showing the very heavy flywheel, which stores plenty of torque, and the clutch assembly within it. Note also the detachable end-caps on the conrods to allow for ease in fitting the standard, split roller big-end bearings, which have been replaced by car-type slipper bearings in the Minogue machine. These simple bearings have proved to be entirely reliable.

The original big-end bearings were split, caged needle rollers, which were used in other Zundapp machines and by Moto-Guzzi, among only a few other manufacturers, but Vin replaced these some years ago with the more popular (and more readily obtainable) plain-metal bearings. Modern-day, thin shell slipper bearings were not readily available in the size needed, but the thick white-metal bearings which have been employed have stood up to the wear and tear quite well, with little modification needed to the oiling system.

The one-piece crankshaft has four throws – each conrod has its own big-end journal – and is very rigid, supported on the front by a large bronze main bearing bush and at the rear by a very substantial ball bearing. On the front of the crankshaft, just outboard of the huge bronze bush, a small 'half-time' sprocket drives the camshaft by chain, the shaft also supported on the front by a bronze bearing bush with a roller bearing at the rear.

A large fibre gear bolted to the front of the camshaft, adjacent to the drive sprocket, indirectly drives the 6-volt, 50-watt generator nestling above the engine. A voltage regulator is built *in situ*, with the twin components contained within a large, cast aluminium compartment which dominates the top of the engine cases. At the rear of this large compartment, which includes a Minogue-special fluted alloy cover, sits the single 22mm Amal carburettor and its attendant steel-mesh air filter. It couldn't be further away from the inlet valves unless it was towed behind the bike on a trailer, and you can well imagine the tortuous, meandering path of those long, long inlet tracts!

The front end of the crankshaft employs a small gear outside the cam-chain drive sprocket which then meshes with a double-sized gear beneath it, the latter driving the double-action oil pump which sits in the oil pan beneath the engine, while further out again, almost on the tip of the well-overhung crankshaft, is a small skew-gear which drives a four-lobe distributor accompanied by its ignition coil, all of which are enclosed by yet another large, highly polished semi-triangular Zundapp/Minogue-pattern alloy cover. Fortunately, the end of the long shaft is located in a bronze bush and an outrigger ball bearing which serve to overcome any possibility of the shaft flexing.

If the timing end of the crankshaft is busy in the extreme, then the drive end is almost dull, for it simply employs a large flywheel bolted to it which contains a two-plate dry clutch. The plates were originally inserted with cork but have since been modified to take a bonded-on fibrous material. The engine speed clutch has proven to be absolutely trouble-free after several years of hard work.

The four-speed transmission is very unusual and almost unique, for it uses four sets of *chains and sprockets* of differing ratios instead of the usual cluster of gears. Double-row roller chain is used and the eight sprocket centres are very close indeed, the gear selection by sliding dogs which engage in long slots on the side faces of the sprockets. Zundapp used this type of 'gearbox' on many models right through to the legendary K601 'Elefant' flat twin of the mid-1950s – the machine which loaned its name to the world-famous motorcycle rally.

This unusual transmission was designed by Xavier and Richard Kuchen, the latter also designing the 1950s, 350cc shaft-drive Victoria Bergmeister, the only other *marque* – as far as I can ascertain – to adopt chains and sprockets inside a multi-speed 'gearbox'. This system was obviously a Kuchen quirk, but it remains a very workable arrangement.

Zundapp's gear change is by hand, the long lever having an H-section gear-gate like a car's four-speed gearbox, which means somewhat leisurely gear changes – which is just as well, for the gears (?) grate if too heavy a hand is used before the large flywheel slows down after the clutch has been withdrawn. Instead of being mounted in a 'gear gate' on the right-hand side of the fuel tank, which was an almost universal siting in the thirties, the long, free-moving gear lever emerges directly from the top of the gearbox, the initial impression given is that changing gears might be similar to stirring the breakfast porridge with a wooden spoon. But there was a surprise in store, for the changes could always be made with absolute certainty whether changing to higher or lower gears, as I could actually *feel* the changes occurring through the tip of the long lever as the dogs slid into position. All it needed, of course, was just a little practice!

There is no adjustment in the 'box' for chain wear, but this should make little difference because of the very close proximity of the sprocket centres, but the more flexible (if that's the word!) drive which ensues through chain-and-sprockets probably offers its own form of shock-absorption.

The shaft final drive is not enclosed as it emerges from the top of the gearbox on the machine's right-hand side, but the crown wheel and pinion is, of course, enclosed within the rear hub. Happily, the kick-starter works through a set of bevel gears to provide a 'normal' movement even though the crankshaft spins across the frame, but the lever is a bit awkward because it is on the machine's left side. Still a darn sight better than the always-difficult sideways action of the early BMW kick-starter!

The long and rakish frame was originally designed by Libby Owens of the British Coventry Eagle company, which used this frame design in its own machines. The frame was made under licence by Zundapp and later pinched by several other European manufacturers. Fabricated from steel pressings welded and riveted together, the frame is quite light in weight yet immensely strong because of its solid box-section and the great emphasis placed on rigidity at the steering head. There is no rear suspension, though a sprung saddle is of course adopted, while the girder front forks are mounted well ahead of the machine on the usual links and mounting spindles.

Front suspension is by a pair of short, supple springs just ahead of the steering head, with a clever, lever-operated hydraulic damping system enclosed in a short cylinder mounted between them. The fuel tank actually sits half inside a

Gear change lever is not 'gated', but sits firmly in place for quick and easy gear changes. And no, it does nor flop about like a wooden spoon might when stirring the breakfast porridge, even though it looks as though it might.

cradle formed by the frame pressings behind the steering head, the tank dominated by a gigantic filler cap at the front with a small, lockable compartment on the top rear of the tank for cut lunches, hip flasks, touring maps and the like.

In the fashion of the time, the clutch and brake levers emerge from inside the ends of the handlebars, which were to allow a straight-pull for the control cables with consequent longer cable life and ease of operation. Instruments are limited to a speedometer inside the headlamp shell and a small amber ignition light alongside the key. The key pushes straight down into the headlamp shell to turn the ignition on, and can then be operated as a headlamp switch knob to turn on the 6-volt lights — such as they are! To complete a very clean handlebar area, a large two-bar lever fits in the centre of the steering head to allow hand adjustment for the friction steering damper which was universal on pre-war motorcycles of this size.

The K800 was originally fitted with the coupled-brake system, which was also very much in fashion at the time, with a separate front brake cable attached to the rear brake lever, thus operating both brakes together whether you liked it or not. Vin Minogue doesn't like this idea any more than I do and has happily detached the rear cable and re-routed it for a separate control, while provision is there to re-attach it should he wish the machine to be absolutely as it left the German factory.

Bore and stroke are 62 x 66.6mm, giving a capacity of 797cc. The compression ratio is a very modest 5.8:1, and the engine develops a lazy 20 kW at a low 4300rpm. The low compression and heavy flywheel allow the engine to be started easily and it surprises by firing in about half a kick, to idle with a deep and lumpy exhaust note. Minogue's own pattern mufflers are fitted, which employ dual inlets for each pair of thin-diameter pipes. They are patterned on the original design, with careful measurements taken from photographs and the rusted and burnt-out shell of a surviving muffler.

Firing the bike up led to more pleasant surprises: unexpectedly the clutch action is very light indeed, and the gear change dead smooth. The different ratios (it's hard to call them 'gears') are easy to select unless the change is rushed, and each time a higher gear is selected (which seems to take a long, long time and a long, long stretch) the bike responds to the throttle by leaping forward with great vigour. For some reason the bike's ratios are for sidecar duty and as such are lower overall than standard solo gearing. This no doubt accounts for some surprisingly brisk acceleration, but there is no mistaking the really strong grunt at very low engine speeds from the lightly stressed motor; again, very much the 'fashion' of motorcycles built at the time. Solo gearing employs nine teeth on the shaft pinion and 41 on the crown-wheel — with a final-drive gear reduction of 4.55:1 — while the sidecar gearing, with eight teeth on the dive pinion and 45 on the crown wheel, results in a ratio of 5.625:1.

The owner usually takes off in second gear and I tried it several times just for the hell of it — the bike pulling away without complaint, the engine smooth as silk right through the engine-speed range while the magic exhaust sound deepens to a strong, resonant growl. It would have been interesting to ride the bike with its solo gearing because, with the lower gearing and the slow gear change I left the bike in top gear for most of the time, even with some light traffic about. It was as if the bike could be ridden almost as one would drive an automatic V8 car, with very little need to change to lower gears. Just roll the throttle on to go a bit quicker and roll it off as required. Probably because of the four cylinders, engine compression braking is stronger than usual, even in view of the large, heavy flywheel.

Of course, you can change up or down at will, but you gain nothing on hills because of the time it takes, particularly changing up from third to top while still climbing sharply. But to feel that engine dig its heels in and drive hard when changing up on steep climbs remains one of the Zundapp K800's strongest impressions. In the main, modern motorcycles are designed to rev hard and to produce most of their power very high in the engine-speed range, so to feel

Reaching for top gear, the power-plant nicely on the boil, the bike steady as a rock on a surprisingly smooth back road. Note that much of the engine's mass is below wheel spindle height. Very clever.

the punchy, low-speed torque of this ultra-low-revving four is a rare joy. Hill climbing is mostly a top gear operation, even if an approach is made from a tight corner or a side street.

Again, most of this is due to the lower gearing, but the throttle response is almost immediate – so much so that it seems as if the twist grip is attached directly to the rear wheel, by-passing the power-plant as if in some form of direct drive. There is no need to pull an overall gear ratio quite as short as this, and in the interest of lower engine speeds while touring, Minogue is about to adapt a small, car-type Austin Seven crown wheel and pinion to the rear hub to return the Zundapp to its more leisurely solo gearing. I'd be willing to bet it would still pull top gear up many of the hills I tried, and with no more strain on the engine or rider.

Traffic is a bit of a pain if it is heavy; particularly stop/start, where the sudden clutch and slow gear changes are very frustrating. It's better to remain in second or third gear in this situation, but even better to whip off along a side-street and try for more open roads somewhere else. I feared the rear cylinders might tend to cook up in this situation, but the owner assures me there has never been a problem in this area, particularly with the cylinder casting canted ever-so-slightly in the frame to allow the heavier barrel finning on rear facing exhausts on the rear pots to be raised slightly into the airstream. In the interest of better cooling for the rear cylinders, there was originally a pair of neatly fluted, streamlined art-deco cowlings fitted on either side of the engine near the footrest and just behind the rear cylinder heads, their clear purpose to direct additional air to the rear cylinders. These items were obviously not readily available ex-factory and, as it happens, even in the hot Australian summers, they are apparently not really necessary. They were of course a cosmetic enhancement as well, and would neatly fill in the open space at the footrests, but really are not missed. They could have been fiddly components to fabricate, but certainly not beyond the power of the owner to make them by hand, but as Vin stoutly maintains, in his opinion they are 'surplus to requirements.'

Typically, the girder front forks chatter a bit over corrugations, but they work very well (and very visibly) and absorb road shocks with surprising ease. The rear is not quite so happy, and the tail can sometimes step out as the wheel leaps over rough going – not a nice feeling if you are reaching forward at the time to drag that long lever back into third or at full stretch as you thrust it into top. One-handed, of course!

The bike tends to drop into corners, no doubt as a result of the girder fork's tendency to do this allied to an engine which has most of its bulk below the wheel spindles, but this allows flashing through medium-paced corners at speed to be great fun if you keep the power on.

Backing-off in a corner finds the bike trying to fall over a bit further, which I suppose, at worst, tightens the entry line a bit. No, the bike won't fall right over if you keep going, and it can be cranked up again without effort, and flung onto the opposite footrest when ridden with some enthusiasm through a series of sweeping Ess-bends. It is a quirk which feels odd at first, but which is probably an asset; especially if a corner might happen to tighten up on the exit, or be slower than it appears on entry. Unfortunately, it could be a liability if you have the wick turned up a bit and the road surface is very choppy, for handling can suffer once the rear wheel starts skipping along the top of the bumps.

Brake levers are unaccountably spongy and don't inspire much confidence because of their feel, but the brakes are really quite effective – the rear inducing a yelp from the tyre if you stand on the pedal with too much enthusiasm. Heavy braking while cranked hard over in a corner on rough surfaces would no doubt be quite dramatic and a good test of rider reflexes and skill!

Even with no rear suspension the bike is quite comfortable, the supple, rubber-topped spring saddle as usual coping very well over almost all

Because of the very low-slung powerplant, with its extremely low centre of gravity and no top-hamper, one of the greatest features of the Zundapp 800, whether coming ...

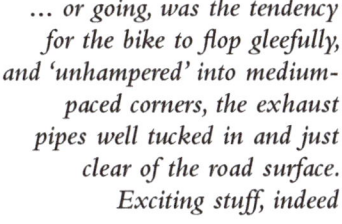

... or going, was the tendency for the bike to flop gleefully, and 'unhampered' into medium-paced corners, the exhaust pipes well tucked in and just clear of the road surface. Exciting stuff, indeed

road surfaces. In keeping with this type of seat, as usual the feeling is one of instability at first acquaintance (only because of modern dual-seats which are, of course, rigidly mounted), but the infinitely variable, flexible feel of the seat soon comes into its own. There might be an argument in favour of a rigid frame with this type of saddle, particularly with shaft drive, but this leaves the rear wheel free to leap about when road surfaces are grim, and the rear wheel obliges by doing just that … and with some enthusiasm at times.

Top speed of the bike is claimed to be 135km/h, pretty good for an open-road machine of this vintage, with fuel consumption around 18.2km/litre, which is also quite good – if no surprise in view of that tiny, single carburettor. Minogue claims he can run the bike flat-out on the open road for long periods of time, and it covers the ground in very short order and with very little drama. I didn't have the machine long enough to put it through its paces like that, nor would I be willing to do so in view of its age and rarity, but it remains a delight to have ridden it and to have experienced the sort of machine which was near the top of the class in the first third of the 20th century.

The engine type was as rare then as it is now, and it's a safe bet there aren't many Zundapp K800s in the world today, though you can only wonder what happened to all the ex-army machines which must have been around at the end of the war. I understand there is at least one other example of this model in Australia, and there may well be more of them unearthed – literally! – In other countries.

Happily, though it remains a rarity, Minogue's K800 is often ridden by him and exhibited at rallies and vintage displays across the country, providing us all with a view of German expertise at its best and a machine which is assured of its place in the history of motorcycling through the years. Let's hope the K800, and the few others which enjoy the same aura and the same rarity, will always be with us to allow comparisons to be made with modern motorcycles and to provide yardsticks to measure the progress of motorcycle design.

TECH SPECS

Make: Zundapp

Model: K800

Years of manufacture: 1933-39/40s

Type:
Horizontally opposed side-valve four-cylinder, with cast-iron cylinders, alloy cylinder heads. One-piece forged-steel crankshaft, employing forged steel conrods with detachable end-caps. Original 'split' caged roller big-end bearings replaced by white-metal big-end slippers. Main bearings consist of large phosphor/bronze bush and substantial ball and roller bearings. Oil contained within a wet sump, with lubrication by double-action plunger oil pump.

Bore x stroke: 62 x 66.6mm x 4

Capacity: 797cc

Power @ rpm:
26BHP (20Kw) @ 4300rpm

Carburation:
Single 22mm Amal carburettor, with wire-mesh strainer

Electrics:
Crankshaft-mounted 6-volt generator, to lead-acid wet battery. Ignition is by distributor, coil and points

Transmission:
Through engine-speed, multi-plate clutch to four-speed, hand-change 'gear' box, with reduction ratios by a series of four 'sprocket-and-chain' transmission, to final drive by shaft.

Gear ratios (Solo):
1st – 13.6:1; 2nd – 6.75:1; 3rd – 5.25:1; 4th – 4.55:1

Frame, suspension, wheels, brakes:
Libby Owens-designed Coventry 'Eagle' one-piece, pressed metal frame welded and riveted into a box-section. It is made by factory under licence. Very heavy bracing at stress points around steering head, rear axle and gearbox. Substantial duplex down-tubes at the front, with additional gussets at the rear of gearbox to meet descending frame rails from below single saddle. Suspension at front is by girder forks with dual compression springs and centrally located hydraulic damper. No rear suspension, but single saddle is mounted on long-travel dual compression springs. Drum brakes front and rear are 7-1/2" (187mm) diameter, with 350 x 19", block pattern tyres on front and rear.

Dimensions:
Length – 2165mm; Wheelbase – 1375mm; Saddle height – 680mm; Ground clearance – 160mm; Weight: 193kg

Fuel consumption: 18.2km/l

Top speed (suggested): 135km/h

Machine loaned by:
VIN MINOGUE, Melbourne.

1975 Bimota SB2 Frame, Running Gear

1972 SUZUKI 750cc DOHC POWER-PLANT

The first so-called 'Safety Cycle', with its two wheels more or less the same diameter, was invented sometime around 1876 by a man called Harry Lawson, the new invention said to have heralded the death of the dangerous 'Penny Farthing' cycle. This was followed by the first commercially successful safety cycle, which was made by John Starley in 1885. However, the horrendous Penny Farthing managed to hang on, in a wide variety of forms, for several years thereafter, including an odd machine with tiny front wheel and huge rear wheel which was made in America. To digress, an American named Lucius Copeland, a man who should have known better, fitted one of these back-to-front penny-farthing monsters with a small steam engine in 1884 (clearly those strange devices were still on the nation's roads eight years after the first safety cycle had been invented) to provide motive power to the huge rear wheel as a kind of crude motorcycle. The most unwieldy device was of course 'steered' by the tiny farthing which stuck out in front!

Copeland was once timed at a brisk 12mph on the thing, but there seems to be no record anywhere of how he climbed onto the device, how he got off it again, or how well it handled – that is, assuming it handled at all!

But it was up to George Singer, of sewing machine fame, to design the simplest, but most profound, invention in the interests of cycle safety a few years later (the precise date seems to be still uncertain) when he patented an all-new front fork design, in which the forks were curved at their ends where the front axle was accommodated. This accomplished two things; first, the forks could flex slightly and thus take some of the brunt off bumps and potholes, but much, much more importantly they were far safer than the straight forks which were in existence at the time.

This is because this new invention introduced the first – if accidental – *trail angle* to the front forks on two-wheelers, which forever changed the fortunes of anyone who ever rode a bicycle; or any other two-wheeler. So profound was this apparently simple design that even to this day the curved front fork is to be seen on millions of bicycles the world over. On mountain bikes, with their sprung front forks, the trail angle can often be, just as on a motorcycle, attended to by the angle of the frame's steering head in relation to the angle of the front forks themselves.

The trail angle is measured by taking a line from the centre of the steering head downwards to the roadway, and another vertical line from the front axle to the road. The difference between the two points is the trail angle, which is usually measured in degrees, or inches, with an angle of 20-24 degrees, or 3-4 Imperial inches, said to be ideal for high-speed cornering. Simple indeed but, whether the design was accidental or not, it is critically important to the (safe) handling characteristics of the simple bicycle, and to any other machine which employs a wheel at each end – including motorcycles.

Attendant upon the new fork design came the so-called 'diamond' frame, which embraced the steering head and the rest of the tubular frame, and which of course complimented the new fork design. Thus, bicycle frame designs, even to this day, have remained almost static, because they still retain the headstock and diamond frame design which was invented, and modified slightly, way back in the last few years of the 19th century! Motorcycle frame design has remained stuck within the same time-warp, for they still retain precisely the same headstock and diamond frame that the lowly push-bike has employed for more than a century.

Telescopic front forks today are pretty much the same as those which found some acceptance on German machines in the mid-1930s (although earlier examples were to be seen on machines built more than a decade prior to that), while rear suspensions have changed from the simple, un-damped plunger type which abounded from the mid-1930s until the mid-1950s, to the swing-arm rear suspension in universal use today. Again, swing-arm – or pivoted fork – rear suspension was employed on Granville Bradshaw's ABC motorcycle, the American Indian, and several other motorcycles back in the 1920s, so that is not a new idea either.

Bradshaw's 1919 500cc OHV flat-twin ABC employed leaf-springs on both ends. Note rear swing-arm pivot just behind the gearbox, attached to a vertical mudguard stay allied to the leaf-springs mounted horizontally above. The rear guard naturally moves with the rear suspension.

Such a rebel is the Italian **Bimota** company, which has employed hub-centre steering in its Bimota 'Tesi' racer along with the occasional road machine, and the later arrival Vyrus, another bespoke manufacturer, which supplies motorcycles with hub-centre steering and their own futuristic frame design, with an owner's choice of engine, to well-heeled enthusiasts the world over. Vyrus is a five-man operation, which to date cannot hope to keep up with the demand for their odd-looking, if extremely functional and brilliantly handling, hand-crafted motorcycles.

It is a simple fact that motorcycle frame design has remained static over a great many years, and remains less than ideal, regardless of the enormous number of motorcycle factories, large and small, which have existed during the century and more that followed the first powered two-wheelers which appeared at the tail-end of the 19th and early 20th centuries. We have seen fully triangulated frames, semi-triangulated frames, frames with engines acting as stressed members. We have seen frames in which the 'spine' – often in pressed metal – is the focal point of design. We have seen frames in which the cast steel or alloy front downtube is the main member and we have seen motorcycles like the Vincent where almost no frame exists.

But in view of the very high performance of which today's motorcycles are capable, it is true to say that the old-fashioned, cycle type frame has come about as far as it can come: perhaps it does the job well enough, but the overall package is still less than ideal. Anybody who has had to fight a frightening high-speed tank-slapper, or had to contend with a rear end waving about like a puppy dog's tail can surely bear testimony to that fact. The once-ubiquitous steering damper of fond memory was installed to try to take care of a wandering front-end, which again ably demonstrates the point.

Radical rethinking will surely see the re-adoption of the hub-centre steering at some point in the distant future. This long-ignored concept is nearly as old as the safety cycle frame, being a standard fitment on the 1910 James, the Zenith Bi-Car and the 1920s Ner-a-Car motorcycles, among several others, all those long years ago. Quite apart from Bimota and the much later Italian Vyrus, the Yamaha GTS1000 is another modern motorcycle which employed hub-centre steering, while the Elf/Honda endurance road racer provides yet another example. Unhappily, the Yamaha GTS was not a success.

The major advantage of hub-centre steering lies in the fact that this design totally separates the functions of steering, braking and suspension, for when the front brake is applied to a machine fitted with telescopic forks, the suspension closes up under the 80% weight-shift to the front wheel, which badly compromises the suspension while radically altering the trail angle, wheelbase and steering geometry at the same time, which in turn plays a crucial role in controlling the machine; particularly at very high speeds.

It has become obvious that the standard chassis and running gear is not up to the demands of the modern GP race speeds, with the inevitable result that specialist frame builders and engine tuners have lately appeared with all kinds of weird variations; hub-centre steering now and again, but confined, for the time being, almost entirely to frame design at the rear suspension.

Oddly, even though the **1975 SB2 Bimota Suzuki,** the machine in this test report – the only one to enter Australia at the time – takes the rear suspension and engine placement design to its almost ideal conclusion, the brilliantly conceived frame retains telescopic front forks, when it might well have provided the perfect marriage of frame and engine support were hub-centre steering to be employed. The powerplant fitted into this particular Bimota frame is a 'simple', bog-standard DOHC 750cc four-cylinder Suzuki from 1972, the plot enclosed within a slim, close-fitting and all-embracing fairing which gives the machine a very futuristic appearance.

The Bimota frame, which was built to embrace the 750cc Four-cylinder Suzuki power-plant, was imported into the country direct from Italy by Ron Angel, who was using Bimota frames on his racing Yamahas. The new assembly was purchased from Angel by Norm Sharp, at the time the manager of Angel's motorcycle outlet in Richmond, an inner Melbourne suburb. Sharp just happened to know of a 750 Suzuki engine which was lying about, and he wanted to slot it into something a little removed from the norm – sorry about that awful pun! – and so, the Bimota kit seemed to fit the bill very nicely.

Considering there is usually no such a thing as a simple, bolt-on modification, Sharp was surprised when the kit arrived to find that the entire frame and running gear gleefully wrapped itself very closely around the engine without needing to attack it with much more than a few simple tools.

But there have been a few designers who have flown in the face of fashion, embracing – even if only for a short time – such 'way-out' designs as hub-centre steering and somewhat radical rear suspension systems, their stated aim being to provide a far better balance of comfort and first-class handling than even the best of the mainstream machines could hope to achieve.

But it was more than just a 'mere' frame, for the Bimota kit included some great fibreglass mouldings which Michelangelo would have been proud to have sculpted, and some of the finest running gear money could buy. It would need to be very exceptional, of course, for the rolling-chassis alone cost Norm a trim $5,000 back in 1980, *without engine or electrics!*

The kit included Ceriani front forks, Brembo disc brakes all round and fat Michelin tyres fitted front and rear, attached to a pair of strong, well-ribbed genuine magnesium-alloy wheels. Frame rails were all in lightweight chrome-molybdenum tubing, with foot control pedals and linkages specially fabricated from alloy billets and forgings. When spending that kind of money for a complete kit in those days, one would expect to get the best, and there is no doubt Norm Sharp got precisely what he paid for. In a phrase, the SB2 Bimota was – and indeed remains – a brilliantly conceived example of the engineer's art.

The frame is actually in two pieces, with the engine forming a stressed, load-carrying member which locks the separate frame components into a single entity. It's not unlike the Ducati layout of the period, but is even more like the classic Vincent. The forward section of the frame contains the steering head, with a pair of slightly curved down-tubes which bolt directly to the engine crankcases at its top mounting holes

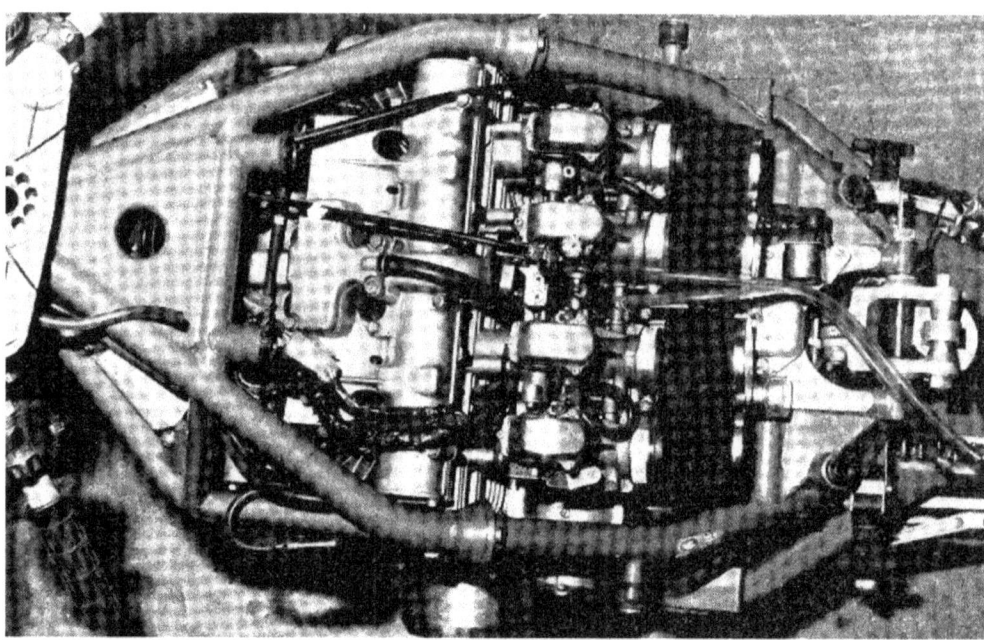

Looking down on the Suzuki 750 power-plant shows how closely it fits into the frame. Note the two-piece frame tubes, with bolted-on, 'cup-and-cone' ends, just behind the double overhead camshaft housings. This was necessary to have the engine fit so neatly into the narrow frame. Note the heavily braced steering head area and vertical spring/damper unit at the rear.

The light-gauge chrome-moly tubing is heavily splayed down and back from the steering head for maximum strength, with dual, upper tubes further splayed out to embrace the top of the engine very closely indeed; so closely, in fact, that the little chrome cover plates which cosmetically dress up the ends of the twin overhead camshaft housings needed to be removed so that the engine would fit!

The area around the motorcycle steering head is the centre of many a motorcycle's handling woes: not so with the Bimota, for the design incorporates no fewer than *twelve* tubes and braces which run into the area, converging from the top of the crankcases and above the engine to completely enclose this highly stressed area. The steering head is further strengthened by a solid, triangular gusset plate welded across and just behind the junction of the top frame tubes.

All the frame tube's ends are smoothly 'fish-mouthed' – or scarfed – where they meet one another, and the welds – and/or brazed joints – are so neat as to be all but invisible. Small brackets are welded to the inside of the curved down-tubes to carry the Suzuki's twin ignition coils, while immediately behind the strengthening gusset at the steering head are a pair of horizontal bosses holding Silentbloc steel-bushed rubber grommets; they mate with a pair of *vertical* bosses on the rear sub-frame to help locate the one-piece tank-seat assembly.

The two frame pieces meet just behind, and slightly below, the rear of the camshafts with a pair of tapered 'cup-and-cone' joints, whose inner surfaces are very carefully machined. The conical joints are locked together by three Allen-head set-screws; the male and female tapers assuring perfect alignment.

If the forward section of the Bimota frame is a work of art, the rear section approaches pure genius. From the conical joints we've just noted, the widely splayed top frame rails sweep straight back to a point above the engine's gearbox, where they then curve downwards and inwards to be triangulated, braced and gusseted where the mono-shock rear suspension is mounted. The shock is a vertically mounted DeCarbon car-type racing spring/damper unit and it sits in a neatly fabricated – and suitably strengthened – 'burrow' on top of the swing-arm. It is connected to the frame by a rocking beam and Heim-type aircraft couplings held in place on self-aligning tapered mounting collars and a single, large-diameter Allen-head bolt.

The top mounting point for the shock's rocking beam is again firmly braced, the dual triangulated members upon which it is mounted gusseted with steel plates in the vertical plane, while yet another bracing tube is heavily gusseted in the horizontal plane. Small tubular girders are welded and heavily braced to make the entire, highly stressed swing-arm and single shock-absorber mount rigid in every plane.

Perhaps the Bimota's most brilliant single feature is the swing-arm which pivots co-axially with the countershaft sprocket at a point exactly half way between the axis of the two wheels.

The swing-arm is fabricated from hexagonal box-section chrome-moly tubing and it pivots on tapered roller bearings which are located in machined housings. The pivot bearings are carried outboard of the frame itself in specially braced and immensely rigid housings; the swing-arm splayed widely (parallel to the rear axle) in this area and very heavily strengthened at the pivot point, and at the lower mounting point for the vertical rear suspension unit.

With the swing-arm pivot point outside the final drive sprocket and in direct line with it, the rear suspension can go about its business without relaying shock loads to the frame or the rider, and of course the chain tension remains constant throughout the 135mm of wheel movement; a bonus in longer chain life from a more lightly stressed rear chain. Constant rear chain tension is not possible with 'normal' swing-arm rear suspension.

The rear axle is located on eccentric bosses and is locked into the tail-end of the swing-arm by big-end-like caps, which allows very accurate chain adjustments to be carried out in a matter of seconds; one simply loosens the two clamps, inserts the special two-prong tool in the holes in the face of the eccentric adjusters and nips up the slack. As the chain tension is constant throughout the entire range of rear wheel movement, there is no need to bounce on the seat when adjusting the chain or have someone check for the tight spots — there simply aren't any!

Un-clothed, the frame looks very odd indeed, but the icing on the Bimota cake is the three-piece set of fibreglass mouldings which completes the SB2. The tank, seat and rear guard form a one-piece moulding in well-sculpted glass-fibre, the entire unit held in place by spigots glued to the moulding and slipped into the four rubber-bushed bosses behind the steering head and directly above the single rear suspension unit. When securely in place, the large moulding is locked by a pair of rubber securing straps like those old car-type 'bonnet' clips.

To remove the tank/seat assembly, it's only necessary to undo the rubber straps, remove the two fuel lines, unhook a pair of battery leads and a threaded electrical socket acting as a junction box, and the whole assembly lifts straight off. It is solidly mounted but simplicity itself to remove and replace; it takes about four minutes with practice.

The race-type fairing is in two pieces, the upper one containing a powerful headlamp, a pair of moulded-in blinkers and two very sporty

Behold the 'simple', upright spring/damper unit and its complex linkages. This allows a longer swing-arm to be mounted co-axially at the final-drive sprocket and a constant chain tension throughout the 135mm suspension's movement. This can't be achieved with swing-arm suspension

With the two-piece fairing and fuel tank removed, which takes but a few minutes, the 'naked' bike looks to be half-starved. But it then allows for simple maintenance to be a carried out effectively. Anything which may need attention is now clearly on display.

(but not too efficient) mirrors, the lower part enclosing the engine unit.

With its clothes on, the Bimota SB2 Suzuki is one of the very few motorcycles which really looks to be doing the Imperial 100 mph while standing still.

The Italians have spared nothing in building the Bimota rolling chassis, even to the startling paint-work, which is fire-engine red, virginal white and funereal black. The bike is an eye-catcher at every intersection, and a downright embarrassment whenever you leave the thing parked anywhere. People fall all over it!

Quite apart from the frame and its attendant fairings, the small Bimota firm has spared nothing in cycle and running gear either. We've noted that the rims are magnesium alloy, the front wearing an 18-inch sports/racing Michelin tyre, the rear a fat 130 x 80-H18 in Michelin's M48 'grooved slick' pattern.

Front Ceriani forks provide 120mm of perfect two-way damping, a little on the short side for bomb craters and odd humps in the road but extremely forgiving of riders who ride on any other road surfaces, for the suspension system is as perfect a match as you could hope to find. The single, DeCarbon spring/damper unit has a fine pitch threaded collar adjustment to pre-load the heavy-duty spring, while the two-way damping is similarly infinitely adjustable. Unfortunately, the shock has to be removed to carry out these adjustments because the bits are hidden in the housing which surrounds the unit and it was a thus a bit of a chore to set the rear-end up before

I rode the bike.

I hope the unit retains its 'tune' once it is adjusted, for it was taken off, tested and replaced several times before it was spot-on for my weight. It comes off easily enough, simply by removing the top mounting bolt and the lower bolt; the double tapers allowing the unit to be self-centring when it is refitted.

The Bimota fits Brembo discs all round, the two front units serviced by dual hydraulic lines which spring from the specially milled lower triple clamp – a neat Bimota modification. The upper clamp is also milled from solid aluminium, and it employs a large, movable eccentric which mates with a similar one on the lower clamp to allow for a two-way setting to alter the trail. It can be set to provide 97.5mm or 117.5mm of trail, presumably for different types of racing circuits, with the dual eccentrics locked after adjustment by little grub-screws.

Steering head angle is 24 degrees, while the fork stanchions are fitted at 28 degrees, which helps reduce the sudden trail changes when braking heavily, particularly if riding at speed over choppy surfaces. In its own small way, this adds to the overall magic handling of the Bimota Suzuki, particularly when diving late into tight corners and cranking over with the brakes still partially applied.

Sadly, the Bimota is set up for Endurance Racing and has all the essential hardware fitted for this purpose, from low-set clip-ons and very rear-set footrests, which are combined with the world's worst seat to make for a ride which is on the wrong side of uncomfortable. It is a no-compromise riding position, as it should be for the bike's intended purpose, but there are some areas in which it could be better set-up in the sole interest of rider comfort.

The seat, which swivels upwards to allow access to a small compartment in the tail, is merely a thin fibreglass moulding covered by a thin layer of suede leather. It is a genuine ball-tearer, in the true sense of that old Australian expression. It isn't helped by having the metal footrests so far back that one cannot stand on them to take the edge off a rapidly approaching bump, or a set of low handlebars which place too much strain on the wrists and the back of the neck.

It is not an ideal weapon for blasting interstate, though an inch or so of padding under the seat and a set of Bultaco-like clip-ons which sweep up from the fork tubes would transform the machine's comfort beyond all belief. This is not to say that the bike is uncomfortable as far as its *suspension* is concerned, for it is in fact very well sorted out in that department, especially the rear suspension, it is just that a short-statured rider like myself would need to make his own adjustments to deeper seat padding and the higher level of clip-on handlebars. It should be noted, however, that the SB2 is essentially a racing chassis, so comfort over short distances may not be a pre-requisite.

Quite apart from the Bimota's riding position (perhaps some Italians have detachable reproductive organs, which could explain that little cubby-hole behind the seat?), there is nothing that can be faulted in the overall design and manufacture of the Bimota. The paint finish, the clean lines of the fibreglass mouldings, the magnificent welding and finicky attention to the smallest detail all stamp the machine as something very much removed from the mainstream; as indeed it is.

Neat little touches abound, like the tiny cam which fits on the mounting plate directly above the rear brake lever, which can be loosened and revolved around its pivot to alter the angle of the lever. It allows the brake lever to be fitted very precisely to the requirements of the rider, regardless of the length of leg or foot. There are small brackets to fit the original Suzuki coils and the other electrical ancillaries like blinker relays, rectifiers and so on, and everything, but everything, from the original Suzuki fits without the slightest hassle. Everything you need to fit the Suzi motor comes with the bike, and the same doubtless applies to the Kawasaki and Ducati versions.

The rolling chassis includes a four-into-one exhaust system, which naturally fitted without the slightest difficulty. It's a tuned unit, intended to fit the bog-standard Suzuki and is typically matt-black in finish, with a deep, booming exhaust note which befits the image of this road-going racer.

So, the Bimota-Suzuki looks great, is built to the most exacting standards, sounds terrific and takes a giant leap forward in frame design, but how does all this relate in terms of open-road performance?

It is true to say that my own self-imposed limitations were well below the machine's potential. I have seldom cranked a heavy bike over to the angles I cranked that Bimota, never before run through a 40km/h corner at more than twice the posted speed, seldom braked so hard over rippled surfaces on the fast entry to a very slow corner, and never felt as secure while doing so. I will except the 1300cc Munch Mammoth from these statements as a matter of course!

The Bimota transported me to a dimension of motorcycling I have seldom experienced, even with such great handlers as the Ducati Super Sport and the trim little Moto-Morini 500. The odd little dips and hollows you so often find on-line, and the occasional off-camber exit from medium paced corners – which become fast corners with the Bimota! – do little but cause a groan from the front forks and a nudge up the backside from the hard seat. They have no effect whatever on a tight line, though I must say that on occasion, when I buttoned off the power after an over-exuberant exit from a decreasing-radius corner, there was a tendency for the bike to shrug its shoulders when dropping into small holes or stepping over small humps.

Keeping the power on and holding the bike down at the most absurd angles soon put a stop to that sort of behaviour.

If you think a 'mere' four-cylinder double overhead camshaft 750 engine in a trick frame is a waste of time and effort when there are many 1000cc donks about –particularly when that 750 engine remains bog standard – then think again.

Regardless of how large or how highly tuned an engine may be, the name of the game in either fast road touring or out-and-out racing is to brake late, accelerate early and corner hard, leaving the long straight bits to those whose machines may be a bit quicker in a straight line. Then you reel 'em in again in the next series of corners or over the next bit of choppy road. Boy racer stuff? Boy racer stuff indeed!

Quite apart from the great handling and impressive braking the Bimota frame bestows upon its fortunate owner, there are several other factors which make the Italian frame a Very Good Idea. Its wheelbase is 1365mm, some 110mm shorter than the GS750 – making the bike easier to toss from side to side – while the seat height is almost 50mm lower. The complete unit weights a full 30 kilograms less than the original Japanese machine; and that is with a fuel tank almost full!

While there has never been a frame quite like the Bimota before, there is never likely to be one again. Bimota abandoned the complicated, older design in favour of a simple – that is to say cheaper – and slightly more conventional design. The two-piece construction, with its clever conical joints, has gone in favour of a one-piece frame, the handlebars are (thankfully) a couple of inches higher than before and the tank and seat are now two separate items, the seat (at last) somewhat more heavily padded.

Perhaps it's unfortunate that because of the whims of fashion or the depth of the market's pocket, compromises sometimes have to be made. But the new Bimota, for all that, is very similar to this one and retains all the best features, so there has been no compromise in the bike's great attributes, even after major design changes have been made to much later models.

But you could be the first on your block – in fact the only one on your block – to have owned one in 1980, as Norm Sharpe placed the Bimota-Suzuki up for sale not long after my test report was finished. He told me that he hoped no one would actually buy the bike: someone did, but the by-now elderly bike is still around, for it was spotted on Phillip Island at the GP races only a couple of years ago. It appeared to be very well kept, for Norm Sharp tells me it still looked to be as trim a machine as it was when he sadly waved goodbye to it all those years ago.

The small Bimota concern built very many, almost 'one-off' motorcycles and frames, similar to the road test Suzuki featured above, many of them with the brilliant hub-centre steering design. This road-going version of the successful Tesi racer, with its hub-centre steering, is just one example of the marvellous work a small band of dedicated enthusiasts can achieve, often on an almost shoe-string budget. The history of motorcycling is littered with very clever people like these, who have enlivened the industry on almost every level since Day One.

1935 11-50 Brough 'Superior'

1100cc JAP SIDE-VALVE VEE-TWIN

During the 1920s, 30s and occasionally into the 1940s as well, there were a great many large-capacity Vee-twin motorcycles made by an equally large number of motorcycle factories in England, France, Switzerland – yes, Switzerland – and America; particularly in America – and now Japan – where large and dominating Vee-twin motorcycles are still being made, and in huge numbers at that. Often intended for sidecar use, but certainly just as well favoured as punchy, low-revving roadsters, or quite often speed record holders as well, many of the large factories in England between the two World Wars had large machines of this type at the top end of their catalogues. Many of the factories made their own engines, but the once-ubiquitous British JAP (J.A. Prestwich) factory must have supplied many thousands of their proprietary engines to manufacturers large and small, as indeed gearbox manufacturers such as Burman, Sturmey-Archer and Albion did, and again in their many thousands.

Perhaps the smallest manufacturer to utilise the services of JAP in supplying engines of various sizes, and most of them very large capacity at that, was the inimitable George Brough, a former racer and record-holder whose machines were always hand-made to the most exacting standards, so much so that there were said to be no two Brough 'Superior' motorcycles which were alike. It must be said, however, they were assuredly similar, inasmuch as they shared a common name, and many common cycle parts as well, including the huge Castle leading-link front forks, which owed some of their basic design to Harley-Davidson. But a client's Brough would often be made to 'special order' and thus tailor-made to suit almost any of the demands or requests which any potential owner may make. The motorcycles were always frightfully expensive, which added to their appeal and their comparative rarity, the machine in its day often referred to by some contemporary motorcycle journalists as the 'Rolls Royce of Motorcycles'.

However, by today's 21st century, multi-coloured and heavily chrome-plated standards, the subject of this analysis, a booming, punchy 1100cc side-valve **1935 11-50 Brough Superior** (of which, just 308 were built from 1933 to 1940), may seem drab in the extreme. In its day, however, the bike glorified in its black-on-black colour scheme, with the odd touch of chrome or nickel plate to relieve it. This was by no means a rarity in the 1930s so one might expect a motorcycle thus equipped to be lost in the crowd somewhere if it stood in line with a bunch of modern motorcycles.

Perhaps so, but for the enthusiast the Brough remains one of the most revered pre-war Classics for reasons very far removed from the current aesthetics of candy-gloss and gleaming metal. The bike is certainly low-key as far as its general *appearance* is concerned, but it proves – as it always has proven – to be a machine of lasting character on much closer acquaintance. A Brough motorcycle of some description (often a prototype, or a very-limited production machine) was often exhibited at the Olympic and Earls Court Motorcycle Shows in the 1920s and 30s, but a new Brough motorcycle was seldom to be seen on display in the showroom of a motorcycle sales outlet.

Although very well known to motorcyclists in that era, the marque was never available in anything like large numbers because, as we have seen, a Brough was always hand-made, and often to very special order, by George and his small band of dedicated enthusiasts who made the machines literally from the ground up. In this way every Brough Superior was built to suit its prospective owner, as good a reason as any to refer to the bike as a two-wheeled Rolls Royce.

No less a personage than T.E. Lawrence (Lawrence of Arabia) owned no fewer than eight Brough Superior motorcycles over a span of some 10 years, most of them the Super Sports SS100, which carried a written guarantee of a top speed in excess of 100mph. Lawrence's written account of his unofficial 'race' against a Bristol bi-plane back in the 1920s makes for fantastic reading, and should be eagerly sought-after and excitedly read by anyone who ever rode a motorcycle of any description. Unhappily, he was killed while riding an SS100 in 1932, while

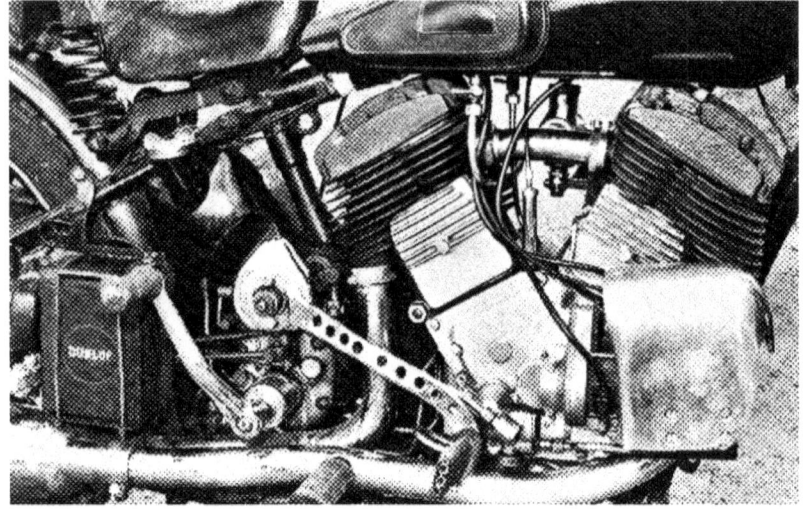

Machine's right side shows the big, side-valve engine at its best. Note the T-shaped inlet manifold between the cylinders, the tappet inspection covers below the cylinder heads and alloy casting to cover the Lucas twin-mag/dyno unit under the front cylinder, driven by bevel gears, instead of the usual sprockets and chain.

his latest SS100 machine was even then being built in the small factory.

In all, there were just over 3000 Brough motorcycles made from the first, 'home-made' effort in 1921 to the last one made in 1940. The small factory's busiest year was 1927, which saw just 226 machines built. Every one of them was assembled and tested, then dismantled to the last nut and bolt to then be painted or plated, before being re-assembled and tested yet again: how's that for attention to minute detail?

At the start of hostilities in 1939 the factory was contracted to make components for Rolls Royce aircraft engines, so motorcycle manufacture virtually ceased, but after the War Brough continued to make spare parts for its machines right up until 1969. At last count, there were claimed to be more than 1000 Brough Superior motorcycles still in existence, many of them still ridden on a regular basis in rallies and similar events. A few others are displayed in museums.

It was said that George would often invite prospective owners to his home for dinner to assess their worthiness to buy one of his machines, and he would quietly make visual measurements of the clients who were lucky enough to pass his secret tests. If the potential customer was accepted, it was assured that, as a proud owner, he would find his new machine a near-perfect fit for his physical dimensions; and indeed, his personality as well. You could say it was a much more relaxed era in those dim, dark days beyond recall; it was an atmosphere which placed the 'bespoke' Brough securely upon its stately plinth even when there were a few other 'hand-made'

The machine's left side features the alloy primary drive cover, unique in being split horizontally. Note the large-bore, 29-type 'variable-venturi' Amal carburettor which feeds the dual manifold. The rear drive chain's width behind the clutch dome indicates the huge final-drive sprocket, demonstrating the engine's very wide spread of low-speed grunt.

motorcycles to be found.

I have long admired the Brough Superior as something removed from the norm, and the chance encounter I made with the owner of a 1935 Brough saw me in the wilds of Yarrambat, outside Melbourne, where the opportunity to actually ride the model was presented. The bike belonged to Melbourne businessman, Jim Cooper, who commuted to the city daily from his Yarrambat retreat, where he and his wife Margaret also tended their farm and bred a small herd of pedigree cashmere goats. Jim has been into motorcycling for many years, and has owned Ducati, BMW and Honda machines. In his garage sat the big Brough, a couple of elderly Nortons, a belt-driven Levis two-stroke and a magnificent 1913 Rolls-Royce car.

The Brough is in very good condition, but at first sight is not very remarkable and could probably have passed for just another old motorcycle – were it not for its reputation and the name on the uniquely shaped petrol tank. Long and thin, the low-slung Brough Superior exhibits a wheelbase perhaps half-a-wheel longer than a Ducati Darmah (and *that's* a long motorcycle!) and very little ground clearance, though the comparatively narrow crankcases allow for plenty of cornering clearance.

It is the 11-50 model, the bike fitted with an 1100cc side-valve JAP engine, the type of British-made power-plant, which was fitted to many hundreds of motorcycles, in all guises from 350 and 500cc singles to big side-valve or overhead-valve Vee-twins. The same company's 500cc single-cylinder Speedway engine has become legendary: mounted in a variety of frames and running gear, the JAP Speedway engine was unbeatable in its heyday.

The side-valve Vee-twin engine design, brought to a peak of efficiency by JAP, and later by Harley-Davidson in its K-type flat-track racers, has gone into history as one of the most popular engine designs of its era, and can still be seen performing yeoman service in many a chopped WLA Harley. But it has its limitations, particularly in the local hot spots around the exhaust area, and the inefficient, tortuous shape of the inlet tract.

Valves were carried in the *side* of the cylinder barrels, with their stems down and heads uppermost, the entire valve gear carried over the top of the timing-gear case, from camshaft and followers, tappets and of course the valves themselves.

Barrels and heads of the 11-50 were made of cast-iron, the flat heads detachable – which was not always the case with this type of engine – and the barrels very heavily finned in the area of the exhaust ports. At the base of the right side of the twin cylinders were two large cover-plates which allowed easy access to tappets for annual (?) servicing.

The 11-50 engine was introduced by J.A. Prestwich in 1933 with the cylinders disposed at 60 degrees, but George Brough specified a *50-degree* Vee-twin, in the interests – he said – of 'a more even torque delivery'. In other words, he wanted a smoother motor, but he may have enjoyed an incidental advantage in a slightly shorter wheelbase with the pots a bit closer together.

That first 11-50 had plain covers over the tappets, but later models were fitted with finned covers and a slightly heavier finning to the exhaust area, both for cosmetic appeal and to provide better cooling. From the heavily finned exhaust area, two thick, 50mm exhaust pipes took the hot charge into the large, fish-tailed muffler which was so much the trade-mark of the mid-1930s British motorcycle.

The front pipe swept out and around a polished alloy cowling which shielded the Lucas mag-dyno unit, that famous double instrument which provided sparks for ignition from the magneto and electrical current for lights from the 6-volt generator, which sat upon it 'piggy-back' fashion. The magneto was driven by a set of bevel gears from the camshaft, and sat alongside the engine under the forward cylinder, unlike many other Broughs which had the instrument driven by chain and usually mounted ahead of the forward cylinder.

The bevel gear drive seemed an unnecessary complication, and was certainly noisier than chain-drive, but the slight whine from the bevel gears didn't impinge on general engine noises. The drive was direct to the magneto, which in turn drove its dependant generator by a fibre gear-wheel, and there was of course no adjustment to either the driving or driven gears.

A single, 29-type AMAL carburettor was fitted to the left side of the engine between the two cylinders and was typically unfiltered. The simple, slide-type variable-venturi carburettor fed the cylinders through a T-shaped single manifold which made for a very tortuous path for the inlet charge. Fuel was drawn into the 'T' and made a sudden, 90-degree change in direction to one or the other of the cylinders, where it would go up and over the valve head and then down into the cylinder. Little wonder the side-valve engine disappeared in favour of the simpler overhead valve (and the much more efficient single, or double, overhead *camshaft*) layout for four-stroke machines.

If the side-valve engine is not the most exciting performer by modern standards, then it remains an extremely acceptable engine when its virtues are spelled out. The big JAP engine – made by the English J.A. Prestwich Company, which also built, amongst a great many other power-plants, the all-conquering JAP Speedway engine of fond memory – was fitted with a large, caged roller big-end and fork-and-blade conrods, with huge ball main bearings to support the massive crank assembly. The alloy pistons were fitted with four rings and employed a compression ratio of only 4.7:1. Peak power of the almost totally unstressed motor was 23.1 kW (28.5 BHP) at an easy 4000rpm, though the engine was still delivering 21.2 kW (27.5 BHP) at an unstrained 4600rpm. Peak torque was 59.8 Nm (44 ft/lbs) at a casual 2000rpm.

Although modern pundits will decry the design of the older side-valve engine, it is nevertheless true to say that in terms of low-speed pulling power and sheer grunt higher in the scale, very few modern (high-revving) engines could hope to live with this nigh-indestructible old Thumper. In fact, the torque curve of the 11-50 JAP engine was dead flat throughout 2000rpm, from 2000 to 4000rpm, and then it just began to drop away. The makers specified polished ports in the standard engine, whether it needed them or not, and the donk was a long-stroke design at 85.7 x 95mm bore and stroke. The similar, if more sporty, **SS80** side-valve was in a slightly higher state of tune and enjoyed a touch more power.

Dry-sump lubrication was used, with oil circulated by a double-geared oil pump from a separate oil tank under the nose of the single saddle. Essentially a total-circulation system, some oil was burnt with the inlet charge after it had circulated throughout the engine. The four-speed, foot-change gearbox and the primary chain had their own oil supply, the latter contained within an unusual horizontally split alloy chaincase.

The frame was of the full-cradle type, necessary to support a fairly heavy engine, and was finished without a sign of a weld at any joint. You could be forgiven if you thought the whole series of steel tubes and forged gussets which located them had been glued together. It was a far cry from current methods of daub-welding which is evident on some modern machines.

No rear suspension was used, and the chore of absorbing wheel shocks rested (and surprisingly well) on the near-universal single spring saddle yet again; the device fitted to almost everything on two wheels back in those days, whether rear wheel springing was adopted or not. Front forks were the busy, and agricultural looking, but nonetheless celebrated, Castle forks which Brough used to great advantage, and which even today excite comment when compared to the more flexible telescopic forks which have since been universally adopted. Essentially, they were claimed to be a 'copy' of the leading-link forks used on Harley-Davidson machines but were said to be an 'improvement' upon them as well.

Ignition advance and retard were manually controlled, which is old hat these days, but handy when it came to booting such a large engine into life when it was still cold and the morning chill was still in the air. No choke was used, but an air-control slide could be dropped into the venturi to act as a device to enrich the fuel/air mixture if the weather was cold enough.

Dual fuel taps under the base of the large, and very distinctly shaped, tank fed petrol through copper pipes into the separate float bowl of the ancient carburettor, and a swift tickle on the copper float raised the fuel to an acceptable level before that long, swinging kick was applied.

In passing, it may surprise – in fact, horrify – enthusiasts of the marque to be informed that the single most important item of equipment on this 'Rolls Royce of motorcycles' was made in, of all places, a local jam-tin manufacturing facility! It is true, for without a fuel tank there would naturally be no fuel to feed the engine, so the bike could not be started, much less ridden away!

But then, hey presto, when it came to firing up the old iron, the engine started easily on its first kick after finding the right position with the kick-starter and easing the low-compression pistons over their compression strokes.

For some reason, photographer Graham Monro was surprised to see little me kick that big, black beast over in one, and was not reassured when I pointed out that I had kick-started two or three (thousand) large engines by a similar means in the 'good old days' – long before there was a little starter-motor button to make the job a whole lot easier. He said it was a fluke, so I did it all again, and with precisely the same result. I don't think he really accepted that either, but he had to admit the engine appeared to be running, if only because of the deep thump from the well-silenced exhaust and the wisp of oil smoke which hung in the air.

Clutch action was easy, but the foot gear-change was a little tricky because of some wear in the external linkages and selector mechanism. As often is the case with the early positive-stop gear-change mechanism on this age of machine, it was necessary to 'pre-load' the foot-change gear lever a little before selecting first gear, and that applied to all the following changes as well.

Gear ratios were typically high, as befits a punchy, low-revving engine, but they were surprisingly close ratio as well. The standard low gear was 10.59:1, with top a high 4.2:1, although JAP had once specified a 'one-off' special with a top gear of a staggering **3.75:1** with special gearing.

That single, high-geared, specially prepared machine was displayed in 1935 as an exercise to point out to the frank disbelievers that a side-valve engine could cut it with the best of them. The specially tuned SS80 model pulled 162km/h (101mph) in a special test, with the engine buzzing at 6066rpm – very high engine speeds indeed for a side-valve engine: higher in fact than some overhead valve engines of the period! The same machine then astounded the multitude by pulling away with no fuss from 19.3km/h (12mph) in top gear, with the engine pulling like a tractor at only **760rpm!** The bog-standard 11-50 could happily lope along at 145km/h (90mph), according to the Brough biographer, but some indication of the JAP 11-50 engine's performance can be gauged from its ability to pull a sidecar to a top speed of 122km/h (76mph), whether riding the outfit uphill or down.

My first impression on pulling away from rest on Jim's 11-50 was one of incredible pulling power from virtually nothing and the ability of the long machine to execute tight, feet-up turns from less than walking pace with the engine plonking away like a well-tuned *'Observed Trials'* machine. Here was a big, punchy engine from the 1930s with no counter-rotating shafts or funny little bob-weights spinning about inside it, smoothly driving a large motorcycle in tight little figure-of-eight circles over rutted and unsealed clay surfaces with hardly a flicker on the speedo. It was quite a test, but the bike was as stable at that snail's pace as if it had a set of invisible training wheels fitted.

Then, without touching the clutch, I tweaked the throttle open a few degrees and spun gravel as the bike hared off down the dirt road, leaving a tiny furrow behind it. There was no hint of drama as I slowly selected second, then third and finally top gear, the bike's startling acceleration building up without slackening of pace. The bike rocketed up the road like a great mobile armchair,

The Castle front forks look to be very agricultural and could be heard as well as seen as they soaked up the roughest of surfaces with contemptuous ease. This was assisted by shock and rebound springing, and friction adjustment by handwheels on fork legs. There was very little 'shock' transmitted to the handlebars as the forks worked their magic. Very surprising!

the seemingly crude, undamped Castle forks soaking up the odd potholes, ripples and bumps with an ease bordering on the contemptuous. The front forks were chattering about and were certainly noisy in their operation, but they were nonetheless very, very effective.

Those Castle front forks, whose action had to be experienced to be believed, were of the bottom-link type – as we have said, probably 'borrowed' from Harley but, if so, they have been vastly improved upon – with shock and rebound springing and hand-adjusted friction damping which, by current standards, seemed crude and unsophisticated. However, the forks accomplished the dual tasks of providing a comfortable ride and keeping the front wheel tracking straight and true with consummate ease, even if they were a mite noisy. The whole experience was a revelation and made me wonder just how good modern telescopic forks really are with their long, unsupported fork tubes with their inherent flexibility. It is little wonder that the fastest of all Australian Speedway outfits have nearly all worn Castle girder forks up front because the assembly, although apparently flimsy, is strong and flex-free and able to soak up heavy side-thrust loads as well as ironing out most of the bumps. I have asked often enough, but never been told where the machine's owners had managed to secure these great forks.

The 'agricultural' forks allowed for quite good handling, a surprisingly comfortable ride and almost total absence of front-end 'wander' even over rock-strewn surfaces. The unsprung rear-end of the old warrior bounded about a bit but didn't exert much effect on the general 'feel' of the bike, probably because of the single saddle's springing.

One cannot advocate a rigid rear-end, but at least you know what you've got – or haven't got – and (as I have noted all too often) that a little sprung saddle can work miracles over some very heavy going. The less said about the hard rubber pad which was bolted to the rear mudguard and masqueraded as a pillion seat in those days the better. I didn't try it, and I'm very happy about that.

However, the tail-end of the big Brough seemed to be airborne on the odd occasion, particularly over some of the sharp rock outcroppings we rode across – although photos didn't back-up the feeling, and the riding position was almost perfect for me, which was a surprise considering I had never had dinner with old George; but somebody of about my size must have done so. No doubt the positioning of footrests, handlebars and control levers, and their relationship to the saddle position, would differ slightly on just about every Brough that came from the works if we believe the well-documented stories. But for all practical purposes I found myself totally at home on the bike after travelling only a few metres. The bike was, naturally, even better over sealed road surfaces.

By the look of the mounting bracket for the handlebars they could never be changed, even if you wanted to do so. However, there was some adjustment to control levers and some of the simple switchgear.

Instrumentation was almost non-existent with the on/off headlamp and dipper switches ready to hand; but there was not much more to it than that. Today, instrument warning lights are standard on everything from off-road Enduro machines to little commuters, but such was the attitude that prevailed all those years ago that even the two-wheeled 'Rolls-Royce' never fitted these by-now bog-standard goodies, nor saw the need for a starter motor or LED trouble-shoot read-out panel. You could say they never thought of it, but the fact is that such things existed way back then, even if they were more basic. One little-known example is the electric starter-motor/generator fitted to some Indian 'Power Plus' motorcycles from way back in 1916!

Brakes were spongy on the heavy Brough, but effective enough to pull the bike up in leisurely fashion and its loping, slightly out-of-step gait was a feeling you just do not get these days – unless you happen to ride something like a chopped flat-head Harley; or possibly a lumpy Cruiser motorcycle: or, maybe, a horse at full speed. At a time when there was probably at least one big Vee-twin machine in almost every catalogue from AJS, Matchless, Royal Enfield, Coventry Eagle, Montgomery, BSA and several others, the Brough was said to stand supreme. It looked little different except for that oddly shaped, hand-made petrol tank and it quite probably felt little different on the road, but for some inexplicable reason it enjoyed a mystique all its own. The bike was available in side-valve form, like this example, the more potent side-valve SS80, or the legendary SS100 overhead-valve Sports iron which really made the marque's name. But the old 11-50 Brough Superior remains a fast and clearly long-lasting machine which is even more eagerly sought-after in the 21st century than it was more than almost a century earlier!

TECH SPECS

Make: Brough Superior

Model: 11-50

Year of manufacture: 1935

Type:
50-degree JAP Vee-twin side-valve design. Cast-iron heads and barrels, with valves contained within the sides of cylinder barrels. Caged roller big-end with single crankpin and fork-and-blade connecting rods, with large ball main bearings. Alloy pistons with four compression rings.

Bore x stroke: 85.7 x 95mm x 2

Capacity: 1096cc

Comp ratio: 4.7:1

Power @ rpm: 28.5BHP @ 4600rpm

Torque @ rpm: 44 ft/lbs @ 2000rpm

Ignition:
Lucas twin mag-dyno, dual instrument for ignition, lighting, battery

Carburation:
Single, T-shaped manifold, single 29-type AMAL, unfiltered

Lubrication:
Dry sump, oil system from separate tank via double-gear oil pump, to engine alone. Separate oil in gearbox and chain case.

Transmission:
By chain in oil-bath primary chaincase, to multi-plate clutch and four-speed foot-change gearbox with external, positive-stop linkage.

Gear ratios (overall):
1st – 10.59:1; 2nd – 6.13:1; 3rd – 4.83:1; 4th – 4.2:1.

Performance (claimed):
Top speed – 90mph. Fuel consumption – 60mpg. Oil consumption – 2000mpg.

Machine loaned by:
JIM COOPER, Yarrambat, Victoria.

1952 Model C Nimbus 'Bumblebee'

750cc OHC FOUR CYLINDER, SHAFT DRIVE

You could be forgiven for thinking that a European motorcycle powered by a multi-cylinder 750cc overhead camshaft engine would be something of a road rocket, and this would certainly be true of any modern-day motorcycle. But this is not always the case, as evidenced by the **1950s Nimbus,** a Danish motorcycle made during two entirely different eras, the latter machines featuring an in-line four-cylinder 750cc OHC engine employing shaft drive, with modern-day telescopic front forks and rigid frame on the later models.

Torsionally rigid in all planes and somewhat 'agricultural' in appearance, the simple frame of the later incarnation of the Nimbus was made of 40mm x 8mm 'flat' strip steel and several interconnected plates, all of which were carefully *riveted* together with not a single weld in sight. As simple as that odd-looking frame was in the later models – some 12,750 of which were built from 1934 to 1959 – it remained strong enough to hold itself firmly together against the weight of the power-plant and such powerful forces as engine vibration, tension and compression from employing no rear suspension, along with torsional, shear, side-thrust loads from a sidecar which was often fitted and 'twisting' forces which would have been generated by the action of the *rigid* shaft drive mechanism. Naturally, with no rear suspension, the final drive shaft needed no complex universal joint, managing to get by with a small 'shock absorber'(?) just ahead of the crown wheel and pinion drive gear contained within the left side of the rear hub.

The handlebars were not the usual tubular steel either, but were fabricated from metal pressings, a small instrument panel incorporated in the centre. The left handlebar grip was unique, and really quite clever, for it was a throttle-like twist-grip with four positions, which controlled the headlamp functions including on/off, and dipper control for high or low beam. Brilliant thinking, and a one-of-a-kind as well!

During the entire history of this most interesting motorcycle, it always presented just one model (with several minor variations on the theme, of course) and always employed an air cooled, in-line four-cylinder engine to propel it. Earlier machines built from 1919 to 1928 varied in basic engine design, the first examples employing the then-fashionable **'i.o.e.'** design (overhead *inlet* valve over side valve *exhaust*), with four separate barrels and a fat top tube welded in place to double as the fuel tank: hence its nickname 'Stovepipe'. Towards the end of the first few years of manufacture, with just 1252 machines made – for it was probably a more interesting, expensive sideline than a serious attempt at motorcycle manufacture – later models in that first series adopted the much more efficient overhead valve engine design for inlet and exhaust valves.

The machines were built in Copenhagen by the Danish 'Nilfisk' vacuum cleaner company which was founded by two close friends, Hans Marius Nielsen and Peta Andersen Fisker, who just happened to be enthusiastic motorcyclists as well as door-to-door vacuum cleaner salesmen. Obviously, the Nilfisk name incorporated the first few letters of the surnames of the two men. Perhaps happily, or perhaps not, their vacuum cleaner sales (which were usually domestic appliances but also heavy-duty industrial types) must have risen to such heights that the manufacture of the early series of quite expensive motorcycles had to be abandoned, if only for the time being.

The Nimbus motorcycle name was resurrected in 1934 with an all-new overhead camshaft design employing hand gear change, and its new, 'flat-strap' frame with separate fuel tank but was otherwise entirely recognisable as it pressed on until its demise – along with another four-cylinder motorcycle, the 1000cc Ariel Square Four, and hundreds of other world-famous marques – towards the middle of 1959.

Motorcycling at that time was at its lowest ebb, with hundreds of famous factories either closed or feeling the cold breath of Doom at the back of their collective necks.

Available records indicate that almost 50% of the Nimbus motorcycles built during that latter period were sold to the Army, Police Force, and the Postal service, many of them with factory

Around 25% of Nimbus production was sold to the Postal Service, the bright yellow machines fitted with matching Nimbus side-boxes. This must have assured the nation of a very swift delivery of posted parcels, as well as other materials.

built sidecars attached. The Postal service used many bright yellow side-box combinations for the speedy delivery of parcels, while Nimbus sidecar outfits were also quite popular amongst more 'everyday' motorcyclists.

At the very end of its tenure, some of the newer machines were *said* to have been built from a huge range of spare parts which were still in stock (which is still not proven) while it has been reported that there is still a large range of spares available to service the nearly 4000 Nimbus machines which are still registered in Denmark, as well as several hundred which are claimed to still be on the roads in other countries, including a few here in Australia (**NB:** *I recall a gleaming 1957 Khaki-green Nimbus displayed in Australia's Hamilton Island motorcycle museum of fond memory*). There are at least two Nimbus motorcycle clubs in England, as there are two in the US and another in Canada.

Nimbus motorcycles were very rarely, if ever, exported and even then, clearly in miniscule numbers, but there are reported to be around 300 of these machines in America alone, with around 500 all-told in several nations outside of Denmark. How they managed to get to some far-flung nations – including Australia – and to have remained there for so long, is anybody's guess. This is not to say that the machines were not up to the task, for a high percentage of the later machines are clearly still out there somewhere and, one may safely assume, are probably ridden on a regular basis, which bears mute testimony to their practicality, ruggedness and reliability.

Indeed, it is little short of amazing that such a large number of the small production run of motorcycles which were last manufactured more than 60 years ago should still be in existence, for this seems to have happened to no other motorcycle of which I am aware. I wonder how many other Nimbus machines may lie quietly in a variety of motorcycle museums scattered about the world. How many more, one imagines, may lie hidden in old garages or chicken-coops as they patiently await discovery and, hopefully, a full restoration?

Oddly, in view of the later machine with its rigid frame, the earlier machines made from 1919 to 1928 employed a modern-looking swing-arm rear suspension with minimal travel, due to its pair of short, undamped coil springs. In many ways the design of that rear suspension was ahead of the game, as its in-line four-cylinder engine was. But the advanced Nimbus which appeared just after WWI was by no means the first machine to be powered by an in-line four-cylinder engine, nor the first with an early type of cantilever rear suspension – nor shaft drive, for that matter.

This is the shaft-drive, three-speed, 1924 Nimbus 750 Four, many years ahead of its time. The engine was an inlet-over-exhaust valve design. It adopted an enclosed, short spring above the front guard and swing-arm rear suspension, hidden by the small saddle bag. The pillion passenger enjoyed a well-padded saddle perched upon its own set of leaf springs A tiny kick-starter can be seen halfway along the very large crankcase casting. It really was a first-rate machine.

The American Flying Merkel employed cantilever rear suspension on its board-track racers from just before WWI, while the Belgian FN motorcycle factory introduced an in-line four with shaft final drive as far back as 1908, but the earlier Nimbus was the only machine of that era I am aware of which displayed *all three design features* in the one motorcycle. Incidentally, front suspension on the earlier Nimbus was usually by trailing link forks, sometimes with a single, enclosed coil spring mounted just in front of the frame's headstock.

Even though rear suspension was not specified as part of the later machine's design, the new Nimbus employed a comfortable, well-sprung single saddle and modern-day telescopic fork, and has since been credited as having invented this type of front suspension. The Scott company, which manufactured high-performance two-stroke twins, employed a 'kind-of', semi-telescopic front fork in 1908, but Nimbus was the first motorcycle with a *'recognisable'* telescopic front fork assembly. It was adopted in 1933, almost a year before BMW fitted hydraulically damped telescopic forks to its R12 machine and let the whole world know all about it by patenting the 'new'(?) design. The original Nimbus telescopic forks had no damper control but were well greased at assembly, while from 1939 onwards hydraulic damping was employed to control the movement of the long coil springs: that same year saw the long-overdue modification from hand to foot gear change as well. The forks were progressively improved so that, by 1948, the newest design (the so-called 'high fork') was adopted as the final modification, the latest front forks said to be amongst the best of modern-day telescopics. Front brakes were also progressively enlarged from 150 to 180mm over the years.

The later OHC Model C, like its advanced A and B predecessors, was quite brilliant in concept and execution, the semi unit-construction power-plant on the later machines clearly designed along the lines of a small, four-cylinder motorcar engine. The large, four-in-line, cast-iron, lightly finned cylinder barrel and upper crankcase half, with its 'bell housing' at the rear to accommodate the large flywheel and dry clutch assembly, was cast in one piece along with the in-situ inlet manifold; a design long employed in motorcar engines. There is an alloy, 2-litre sump bolted directly beneath, the deep casting containing sufficient oil to lubricate both engine and gearbox, while claiming to provide limited assistance in cooling the engine as well. Oil-cooled motorcycle engines were by no means unknown in those days, the eccentric British engine designer, Granville Bradshaw, creating several successful oil-cooled power-plants for motorcycles in the 1920s and early-1930s.

A long alloy casting which bolts atop the one-piece cast iron cylinder head contains the overhead camshaft, the shaft supported at each end upon large bronze bushes – with a much larger bush at the more highly stressed front-end, of course – while the tips of the valve rocker arms, with their screw-and-nut tappet adjusters, peep shyly from specially sealed holes

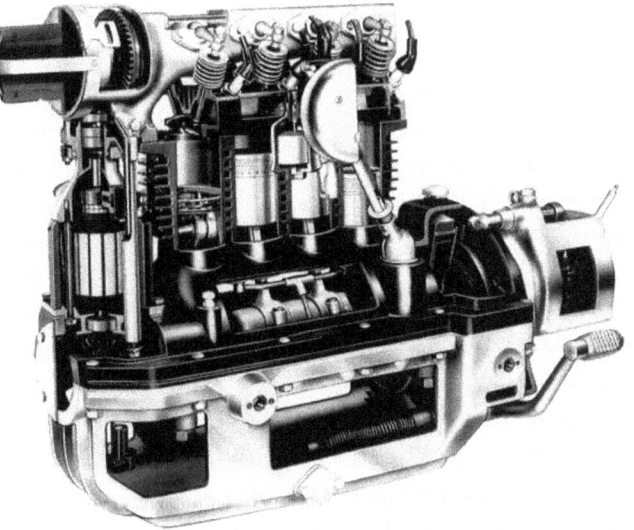

This cutaway drawing shows the neatness of the Nimbus design. Note the vertical generator and its armature drive, the shaft of which drives the overhead camshaft as well. The thick crankshaft can be easily seen, along with the large ball bearings which support it. The large sump provides a clue to the likelihood of a degree of oil colling as well as effective lubrication. The small lever under the gearbox is the 'sideways' kick-starter.

in both sides of the alloy casting. The valves and attendant springs upon which they operate remain fully exposed. The enclosed camshaft is driven by a vertical shaft and bevel gears with three different types of gear teeth employed on occasion. This was said to be depending on subtle differences in cylinder head design and the types of pistons used – some of the latter using the very efficient four-ring design, with a lower oil ring at the base of the long pistons. The design of the various bevel-gear teeth was reported to be straight-cut, 'angled' or helical. Naturally, the valve timing marks on various gear teeth were slightly different, and of course were not interchangeable.

One of the most brilliant design features of the Nimbus engine is the armature shaft located in the centre of the most unusual (and probably unique?) **upright** generator, the component mounted directly in front of the engine. The thick armature shaft also serves duty as the vertical shaft to drive the overhead camshaft, the generator shaft driven from the engine's crankshaft-mounted half-time pinion by its own pair of bevel gears with similarly angled gears driving the overhead camshaft. Very clever, indeed, though almost up-staged by the engine's horizontal distributor, with attendant ignition coil and contact points, which is driven off the front of the camshaft just above, and ahead of, the 6-volt, 70-watt generator. The spark plug leads are then conducted along the upper surface of the camshaft casting and through a small metal clip to the four, easily accessed spark plugs: clearly, routine servicing tasks, like checking and/ or setting tappets and contact breaker points, as well as cleaning or checking spark plugs, must be simplicity itself.

The same applies to the odd-looking, small-bore brass carburettor and its small, steel mesh air filter. The strange carburettor, which features an accelerator pump and special jets, sits in the centre of the cast-in manifold on the left-hand side of the cross-flow, hemispherical combustion-chamber engine. The air filter cover is easily removed by unscrewing three screws to allow for cleaning, re-oiling the steel mesh filter and other simple maintenance tasks. A small, angled tube from the crankcase breather allows oil mist to enter the manifold to provide lubrication for the inlet valves; the naked exhaust valves requiring an occasional small squirt of kerosene or light oil from outside, a process at once absurdly simple and yet (I suggest) urgently required: yet another plus for simple maintenance.

Lubricant from the large sump is fed under pressure from a small-submerged pump adjacent to the crankshaft pinion from which it is driven, feeding high-pressure oil from a sump-based filter through a T-junction at the centre of the crankshaft and through drill-ways into the big-end bearings. The lubricant is then flung under centrifugal force into the large crankcase through other drill-ways in the crank cheeks, where the oil mist thus generated lubricates other crankcase components, including the two large, heavy-duty ball bearings which support either end of the crankshaft. Oil is also directed

The overhead camshaft assembly, which is driven by shaft and bevel gears. The forward-facing distributor is also driven by the camshaft bevel gear – very clever. Spark plugs were placed between the 'naked' valve rockers, with their attendant tappet adjusters. These clever features would make for very easy servicing.

up a special vertical tube to lubricate the overhead camshaft, from where it drains back to the sump under gravity through a smaller tube which is cleverly sited within the camshaft's oil-feed tube. Another special oil line feeds lubricant under pressure into the bolt-on alloy gearbox, by-passing the dry clutch, which is located in its own weather-proof chamber immediately ahead of the gearbox. The gearbox drains oil, under gravity, back to the sump.

The shortish, chunky crankshaft employs very substantial big-end journals, the two in the centre parallel, with the innermost pistons closely attendant and at 360 degrees as they rise and fall together. The two outer crank cheeks have their pistons similarly disposed at 360 degrees, and oppose the centre pistons' travel by 180 degrees, with the firing order 1,3,4,2: all of this designed to help overcome the 'rocking couple' which automatically occurs with 180-degree vertical twins as well as some four-cylinder engines.

In similar fashion to the 1920s Austin 7 side-valve car engine, the Nimbus crankshaft has no centre main bearings, but the crank is very well supported at each end by the large, heavy-duty ball bearings we have mentioned and which are very well lubricated: the front bearing, in view of the added stresses of the various drive gears the engine employs, reported to be more robust. Some owners may have replaced the front bearing with a roller bearing as a 'fail-safe' measure during major overhauls, for the roller bearing clearly presents a larger bearing surface than the ball type: perhaps not necessary but, arguably, not such a bad idea.

Modern-day, high-performance motorcycles usually employ crankshafts with up to five main bearings for support, but it should be noted that the Nimbus crankshaft might not be subject to the 'flexion and whip' phenomenon one might expect, for the Nimbus engine was obviously designed to be very much a 'Gentlemen's Tourer' power-plant – which gives a different meaning to the term 'GT'. It produces its light 22BHP at a leisurely 4500rpm, which is almost a fast idle by modern standards. A modern, 750cc DOHC Four might develop more than four times this power, but at astronomical engine speeds, often spinning at three times the revolutions of the much more casual Danish motorcycle.

Steel connecting rods are drop-forged and similar to the types used in motor cars, employing the narrow, 'I-beam section' design common in automotive application, unlike the con-rod profiles used in most modern motorcycles. The shortish rods feature a large, big-end eye, with detachable end-caps, and are cleverly drilled to allow some high-pressure oil to be flung up the inside of the low-compression pistons to help lubricate the little-end and, I suggest, to minimally assist in engine cooling. Slipper type, white metal big-end bearings are of course employed. Bore x stroke dimensions are almost square at 60 x 66mm, allowing for comparatively low piston speeds, again handy in such a low-revving, lightly powered engine.

The machine's wide-ratio three-speed gearbox, with left-side foot gear-change pedal, might also provide a clue to the engine's handy pulling power at quite low engine revs, thanks to the engine's 'soft' cam profiles, small carburettor and 5.4:1 low-compression pistons in earlier models. Slightly higher domed pistons were adopted in 1936 which raised the compression ratio to 5.7:1, which in turn raised the power from a casual 18BHP to its current, easy-going 22BHP level. Intended initially for the Sports model with upswept exhaust system, the higher ratio pistons were then adopted as standard ware. However, the bike was clearly not designed to be ridden with any urgency, but to be enjoyed to the full in a much more 'leisurely' fashion. Its top speed is claimed to be just 135km/hour, but it is suggested that this should be for short periods of time only, with the much more legal speeds of around 100-110km/hour said to be the norm. I suggest there is a very good reason for this.

If the iconic Danish machine has an Achilles heel it would probably be in the design of the exhaust system which, unlike the four separate pipes which would normally be fitted to other four-cylinder machines, is again more car-like, for a casting bolts directly onto the right face of the engine as a one-piece manifold, encapsulating all exhaust outlets into the one component. The manifold and upper section of exhaust pipe has a chrome-plated heat shield to cover it, but the rearmost cylinders are thus subjected to the furnace-blast of high-temperature exhaust gas conducted from the front pots through the one-piece manifold. This of course adds to the hotter air from the cooling fins of the front cylinders which are circulating rearwards along the lightly finned, one-piece crankcase/cylinder casting. The exhaust system resembles a 'Lazy S' as the waste gases are then routed through a long exhaust pipe and into a similarly long muffler with small fins at its end.

How the Nimbus would cope with being ridden briskly during a 40-degree Australian summer day might be of interest, for I imagine that burnt-out exhaust valves and/or cracked exhaust valve **seats** may not be unknown in this parlous situation. But we must remember the bike was designed to be ridden in a fairly cold, and mostly flat, country where the serpentine exhaust system may have presented few problems: and remember the Nimbus was not intended to be exported. But I believe that later machines were tested in Denmark by the factory with alloy rocker covers fitted, which removed the (essential?) cool air flowing over the exhaust valves, with the result that over-heated, burnt valves became a problem: naturally, the newer modification never got past the prototype stage. Water cooling would have made an enormous difference, of course, but would have added extra weight and more complexity to the design, and may not have been necessary in Denmark, anyway.

Almost at the end of the machine's tenure in the late 1950s there were a couple of prototype Nimbus machines in the pipeline, one of which was said to employ a four-cylinder engine with rotary valves, the other a smart, if odd-looking, twin-cylinder OHC engine fitted into a newly designed frame with Earles front forks and swing-arm rear suspension. The rotary valve machine never made an appearance, while a few prototype vertical twin motorcycles were built, but never reached production.

Unhappily, there is no technical information available on the prototype, all-alloy (?) 1956 OHC vertical twin, but there is just one photo of the machine which shows it to be an in-line design very similar to the four-cylinder model, and it looks to be of about 500cc engine capacity. However, as a prototype, it might have made good sense as a cost-cutting exercise to utilise the pistons, conrods and *half* the crankshaft of the four-cylinder 750 to create an odd-capacity, 180-degree 375cc twin.

The overhead camshaft of the twin-cylinder prototype is apparently driven by chain at the front of the engine for the generator is gone – and with it the armature shaft, of course – and what is probably an alternator is mounted at the front of the large crankcase casting, where it is probably driven directly from the crankshaft. Curiously, the two cylinders are in very close proximity (which would probably preclude over-boring the cylinders to, say, 70mm, to create a 'full-size' 500cc twin) the one-piece, 'figure-eight' barrel exhibiting very light finning, which leads me to the reasonable assumption that the engine may have been *fully* oil-cooled, not 'oil assisted' as in the four-cylinder model. The alloy casting which encloses the OHC drive mechanism on the prototype twin would inhibit air-cooling for the tiny cylinder fins to a large degree, while the large-capacity sump adds another clue to the assumption of an oil-cooled engine. However, the little-known photo shows no oil-cooler, which may still exist, of course, if out of sight on the machine's opposite side.

The rare photo of the newer Nimbus is from the machine's left side so the exhaust system cannot be seen, but part of an angled exhaust pipe on the right-hand side can just be seen which gives the clear impression of a similar 'Lazy S' serpentine exhaust system to the 750 Four – it is sited just to the rear of the odd-looking carburettor – which may again place the rear pot at a disadvantage of over-heating.

As we are aware there is nothing new about oil cooling for internal combustion engines, in fact some 45 British factories made motorcycles in the 1920s which were powered by 350cc

In the Nimbus Museum is this 1950s prototype Nimbus twin, with Earles front forks, swing-arm rear suspension and crankshaft-driven alternator. The chaincase for the overhead camshaft chain shrouds the very shallow air-cooling fins, leading to the thought that the 375cc engine – if that is its capacity? – may be oil-cooled. Just one photo exists, and there is no information on the machine to be found anywhere. This all-new Nimbus twin must surely remain unknown outside the museum.

oil-cooled Bradshaw engines, while this type of design was utilised in more modern eras as well. In the 1980s, Suzuki initially employed oil cooling for its GSX-R sports model, before adopting more 'normal' water-cooling. The latest Bonneville Triumphs are essentially oil cooled, with large, 'cosmetic' air-cooling fins on heads and barrels, while BMW designed an 'oil-head' cooling system for a short time on its R-series 'boxer' twins. There are many other examples, including the huge, oil-cooled, suitcase-shaped 750cc OHC four-cylinder alloy engine which powered the massive 1927 German Windhoff motorcycle.

It is clear that none of the prototype Nimbus machines survived the earlier stages of development for, as we know, the motorcycle trade was almost on its last legs in the late-1950s and was lucky to have survived the onslaught of the dreaded Mini, the accursed Volkswagen and several other cheap 'bubble' cars. Not an ideal time to be introducing new models into a shrinking marketplace, one would have thought, which is probably the reason why the new Nimbus twin quietly disappeared.

Clearly, no one thought to mention this sad state of affairs to the burgeoning Japanese motorcycle factories, in particular to a Slumbering Giant called **Honda!**

One of the few Nimbus machines in Australia is owned by well-known Sydney motorcyclist/businessman Anthony Gullick, who graciously offered me his prized **1954 Model C NIMBUS** for an all-too-brief test ride. The bike looks to be more in pristine than in outright 'showroom' condition, which indicates it is ridden often enough, rather than being locked away somewhere, and its odd 'Vintage' look, I am sure, would create many a questing glance from modern-day riders, most of whom, it is safe to say, would never have known of its existence, much less its country of origin.

Please note that *I was unable to take advantage of Anthony's offer,* but I did enjoy a ride on a model of similar Vintage, which I discovered entirely by accident in a Northern Sydney beach-side suburb many years earlier. It was cautiously loaned to me for a half-day's test, which I underwent, taking copious notes as well, but unhappily there were no photographs taken at the time. The following paragraphs are from some of my notes on the Nimbus, and should thus be applicable to the Gullick machine as well.

Naturally, there is no starter motor, but the engine fires up easily enough in one or two kicks because of its very low compression ratio and heavy flywheel, its small kick-starter an almost anonymous little left-mounted pedal which peeks out from the gearbox and which, early BMW-like, has to be booted out sideways.

Some riders may be able to operate the little pedal with their left heel while normally seated, but my short legs would never allow that, so I needed to stand alongside the bike to boot it over with my right leg. It would be even easier if the bike was on a centre stand at the time, with me standing on the footpath, rather than prodding at the little pedal while jumping on it sideways.

The engine idles smoothly enough, with a nice, almost comforting burble from the long muffler, a sound which earned it the nick name of 'Bumblebee', and which becomes even more 'bee-like' when on the move. If someone tried hard enough, one could be too-easily hypnotised by the sight just under one's thighs of the eight valves jumping about all over the place when the engine is running, but it's clearly better not to go there. The bike is equipped with a wide-ratio three-speed gearbox, the smooth left-foot change employing the near-universal one-down-two-up pattern, with gear changes at once positive and smooth, whether moving up the range or coming back down again. Clutch action is light and progressive, the gear ratios perfectly in step with the engine's modest power output, with the pleasant surprise of acceleration which is certainly on the brisk side.

Clearly the odd, small-diameter brass carburettor which, when compared to similar components fitted to later motorcycles, looks to be home-made and perhaps might not work at all, is absolutely up to the job: it is probably ideal for the task when employed with such a lightly tuned engine.

As its 'tech specs' indicate, the Nimbus is not an urgent, high-revving machine, but its gentle, loping gait allied to an old-fashioned 'sit-up-and beg' riding position is at once a relief, relaxing in the extreme and a joy to experience: for many of us this more casual, no high-drama, no-histrionics type of machine typifies a design more in keeping with the mid-1930s than into the late-1950s. There is of course a place for the very high-performance machines which proliferate today, and we ride these sports models as often as possible for a buzz, but it becomes something of a relief to ride such an unpretentious motorcycle for a change.

In view of the fact that Nimbus was the first motorcycle manufacturer to employ 'modern day' telescopic forks more than 90 years ago, more than a year earlier than the more famous BMW (who always claim to have been the first). It's no surprise that they work so well on the Nimbus, ironing out road irregularities with almost contemptuous ease. There was no rear suspension and thus, one would have thought, a good boot up the backside every now and again would be inevitable when traversing irregular road surfaces, but this was not the case. Oh, the rear wheel could be 'felt' as it hopped about a bit over some very 'uncertain' road surfaces, but the odd-looking, well-padded single saddle gave a surprisingly good ride, aided by the standard rubber bands (?) upon which it's mounted, which added their own well-damped, progressive springing to the rear end. It reinforced my oft-mentioned view that a well-sprung single saddle could give almost as good a ride as a machine with swing-arm rear suspension, if the well-sprung rear-end of the bike was surmounted by a nigh- bulletproof, unyielding dual-seat: as is/was all too often the case. The 180mm drum brakes, equipped with their long pivot levers, proved to be surprisingly powerful, and were well capable of hauling the machine to a standstill in very, very short order. In fact, all these components, from a modern/ vintage engine design to a supple suspension, from simple carburation and electrical generation to an overall 'nuts-and-bolts' appearance were cobbled together to make an entirely acceptable, easy-going machine, 'agricultural' in appearance though some modern-day riders might suggest it is, when looking down their collective noses at it.

To each his own, of course, a statement which obtains to the entire machine, 'old-fashioned' though it clearly is, and by no means to everyone's taste. But it is still a fine motorcycle which enjoys its unique place in the History of Motorcycling, and to which many of us gleefully doff our helmets in acknowledgment. Well done, Nimbus, and well done, Anthony.

TECH SPECS

Make: Nimbus

Model: Model C

Year of manufacture: 1954

Type:
In-line, OHC four-cylinder, featuring one-piece, cast iron cylinder barrel/upper crankcase half/inlet manifold. Cast iron cylinder head employs two valves per cylinder, all eight valves and valve springs un-enclosed, with adjustable screw-and-nut tappets. The cylinder head is topped by a large, bolt-on alloy casting, the enclosed camshaft supported upon two large bronze bushes and is driven by the forward-mounted, vertical generator's armature shaft via two sets of bevel gears. An alloy oil sump bolts to the base of the engine casting, oil circulating by a submerged gear-type oil pump through an external pipe to the camshaft, draining back to the sump by gravity. High-pressure lubricant is also delivered to the crankshaft and supporting pair of large, heavy-duty ball bearings through a number of internal oil lines, drillings and oil galleys within the large crankcase casting; oil mist also assists. A separate oil line is routed to the gearbox, oil returning to the sump by gravity. The chunky crankshaft is a steel forging, with car-type connecting-rods having detachable end-caps and white-metal slipper bearings.

Bore x stroke: 60mm x 66mm x 4

Engine capacity: 746cc

Compression ratio: 5.7:1, with four-ring alloy pistons

Power @ rpm: 22BHP @ 4500rpm

Carburation:
A single, oddly designed, 26mm small-bore carburettor, with accelerator pump and oiled, steel mesh air filter. Oil mist from crankcase via special tube intended to lubricate inlet valves.

Electrics:
Unique, vertically disposed 6-volt generator to lead/acid battery. Ignition by battery, contact points and coil

Transmission:
Through dry, single plate car-type clutch to separate, bolted-on three-speed gearbox, with left foot gear-change; one down, two up design. Shaft final drive is through crown wheel/pinion, with rear mounted 'shock absorber' on drive shaft.

Gear ratios:
(Solo) 1st – 9.89:1; 2nd – 6.39:1; 3rd – 4.23:1. (Sidecar) 1st – 11.90:1; 2nd – 7.69:1; 3rd – 5.12:1.

Wheels, tyres, brakes:
he 19" wheel rims are laced to 180mm drum brakes on front and rear, fitted with 350 x 19 tyres, ribbed on front and block pattern on rear.

Dimensions:
Length – 2200mm; Width – 720mm; Height – 1100mm; Wheelbase – 1453mm; Weight – 185kg; Fuel tank – 12.5 litres (with 1 litre reserve) Fuel consumption – 5.6 l/100km.

Machine offered for test owned by: ANTHONY GULLICK, Sydney.

1939 Levis 500cc OHV 'Springer'

Many years ago, the Levis Engine Company in England changed the spelling of its name. It added an 's' to the end of its name simply to avoid the constant mispronunciation and inevitable association with the popular garment label. It must be at once a sad reflection on a machine which was once amongst the better-known British motorcycles, as well as a testimony to the power of the advertising man's persuasiveness. Could a classic old British single-cylinder motorcycle really be confused with a pair of trousers?

It was not ever thus, for the Levis was a well-sought-after machine, from the time it was raced as a 175 two-stroke single to its demise during World War 2. In the immediate post-war years, Levis manufactured air-cooled industrial engines and small air compressors.

When I was a beardless youth there was a character who owned a Levis 600cc single, living not far from my place in the wharf-side Sydney suburb of Woolloomooloo. We all thought it was an overhead camshaft engine simply because it had a single, chromed tube running alongside the cylinder, and we assumed it carried the cam drive inside it in a similar fashion to the Norton 'International'.

I learned many years later that the 600 was a rare bird indeed – the larger models were mostly five-hundreds – and that it was in fact an overhead *valve* engine with the pushrods carried in that single tube. The engine looked simple enough, with nothing but a tall cylinder mounted on an almost round crankcase, with a Burman four-speed gearbox – the formula for the classic British single, though in this case a full 600cc – an engine capacity well-known to sidecar drivers pre-war and in the immediate post-was era. It is also worthy of note that the 600cc Levis was capable of just over the Imperial 90 miles/per hour (153km/h) in 1938, a very good performance indeed for a large capacity single cylinder motorcycle in those days.

But I had not clapped eyes on a Levis almost since I fled the 'Loo for Sydney's West, and it came as something of a surprise to discover not only a pristine example of the marque alive and well in suburban Sydney but to further discover that the bike was a very rare 1939 Levis, one of only seven 500cc models which came to this country with *plunger rear suspension* and the only one still in existence. To me it made this test doubly interesting, for the opportunity of riding such a rare example of all that was good in British pre-war motorcycling was tinged with the knowledge that here was a rare motorcycle indeed

It could never pass for anything but just what it is, forever stamped with the indelible 'Made in England' mark, as British as the Union Jack.

The Levis features a simple, long-stroke engine with cast iron head and barrel, that long, chromed tube up the right side of the tall, thin cylinder barrel carrying the long pushrods which control the enclosed overhead valve gear. In this, the Levis differs from some of its fellows, for several pre-war 500 singles still had the overhead valve gear completely exposed.

Neat little alloy covers can be removed in a moment for the *annual* chore of glancing at the tappets; and the valve gear is neatly contained within cast extensions on the iron head, with the covers locked in place by spring clips. Sealed and totally free of oil leaks, it must make for simple, swift maintenance.

The separate-bowl Amal carburettor lies on its side, with a horizontal float-bowl like that fitted to pre-was Tiger 90 Triumph 500cc singles (I would like to find one of those, too, please!) again making for simple tuning and even simpler routine maintenance.

Twin exhaust ports are a feature, as they often were with this type of engine all those long years ago, but the upswept design of the exhaust pipes lends a sporty air to the machine.

An external Pilgrim pump supplies oil to main and roller big-end bearings, with oil mist taking care of much of the lubrication in the very lightly stressed engine. The Pilgrim pump is very similar to the type fitted to JAP speedway engines and is of the total-loss type. Yes, the oil circulates through the engine then most of it ends up back in Mother Earth, after some of it finds its way into the combustion chamber, as we shall soon see.

Part of the publicity blurb covering the machine neatly counters any opposition to this primitive oiling system by pointing out the great advantages of a 'constant supply of *fresh, clean oil*', rather than: '*lubricating the engine with a thin valve grinding paste*' (?), as the blurb goes on to say. Clearly, Levis were yet to discover the joys of the two-sided scavenger-return oil pump, much less modern-day detergent oils.

The single pushrod tube gives the impression that the engine is an overhead camshaft design, which the Levis is not. Note the external, 'total loss' Pilgrim oil pump directly below the curved exhaust pipe, and the rare Miller mag/dyno unit directly underneath the carburettor.

If the oiling system is simple, it is none-the-less very effective, and is quite like modern two-stroke systems. Oil under pressure finds its way along the hollow engine mainshaft to feed the big-end bearing, then up the inside of the connecting-rod (which is drilled from big-end eye to gudgeon-pin hole) where it then throws out through the lower skirt of the piston to the cylinder walls. No oil ring is fitted, the pressure beneath the descending piston forcing some oil past the two compression rings where it is burnt in the combustion chamber.

Main bearings are pressure-fed from the oil pump, and the timing gears are similarly fed. Oil which finds its way into the crankcases mists with heat build-up and is cunningly allowed to rise through the long pushrod tube to provide positive lubrication to the entire, fully enclosed valve gear assembly.

The valve guides allow oil to run between them and the valves, which of course provides them with adequate lubrication as well.

But it is the tiny attention to detail which distinguishes this basically simple engine, for each moving part has its own specially machined 'reservoir' of oil lying in wait for the next cold start.

Each of the timing gears in the tiny timing case has a neat little pocket machined underneath it to catch a supply of oil so that the instant the engine spins over the oil is picked up and distributed by the teeth of the gears themselves. Similarly, the valve guides lie in little puddles of oil which are distributed to lubricate the upper cylinder and valve stems almost as soon as the valves begin to rise and fall. Small pockets of oil also allow main bearings to be half-immersed in the lubricant, and the big-end bearing receives the first blast of 'cool, fresh, clean oil' as soon as pressure is applied to the kick-starter. Overall oil consumption was said to run to 2,000–2,400 miles per gallon, though an eye would have to be kept on the oil level in the tank in view of a complete lack of any system to warn of low supply. Oil is fed to the pump from the oil tank under the nose of the single, spring saddle, and flow adjustment is by screwing a knurled knob on the side of the pump. The flow is viewed through a clear mica window atop the pump body. As I have noted, there is of course, no 'scavenger' return feed to the oil tank.

The mufflers are detachable and in four pieces to facilitate cleaning, just like modern two-strokes, but with a heavy burn-proof centre spiral of some 4mm thickness.

Such was the easy-going nature of the old, big single that such an engine could run for many, many thousands of miles with little or no attention, the essentially slow-revving design allowing adequate oiling to even the most highly stressed components. The answer lay, of course, in the very large ball and roller bearings with which this engine was equipped, which is why many a road-going engine could be highly tuned for racing without the need to drastically modify its basic design, and why they always remained very reliable; even when put under the high pressure of racing.

To complete the trad British picture, the 500cc Levis mounts a rare Miller mag-dyno unit behind the cylinder barrel, directly beneath the odd carburettor, the component driven in typical fashion by an enclosed chain from a small sprocket on the right end of the timing-side main shaft. The dual electrical instruments were fitted to many British motorcycles, the magneto driven from the engine and itself driving the generator, which was mounted to the top of the magneto outer case, located by a metal strap and clamping bolt. However, the Lucas mag-dyno was a far more popular component, fitted to many thousands of pre-war motorcycles, while the Miller component was much rarer.

As ever, the component was totally trouble-free, supplying plenty of fat sparks for ignition and enough current to keep the standard sized 6-volt battery honest. Not a hard task, with just head and tail lamps to supply.

The picture is completed by the nigh-universal Burman four-speed gearbox, separate from the engine and driven by chain in a large semi-oil bath case on the machine's left side. The clutch is essentially dry, again standard practice on British machines, with the case merely to provide lubrication to the primary chain. Adjustment to this chain was affected by slackening off the gearbox mounting bolts and sliding the gearbox back in its slotted mounting plates.

In other words, the 1939 Levis is very, very similar to just about every other 500 single which went before or was to follow. Where then is the mystique?

Ah, the word is *character*, not conformity, for the British 500 single existed in many names though similar in form and specification. But you could never confuse, say, a Velocette MSS with an Empire Star BSA, or even a model J Royal Enfield. Or an ES2 Norton with a 500cc Triumph Tiger 90.

By the same (but modern) yardstick, one cannot compare the A1-R Kawasaki to the GS1000 Suzuki or CB900 Honda without finding great similarities in specifications and yet total differences in feel, character, and general performance.

Girder forks are fitted to the Levis front end, but the machine makes a total departure from its fellows in the adoption of a rear suspension system which is without peer anywhere in motorcycling.

It is the tried-and-true plunger suspension system which sees a rigid rear frame assembly with the rear wheel axle carried in the centre of a set of springs which allow shock and rebound movement of about 75mm. Springs carried in a housing above the axle absorb road shocks – well, *some* of them! – while shorter springs housed beneath the axle mount allow some form of shock absorption when the wheel falls into small potholes.

The system worked well enough but was not without its many faults, for the inevitable differences in spring tension and efficiency of the sliding members of the plungers themselves would sometimes allow the rear wheel to get itself mis-aligned with the front. Usually, the lack of any form of damper control meant that the rear wheel could patter all over the place like so many tiny feet, often leaving a series of short, black crescents on the roadway when cornering far too quickly. It could get very busy at high speed over choppy surfaces through corners, let me tell you!

But the Levis has a brilliant system of damping for its lookalike plunger rear – somewhat primitive, perhaps, but very clever indeed and apparently quite effective.

A piston is fitted above the upper springs atop each plunger, the area directly above being filled with a mixture of oil and grease. From each plunger an oil feed line is routed to move the incompressible material to the centre of

This is a small section of the plunger rear suspension tubing which contains the oil/grease mixture which, under pressure generated by the suspension's action, helps dampen the oscillation of springs. Here, it is entering the area in which the friction material is located.

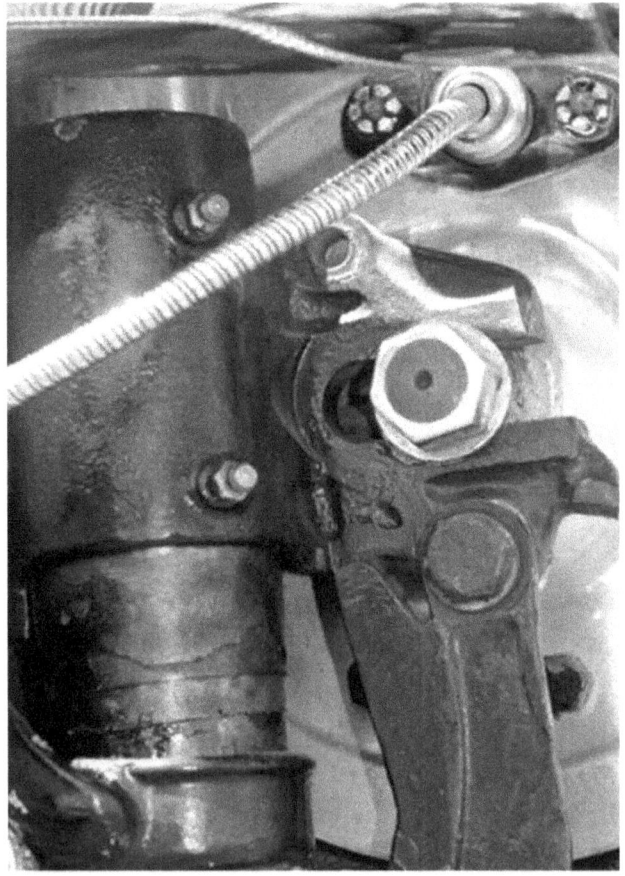

Because of the upswept exhaust pipes, it was very difficult to get a clear photo of the plunger rear suspensions, but here we can see part of the rear plunger. The damping system has its tubular piping attached to the front of the two plungers, where it could not be easily seen. The owner could not be persuaded to remove one of the exhausts to obtain a better shot.

each plunger just above the rear axle, with the two individual plungers inter-connected by a branching pipe which balances the fluid pressure between the two separate plungers.

In operation (let us hope this is easier to explain) the compression of the shock springs forces the pistons to apply pressure to the oil/grease mixture, which in turn – and immediately – applies this pressure to a flat-faced block in each plunger. The block, which is covered with a brake-lining type material, bears on an opposing member within the lower section of the plungers, applying a simple form of hydraulic control.

Though essentially simple, the 'damper' system is brilliant, allowing some control over the oscillation of the rear springs and – through the coupled pipes – assuring an even wheel movement with both plungers operating almost as one. The heavier the bump the firmer the pressure upon the spring housing and the more effective the damper medium, almost like the later, more sophisticated oil or gas dampers in combined shock/spring units.

On the road, this unique rear suspension is surprisingly comfortable and allied to the trad sprung single saddle gives an even, 'floating' ride which is very definitely better than a number of modern machines.

The old girder forks play their part in the handling/comfort game as well, and overall comfort would have to be considered outstanding, though the front end tends to chatter a bit, the single spring hard at work and the simple friction damping exerting some measure of spring control. We never ventured off the tar-sealed roads, but it would be a safe bet to say that handling would probably be skittish under these circumstances.

As I have mentioned on other occasions, a trait of the girder front forks is the tendency for a machine thus fitted to fall over alarmingly into corners. It is no bad thing when you get the feel back again, and it shows just how heavy the steering of modern motorcycles can often be, but the first time a tight, feet-up turn is attempted it is a surprise to find yourself doing a trim one eighty and heading off down the road

The Springer was as nice a pre-war 500 single as any of its better-known Brethren. The ride was greatly enhanced by the unique – if a little primitive – damping system employed on the machine's plunger rear suspension, which worked well, but was too difficult to photograph effectively.

again in about half the distance you think it's going to take!

This trait comes into its own when the whips are cracking, and it works fine with the relatively good ground clearances to allow very high cornering speeds without leaving your own side of the road! The first time I heaved the lightweight, spindly looking 500 into a left-hand corner it was a giant surprise to find myself almost running off the road on the *inside* of the corner!

Though people would argue otherwise, the old single's engine is very smooth indeed on the move, the top-gear punch something to experience and the easy, loping gait so very relaxing. This is not to say that the pre-war single is not a fair road performer, for it cracks along very briskly and exhibits a level of acceleration which would surprise many. Top gear acceleration is something to marvel at, with the gearbox used mostly for upward changes and then left pretty much alone.

In traffic the ultra-light steering could be a headache simply because it would take some getting used to, for the instant response of a turn of the bars or a minor amount of lean sees the bike dive well to one side or the other. What it means, simply, is that some of the more ham-fisted riders of modern machinery would have to go back to school to learn a smoothness and subtlety of movement they might have thought exclusive to Observed Trials riding.

What vibration there is seems to be most obvious at idle speeds, with front forks jumping about, some harmonics in the single fork spring and a tickle through the bars which causes your nose to itch.

Handling is generally good but takes a little getting used to and is at first a little tenuous. The front forks are mounted to the frame by four long bolts and side plates in much the same position as modern telescopics but are much more flexibly attached. The front-end thus feels a little more 'remote' (for want of a better word) and out of touch at first acquaintance, but soon proves to be more stable and effective than its 'nuts-and-bolts' installation initially suggested.

Couple this to the loose feel of a single saddle which is attached at the nose and spring-mounted to the frame and one has a totally different feel to the rigidly mounted dual-seat and firm telescopic forks of today's motorcycle. Its flexibility takes a little time to become accustomed to – again! – and is part of an earlier design which had been almost forgotten.

The feel of a sudden dip in the road, particularly on the apex of a tight, fast corner, is exciting to say the least. The forks take it with a grunt and a shudder, the rear suspension does likewise, the saddle takes the edge right off whatever is left and then gives a gentle nudge in the behind as it is returned to its normal position by its mounting springs. It all works well, and in harmony, but that last little nudge is an odd one and, as I said, takes time to get used to (again)!

With practice you can scurry over some quite rough roads at some good average speeds, letting the saddle take much of the brunt of the attack while relaxing and taking it all in; it's a little like riding a horse at high speed!

Brakes are up to the mark and stop the bike with ease because of its comparative light weight, but there is some choppiness of ride from the front end and the occasional protest from the tyre if the surface is rough. The rear end works equally well and is thankfully free of much of the rear-wheel hop often associated with plunger rear suspension.

Clutch action is commendably light and progressive, with the typical notchy gear change of the Burman box. At least it is reliable, though the gear changes must be made with care and some deliberation.

The old Levis owned by Alan Pride is in showroom condition and carries its name proudly on a logo – which used to be a transfer – framed on the chrome-panel tank by a fetching red flash to relieve the overall black stove-enamel job.

It gleams like a jewel, though its appearance is essentially Spartan, along with its appointments. The bike is probably a whole lot better than it was when it was new, and in fact its paint job surely is, because of modern enamels and baking techniques. The bike is one of the real rarities in this country, though the casual observer may dismiss it as just another British single. Essentially it is, but it remains a rare example of a little-known machine, with more than a few differences from its fellows to have it stand alone.

TECH SPECS

Make: Levis

Model: SF500

Year of manufacture: 1939

Type:
Air-cooled 500cc overhead valve single-cylinder four-stroke with totally enclosed valve gear controlled by pushrods. Cast iron head and special molybdenum cast iron barrel. Two-valve cylinder head, twin exhaust ports.

Bore x stroke: 80 x 99mm

Capacity: 498cc

Compression ratio:
6.8:1 (8.1:1 optional for racing)

Carburation:
Single, horizontal Amal 29 type carburettor, with separate float chamber and no air filter

Ignition: Miller mag-dyno

Lubrication:
From separate oil tank to adjustable, sight-feed Pilgrim oil pump, fitted outside the timing case. Pressure-fed main and big-end bearings, with upper cylinder and valve gear lubricated by oil mist. Total-loss lubrication system, with no scavenger return.

Transmission:
By enclosed ½ x ⁵⁄₁₆" chain in oil bath case to multi-plate dry clutch and separate four-speed gearbox. Right foot change, one up, three down.

Gear ratios (overall):
1st – 13.4:1; 2nd – 8.9:1; 3rd – 6.4:1; 4th – 4.6:1.

Frame & suspension:
Welded tubular steel frame, single downtube with bolt-on full cradle engine support and special heavy-duty steering head bearings. Front suspension by spring-loaded girder forks with adjustable friction damper plates. Rear suspension by plunger assembly containing shock and rebound springs controlled by grease/oil operated friction pads.

Wheels, tyres, brakes:
Steel wheel rims, 300 x 21 rib front tyre, 400 x 19 block rear. Brakes: 175mm diameter front and rear. Girling drum brakes with alloy back plates and direct control by wedge. Rear hub fitted with rubber cush-drive and quickly detachable wheel.

Dimensions:
Wheelbase, 1375mm; ground clearance, 125mm; weight. 175kg; Tank capacity 18 litres.

Performance:
(from original road test, November 1939): Top speed – 138km/h. Standing quarter – 14 sec. Braking from 50km/h – 11.8m. Fuel consumption – 17km/l.

Machine loaned by:
ALAN PRIDE. Sydney.

1975 Benelli 'Sei'

750cc OHC SIX-CYLINDER SPORTSTER

1975 BENELLI 'SEI'

It is impossible not to be mightily impressed by the Benelli Six even at first glance. Strangely, the overall size is much smaller than photographs would indicate, for the bike is not much bigger than the Honda 500 Four it so closely resembles.

Wheelbase is shortish by most standards and the weight is a surprisingly low 220kg. Allied to these dimensions are low saddle height of only 780mm and a set of well swept back handlebars in a sports bend.

If the Benelli is somewhat smaller than anticipated, the size of the engine is not. At first acquaintance it seems to be almost literally bursting out of a frame which is apparently too small to accept it, but this is obviously due to the transverse mounting of the beautiful six-cylinder power-plant.

There is no doubting the ancestry of the engine, for it is quite clearly pinched from the neat little Honda 500 Four – a fact to which its creator, Alejandro de Tomaso, quite happily admits.

Externally, the engine castings are virtually identical to the Japanese machine, while the Benelli 'Sei' features the same bore and stroke dimensions, and similar valve and bearing sizes. It has been said that engine parts are freely interchangeable between both marques, but this is impossible to ascertain at this point of time.

Be that as it may, the overall finish of engine and gearbox shriek of the excellent Japanese design – which is not altogether a bad thing, whether one gets away with it or not. Of course, the Japanese are not above pinching the odd design feature themselves, so they are perhaps not in the ideal position for the pointing of scornful Oriental fingers.

The test machine I rode employed a contrasting panel cleverly blacking out the front of the fuel tank, where the occasional stone may chip the surface. Removable side panels are finished in the same shade, their removal allowing most of the ancillary electrical components to be easily serviced.

Mudguards were unusual in styling, heavily chrome plated and valanced in an older 'knife-edge' styling not often seen on modern machines.

Impressive rear view (which most other road users would see, however briefly) shows the six impressive megaphone-shaped Benelli mufflers to advantage. The exhaust sound was well muted, but still very impressive indeed!

Exposed-tube front forks are adopted, and blend well with a large chrome headlamp to add to the machine's sporting image. What can one say about the sexy 'mega' mufflers which sprout – all six of them! – from the tail end of the bike, except to remark that they look like nothing you've ever seen before; and the sound is like something Beethoven or Mozart might have striven in vain to compose?

The exhaust note alone is enough to sell the bike if it was recorded and handed out to pretenders and intending purchasers alike, for the sound is sweet music to all. Well muted and in no way offensive to the unfortunate majority to whom two-wheeled motor vehicles are distasteful, the sound is V12 Jag, or perhaps full-bore Ferrari. There is no way it is the usual sound of the trad motorcycle!

With the hot engine tinkling at him as it cooled down at Melbourne's Sandown racing circuit and cries of 'Geez, it red—lines easy' and 'Hey, you can get over nine thousand out of it right through the gears' ringing in his horrified, Vintage ears, your tester approached the Six with more reverence than some of the more idiotic of the previous test riders clearly did, to find it had to be kick-started because the battery was flat. This proved to be no chore as the engine fired up halfway through the kick, idling reliably, if more than a little on the lumpy side which, I must say, was no surprise.

The Benelli's clutch lever was spongy in feel and did not surprise by exhibiting signs of both grab and slip – pointers to a dangerously overheated, badly abused component. I heard it said that 'shades of the old Honda clutch slip problem' was clear, but the jackass who uttered those asinine words was swiftly acquainted by me with the facts of his almost total lack of knowledge. Naturally, he did not agree, but he clearly knew not what he was talking about, so I just nodded politely and let it rest.

The bike was guarded menacingly by this writer and allowed to cool before any spirited riding was attempted, but two or three magic laps at far more reasonable speeds – the clock showed only 1,600km on its face, after all! – whetted the appetite for the week-long 1,000-kilometre road test which was to follow. The bike promised an easy, smooth performance beyond experience and belief with thoroughbred handling and powerful brakes to match, but how it had managed to survive the Baptism of Fire by two or three, over-enthusiastic, uncaring – and clearly moronic – riders who had thrashed the machine mercilessly for far too long, still escapes me.

It very nearly came to nothing, for one of the two Benelli 'Sei' on site was dropped very shortly thereafter by a member of the television crew which was there to film my on-course report of the new Suzuki RE5 rotary motorcycle, which was being recorded for the ABC TV *Torque* motoring programme, with myself as its first motorcycle compere. Why Peter Stevens, the machine's State distributors, allowed that person

The original road test of the Benelli Six was published in REVS Newspaper in 1975. In 2020, some 45 years later, I am re-acquainted with the Benelli Six at Surfside Motorcycle Garage, in Brookvale, a Sydney suburb. It was a heart-warming day, but the owner could not be contacted to possibly(?) allow a brief, if near tearful, ride.

to ride the bike at all was a mystery, but it might well have been the fact that it was a member of a television crew who had asked could he ride it.

The bike was being ridden very briskly along the top section of the Sandown circuit at the time, when the rider pitched the bike down the track, badly graunching the bike's left side ... and his left side as well. The damage to the bike was superficial, being confined to the usual bent handlebars, broken mirror, and blinker, scratched paintwork and a badly kinked gear lever. The bike was unrideable, but the prang bore mute testimony to its inherent strength. Though basically light, the Benelli was clearly strong in all the right places, which matters greatly.

The one-piece alloy cylinder head contains what is probably the longest camshaft ever fitted to a road-going motorcycle, the shaft supported upon two bearing 'pads' on its ends, and two closely spaced inner bearings which support the shaft at its centre. The single overhead camshaft is driven by chain from the centre of the crankshaft, and is automatically controlled by a spring-loaded tensioner, the cylinder head's centre bearings providing the support essential to counter any possibility of the long camshaft unduly flexing.

Three inlet manifolds are fitted with three 24mm Del'Orto carburettors of just 24mm diameter —each of the six pots is, after all, only 125cc capacity – the outer pair sporting odd, longer lengths which are well angled to keep the carbs as far inboard as possible. I felt this could have easily resulted in the rare 'induction bias', but this seemed not to be the case. There are 29mm carbs listed, but (according to the brochure handed to me at the time) the machine I was riding employed the smaller-diameter units. Three-ring pistons of a high 9.8:1 compression ratio are fitted to short, chunky connecting-rods, which in turn are clamped to the rigid, one-piece crankshaft, with slipper bearings of lead/indium/bronze material interpolated. Similar bearing material is adopted for the *seven* main bearings which support the crankshaft.

Primary drive is taken from the centre of the crank via a Hy-Vo 'toothed' chain through gears on the crankshaft and clutch drum. Both drive and driven gears employ rubber inserts to provide a degree of primary transmission shock absorption. The clutch is of the immersed wet, multi-plate type and rejoices in having eight friction plates: just as well, in view of the severe caning the clutch had endured.

Cleverly, the crankcases are only 40mm wider than the smaller 500 Honda Four – though they do look much wider – a situation achieved by the neat ploy of driving the alternator by a special jackshaft directly behind the crankshaft. The shaft is driven by the centre crankshaft gear which seems to be a multi-purpose gear, for it drives almost everything else inside the engine!

The oil pump is similarly gear driven and is of the Eaton type – like the pump fitted to several top European machines, including BMW. Its pumping capacity of 1478 litres per hour at 6000rpm would appear to be ample for a machine with one oil supply to cope with the demands of engine and gearbox combined.

The gearbox is a normal five-speed component but looks tiny tucked neatly behind the wide crankcases. Though split horizontally with the crankcase for major servicing, a large end cover on the box's right side directly beneath the high-mounted alternator allows access for a wide variety of servicing or essential repair. The crankcase sump filler plug is fitted at this spot and its removal allows the kick-starter spring to be clearly seen, a pointer to this component's easy replacement in the unlikely event of failure.

Final drive emerges from the machine's left side and is via a 17-tooth sprocket to a 42-tooth sprocket driving the clutch through yet another neoprene cush-drive hub; a reduction of 2.47.

The engine assembly is mounted very low in the frame, with the crankshaft centreline virtually at wheel-spindle height; an ideal set-up if the interests of an acceptably low centre of gravity are to be considered.

In the case of Benelli, this low mounting also allows the essential routine maintenance tasks to be more easily carried out, for tappet settings and spark plug replacement can be achieved without the fuel tank or other components or ancillary equipment being removed.

Of course, the work is made easier if one insists on removing the fuel tank, a task accomplished in a timed 45 seconds by merely lifting the seat and releasing a rubber mounting strap, slipping off two fuel lines and sliding the container backwards off its forward buffer rubbers. With the tank removed, the entire engine assembly can apparently be stripped without removing it from the frame.

Similarly, the points, which mount on the end of the crankshaft under the screwed-on outer cover, can be rapidly serviced and re-timed, if necessary, in a few minutes. Obviously, this scary looking engine can be simply and rapidly serviced by any reasonably competent enthusiast; a large plus-point in any motorcycle design.

If the power-plant is distinctly Oriental in appearance and ancestry, the rest of the machine is very definitely Italian – from its thick cast iron, twin front disc brakes, its lipped Borrani alloy wheel rims and its sports handlebars, to its angular Latin styling.

No engineer's drawing board run-of-the-mill Superbike, this model features the bold styling of Ghia, one of Italy's best known automobile artists. Side on, the unusual treatment blends engine, frame and suspension into an attractive package topped well by the 22-litre petrol tank and thin 'banana' seat. Completing the urgent lines of the Benelli Sei is a six-trumpet exhaust system which promises to be the most pretentious this side of a Formula 1 racing car!

Marzocchi front fork and rear spring/damper units are standard fittings, the forks blending particularly well with the 'sports/tourer' image. These features are enhanced by the all-new Italian switchgear, which fits almost unobtrusively within easy reach of a rider's thumbs.

The only real criticism one can aim at their design is the odd practice of enclosing the wires within the handlebars themselves. True, they are very neat as they are hidden from the baleful glance of the passing peasantry, but the priceless asset of easy accessibility is lost to the whim of fashion's decree, for it means that a handlebar change necessitated by desire or accidental damage is made a major chore instead of a 10-minute exercise. A definite black mark.

But there is no denying the attractive appearance and the efficiency of the new switches; the left side controlling the blinkers, horn/overtake flasher (a double-sided rocker switch) and main light, parking, and dipper switches. The right-hand switch controls the electric starter and includes the now universal 'kill' button.

The excellence of design does not end there, for atop the handlebar clamp sits one of the neatest instrument panels it has been our pleasure to gaze at. The entire assembly of seven warning lights and twin speedo/rev counter instruments is contained within a neat crack-black oblong box canted back at just the right angle to make the whole system easily readable at a swift glance.

The speedo face sits to the left with a green blinker warning light above it, with its matching rev counter on the opposite side below a similar blinker warning. Between the two faces a row of multi-coloured idiot lights indicate high beam, oil pressure, lights on, generator/ignition and neutral gear selection.

Only the generator warning light (which seemed to spend a lot of its time glowing at anything below a fast idle) was clearly visible during daylight hours. The neutral light – which only the naff should trust, or even refer to – was less than useless, and the blinker warnings were similarly invisible: I imagine the dead battery was the culprit? The blinker warning lights were positioned directly above the blinkers themselves, which could be clearly seen, thereby rendering the green warning lights somewhat superfluous.

So much, again, for the dictates of fashion. At night, the lights on the panel glowed a little more reassuringly, but again were not necessary; one has only to glance at the road ahead to see that the headlights are on in the dark, and high and low beam seemed to make little difference to the amount of road one could see, making the high beam warning almost 'surplus to requirements'.

The oil pressure light could, of course, be handy but it happily went out the moment the engine fired up and never so much as glowed fitfully whenever the engine was running.

The bike was picked up on a windswept and watery Melbourne evening and ridden home through heavy late-night shopping traffic, an ideal – if unintentional – time to check its behaviour in less-than-ideal conditions.

It was noted that the front disc brakes worked very efficiently indeed despite the streaming roads, due entirely to the material from which the discs are manufactured.

Cast iron enjoys a far greater co-efficient of friction than stainless steel, and the friction material in the pads can thus be made to work more effectively. The only disadvantage of cast iron is the fact that light surface rust appears often in wet or humid weather, though it does scrub off with the first application of the brakes.

Of course, the Italian factory could follow the lead of Japanese contemporaries and overcome the rust problem by fitting stainless steel discs, but the material is nowhere near as efficient in the dry weather and lethal in the wet, when it hardly works at all!

Wet weather riding was made more enjoyable by the adoption of the new Pirelli Super Sport tyres featuring the Dunlop K81-type tread pattern and sports profile – perhaps not surprisingly, for Dunlop now controls the Italian tyre manufacturer. A healthy 3.50 x 18 ribbed pattern graces the front alloy rim while the rear is a huge 4.25 x 18!

The machine was to endure several days of miserable weather before the first stint on dry roads, and it never disgraced itself by so much as a wag of the tail – even though the occasional close shave was experienced: as usual!

On dry roads, the big six was at last able to show its true form and demonstrated its potential in no uncertain terms. With a speedo reading 1,700 kilometres it was at last decided to give the machine its head on several suitable stretches of road, with very gratifying results indeed.

It hummed smoothly for hundreds of kilometres with the needle well into the three-figure mark, returning an average (on almost

This grainy shot of the bike, taken when ridden at high speed through this glorious, opening right hander, shows just how stable this machine was, for its rider appears to be entirely happy with its performance, and seems to be entirely at ease. As it happens, he was, and on the lookout for much more of the same!

traffic-free roads) of just under 130km/h on one run of almost two hours duration with the excellent fuel consumption figure of 7.5 litres per 100 kilometres.

At very high cruising speeds there is a slight tendency for the machine to wag its tail, particularly when cornering hard over rippled surfaces, but at no time was there cause for alarm for the bike would not be tossed offline under any circumstances.

The almost total lack of flywheel effect experienced with this six-cylinder engine could be upsetting at times as engine braking was of a very high order.

In many instances, a quick downward gearchange when the throttle was rolled back slowed the machine very dramatically – almost as effectively as if the rear brake were applied – and this proved a boon on occasions. But it had an unsettling effect on handling if the throttle had to be snapped right off at lurid cornering angles, for the sudden braking effect caused some twitchiness. When it was being driven hard and deep into corners under full stick, the Benelli cornered on rails and could rarely be made to ground.

On right hand corners, the leading edge of the outer exhaust pipe and the footrests touched as one, and on left handers the limiting factor was the small prop-stand bracket. It should be stressed that the machine would touch down only on extreme angles of lean, and even then, was in no way thrown off-line. In most instances – even at high touring speeds – this was never noticed. (The feel of the engine at speed must be experienced to be believed; it buzzes away beneath you like Aunty Maude's new sewing machine, enjoying almost instantaneous throttle response from as low as 3500rpm through to your tester's mental maximum (during the bike's running-in period, *if it still applied!*) of 6500rpm. The bike accelerates like a true projectile, covering a measured 400 metres in a very useful 12.8 seconds, down a little on the quickest of its Oriental opposition to be sure, but giving nothing away in terms of high point-to-point average speeds: where, it could be argued, it matters most.

The unlearned who consider sheer speed the sole criterion of a machine's worth, will doubtless be more than a little put-out by the model's refusal to beat the top straight-line chargers in sheer acceleration, or speed, but the more experienced rider will enjoy its great, exuberant cornering style, which is where it really comes into its own.

The bike feels strangely like the popular Yamaha RD350, except that it handles very much better. There is no way it feels like a big, six-cylinder 750 when on the move!

Oddly, the bike did not seem happy carrying a pillion passenger. It was hard to define, but handling seemed to suffer somewhere, although performance was hardly impaired. Perhaps the impressive handling lost its edge a little, or perhaps the shortish seat tended to see the rider slightly too far forward for maximum comfort, but the fact remains that the bike in some strange way lost some of its charm when called upon to carry somebody else behind its starry-eyed pilot. Very strange!

Cold starts first thing in the morning tended to be dramatic to say the least. The engine refused to fire at all unless full choke was employed, whereupon the engine would run straight up to 3000rpm, on the high side for most people's taste, including mine.

The exhaust could hardly be called offensive, for it was well muted, but it was remarked upon by the occasional interested bystander. To add further to the drama, the clutch could not be fully released first thing in the morning with the result that the machine would leap up the drive when selecting first gear.

Even the old British-bike ploy of pulling the clutch lever in and working the kick starter several times before starting the engine would not release the stuck, cold clutch. In fact, on one occasion, the engine fired up on the kick starter with the clutch lever pulled right up to the handlebars! In fairness, it should be remembered the clutch received a merciless thrashing at a very early stage, and it would not surprise to find the plates warped through overheating.

When warm, the engine idled smoothly but a slight maladjustment in carburation saw engine revs fluctuate between 1200 and 2000rpm as though an unseen hand were operating the throttle.

The engine was quiet, except for some noise from the cam chain and valve gear, and a loud chunking sound from the alternator. The latter was traced to backlash in the jackshaft driving this component, which probably occurred when the machine was so badly abused.

Gear selection was always crisp and easy, with no bumps or grinding noises from the transmission when changing up or down. The lever itself moved through a very short travel, with the result that gear changes could be made as quickly as hand and foot could move.

But the movement was a little more 'notchy' than it should have been, resulting in the occasional missed gear on downward changes. If the machine were brought to a stop before neutral was selected – yes, one should never do this! – it could be difficult to change up from first or back from second gear.

Suspension was very comfortable, if firm, and allowed long high-speed trips with no discomfort. The seat, also firm, was comfortable, the bike – again – turbine smooth.

At $3,300 *(that is new, in **1975**, be it remembered!)* the Benelli will probably appeal only to the enthusiast able to afford the initial purchase price and the cost of keeping such a machine in good running order – though it probably will not cost as much to maintain as some of its Oriental opposition – but it should enjoy reasonable sales amongst Superbike enthusiasts.

Perhaps it could lose a little in terms of initial acceleration, but it does come on very strongly when called upon to do so. It can be viciously fast and will bow to very few machines when braking late, the corners are there, and the whips are really cracking. The brakes are superb, in that distinctly undramatic manner; they too, are at their best only when they need to be. In fact, it could be very easy to underestimate this Latin flying

The Benelli Six looks just as impressive head-on as it does going away. The engine hangs out of the frame a little too far for its own good, but the machine proved its strength when it was dropped at speed on the Sandown circuit and escaped with only minor damage. The rider who dropped the bike, it must be said, suffered a little more damage.

machine – it has been done before, with lesser machines than this one: it is a true Jekyll-and-Hyde performer, no doubt about it.

It will hum along discreetly in top gear at an easy 3000rpm, for all the world like the mount the village vicar may use to tour a far-flung parish. But slip into your leathers and take the bike out to your local racing circuit and screw it hard through its five gears and you will have to hang on with everything you possess, for the discreet hum soon becomes a snarl, then a shriek and then you are suddenly very hard to catch.

It is not, of course, all things to all men, and there are those who would throw up their hands in horror at the complexity of the machine's design, but it is certain to find its small niche in the ranks of the Superbikes – if only because it dares to be so very different.

Almost inevitably, the engine was increased in 1979 to 900cc by altering the bore x stroke, the great sight of six mufflers on the 750 changed to three exhausts either side blending into two long mega mufflers. It was not nearly as dramatic a sight as the six trumpets on the 750, and the bike only delivered about five extra ponies, the smaller exhausts possibly to blame. Some 3,500 of the 750 were sold, while just over 1,900 of the larger model were made from 1979–1987.

TECH SPECS

Make: Benelli 'Sei'

Type:
All-alloy, six-cylinder air-cooled overhead camshaft design, with alloy heads and barrels. Overhead camshaft driven by single row chain from centre of crankshaft. Steel conrods connected to crankshaft by lead/indium/bronze slipper bearings, with seven-bearing crankshaft supported upon lead/indium/bronze slipper bearings.

Bore x stroke: 56 x 50.6mm x 6

Capacity: 747cc

Compression ratio: 9.8 to 1

Power @ rpm:
55Kw (76BHP) @ 9000rpm

Carburettors:
3 Dell'Orto 24mm (NB: some listed as 29mm)

Ignition:
Three contact points, three double coils.

Primary drive:
Through gears, via wide, Morse 'Hy-Vo' toothed chain

Clutch: Wet, multi-plate

Gearbox:
Five-speed, foot change on left side, constant mesh

Gearbox ratios:
1st – 12.43:1; 2nd – 8.98:1; 3rd – 6.99:1; 4th – 5.74:1; 5th – 4.92:1.

Final drive:
Heavy-duty chain; final ratio, 2.47:1 (17/42th sprockets).

Frame:
Duplex, full cradle, stiffened at swing-arm pivot point and steering head.

Suspension:
Front, Marzocchi telescopic forks, with two-way damping. Rear, swing arm and Marzocchi spring/damper units, with five pre-load settings.

Brakes:
Front, twin discs, hydraulically operated, 280mm diameter. Rear: single-leading-shoe drum brake; 200mm dia. Borrani lipped, light-alloy rims.

Dimensions:
Length – 2100mm; Width – 760mm; Height – 1070mm; Seat height: 780mm

Tyres: Front:
3.50 x18 Pirelli Super Sport ribbed; Rear, 4.85 x 18 Pirelli Super Sport block.

Performance:
Maximum speed: 205km/h, Standing 400 metres: 12.8 sec.

Fuel consumption:
7.5 litres per 100 kilometres. Fuel Tank: 22 litres (295km range)

Machine loaned by:
PETER STEVENS MOTORCYCLES, Melbourne, Victoria.

1946 Triumph Tiger 100

500cc OHV VERTICAL TWIN

Edward Turner's 1937 500cc overhead valve Triumph Speed Twin certainly made history as the forerunner of a great many similar vertical-twin four-stroke engine designs which were to follow for many years thereafter. Other British factories, BSA, Norton, AJS/Matchless, Sunbeam and Ariel, and several German factories followed, as did the Americans with their 'lightweight' Indian motorcycles in the 1940s, and later still by all the Japanese manufacturers. The latter usually employed the much more efficient overhead camshaft – and sometimes *double* overhead camshaft – design. The new Amaranth-Red 5T Triumph design was hailed far and wide as something removed from the norm, which it was, while many believed it to be the first-ever vertical (or parallel) twin from Triumph – which it was not.

The first-ever vertical twin engine which was *expected* to be used in a Triumph motorcycle was a 440cc side-valve engine originally designed in France in 1910, four years before the First World War. In 1913, an enlarged, *603cc* side-valve parallel twin replica of the French/Belgian engine was redesigned by Maurice Johann Schulte, one of Triumph's original German founders, with the intention of slotting the power-plant into a Triumph frame and running gear, and then introducing it into the Triumph catalogue.

War World 1 intervened, and the engine was quickly abandoned, the Triumph factory instead manufacturing many of the more prosaic, if quite reliable, Schulte-designed, B-model single-cylinder side-valve motorcycles which were supplied in their thousands to Despatch Riders from England and Allied countries. It has been claimed that almost 30,000 of these belt-drive Triumph motorcycles were supplied to the Allied forces during the run of the 1914–18 war. The almost unknown, original French twin-cylinder engine, along with the Schulte derivative, quietly disappeared – at least from the Triumph list – but is supposed to have resurfaced briefly after the war. There seems to be no evidence anywhere of its re-appearance, however, and there seems to be no evidence that one of the French-made vertical twins was fitted to any of the aviator Louis Bleriot's motorcycles, which were manufactured from 1920–25.

But again, Turner's 'all-new' Triumph engine was by no means the first Triumph vertical twin to feature in the factory's catalogue, because their first *production* parallel twin was the little-known '650cc' (645cc) overhead valve 6/1 model, which was designed by the brilliant Val Page in 1932, the machine built in 1933, four years prior to Turner's Speed Twin. The 6/1 engine was a semi-wet sump design, the oil located within a separate container inside the large crankcase, the engine featured un-enclosed valve springs and rocker arms, with the primary drive by double-helical gear – which meant the engine ran backwards in relation to the road wheels.

The semi-unit construction engine employed a four-speed hand-change gearbox which was bolted directly to the rear of the crankcase instead of being mounted separately, the motor was slightly offset to the right in its frame, while the unusually wide crankcases and low-slung mounting allowed little cornering clearance. This was not considered to be of much importance because the new twin was intended to be a dedicated sidecar machine, and was usually offered, and ordered, in that form. It has been said that only around 200 of these machines were ever built, for they were never popular, but the true figure was probably somewhat higher than that.

Not long after it was introduced, a new 6/1 *outfit* made an impressive attempt on Britain's coveted Maude's Trophy by circulating the steeply banked Brooklands track in England for just on 500 miles at an average speed of 60 mph, and then competed in the tough International Six Days' Trial (ISDT), where it won a top award. In view of this great performance, and the machine's demonstrated endurance, the *sidecar* duo was happily awarded the Trophy.

When Page left Triumph early in 1936 to work for BSA, Turner, who was always noted for his briskness and terse behaviour, summarily removed the new twin from the 1936 catalogue (some said in a fit of pique at Page, his former boss for some years at Ariel and, later, at Triumph) to concentrate his attention on the single-cylinder Page-designed range of 250, 350 and 500cc overhead valve single-cylinder machines, while he also had in mind his very own twin-cylinder design. He cleverly smartened up the dowdy-looking, mostly dark-coloured single-cylinder machines with all-new upswept exhaust pipes, enclosed valve gear, revised gearbox design and bright silver-and-chrome livery to re-introduce them as the smart-looking, *apparently* sportier Tiger 70, 80 and Tiger 90, the new nomenclature hinting at their respective top speeds. They then became very popular machines – in particular, for some strange reason, the 350cc Tiger 80.

Turner was mostly a self-taught designer, perhaps more of a very clever 'ideas man' than the brilliant designer which some claim he was, often relying on his experienced band of highly qualified engineers to help develop his original designs. This included Val Page himself, it must be noted, who, among many other things, helped bring to fruition Turner's best-known motorcycle, the 500cc OHC Square Four Ariel of 1930. The first Speed Twin in 1937 needed an enormous amount of input from the brilliant engineers Bert Hopwood, and later Doug Hele, before it could give of its best, for its initial design left much to be desired, although its basics remained mostly unaltered.

For a start, its cast-iron cylinder barrel was attached to the crankcase at its flange by just six studs, which resulted in massive oil leaks from that area, followed by the occasional crack appearing in the base flange with some of the studs popping out of the 'cases. This was hastily corrected in later models during early 1938, the barrel now well secured by the *eight* 3/8" base studs, with their locking nuts, it always needed. One cannot help but wonder what Val Page – who was probably the finest motorcycle designer the Brits ever had – thought of all this, for his earlier 6/1 Triumph employed the same eight-stud layout which Turner was forced to use on the later Speed Twins. **Ouch!**

For some unknown reason, the 500cc twin's four OHV rocker box caps, which could be easily removed to inspect and adjust the tappets, would very often just as easily vibrate loose and simply fall out. Another problem, which continued into the later models in the 1950s and even beyond, was the apparent lack of a good supply of oil to the curved crown of the cam-followers which bore directly upon the two camshafts, the latter sited just beneath the base of the front and rear of the cylinder barrel. This resulted in premature wear on the tip of the followers' crown, for the oil supply to this very highly stressed area – though *seemingly* quite voluminous – was clearly not effective enough. The first Speed Twin employed a small oil return feed from the rocker box to the centre of the two external pushrod tubes in an apparent attempt to supply more oil to the base of the followers, but it still did not work quite as well as it should have.

The much-modified 1938 Speed Twin Triumph was a huge sales success, however, and this led to Turner introducing a sports derivative for 1939, the striking silver-and-chrome Tiger 100 machine, which was to remain in the catalogue, with little more than the changes dictated by more modern styling, and other simple cosmetic changes or minor engine details, until the all-new unit-construction machines were designed in 1963. The 1939 sports 500cc twin employed a one-inch single Amal carburettor in place of the Speed Twin's 7/8" component, with the compression ratio raised from 7.2:1 to 8:1, thus imbuing the new Tiger 100 model with a genuine 100mph performance. The bike also employed a pair of neat, tapered megaphone mufflers, the tail-ends of the mufflers quickly detachable, which then supplied a young Clubman racer with a competitive road race motorcycle at reasonable cost.

Girder forks were employed up front, the rear end remaining unsprung as usual, the ubiquitous sprung saddle helping to iron out the rough bits. The two separate camshafts were both gear-driven, while the almost universal Lucas Magneto-Dynamo (Mag-dyno) unit sat beneath the single carburettor, the entire gear train contained within the trim, highly polished alloy case on the machine's right side which was always such a feature of the engine design.

The Turner parallel-twin design closely resembled many of the 500cc twin-port/dual exhaust pipe *single*-cylinder machines which abounded at the time, the fat, symmetrical exhaust pipes and large mufflers framing its substantial-looking cylinder block and large alloy engine castings. The later Tiger 100 was, in fact, the first *roadster* whose engine achieved 1BHP per cubic inch, its 500cc (30 cubic inch) engine pushing out a handy 30BHP, its T100 designation again hinting at the bike's stated maximum speed.

Unhappily, the bike's introduction saw the demise of the *Tiger 90*, Triumph's potent 500cc single, which was then, and even now, to those of us who have ridden one, very sadly missed. To add insult to injury, the Tiger 100 motor was slightly narrower than the Tiger 90 single, weighed a couple of pounds less and was designed to fit into the Tiger 90 frame with virtually no alteration, and it sat there smirking at the world as though it had every right to be there, in fact as if it had grown there in the first place. It was crying shame, but if that was progress (?) then so be it.

No sooner had the new twin arrived and made a place for itself on street and starting line alike, than war broke out and little more was heard of it until hostilities ended some six years later. But the basic engine was by no means forgotten, for the Triumph motorcycle engine formed the basis for a more highly tuned, all-alloy version which was designed and built in 1942 and found its way into British bombers as a stationary power-plant for the generation of electricity to power the radio, instrument lights and other ancillaries. It probably provided a small blast of hot air from its heavily cowled, fan-cooled, all-alloy engine as a form of crude air-conditioning as well, while it was certainly called upon to perform other duties while on bombing runs.

Not long after the war ended in August 1945, the Triumph factory was almost ready, certainly willing, and of course able, to return to the production of its series of twin-cylinder motorcycles, but there were no single-cylinder machines in the new catalogues, even though their nippy little 350 single, which was built during the war, could so easily have been fettled to appear in civilian guise. In September 1946, a highly tuned 500cc Triumph Tiger 100 fitted with the all-alloy head and barrel from the Air Ministry stationary (Bomber) engine was ridden by Ernie Lyons to a win in the 500cc Clubman's race on the rain-sodden Isle of Man. This was a marvellous achievement, since the original Triumph factory in Coventry had been flattened by a German bombing run in 1940 – two years before Turner designed the Air Ministry stationary engine – the factory quickly relocating to Warwickshire to continue to make 350cc single cylinder machines for Army despatch riders, before it was finally shifted to Meriden, where it remained for many years.

A factory replica of the Lyons all-alloy Tiger 100 then became the Limited-Edition GP Triumph, a Clubman racer machine which was a

This is the 45BHP G.P. Triumph of 1946–52, the only true racer the company ever made and specially tuned by the factory. The all-alloy engine was originally used in Allied bombers in WWII to drive a generator for lights and instruments, but the machine proved to be competitive for Clubman racing, if not fast enough for the Grand Prix events.

handy iron to race in those types of events but was never going to be fast enough to compete in serious GP events. The GP Triumph was built in small numbers, because Turner had shown no interest whatsoever in racing any of his machines: even so, Triumph twins were to become very successful for many years thereafter in all spheres of motorcycle sport, particularly in Australia, and later in America.

Triumph's recovery after the war was swift and dramatic, with the first roadster Tiger 100 machine arriving in Australia, in small numbers it must be said, in early 1946. I recently found one of these rare, **1946 500cc Tiger 100** machines alive and well (in fact probably better than new!) in Melbourne, where we fell upon it with shouts of almost unrestrained glee.

Just after the war, Australia was the biggest importer of British motorcycles in the world, with virtually all the machines which arrived here being marked 'For Export Only', as they were not readily available in the country which actually built them. It is not hard to see why this had to happen, because steel, aluminium and other materials were hard to come by for any industry, so the supply of new motorcycles which left the various factories was more a trickle than a flood, the new machines still tracing their origins back to the 1920s or 30s. Besides which, the British nation was still in all sorts of strife economically, which is why the 'Export Market' – and, of course, not only for motorcycles – was so critically important to the British economy.

The sleeping giant America was not yet fully aware of the fact that the Brits had made some of the finest motorcycles in the world during the years between the two World Wars, and that they had staged such a remarkable recovery after the devastating bombing raids they were forced to endure during the Second World War. It was not until the early months of 1948 that motorcycles from England began to arrive in large numbers in the States, and by 1950 the American market for motorcycles made in Great Britain, and later from European manufacturers, had become the largest in the world. But this was certainly not the case just after the war finished.

Even after dusk the Tiger glowed like a jewel, helped of course by the flash. But it's a safe bet that the machine could be found easily on a moonless night in mid-winter in the centre of a five-acre paddock, for it shone beautifully like nothing I have ever seen before, nor since.

As we expected, and have noted with many Classic motorcycles before, the 1946 Tiger 100 we rode has enjoyed a new lease on life at the restorer's hand (in this case the machine's owner Leigh McCracken) and looks in better than showroom condition. This is due to more modern techniques in paint and chrome finishes and to better polishing agents for alloy castings, for the bike gleams in the sunlight so much that it might well inflict some injury to a casual observer's eyes if the sunglasses had been left at home. It looks at least as good at dusk with a magnificent sunset, too, as we can clearly see.

I had enjoyed a close working relationship with those British twins around that time, because I started work at the Triumph importers in Sydney in 1948, just two years after that first 1946 Triumph appeared in the firm's showroom; I was fresh from school and as eager as a young puppy dog. Too young to hold a motorcycle licence of course, but not too young to occasionally sit upon those gleaming machines in the showroom to pretend I was out on one of the King's Highways somewhere.

While most of its fellows were suffering black – or similar – paint jobs, the Tiger glorified in Turner's brilliant silver paint job on the fuel tank and large mudguards, with neat, pale blue pin-striping and chromed tank panels, well offset by highly polished engine, gearbox, and primary chaincase alloy castings, augmented by a glossy, jet-black frame and separate oil tank. It looked a gem on the showroom floor, and almost as soon as the machines were more readily available in Australia, the gleaming Tiger became a favourite pursuit motorcycle used by the NSW Police forces.

The 1946 model differs from the pre-war machine only in minor detail, its rather slim telescopic front forks replacing the earlier girders, the later model employing separate magneto and 6-volt generator, instead of the twin mag-dyno employed on the earlier machine. The steering head angle was yet to be altered to accept the different trail angle of the telescopic forks, but all the other frame components, running gear, engine and gearbox were virtually identical to the 1939 model – including the rigid frame, for there was no rear suspension on the immediate post-war machines.

The oil tank on the 1946 model still had the small flat pressed into the front of it to allow clearance for the mag-dyno unit, which was no longer there, an anachronism which was corrected before the 1948 models I saw had arrived. The timing case has been subtly altered as well, being slightly extended at the front to accept the fitting of the separate 6-volt Lucas generator, driven by gear from the exhaust camshaft, the sports BTH magneto (BTH did not make a mag-dyno unit) sited on its own at the rear of the case, just underneath the carburettor where the original dual instrument was located.

Unusual for a sports motorcycle, at least by today's standards, the Triumph engine's bore x stroke measurements remained somewhat 'under-square' at 63mm x 80mm, with the slightly higher compression ratio than the 'cooking' Speed Twin, while its 6-Type, single Amal carburettor was also slightly larger than its Amaranth Red stablemate. Again, this was not terribly exciting by today's standards, but was clearly ahead of its rival machines way back in 1946.

As usual with British vertical twins, the pistons rise and fall together, for the crank is spaced at 360 degrees, while the two aluminium-alloy conrods feature detachable steel endcaps lined with a light flash of white metal. The rods bolt directly to the crankpins, as no big-end bearing slippers are used. The crank remains a bolt-up design, the two separate, forged steel crank cheeks bolting to a large, centrally placed flywheel – a design feature employed by Triumph in the design of their vertical twins since Day One. The crankshaft material is composed of manganese/molybdenum alloy steel, the steel big-end caps drop-forged and made from nickel-chrome steel of some 100 tons tensile strength.

Triumph's chunky aluminium connecting rods are forged from RR56 alloy, itself immensely strong with a tensile strength of 32 tons per square inch. Thinner steel conrods could easily have been used, of course, as used in the smaller, 350cc 3T model, without being any heavier, but the extra thickness of the alloy rods allows for immense strength, with its attendant reliability when – no, not *if*, but *when!* – a motorcycle engine is pushed to its limits.

The Triumph crankcases are barrel-shaped, for all the world like a beer keg turned on its side, split vertically and very strong, the left side of the engine dominated by the large, domed and highly polished primary chain-case which contains the single-row 1/2" x 5/16" primary chain driving the multi-plate dry clutch. The chain-case contains just enough oil to cover the bottom run of chain. Blessed with the best clutch assembly of all the British motorcycles, Triumph also enjoyed one of the best gearboxes, the four-speed 'box separate from the engine, with the chain tension adjusted by slackening off its mounting bolts and sliding the gearbox backwards within its mounting plates. The gear lever is on the right side, which was usual practice with British and Italian motorcycles at the time, with the gear change pattern down-for-down, and up-for-upward gear changes.

A highly polished, heart-shaped timing case on the engine's right side contains no less than six timing gears. The small half-time pinion on the end of the crankshaft drives a large idler gear, which in turn drives the camshafts through a pair of similarly large gears, the two camshafts, as we have remarked, located at opposite ends of the base of the one-piece, cast-iron cylinder barrel. The camshaft gears, in their turn, drive the magneto at the extreme rear of the timing case, and the separate generator at the front of the case.

The inlet camshaft also drives a twin-plunger oil pump which is bolted to the inner face of the timing case; the drive through an alloy block retained by the two plungers and driven by an offset pin on the end of the nut which locates the camshaft drive gear. Oil is fed to the crankshaft and big-end bearings through a small bush in the outer timing case, at the end of the engine mainshaft, the oil at some 60 psi and a very high volume. A simple relief valve allows some of the lubricant to be routed to the timing case and thence into the crankcase to be returned to the oil tank. On its journey, the oil lubricates the two large mainshaft bearings upon which the crankshaft rests.

Some of the scavenged oil returning to the crankcase is rerouted by a small by-pass pipe to lubricate the overhead valve rockers in their Y-alloy rocker boxes, the residue then draining down through the pushrod tunnels and thence to the crankcase again. For some odd reason, the 1946 Tiger has no rocker-return oil leads routed to the pushrod tubes; they were to return in later models with no reason given (that I can remember) for their disappearance on the immediate post-war machines. The oil dribbling down the inside of the pushrod tubes provides lubrication for the camshafts, pushrod ends, and the cam-followers contained within their special cast-iron blocks which are pressed into the base of the cylinder barrel and locked in their various positions by a pair of small set-screws.

But the cam-followers continued to wear on the rubbing face which bore on the two camshafts, even though the area appeared to be well lubricated. The State importers for whom I worked at the time kept all the worn-out items thrown at them over the spare parts counter by irate owners and had their bearing faces specially tipped with Stellite, an extremely hard alloy steel, thereby enjoying a neat little earner while supplying a crying need at the same time. In later models the problem was overcome to some degree by Stellite-tipping the followers at the factory, though the highly stressed components can still tend to wear prematurely.

A small instrument panel is set into the top of the gleaming fuel tank – another pre-war feature which was carried over from 1946 to 1948 – the rudimentary instruments consisting of an ammeter, light switch, oil pressure gauge and a handy little 'trouble light' for use if working on the machine at the side of the road after dark! The speedo sits alone, above the small-diameter headlamp and slightly ahead of the friction steering damper. Naturally, there are no

The instrument panel, like the original 1938 machine, sat in a panel recessed on top of the fuel tank. The panel contained a headlight switch, ammeter, oil pressure gauge and a 'trouble light'. The latter, sited just above the instruments, could be taken out and, at the end of a long cable, be used for emergency repairs on the side of the road at night(?).

warning lights in the instrument panel, with no electric starter and no blinkers either. There was no provision for a stop-light warning in those days, and rear vision mirrors were not required by law either, but after-market switches, mirrors, and special tail-light with two filaments were of course readily available and were quite often adopted by careful owners. The McCracken Tiger has both these accessories fitted.

There is no ignition key; you simply turn the fuel on, tickle the old Amal carburettor to raise the fuel level in the float bowl and jump on the kick-starter. The engine fires up in a couple of kicks and immediately settles down into a reliable idle, with the inevitable vibration at footrests and handlebars.

I would have bet money on it, and won with ease, for immediately the engine fired up the carburettor throttle slide started tinkling like a little bell, almost like an old friend ringing up to say hello again after all those years. You see, there is quite a strong pressure pulse through the short, Y-shaped inlet manifold from the single carburettor to the two cylinders and this pulls the slide against the carburettor body on the inlet phase and releases it again when the pressure subsides. Even at idle speeds this happens many times a minute and the slide ultimately wears thin on the engine side and rattles about inside the throttle body at idle. Of course, when the slide is open, and the bike is underway the sound disappears.

Over the years I have seen Amal carburettor throttle slides worn almost to razor blade thinness on the engine side, the outer face virtually unmarked. I might say that even a new throttle slide does not always supply a cure, because the carburettor throttle body can warp to a more oval shape with time and the round slide cannot fit until a small riffler file is used to reshape it, finished off with the diligent application of a light emery paper.

Naturally, the bike crunches into first gear, which was always an odd feature of Triumph gearboxes, and the engine coughed apologetically just off the idle as we moved away – courtesy of the worn throttle slide – but the Tiger zoomed

It's not easy to see, but the front brake cable ended at the top of the long tube through which the naked cable ran, until it emerged at an adjuster. As the forks worked, the tube moved through a small metal clip to locate it and squeaked as it did so unless oiled regularly. Most of these tubes were swiftly removed and a different brake cable adopted.

off with some vigour when the clutch was fully home, and we moved smartly though the gears. It was a joy to ride the old machine, and it proved to handle quite well on smooth roads – if more than a little lumpy over rough surfaces, because of the rigid frame.

Another old friend then made its appearance, the long tube which contains the front brake cable twittering as it slid through the little metal clip which locates it so neatly just behind the front fork leg. The old cure of a finger in the oil tank and a quick wipe over the tube silenced it immediately, and the difference, as ever, was remarkable. As it happens, most owners threw the tube away, for it had to be oiled often and proved to be more of a nuisance than a help: a modified front brake cable was then fitted.

The brakes were not very remarkable when the bike was new and have not improved much with age, so much so that the front one was just about up to the job, the rear brake falling a little short. Both brakes are drums, of course, and small diameter at that, but there always seemed to be plenty of leverage from the long rear brake pedal and the long brake arms on both brake plates, so the reason would have to be found in the brake lining material itself. In racing, these 7" brakes could be made to work very well, but it needed special racing material like Ferodo MZ41 lining on the brake shoes and some very judicious fitting upon re-assembly.

Underway the engine is quiet while the exhaust note is a joy to listen to. Vibration is always present, but certainly bearable, felt mostly through the footrest and handlebars. The bike is a willing performer and has always rewarded the 'press on' rider with spirited acceleration and a top speed we are aware of but did not fully explore. The bike goes precisely where it is pointed, the rigid rear end hopping about over bumps, while the telescopic front end, though a bit firmly sprung, absorbs just about everything it passes over.

If an owner so desired, the strange Triumph sprung hub could be ordered as an option to provide a crude form of rear suspension, and this device – which was simply attached by removing a rear wheel and replacing it with a wheel containing the suspension medium *inside the centre of its hub* (?), which allowed about 30mm or so of limited suspension movement. It provided an equally limited degree of comfort, but the handling suffered because a machine fitted with a sprung-hub rear wheel felt as though the rider was traveling on a motorcycle with a flat rear tyre! The sprung hub was said to be 'designed'

The Triumph sprung hub certainly looked neat enough and could be fitted very quickly, by simply sliding out one wheel and replacing with another, fitted with the awful sprung hub. Happily, it could then be removed just as swiftly if required, which was so often the case!

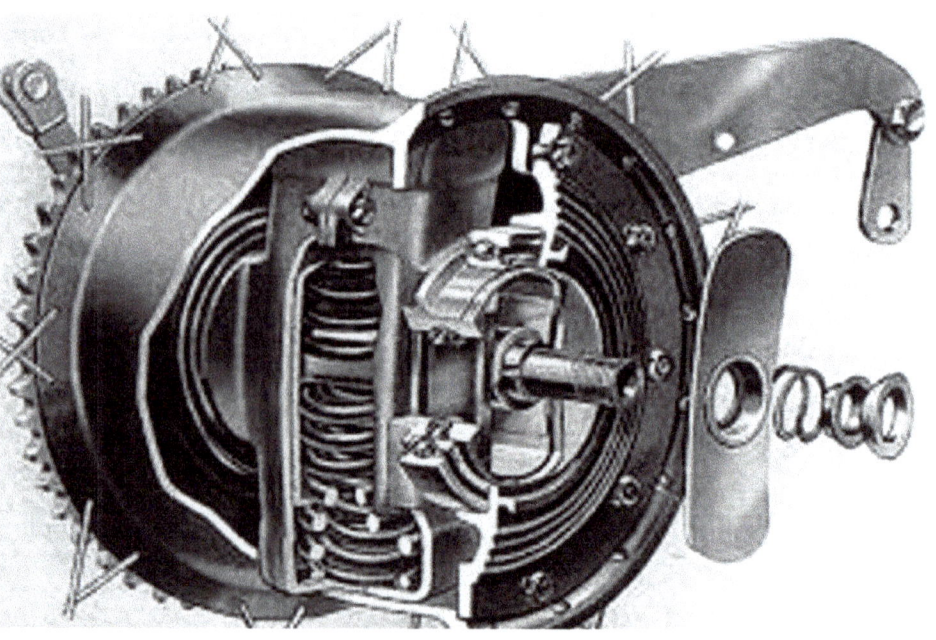

A cutaway drawing of the device, which shows the uncontrolled springs, nestled inside their alloy casting. The sprung hub's designer probably knew more than a little about Dowty's Sprung Wheel, which allowed some eight inches (200mm) of hydraulically controlled suspension, a boon on rough, grass-lined airfields.

by Edward Turner before the war and made its appearance in 1947, but was never very popular: the reason, I suggest, is obvious.

The sprung hub was a shocker, and was reviled by various road test reports which stated the device was, variously 'a pain in the rear end' or, 'the worst rear suspension device ever invented' or, 'was dangerous at high touring speeds'. Although it was Turner's baby, and was fitted to Triumph from 1947 to 1955 – long after most other marques had fitted swing-arm rear suspension – it first saw service as Bill Dowty's 'Sprung Wheel' a pair of which were attached to the rigid undercarriage of the Gloster 'Gladiator' aircraft from the mid-1930s. That 1946 Triumph Tiger 100 certainly does not have many of the creature comforts of much later machines but make no mistake that 500cc Tiger was still a very handy sports machine in its day, specially tuned machines winning a great many road races, while being quite capable of maintaining very high point-to-point average speeds on the open road as well, and for hours at a time. Even with its lack of rear suspension, it could always manage to hold a tight cornering line even over some rough surfaces at speed, but a more pedestrian owner who might not have been quite so addicted to riding at high speeds might order a sprung hub to be fitted to enjoy a little more comfort and be entirely happy with his choice.

The fact that the name, and the basic design, managed to survive for so many years after the war bears testimony to the staying power of the machine, so ably demonstrated by that trim little 1946 model we had so much fun with on that long day, and into the night as well. Even after all its trials and tribulations, including its almost criminal mismanagement many years ago, Triumph has survived, as few of its contemporaries have done, and gone from strength to strength. It must be said that this is no surprise.

I only wish I could find the photographs we took of myself riding the bike; unhappily, they have disappeared somewhere in the mists of time, and there does not appear to be many – if any – of those 1946 Tiger 100 machines about to recapture those riding shots.

TECH SPECS

Make: Triumph

Model: Tiger 100

Year of manufacture: 1946

Type:
Twin cylinder overhead-valve four-stroke, one-piece cast-iron cylinder barrel and cylinder head, the crankshaft designed to operate at 360 degrees, with pistons rising and falling together

Capacity: 498cc

Bore x stroke: 63 x 80mm

Compression ratio: 8:1

Power @ rpm: 30BHP @ 6000rpm

Carburettor:
Single Amal, 1-inch bore, No air filter

Electrics:
Lucas magneto, Lucas 6-volt generator, lead/acid battery

Transmission:
By 1/2" x 5/16" chain in enclosed primary drive alloy chaincase to four-speed Triumph gearbox. Final drive by 5/8" x 3/8" chain.

Gear ratios:
1st – 12.20:1; 2nd – 8.45:1; 3rd – 5.95:1; 4th – 5:1

Frame, Wheels, Brakes, Tyres:
Brazed, full-cradle tubular steel, rigid frame, telescopic front forks. Steel rims, with 7" brakes front and rear. Tyres: 325 x 19 ribbed front; 350 x 19 block pattern on rear.

Dimensions:
Wheelbase: 1410mm; Ground clearance: 127mm; Weight: 170kg; Tank capacity: 18 litres.

Top Speed: 170km/h.

Machine loaned by:
LEIGH McCRACKEN, Melbourne.

1953 Moto Guzzi 'Falcone'

500cc OHV 'HORIZONTAL' SINGLE CYLINDER

The World War 1 Italian pilot Giorgio Parodi was still imbued with that spirit of *derring-do* which was so much a part of the character of young men who flew those fragile aircraft during that short conflict, and he itched to do something more about it than to just sit quietly in the sun scratching himself fitfully while letting the world drift by him. He enlisted the aid of long-time aircraft mechanic and friend Carlo Guzzi and in 1921, after tossing a few ideas back and forth, they founded a small factory on the foreshores of the beautiful Lake Como in Northern Italy and began the laborious process of building their very first motorcycle, the Moto Guzzi 'Normale'.

The machine was a simple, single cylinder 500cc, but with an unusual, forward-facing, horizontal cylinder, a hand gear change on the right-hand side of the fuel tank, a large external 'bacon slicer' flywheel and with the then-*unfashionable* overhead valve exhaust and side valve inlet design: most other marques employed valve gear which was exactly the opposite: overhead valve inlet and side valve exhaust design.

The original, **1920** design was far more exciting, however, for it initially employed a four-valve head and overhead camshafts, which would have been far more costly to manufacture.

They were not to know it at the time, of course, but that first five-hundred single was to continue in production with little more than the normal evolutionary changes in design to engine internals, frame, suspension, and braking systems, for more than 50 years, with the last – and still entirely recognisable – Moto Guzzi 'Nuovo' built from 1969 to as late as 1974! Yes, that last five-hundred single still employed that fat, horizontal cylinder, the same bore and stroke measurements and indeed the external, 'bacon-slicer' flywheel was still to be seen spinning away outside the engine; it was by that time enclosed to some degree, but it still sat out there in the breeze for the entire world to see.

That large, 280mm flywheel, it might be noticed, ran anti-clockwise, because the primary drive in the unit-construction engine was by straight-cut gears direct to the clutch, with no intermediate gear, which meant the engine ran 'backwards' in relation to the direction in which the machine was being ridden. The primary transmission gears were well lubricated, along with the gearbox pinions, because the gear-driven oil pump delivered lubricant firstly to the large main bearings, then to the unusual crowded-roller big-end bearing. The steel connecting-rod employed a detachable end-cap at the big-end; a normal arrangement where slipper big-end shell bearings were to be used, but Guzzi often employed a most unusual 'split' caged roller big end bearing on machines of later vintage. The lubricant is then flung onto the bottom of the piston skirt and, in sequence, squirted under some pressure onto the square-cut transmission gears and into the gearbox. Naturally, the box itself was well lubricated with its own oil supply, incidental to the additional oil, which provided several reasons why this very low-stressed engine was so silent, trouble-free, smooth, and so long-lived.

The first 1921 Moto Guzzi, the 'Normale' with its horizontal cylinder and 'bacon slicer' external flywheel, which enjoyed many improvements over nearly 60 years, while employing the same basic layout. A most remarkable machine.

The oil was contained within a small, triangular tank sited just under the nose of the fuel tank, the lubricant supplied to the gear-driven pump – and returned to the tank – at a junction at the right-hand base of the large cylinder barrel where three separate oil lines are attached to the outer face of the internal oil pump.

An unusual form of cantilever rear suspension was employed from early in 1929, which was operated from a short, triangular-shaped, twin-tube swing arm set-up, which tapered from its location behind the gearbox towards the rear axle. Far from employing an upright swing-arm spring/damper unit, however (which were extremely rare and little known at the time, anyway) the lower sub-frame tube acted by 'pulling' upon a set of springs contained within metal boxes located directly beneath the engine's crankcase castings. The upper frame rail provided the pivot point from its position just below the rider's seat, while the lower sub-frame tubes acted upon an articulated arm which was attached to the long springs under the 'cases. A pair of knee-action friction dampers, sited just outside and at the rear of the single saddle, could be readily adjusted by hand to control the action of the springs. This unusual combination of levers, springs and friction damper control proved to be very effective, even though they appeared to be more than a little on the antique side. This odd suspension layout was to be used very successfully by the Italian factory on Falcone motorcycles for more than 40 years.

A cleverly designed, large centre-stand utilised a set of steeply curved 'feet' and was thus an easy 'roll-on' type, which required very little effort, the rider simply standing on the stand's pedal and leaning back as the bike was moved onto the stand. There was no prop stand fitted, so it was perhaps just as well the centre stand was easy to operate.

I owned a brand-new Moto Guzzi 'Nuovo' in 1972 which was fitted with a prop stand as well as the 'roll on' centre stand, the machine finished in a very swish all-white with thin red piping; with dual mufflers springing from its large diameter, single exhaust pipe. By now it had (mostly) moved with the times, having grown a huge dual-seat, large blinkers and an electric starter and the more modern swing-arm rear suspension with twin, spring/damper units, the while retaining that same fat, horizontal cylinder, and external flywheel – still visible, even if hidden by a small cover. Externally, it was very clearly a single-cylinder Moto Guzzi, but internally, however, the engine was very different, but it remained a traditional, low-revving thumper. The Nuovo served in many guises, for it was supplied in large numbers to various Police forces and the Italian Army as well as being sold in more limited numbers to the public as an easy-going, relaxed tourer. The Falcone never made any claims to being anything other than a simple, honest, reliable motorcycle. It remained so during its entire existence.

Single-cylinder Guzzis created history when one of them won the inaugural 500cc European Championship in 1924, as well as seven other European and World Championships, and as late as the 1950s, Moto Guzzi singles, still featuring their low-slung, 'horizontal' engine, design, won five World Championships in a row, the Australian Keith Campbell winning Guzzi's final honours with the now-defunct 350cc Championship in 1957.

But there was much more to Moto Guzzi than building 'simple' world beating single-cylinder engines, because the factory also built such incredible machines as the rare, three-cylinder, overhead camshaft 500cc sports roadster, which formed the basis for the 500cc supercharged road racer in 1937, and the unwieldy, shaft-drive, liquid-cooled, in-line four-cylinder 500 racer which appeared in 1953 and disappeared very shortly thereafter. Guzzi then upstaged the entire world with the legendary *eight*-cylinder DOHC 500cc road racer (the often-fragile, high-revving little engine designed as a very trim, slim V8, not much larger externally than a heavily finned, *single-cylinder* 500cc Manx Norton) which appeared in 1955. However, most of their racing successes remained with the single cylinder machines which were made in race or sports forms from 175, 250, 350 and of course 500cc capacities. The little 175cc racing machines were ridden in specialised Italian 'street race' events, with the road-going five hundreds augmented by very neat little road-going 175 and 250cc forms called 'Lodola'.

Along with several other Italian manufacturers – Vespa and Lambretta – the Italian factory entered the fashion stakes when Carlo Guzzi built the first of his Galletto (Little Rooster) scooters in 1950, expanding the original 150cc engine to a full 200cc by 1954, the overhead-valve four-stroke (and yes, with a horizontal cylinder and outdoor flywheel), and a somewhat odd, one-sided swing-arm rear suspension. Unlike modern scooters with their 'twist-and-go' automatic transmissions, the Galletto emerged with a four-speed, foot-change gearbox. The Galletto was the first-ever scooter to be fitted with motorcycle-sized wheels, with a spare wheel carried in front of the large front 'apron'. The scooter was, often, fitted with just the single saddle, but with some models featuring a dual-seat. It was a far safer machine to ride than many other scooters of its era, simply because of its better handling engendered by the larger-diameter wheels (which did not fall quite so readily into potholes) and well-damped – if essentially short-travel – suspension.

It is a safe bet that Honda had a good, hard look at Carlo's scooter before it built its first 50cc Super Cub step-thru, you may be assured of that! Quite apart from the small leading-link front forks which Honda pinched from the NSU machines (the NSU 'Quickly' moped, and NSU Max 250) the first of the 50cc OHV Honda step-thru machines employed large diameter wheels and a general silhouette very, very similar to the Guzzi Galletto. Although the Honda's gearbox was a semi-automatic – it employed a centrifugal clutch – its design even embraced the Guzzi's traditional heel-end-toe gear lever for its three-speed gearbox.

All those earlier Guzzi race, sports and small-capacity roadster motorcycles are now the stuff of legend, but during all that time, during fair weather and foul, war, misery, constipation, pestilence and famine, and indeed happy times, that single cylinder 500cc Moto Guzzi Falcone, in its various forms, continued to be built almost exactly as that very first machine was, proving beyond doubt that the original design had much going for it.

One of those Classic Falcone five-hundreds which is used as almost daily transport is the perfect example belonging to George Hempenstall. It is a **1953 Moto Guzzi Falcone,** a typically fire-engine red delight, standard and refurbished to near-showroom condition by George, who bought the bike from a hotel doorman in Rome on a visit to Italy. George, an ex-sidecar racer from Melbourne, builds the very trim Twin-G sidecars when he is not respraying classic motorcycles or removing large dents from motor cars. His bike is just one of the four examples known to be in Australia.

The Galletto, 192cc scooter, with four-speed gearbox, and larger motorcycle-sized wheels, proved to be a popular machine. Far better than many others with doughnut-sized wheels which drop into potholes. Honda took a long look at the bike before launching their 50cc 'Cub' step-thru in 1958.

Please do not attempt this at home, or anywhere else! A little tentative to begin with but, coached by the machine's owner and with help from the valve-lifter, I was able to fire up the Guzzi engine by hand! But once was more than enough.

The Guzzi Falcone is a strange looking motorcycle by any standards and is not an easy machine to ride at first, yet it possesses a distinct charm and character which sets it apart from its contemporaries. Its most striking feature is that heavily finned, horizontal alloy cylinder which catches whatever breezes slips past the heavily valanced sprung front mudguard. Finned longitudinally, the Guzzi motor looks much longer than its oversquare 88 x 82mm bore/stroke dimensions would suggest – which, as we have seen, are the same bore and stroke measurements of the original 1921 five-hundred single. The later machines, such as George's '53 model, used pushrod operated overhead valves which are much more up to date by being fully enclosed and are controlled by hairpin valve springs. A single tube on the engine's right side encases both pushrods, giving the machine the appearance of an overhead camshaft design.

Under-stressed is the best way to describe this big, gentle single. With a soft 5.5:1 compression ratio, the Falcone is simplicity itself to start. With the aid of the clutch-lever sized exhaust valve lifter, the heavy flywheel spins the engine very easily, to the point where the Falcone could be started with ease just by pushing the kick-start lever down by **hand**. I know this because I did it myself – under George's guidance, of course – although I would not recommend it as a daily exercise.

This softness of tune and heavy flywheel allows the Guzzi to idle at ludicrously low revs; almost like a country farmer's chaffcutter. Well, perhaps not quite, because chaffcutters usually rattle alarmingly, and can clearly be heard (and felt) from some distance away. There was no tacho fitted to the motorcycle, so with the engine idling quietly I timed the sucks which slurped through the unfiltered carburettor, added the soft exhaust thumps that swiftly followed and timed it all very carefully on my digital watch. It was a bit like taking somebody's pulse, with about the same result, because the Falcone idled smoothly, and quite reliably, at just on 150rpm. No, this is not a misprint, or a 'typo' – that's *one hundred and fifty revolutions per minute,* **not** *1500rpm!*

As well as lacking a tacho, there is also no speedo, no ammeter, no warning lights, no blinkers, no oil pressure light, and – horror of horrors – no little green light to tell you when you have selected neutral! There are, in fact, *no instruments of any kind* on George's Falcone, and he tells me there never were! Of course, there would have been a small range of simple instruments which could be ordered as options when purchasing a brand-new machine or could be attached later if a rider thought they were necessary, but these 'essential items' were clearly considered to be not quite so essential at the time. Naturally, there is a small switch to turn on the lights, and a tiny button to control the groaning horn, and that is that.

The Falcone is so obviously intended to be leapt upon and ridden briskly away, the factory probably assuming that anyone who did so would hardly be concerned with what gear he or she was in, or what speed one was doing, but would doubtless spend more time watching the scenery and watching other road users flashing about, rather than peering at a battery of winking lights and needles whizzing about over grinning dials. They must have been a bit more relaxed about speed limits in Italy in 1953; but Melbourne – as we all know only too well – is a different story entirely! I confess I was a bit wary about riding a motorcycle which had no speedo fitted, particularly a relaxed machine like that big single, because it was – when I finally came to grips with its vagaries – such an easy ride that I could so easily have exceeded the speed limit on the bike and probably did without realising it.

I wonder what my excuse might have been had I been pulled over to be booked for some transgression, for there might have been a first-rate excuse for having done so. Then again, it might well have been illegal in Melbourne to ride – or indeed to drive – any vehicle which was not fitted with a speedometer.

It might easily have happened, because for a machine in such a mild state of tune, the Guzzi is surprisingly agile, with brisk acceleration and top-gear performance which would shame your grandfather's old 1930s Buick. Of course, I couldn't conduct the 'ear-hole' test of listening to the sucks, and the following thumps, while timing it on my watch as I was riding the bike, but its low-end torque at minimal engine revs was really something to be wondered at. You can wind the engine out hard through the gears if you are that way inclined – I did it once or twice just for fun – but the Falcone engine's bottom-end grunt renders this unnecessary. Bags of torque are stored in that heavy flywheel, and the thick, chunky crankshaft as well, resulting in a distinct lurch (if not a surge) of power when you drop the clutch after changing up. Similarly, if you change back a bit too early, the bike leaps on for a metre or four before engine braking takes any real effect.

It is not easy to ride the bike smoothly if it is revved too hard through the gears, but the engine is certainly up to the challenge should this be your passion. The engine's characteristics are

The engine was well on the boil as we were lining up this great, open right hand corner, the bike eager as ever to be put well and truly through its paces. It seemed to enjoy the exercise every bit as much as its rider did.

so different from almost everything else on the road that it takes some little time to learn how to make the most of the machine's performance, casual though it seems to be at first acquaintance.

The Falcone weighs just 176kg, while the engine produces a modest 18.9BHP at a leisurely 4500rpm, an engine speed at which most modern machines are only just beginning to organise themselves. Probably because of the heavy flywheel and the chain-less primary transmission, the Guzzi engine is smoother than many 500 singles, and in fact could be a bit off-putting when stopped at the lights in heavy city traffic, because at those ultra-low idling revs it doesn't feel as though the engine is running at all!

This was a little disconcerting, because the left-mounted kick-starter is awkward to use, and the prospect of booting the thing over while using that left lever, if the engine had conked out at the lights, was more than a little daunting. Had this been necessary, I suppose I could have climbed off the bike and turned the engine over by hand just to give bystanders a treat, but thankfully it never came to that. I found the easiest way to start the engine was to stand alongside the bike and kick it with my right leg, in the time-honoured manner.

Because the horizontal engine is mounted so low in the frame, with the suspension components underneath all of that, the extremely low centre of gravity allows cornering which is out of this world. The footrests can be lightly touched either side, but by then the tyres are scrabbling at the road surface and are beginning to slide. But such is the angle of lean that your elbows and earlobes are not far behind, and you really should not be that far over on public roads in the first place. The bike handles very well, even over the sort of choppy road surfaces which would find some suspension systems hard-pressed to cope. You can feel the suspension moving about much more than is noticeable on more modern machines, while it can be a bit on the firm side and noisy at times, but the ride is very predictable and quite comfortable.

The old-time single sprung saddle takes care of some of the larger holes and bumps which even the best rear suspension systems have trouble ironing out, but with its long, soft springs and its somewhat flexible mounting, the well-shaped saddle feels very insecure at first. It quite naturally perches above the frame on its own spring mounts, almost as though placed there as an after-thought. Occasionally the two wheels

A pair of spring boxes under the crankcases allow for plenty of suspension movement through linkages to the swing-arm. The chamfered footrest rubber tends to indicate some degree of over-enthusiastic cornering. Please note the awful heel-operated rear brake pedal.

Spring oscillation is well controlled by this knee-action friction damper at the rear. Friction disc material is inserted between metal discs and can be quickly adjusted for weight by the small hand lever in its centre.

get out of step with one another over unusually rough going – Melbourne tramlines are a classic example – but the bike never tries to have its own way. Well, not very often anyway!

This is one of the old breeds and the handlebars, saddle and footrests are ideally situated – in that old sit-up-and-beg style – to allow for total comfort at high touring speeds, and seemingly for hours at a time. There is no weight on the wrists, unlike some modern sports tourers, although the breeze can be a fit busy at close to the entirely naked machine's top speed.

Unhappily, the single saddle tends to bounce about as it performs its natural office over choppy surfaces, which of course adds to the general comfort of the bike, but because of bouncing like this it is difficult, if not impossible, to keep your foot resting lightly on the Guzzi's unusual **heel-operated** rear brake pedal.

Over very choppy surfaces that oddly mounted, heel-operated brake proved to be very difficult to control, inevitably resulting in almost locking the rear wheel now and again under heavy braking, and even more so if changing back a couple of gears at the same time. Perhaps it would have been better not to have ridden it quite so enthusiastically, while braking much more gently, and somewhat earlier. I would have very swiftly modified the pedal to a more standard position had the bike been mine.

Clutch take-up is smooth with the gear change (on the typical British/Italian right-foot side) very fast and reliable, if a little notchy, but it was a novelty to use a heel-and-toe gear change again. As you would expect, it isn't necessary to change gears all that often with a slugger like the Falcone. Even top gear, which is a quite high 'touring' ratio – a tall 4.32:1 on the Falcone *'Tourismo'*, and an even taller 3.45:1 on the Sports model – can still be used in most areas of the inner-city suburbs.

One joy the bike often delivered was a very satisfactory kick in the pants when changing back to overtake or zoom up a steep hill after a slow start from behind a large truck or other impedimenta. It was great fun and required only a gentle stroke of the clutch lever and a lightning-fast nudge of the gear lever with the throttle kept open. As soon as the engine load is eased when the clutch is lightly disengaged the revs pick up instantly, and it is here that the flywheel mass is a boon because the bike leaps away surprisingly quickly when this flywheel effect is then boosted by significantly higher engine speeds allied to a fistful of throttle.

That swift downward gear change is an art I learned while riding a large range of early British singles, and it has always proven to be very effective in overtaking rapidly or storming a steep hill. With the Italian machine's added poke from the large flywheel, it is even more impressive! This 'single-cylinder' swift downward gear change cannot be employed as effectively – if at all! – on modern, multi-cylinder machines, for the higher engine revs would flash almost to infinity much too quickly, resulting in either a loud banging noise or a serious 'lurch' and unintentional 'wheelie' when the clutch is swiftly re-engaged.

Ridden as a Tourer, the Falcone covers long distances with ease and assurance. I suggest the Falcone could corner very much faster than many of its 'casual' owners would be aware of, because of it very low centre of gravity, and it feels as though its Italian Pirelli tyres might be the only limiting factor in this area.

Measured even by the standards of its time, the Guzzi *Falcone* was an unusual machine, and certainty not your average 500 single. Its flaming, Italian racing-red paint job looks great, and it quite deservedly gets its share of attention, from the occasional pedestrian as well as other motorcyclists, when it hits the streets.

It is a little-known machine in Australia, but internationally it is one with a very long and proud history. It was on the roads nearly 40 years before the Japanese first hit the Western world and has really stood the test of time.

I was told there was a sports version of the Falcone kicking around somewhere in Melbourne, which might have given some modern lightweight machines a bit of a fight out of some tight corners, as well as diving headlong into them, and it *might* even be more fun to ride than the 'standard' Tourismo Falcone I borrowed for this report. Somehow, I think I doubt that very much, for the Moto Guzzi I rode was very much a great fun bike and its staid (?) performance was well up to scratch. It gobbled up the miles with ease and assurance, without question filling to near-perfection the role it was intended to fill, which I suggest was that of an easy-going, old-fashioned, relaxing Open Road Cruiser but – in true Italian style – with more than a little sportiness woven into it just for good measure.

The basic design of the 500cc Moto Guzzi single remained from 1921 to 1976, almost certainly the longest-running motorcycle design in history. The horizontal single glorified in several name changes during that time, but pressed on, with little change, until it was 'discontinued' in 1963: there were, in fact, a few which still managed to be built for civilian use, for a small demand still existed.

But the Italian Army and Police forces were having none of this, and so, in 1969, demanded that the factory begin to manufacture the old war horse again, but this time with several changes, most of which, it must be said, for the better. The old-fashioned, cantilever rear suspension was changed for the more normal swing-arm rear suspension, with far more effective telescopic front forks as an added bonus. But the engine design was changed as well, although this hardly seemed necessary, as the old plodder had served with great distinction for those many, many long years. The Army models were finished in khaki, and bore both windscreen and combined leg-shields/safety bars. There were some 13,000 machines all told, ordered for the Army and Police.

The 'signature' outside flywheel remained almost as a matter of course, but was now primly shrouded by a trim alloy casting. With the engine ticking over, the flywheel could still be seen spinning about, but one had to peer over the top of the casting to see this. The 'new' engine was now a wet sump design, with big-end slipper bearings replacing the older split-roller type, a little odd, I thought, for the roller bearing big-end had served the older design well almost since Day One.

The 'Civile', or civilian model, was being made again from 1971, and was usually painted in a dazzling white with a bright red frame, the exhaust running into a pair of long, megaphone-type silencers, which muted the sound nicely, but without losing the 'feel' of the Old Thumper. Around 3,000 of the civilian models were said to have been built during this time, many of them with the optional lector starter. I owned a 1972 model for a short time, which employed a self-starter, and it was a delight to ride, for the bike rode and handled better than the earlier model; a surprise, for I reckoned the machine featured in the above report would have been hard to beat in this area. Sadly, the last of the venerable old singles left the Italian factory in 1976.

TECH SPECS

Make: Moto Guzzi

Model: Falcone

Year of manufacture: 1953

Type:
Horizontally disposed, all-alloy, overhead valve, air-cooled single cylinder four-stroke, unit-construction engine/gearbox, with dry sump. One-piece forged steel crankshaft with large 'bob-weights', while the steel connecting rods have detachable end-caps, with 'split-cage', roller big-end bearings, the chunky, if lightweight, crankshaft augmented by a large-diameter external flywheel. The crankshaft is supported upon a large roller bearing on the drive side, and large ball bearing on the timing side. Lubrication from separate oil tank through external oil lines to gear-driven double-action gear-type oil pump, internal drill-ways and oil galleys.

Capacity: 498.4cc

Bore x stroke:
88 x 82mm, with four-ring piston; two compression, two oil rings

Compression ratio: 5.5:1

Power @ rpm: 18.9BHP @ 4500rpm

Carburation:
Single, 27mm Dell'Orto carburettor, no air filter

Electrics:
Gear-driven Marelli Magneto ignition, with 6-volt generator; dual instrument

Transmission:
By straight-cut primary-gear drive to 12-plate, oil-bath clutch and four-speed foot-change gearbox, with heel/toe gear lever on right side. Rear drive is by 5/8" x ¼" chain.

Gear ratios (overall):
1st – 9.9:1; 2nd – 7.48:1; 3rd – 5.69:1; 4th – 4.32:1.

Frame, wheels tyres, brakes:
Tubular steel diamond frame, with bolted on, full cradle sub-frame to support engine. Rear suspension is by triangulated sub-frame to cantilever operating tension and compression springs located underneath engine, controlled by knee-action friction dampers. Front suspension by hydraulically damped telescopic forks. Wheels are 19" steel rims, laced to seven-inch (175mm) drum brakes front and rear, with 325 x 19" ribbed front tyre and 350 x 19" block pattern rear.

Dimensions:
Length – 2260mm; Wheelbase – 1500mm; Height – 1050mm; Weight – 176kg; Fuel tank – 13.5 litre

Top speed (suggested): 135km/h.

Machine loaned by:
GEORGE HEMPENSTALL, Melbourne, Victoria.

1952 K600 Zundapp 'Green Elefant'

600cc OHV 'BOXER' TWIN CYLINDER

From 1956 the German *Elefantreffen* (Elefant Rally) was named after it, the machines which preceded it saw yeoman service during World War 2 as a sidecar courier and transport motorcycle, while many enthusiasts are happy to declare it to be a better machine in its day than that 'other' flat-twin, shaft-drive motorcycle from Germany, the BMW. This was confirmed by no less an authority than the German Government itself. This occurred when the 750cc flat-twin Zundapp ZS750 and R75 BMW outfits were submitted to the German War Office prior to WWII. The Government of the day insisted that BMW build its opposition's machine under licence because the beefy Zundapp, it was stated, was clearly a superior design. This statement scandalised BMW, who flatly refused to do the unthinkable, but a compromise was reached whereby some 70% of the engine and transmission internals of both machines had to be readily interchangeable.

Following the War, Zundapp's reputation for building a better motorcycle continued, when its first post-war flat twin arrived on Australia's shore in the early 1950s; albeit in very, very small numbers. Prior to the arrival of the larger machines, Zundapp motorcycles were initially small-capacity two-strokes. The reason the larger-capacity German motorcycles arrived late unto the international scene is that, for several years after hostilities ended, the German motorcycle factories which survived the war were restricted to building machines with power-plants of no more than 250cc. At that time, Zundapp machines were imported by Sydney's Tom Byrne Motorcycles, the company, which was later to import BMW motorcycles, even as the small range of single-cylinder two-stroke and overhead valve flat-twin Zundapp models slowly fell from grace. The motorcycle which features in this report was the first large-capacity German motorcycle to be seen in this, or any other country outside of Germany, just after WWII.

The machine to which I refer is the **1952 Zundapp 'Elefant' K600,** a 600cc transverse-twin, shaft-drive mount which was designed just before WWII and enjoyed a later heyday as the beefy, purpose-built KS750 during the Second Word War, the later, smaller-capacity, much more 'civilised' motorcycle probably the first machines of its type to be built in Germany at the end of the war. The post-war machines were always called the *'Green Elephant'* because that was its standard colour scheme, but the bike was also available in jet-black and flaming red but, for some odd reason, was always referred to as the Green Elephant. Why Elephant? The editor of a German motorcycle reckoned the machine had as much low-speed grunt as a 'Green Elephant': and that was that!

The pea-green flat-twin was badly served by a capricious Fate for it is largely unknown today, except to a surprisingly large number of enthusiasts who keep its name alive with the world-famous 'Elefant' Rally in Germany, which has moved about through its various resurrections and is currently held – for some unaccountable reason – in the depth of a European winter in a Bavarian Black Forest at the tail end of January or early February, when heavy snow and sub-zero temperatures are virtually guaranteed. The Rally was originated as long ago as 1956 and attracted just 400 enthusiasts but has later been known to attract up to 10,000 hardy souls each year.

Many of those motorcycles arrive at the Elefant Rally fitted with heavily studded tyres on both ends, with some of the solo machines temporarily fitted with a pair of 'safety', spring-loaded devices like short skis, which attach to frame or footrests, clearly in the interest of having a modicum of control over the treacherous, icy road surfaces which are certain to prevail. The Rally certainly helps in the preservation of a fair number of the now-rare species, the more sporting, 34BHP, KS601 motorcycle – many with sidecars, the more powerful Sports motorcycles manufactured in quite some numbers from 1950 to 1958.

Zundapp deserved a better fate simply because the factory was in the same financial strife as BMW during the late 1950s, and like BMW it was lucky to survive. Unlike BMW

A photo from the Elefant Rally of 2015. You would not need to be crazy to attend this odd, freezingly cold rally for rabid motorcyclists – once described as 'the most bizarre rally ever seen on this earth' – but I reckon it would be to your advantage if you were

It has been said that up to 10,000 motorcyclists attend the great Elefant. I wonder if they would ever run out of attendees, for surely no one would ever wish to go back again after one's first attendance; or would they go back? I suggest quite probably!

however, which stuck with the flat-twin concept with its small model range – with the exception of BMW's 'upright' 250cc single, of course – Zundapp branched out into the manufacture of numerous small-capacity sporting two-strokes. Some of the smaller machines were very nippy, highly specialised International Enduro mounts, allied to a host of mopeds and top-class motor scooters. Quite apart from the large-capacity flat-twins, the Zundapp *'Bella'*, both in 150 and 200cc capacities, was a first-class example of a popular scooter. The very swift little 250cc single-cylinder two-stroke 'Elastic' of the 1950s was yet another first-rate motorcycle.

While the then-struggling BMW factory enjoyed an injection of funds from some friendly banks in late 1959 and sold its aircraft facility to be able to build its equity to the point where its new range of cars and motorcycles began to pay their way, Zundapp soldiered on with much more limited funds. However, the latter continued to build a surprisingly large range of motorcycles from the (very) occasional 750cc and 600cc flagship flat twins to several lightweight motorcycles and tiny mopeds.

The first BMW 250cc singles, which appeared just after the War, and then the later flat-twin motorcycles, were originally imported into NSW by a suburban dealer in the late 1940s, before Tom Byrnes began to import the marque, but neither BMW nor Zundapp machines were to be seen in very large numbers in those days. Thus, the two very similar rivals saw very little of each other in the 1950s and early 60s in Australia, even with the same importer handling both brands. Those earlier machines see even less of each other today!

There are several 70-year-old BMW flat-twins about, but I have only found one 'Elefant', the machine in Victoria. It glorifies in that great pea-green colour which was so much the hallmark of most of the Zundapp motorcycles of that era, including the 250cc 'Elastic', and it looks much more becoming than BMW's basic black-and-chrome colour scheme. The K600 belongs to arch-enthusiast Vin Minogue, who has restored several other Zundapp machines, notably a 1934, 800cc flat-four with shaft-drive and hand-gear-change, which I have also had the good fortune to have ridden, along with a KS750 outfit which saw service with the Germans in North Africa during WWII. I have given that Wehrmacht outfit a good workout over a few days as well and reported upon them both in some detail within these pages.

Vin's K600 is more a clean and purposeful example of the marque than a totally restored gem, but it is nonetheless nicely finished and entirely free of bugs. The BMW-like horizontally opposed engine sits low in its all-tube frame, the cylinders sticking well out in the breeze for optimum cooling, the other engine parts concealed beneath a series of quite large alloy castings. It is an overhead valve design, the bore of 75mm and stroke of 67.6mm, being nicely over-square, seemingly to allow for some spirited engine revs but peak power of a handy 28BHP is generated at a surprisingly low 4700rpm which hints at very good torque from low engine speeds, allied to a long engine life. This is a similar design feature probably resulting from the development work carried out on the high-torque, low-revving WWII sidecar machine. Top speed of the solo, K600 is claimed to be 140km/h, the machine's all-up weight just on 240kg.

Naturally – which seems to occur with just about everything which has ever been built on two wheels and powered by an internal combustion engine – there is a 'Sports' model as well, the **KS601**, the latter fitted with slightly larger-bore carburettors and higher compression ratio, the engine then pushing out a very handy 38BHP at a much higher 6000rpm. The sports model is still lightly tuned, however, but was said to be noticeably much quicker off the mark than the K600 'cooking' version. It would certainly have enjoyed a better turn of speed through the gears while at once delivering a brisker surge of acceleration.

The smooth aluminium-alloy engine castings – one or two of which were of necessity 'home-made' by Minogue because they were either badly damaged or missing entirely – conceal a range of electrical components which were not always carried within the confines of such castings: they include the ignition coil and voltage regulator which sit atop the power-plant. These components were more often carried on other brands somewhere on the machine's frame or hidden underneath the fuel tank. The large upper casting which conceals the ignition coil also carries a wire-mesh air filter at the rear with two long manifolds which direct clean air to a pair of separate 25mm Bing carburettors, in the same style as the BMW twins. Two high-tension leads emerge from the same casting directly below and ahead of the manifolds, with the spark plugs they serve safely out of harm's way on the upper face of the cylinder heads.

A one-piece, steel crankshaft is supported on substantial roller bearings at each end, with the chunky connecting-rods employing detachable end-caps fitted with the almost-unique split-caged roller big-end assembly. This unusual big-end assembly was used in many machines in the Zundapp range – including the two-stroke Bella scooters – and was also adopted by Moto Guzzi for the earlier 500cc single cylinder Falcone.

There is a small helical gear on the front of the crankshaft which drives a large camshaft gear directly above it, with long mushroom-type cam followers bearing on thin pushrods to operate the overhead valves. Valve rockers are very solid and are supported upon caged needle rollers.

A small gear carried inboard of an outrigger bearing drives the oil pump gear, a high-capacity pump which is sited slightly below the engine in a deep oil pan. A small outrigger bearing supports the front end of the crank which has a heavy generator hanging on the end of it, with the ignition contact points – and auto-advance unit – in front of that! It is a long crankshaft, be assured, but it is well supported and apparently trouble-free. Naturally, the opposite end of the crank has the clutch assembly attached, and it is a multi-plate dry clutch at that. It sits all on its own in a bellhousing ahead of a most unusual 'gearbox', the tail-end of the crankshaft assembly supported upon a substantial roller bearing.

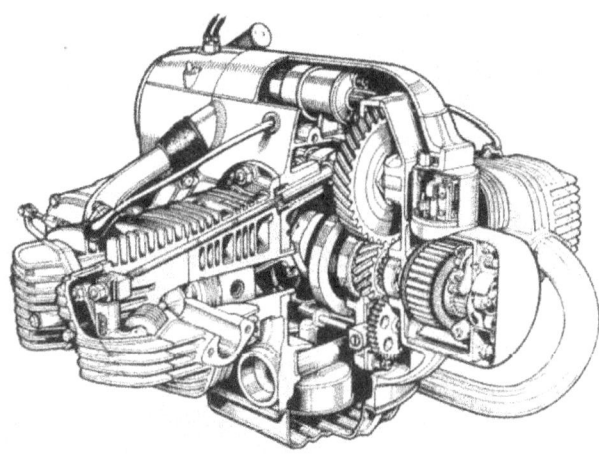

The immense strength of the K600 power-plant is clear from this cutaway drawing, which shows to best advantage its very compact design. Note the alloy casting which covers the ignition coil, air filter and other components, with the crankshaft-driven generator, under its own chrome-plated cover, at the front.

Zundapp employed shaft final drive, with gear drive – as we have described – for the camshaft and oil pump, but the gearbox (a misnomer, for it should be called a sprocket-box) *uses a set of four chains and sprockets* instead of the gears one would normally expect to find! It's quite odd and almost unique, though the system was used in the 350cc shaft-drive Victoria Bergmeister transverse Vee-twin of 1955, as well as Zundapp's trim little 250cc two-stroke singles.

Each of the sprockets in the 'gearbox' has a double row of teeth and of course duplex chains, the sprocket centres so close together that the teeth almost touch. The two rows of sprockets lie side-by-side, the 'box slightly offset to the right of the centre-line of the engine's crankshaft. The entire drive line inside the gearbox is supported upon multi-row ball bearings, the lay-shaft – on the left side of the 'box in line with the crank – having a small skew-gear attached which engages with the much larger kick-starter gear. Unlike the BMW kick-starter, which was such a pain because it was left-mounted and kicked `outwards' very awkwardly, Zundapp attached a bevel gear to the kick-starter shaft which alters rotation and allows the lever to move in a normal manner.

I don't know why the gearbox design employs sprockets and chains instead of the more normal gear train, but there is no evidence of what the 'gearbox' contains when on the move. It could be that the essential backlash in this type of transmission acts as a type of in-built shock absorber when changing gears or backing-off the throttle, because the bike was very smooth on the move and gear-changes were similarly smooth and silent. There *did* seem to be a touch of free-play in the transmission on the over-run, but there could easily have been some wear in the final-drive components in the rear hub to account for that.

The kick-starter is still mounted on the left side of the gearbox and feels awkward to those of us more used to the 'British' kick-starters fitted to the right-hand side but is easy to use in

The unusual, four-speed chain-and sprocket 'gearbox' internals from the Zundapp K600. As far as is known this type of transmission was fitted only to Victoria, Hoffman and Zundapp machines.

view of the assistance of a heavy flywheel effect and the engine's mild 6.4:1 compression ratio. The alloy pistons, incidentally, are the four-ring type long favoured by German designers: three compression and one oil ring on each piston ensuring long service before repairs are necessary. Occasionally, two compression and two oil rings were employed.

It has been said that the weight of pistons on a horizontal cylinder promotes premature wear underneath the piston rings and the pistons' faces on the thrust side because of the additional effects of gravity, but this phenomenon is apparently more prevalent with your old two-stroke lawn mower. This type of wear has not been in evidence with Minogue's Zundapp; or with BMW, Douglas or other horizontally opposed twins, for that matter.

Gear-change is a bit strange, because Zundapp's left-mounted lever employs a cross-over system with a remote linkage to a lever on the right side of the 'box, a system long favoured by the factory on most models, including the 250cc Elastic.

The driveshaft is enclosed within a torque tube on the machine's right side, the bevel-gear drive assembly contained in a very trim rear hub which features a quickly detachable wheel. Telescopic front forks and plunger rear suspension are employed, with a single coil spring under a cantilever-mounted rubber single saddle to take more than an edge off bumps the pliable rear suspension may have trouble ironing out.

The fork legs contain long, thin springs which are well lubricated, the essential damping by an entirely separate, centrally mounted hydraulic damper which sits atop the solid, heavily valanced front guard. The telescopic damper is almost half the length of the forks and contains an elaborate piston and valve system. Although only one-way damped it proved to be very effective indeed and was entirely oil tight.

Zundapp Green is the colour scheme on forks, tank, and the two deep mudguards, the duplex-downtube, full-cradle tubular frame a complimentary black for a very neat and attractive package. The bike kicks over easily, if it is again a bit awkward, but it tends to idle a bit on the lumpy side and vibrates more than I would have expected it to; perhaps the flat-twin BMW has spoilt us all a bit – although the BMW models of that earlier time jumped about at idle as well if I remember aright. However, vibration all but disappears once the machine is nicely underway but returns at idle speeds.

The brakes are of course drums front and rear, the front one being quite potent and progressive, the rear a little touchy when braking while changing back to a lower 'gear' – particularly if the machine happened to be cranked over into a corner at the time! Both brakes are quite large in diameter, with large fulcrum levers on their drums, and the owner/restorer assured me the brake shoes are quite wide as well. This clearly accounts for the efficiency of the front brake, and the touchiness of the rear one as well.

The Zundapp suspension was great, the front forks extremely smooth and quiet, with a long travel even though the front wheel's springing is only one-way damped, controlling only the 'bump' if not the springs' rebound, the initial shock of a road irregularity well controlled, the rebound undamped. Rear suspension is by longer-travel plunger units which were in fashion at the time, the heavy-duty springs controlled and lubricated by grease. The rear wheel travel is about 95mm, and it is a bit choppy on uneven surfaces as a result, but it's perfectly augmented by the supple rubber saddle and the odd, large-diameter single spring upon which it is located. You would expect the seat to twist about because of the unusual single spring, but the solid mounting through its nose takes care of that very well. Overall, the old Zundapp surprised with its comfortable ride over give-and-take road surfaces.

The exhaust note is a subdued burble through the pair of long mufflers, but it becomes more and more urgent as you turn the wick up a bit. It is certainly a very healthy sound at top whack on the open road, but as usual, due deference to the bike's age and rarity forbade me belting it along too hard; or at least not for too long!

We did, however, put the bike through its

paces in a suburban situation and gave it a bit of stick on occasion when out of the traffic stream, to be rewarded by a surprisingly good burst of acceleration and an entirely acceptable turn of speed – but only for a short time, be it understood. The bike cornered on rails over smooth surfaces, the rear suspension a little noisy, the single saddle 'hunting' a little as usual. Under acceleration, the tail-end stepped out a little now and again over Melbourne's notorious tramlines, but was otherwise well behaved, the 'no-name' block pattern tyres fitted to both wheels more than a little suspect. Zundapp fits 19" wheels at both ends, with a fat 350x19 tyre on the front, an even fatter 400x19 on the rear, but the tread pattern and unlikely grip of the anonymous tyres precluded urgent cornering styles.

There was, however, a tautness, a certain Teutonic strength about the machine's general behaviour on the road, almost regardless of the road's surface, which inspired confidence and allowed for high-average 'touring' speeds when we finally reached the Open Road.

The marque is little-known today, as evidenced by the fact that a couple of BMW owners who stopped to stare as we were running a photo session wondered whether the machine was a new Russian machine – Heaven forbid! – or perhaps an odd machine from a small manufacturer, the bike – they may have assumed – probably found in someone's garden shed somewhere. When I pointed out that the name was bigger than BMW during the war, and that the Afrika Korps was well served with many thousands more than the similar machine BMW produced at the time they frankly, and quite obviously, did not believe it.

In fact, you cannot help but remark upon how well the Zundapp could have compared to its similar BMW competitor in the early 1950s when both machines had been brand new, or how well it would stack up today if the factory still made a machine of this size. Unhappily, it does not, though there was talk many years ago of the former giant having the design for an all-new transverse-four, with shaft drive, on its drawing board at one time. Unhappily, it came to nothing, but we thought there could have been some very exciting news in the pipeline someday, for the large Chinese manufacturing company, Xunda Motor Company, bought the entire Zundapp factory, lock, stock, and barrel when Zundapp was declared bankrupt in 1984!

The apparently sudden 'fire sale' came as a surprise to just about everybody – particularly the Germans! – but once it was sold to the Chinese the factory was descended upon by happy Orientals, who stripped it absolutely bare and left nothing but four walls behind. They removed fire extinguishers, all toilet door signs, walls, partitions, jigs, patterns, dies, drawings … in fact, everything which was in any way part of the German factory. The lot was then shipped back to China, and the deal at the time included borrowing the expertise and guidance of a bunch of engineers, designers and metallurgists who were to stay in China for a short time under contract to help set up the manufacture of a whole range of former-Zundapp machines which would bear the Chinese name.

It appears the Chinese had long wanted to seriously enter the motorcycle market but had so far lacked anything which could have been viable on the international market.

Leaving suburbia for a squirt into the country, wearing a genuine Zundapp helmet of unknown antiquity which the owner insisted I wear. The bike proved to be a nice ride, with powerful brakes and a very handy performance. The comfortable, long-travel plunger rear suspension was well augmented by the unusual single spring under the saddle.

What were their plans? Nobody knew, but we might have hoped the Chinese would arrive with a bang with a range of machines to challenge the best available from many of the other motorcycle factories. But they seemed to have squibbed out and were apparently more interested in the range of small commuter and moped machines which the Germans were manufacturing at the time, because the machines which arrived somewhat later were mostly Honda-engine, lightweight scooters, small commuter machines, and a few small electric run-abouts! Happily, that is now all over and done with.

As a later footnote, the Zundapp name, along with some materials, was bought back into Germany in 1999, so we are just beginning to see the proud old Zundapp name appearing on the fuel tank of an 'all-new' German motorcycle. Zundapp, as we have noted, was always considered to be a better machine that its closest rivals, which is why the K600 proved to be as nice a Classic mount as you would ever find.

TECH SPECS

Make: Zundapp

Model: K601

Type:
All-alloy, horizontally opposed overhead valve twin cylinder. One-piece steel crankshaft, with detachable-cap steel conrods and split, caged roller big-end bearings. Aluminium alloy pistons employ four piston rings. The crankshaft is supported upon substantial ball and roller bearings, with extra outrigger bearing at front overhang. Gear-driven, high-capacity oil pump in engine sump.

Bore x stroke: 75 x 67.6mm

Capacity: 597cc

Compression ratio: 6.5:1

Power @ rpm:
28BHP (20.6kW) @ 4700rpm

Carburation:
Dual 25mm Bing Carburettors, with large, wire-mesh air filters.

Electrics:
Noris 6-volt, 70-watt generator, to wet, lead-acid battery. Bosch contact points, dual coil ignition.

Transmission:
Direct from crankshaft through multi-plate dry clutch, to four speed sprocket-and-chain 'gearbox', with final drive by shaft through enclosed bevel gears.

Gear ratios:
1st – 14.63:1; 2nd – 7.92:1; 3rd – 6.03:1; 4th – 4.69:1.

Frame, suspension, wheels, brakes:
Full-cradle, dual down-tube tubular steel 'closed' frame, with frame rails brazed into cast steel lugs, reinforced at steering head, gearbox mounts and other stress points. Front suspension by long-travel front telescopic forks, with one-way damping controlled by short hydraulic unit mounted atop front mudguard. Rear suspension by short-travel 'plunger' units, with pairs of undamped springs within chromed shrouds, springs located above and below each side of rear axle. Shaped rubber single saddle supported upon a single compression spring. Wheels are 19" rims, laced to large 8" (200mm) drum brakes, tyres are 350/400 x 19.

Dimensions:
Length – 2140mm; Width – 1010mm; Height – 740mm; Wheelbase – 1415mm; Weight – 224kg (492lb)

Capacities:
Oil sump – 2.5 litres; Fuel tank – 14.5 litres

Performance:
5.5l/100km; Range: approx. 320km; Top speed: 140km/h.

Machine loaned by:
VIN MINOGUE, Victoria.

1966 Ever Onward 'Bitza'

500cc BARR AND STROUD SLEEVE-VALVE ENGINE

Ever heard of a motorcycle called the **'Ever Onward'**? Chances are you never have, and chances are you never will again, for it was an exceedingly strange machine, finished in a nice two-tone blue, with soft cream tank panels, the name 'Ever Onward' emblazoned upon the sides of its slim fuel tank. It really looked to be quite a machine, as, in fact, it was!

As it happens, the brand name did not exist anywhere on this earth except upon the bike's tank, for it was, in fact, a one-off 'Bitza', made from *bitza* this and *bitza* that. The frame and wheels belonged to a 1924 Norton, the large brakes sourced from Royal Enfield, with a hand-change, three-speed Sturmey-Archer gearbox fitted, while some of the tinware and sundry items came from Douglas, BSA and one or two others.

Nothing new about that, you may safely muse, for Bitzas have been built many times before, and will be built many times again, but the major difference between this and many other Bitzas was the engine, which was totally different from almost every other engine which empowered most two-wheelers, and several four wheelers, no matter where – or when – they may have been built.

Note the gravity-fed oil line from the tank above, aided by hand-pump, which leads to the external, total-loss Pilgrim oil pump on the 500cc engine. Higher-pressure oil is then conducted from the rear of the pump to the oil union below the barrel, where it is sprayed onto the base of the sleeve, then into the rest of the engine. Primitive, but very effective nonetheless; in fact, sometimes too efficient?

The engine was a 500cc four-stroke, but it employed no valve gear; neither overhead valves, side-valves – the norm in the 1920s – nor overhead camshafts, for the passage of the incoming and outgoing gases were carefully controlled by a series of holes cast into the top of the cylinder walls.

And no, as we have already noted, it was *not* a two-stroke engine.

It was instead the distinctly odd Barr and Stroud **single-sleeve-valve** power-plant, a clever, highly efficient, if comparatively rare design, which was supplied from the small Glasgow factory for motorcycle use, complete with carburettor and magneto. All it then needed to build an entirely viable motorcycle was for a small factory to add a gearbox of some type – usually, in those days, the Sturmey-Archer three-speed, hand-change unit – a frame, running gear and tinware; in fact, in much the same manner as our one-off Ever Onward was created.

The Barr and Stroud (B&S) engine was sold in the early 1920s in small quantities, like the far more popular propriety engines supplied by JAP, Anzani, Blackburn, MAG, Villiers, and other engine manufacturers who did not build complete motorcycles, but whose power-plants were fitted to many thousands of machines which were built by smaller factories in England and elsewhere. Though the names of the motorcycles are little known today, the 70mm bore x 90.5mm stroke, 350cc and 500cc (86 x 86mm) B&S single-sleeve-valve engines were fitted to Beardmore-Precision, Omega, Zenith, Rex-Acme, Royal Scott, Grindlay-Peerless and several other motorcycles in the 1920s, the time in which the small, sleeve-valve engines were built.

The factory also manufactured a very few Vee-twin 1000cc B&S engines, only two of which were fitted to Brough Superior motorcycles, while it was said that several of the Vee-twins were fitted to Grindlay-Peerless machines as well. There is one of the Vee-twin B&S Grindlays still in existence which has been beautifully restored and is now on display in Sammy Miller's Motorcycle Museum in Southern England.

The early model, 500cc single-cylinder,

sleeve-valve engine which is fitted into the 1924 Norton frame of the Ever Onward is an odd-looking device, for it employs the usual, if very lightly finned, cast-iron cylinder barrel, but it appears to be a single casting, and thus to have a non-detachable head. It also looks like a two-stroke, because of the total absence of any form of valve mechanism. As we have noted, this is because, unlike every other four-stroke engine on the planet, the inlet and exhaust ports have no poppet valves in them to get in the way of the various passages of inlet and exhaust gases.

If it looks to be in one piece, the cylinder head is detachable and is locked to the barrel by six bolts, and it protrudes some distance into the cylinder, where it is sealed at its base by a thick piston-ring-like seal which bears against the cylinder walls to prevent any by-pass leakage of burning gas.

Because of the total absence of valves in the cylinder head – in particular, a red-hot exhaust valve which can cause pre-ignition – the combustion chamber allows for a quite high compression ratio and an ideal 'squish' combustion chamber, the spark plug placed ideally in the very centre of the casting. This, combined with the long dwell in the port timings, results in very effective 'swirl' of incoming gas, accounting for more efficient combustion and more effective volumetric efficiency, while the *thermal* efficiency is also greatly enhanced, which is why there is such very light cylinder finning. There is a small compression-relief in the cylinder head, which is there to make kick-starting easier. The B&S engines had the cylinder barrel cast in three *pieces*, the barrel's five cast-in ports closed by two separate, semi-circular bolted-on castings which cover them: one of the castings is fitted with a carburettor stub and carburettor, the other a simple exhaust stub.

How then does the thing work, if there are no valves or valve gear to allow the ingress of the highly combustible inlet charge and the egress of the burnt gas after combustion has occurred? It is almost absurdly simple, and yet highly effective.

The 'working' cylinder is a very, very carefully machined cast-iron sleeve in which the piston pursues its path, and it is a very close (around .006-.008") 'sliding' fit inside the bore of the finned, cast-iron cylinder barrel, the barrel having had its inlet and exhaust ports carefully cast in place, with the bolted-on inlet and exhaust stubs we have mentioned. The sleeve is about .095" ($^3/_{32}$ inch) thick and moves through its figure-eight motion of not much more than about 45mm, or slightly over 1½ inches. Thus, at half engine speed, the inlet and exhaust ports are open for a fairly long period of time, which would greatly assist in obtaining both high volumetric and thermal efficiency.

The crankshaft is supported upon large roller bearings on both timing and drive sides in the 500cc design (the 350 employs double-row ball bearings throughout), while the small pinion attached to the timing side of the crankshaft drives a double-sized, drop-forged 'secondary' gear, which has had an off-centre hole bored into it close to the gear teeth, with a small, 'self-centering' ball-bearing inserted. This secondary gear also drives the magneto through a set of three gears in the 350cc engine, or, with a small sprocket attached to the gear, by chain and sprockets in the five hundred.

Thus, due to the rotation of that secondary gear which, as we have indicated, is twice the diameter of the crankshaft pinion, the hole in that gear naturally moves through an 'off-centre' orbit. A thick spigot fits tightly into the hole and is locked in place by a small screw inserted into the centre of the spigot from the opposite side, the 'gimbal' – as it is called – formed as part of the thick base of the moving cylindrical sleeve in which the piston travels. Clearly, the action of that gear as it revolves causes the sleeve to move as it describes a reciprocating and rotating, 'figure eight' path. This action allows a series of *five* heart-shaped holes which are machined into the *moving* sleeve to open and close at very carefully timed intervals in relation to the inlet and exhaust ports which are cast into the cylinder barrel directly opposite each other. To achieve this, the sleeve moves up and down but also rotates around 45 degrees in each direction through its prescribed orbit as it opens and/or

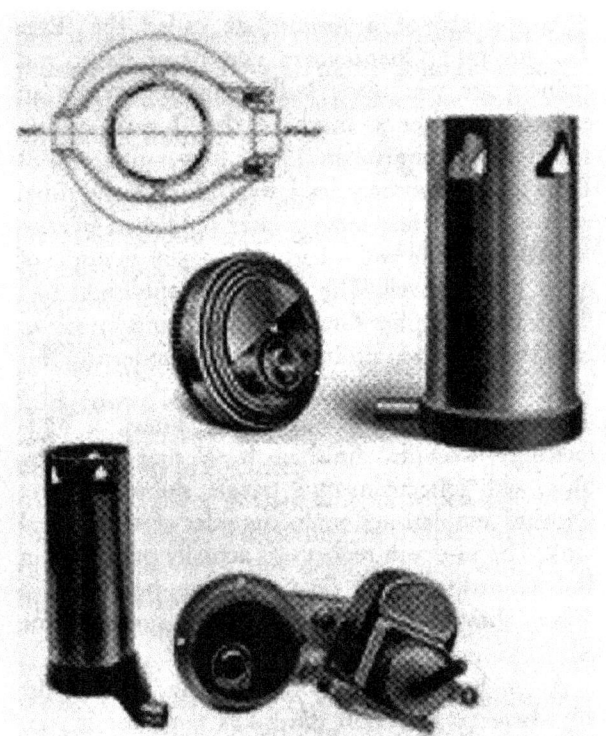

Here are the moving sleeves, the ports in place near the top. The 500cc is above, the 350 below, with its offset hole in the driven gear and the geared magneto drive. Both of the large gears show the offset holes into which the gimbals fit so snugly, allowing the sleeves to move in a reciprocating and oscillating manner almost simultaneously. The odd illustration above apparently shows the sleeve lining-up with the exhaust ports.

closes the inlet and exhaust ports. Try as I might, I could not accurately measure the degree of 'rotation' in which the sleeve moves, but I reckon it is probably just 45 degrees.

Although the sleeve's holes align with ports in the barrel they have no relationship to the moving piston, nor does the piston have any effect on the opening of the ports, unlike a two-stroke engine. An advantage of having several large holes near the top of the sleeve is that their combined area is very large. The ports are thus timed to open fully with no obstruction by 'intruding' valve heads and they can remain open for longer periods of time than is possible with poppet-valve engines. Because of this, the volumetric efficiency of the 'simple' sleeve-valve engine can be vastly superior to the volumetric efficiency of even the very best, and most powerful, poppet-valve engines. The ports in the moving cylinder align with **six** ports in the cylinder barrel, while the rotary action of the sleeve opens ports on the inlet face at one stroke, the exhaust on the other. The **fifth** port in the sleeve functions as *both inlet and exhaust ports during the different strokes,* lining up alternatively with the appropriate ports in the barrel for **three** inlet and **three** exhaust ports.

In the normal four-stroke, poppet-valve engine, the type of engine which powers almost everything on two wheels, there are clear and serious disadvantages. It does not matter how many poppet valves are employed, nor how they are operated, for the valves themselves get in their own way.

Because of their position directly above the piston, poppet valves cannot be opened very far and cannot stay open for very long, and when

Emerging into the daylight from within the heavy fog of burning oil at the first start-up, the engine still pulling like a steam train, with very much more to come, due to its almost linear torque curve. After the engine had warmed up, there was very little oil smoke, the B&S sleeve-valve pulling even better. The bike's owner insisted it had never done that before, saying he was going to pull it all apart when he took it back home again.

they *are* open, they obstruct most of the area of the ports simply because of their 'mushroom' shape and position, and the shape of their attendant valve stems and intruding valve guides. They are also slower to open fully than sleeve-valve engines, and there is also a measurable power loss in poppet-valve engines by having to exert pressure upon many very heavy valve springs, with frictional losses also engendered by the very complex cams, valve gear and attendant components.

The main problem with the earlier sleeve-valve engines was heavy oil consumption, which was evident when the Ever Onward I rode disappeared in a heavy white cloud of burnt oil when it was fired up.

This may well have been caused by excessive wear in the moving sleeve, or the piston rings, for it has been said that oil consumption was usually no more than that experienced with many machines of its era. This is because the Pilgrim oil pump used by B&S – and which many other manufacturers adopted in those days – had no scavenger return and was thus of the 'total-loss' system, the oil piddling out of the base of the crankcase onto the roadway after it had circulated throughout the engine. A similar total-loss lubricating system was employed very effectively in Speedway JAP engines.

The sleeve valve was well lubricated by oil which was pressure – fed and squirted onto the base of its skirt from the outboard Pilgrim Pump, the reciprocating-and-rotating action assuring the sleeve received adequate lubrication almost instantaneously over its entire surface, even in view of its very close tolerances within the outer barrel. This was of course assisted by the fact that cast-iron is self-lubricating to some degree, which was here allied to the matt finish on the exterior of the sleeve, which helped retain oil on its surface. The big-end and main bearings were also well lubricated by a pressure-fed, splash-feed. Oil mist also played its part.

It has also been said that the 'normal' loss of oil at start-up had been successfully addressed in later developments to the engine, but it remained a problem with the Ever Onward for a while,

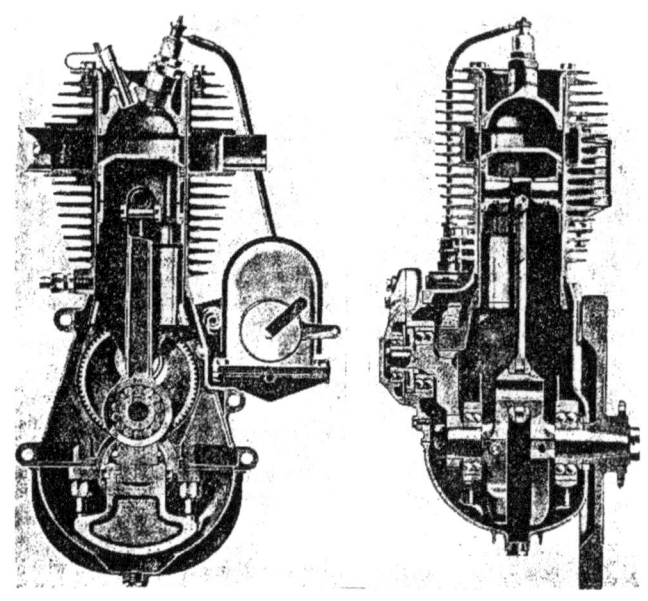

Drawing of the simple, 350cc B&S engine internals. On the side view we can see the oil feed, the piston at top dead centre, the sleeve driven by the very large gear from the crankshaft gear, and moving at half engine speed, the magneto drive to the right. It looks to be at the firing stroke, for both ports appear to be closed off.
Head on: We can see the double-row ball bearings throughout, and single row, crowded roller big-end. The external flywheel indicates it is a 350.

until it had settled itself down after warming up. It was then that the clouds of oil smoke seemed to have almost disappeared, but it still meant that a weather eye had to be kept on the contents of the oil tank. The B&S piston employed two compression rings and a thin scraper, while a piston with at least one genuine oil ring – or preferably two, as in some German motorcycle engines – might have made an enormous difference to the Ever Onward's oil problem.

Sir Harry Ricardo, the brilliant engineer/mathematician who was responsible for the new-fangled octane rating of fuel (among a great many other things) and who designed the four-valve Triumph 500cc single in 1921, was a strong advocate for the sleeve-valve engine, extolling its many virtues in his seminal writings on the design. He was very instrumental in the adoption of the sleeve-valve engine in aircraft during WWII, claiming (rightly) that this type of engine could produce far more power than could any poppet-valve engine of similar capacity.

Complicated, double sleeve-valve engines were used for a time in some early Daimler,

Mercedes, Panhard, Willys-Knight, Minerva, and Peugeot cars in the 1920s, while the multi-cylinder Napier 'Centaurus' with its far simpler, **single** sleeve-valve engine was the most powerful engine ever fitted to any propeller-driven aircraft in WWII. When it was fully developed for aircraft use, the latest, 24-cylinder **supercharged** single-sleeve-valve Napier 'Sabre' aircraft engine developed an amazing 5,500BHP (4400Kw) at just on 4200rpm in bench testing, with well over 4,200 (safe) BHP in normal service. The servicing times for these engines was three times as long as the far shorter intervals in the poppet-valve engines; a bonus for the sleeve-valve designs.

The Napier was only one of a great many aircraft to employ sleeve-valve engines at the time; one of them, the Bristol 'Beaufighter', employed a 14-cylinder Bristol 'Hercules' single sleeve-valve engine. It was nick-named 'Whispering Death' because of its eerily quiet, unsilenced exhaust. Historical records show that some 130,000 sleeve-valved engines for a variety of makes were built in England alone for WWII aircraft, before the jet engine arrived.

The late British engineer Mike Hewland and his team, famous for their work with gearboxes for Lotus and other racing cars, developed a reliable, high-compression, single-sleeve 500cc engine in the early 1970s which returned an astonishing 74BHP (52Kw) on a dyno test! The new engine was used as a test bed, intended as a precursor to a two-litre, four-cylinder, sleeve-valve engine designated for open-wheeler racing. After an interview with Charles Fox, from *Car and Driver* magazine in the July 1974 issue, in which Hewland described his sleeve-valve design but still gave little away, nothing more was ever heard about either of the engines.

But, to keep that enormous 74BHP figure in perspective, it should be noted that one of the most successful 500cc single-cylinder racing motorcycle engine of all time was the 48BHP, DOHC Manx Norton, the best of which returned just on *52BHP* after additional tuning had been carried out. It has been said that one of the great Norton tuners, Tom Arter, once had an engine which (briefly) showed 56BHP on a dyno, but that figure was never seen again, and is thus under some cloud.

But it still cannot compare with the amazing 74BHP – some 40% more than the Norton engine – which the single cylinder 500cc Hewland sleeve-valve engine delivered at a staggering 10,000rpm. It was also said to use less oil on test than the normal poppet-valve engine, doubtless with oil rings on the piston, among many other things. I wonder how the big-end bearing withstood the enormous stresses!

No doubt the latest materials, modern manufacturing processes and far better lubricants were used during the Hewland engine's development; perhaps the metal-bonding dry lubricant, Molybdenum Disulfide, if added to the oil, would have been ideal in helping to lubricate the moving sleeve as well. Hewland had worked on Bristol sleeve-valve aircraft engines during WWII, so he knew the single sleeve-valve engine very well indeed.

In passing, let me suggest that, with its very slim profile, superior handling and subsequent, great power-to-weight ratio, a Featherbed-framed Manx Norton fitted with a 74 BHP Hewland 500cc sleeve-valve engine and, say, five-speed Quaife gearbox, would gleefully eat alive anything on two wheels which ever tried to come anywhere near it!

An American owner of a Briggs and Stratton lawnmower engine, a small, side-valve design, completely converted it to a single sleeve valve, with remarkable results, the lawnmower engine revving to 6,400rpm, and seemed eager to run very much faster. But the engineer was not brave enough to run it any higher in case it blew up in his face, for the engine was never designed to run at anything like those high engine speeds. He found that the ingress of dirt into his prototype lawnmower almost caused the sleeve to seize, which may well have destroyed his pride and joy.

But perhaps the most remarkable thing about the single-sleeve-valve engine is that not one of the major Japanese motorcycle manufacturers has ever shown the slightest interest in it: neither has anyone else, be it known. It may well be that the Japanese had never heard of the design of this most interesting engine, but there may also be a good reason why they never pursued this design in smaller engines, much less spent any time developing it.

An answer could well be that, like the Wankel rotary engine, there are very few moving parts in a 'simple' single sleeve-valve design, which could mean very little profit for the Spare Parts Department in a major dealership, and not much profit in servicing the engine, either. A cynical thought? Perhaps, but that point could easily be made, nonetheless. In fact, it has just been made!

So, after this hopefully interesting dissertation on the remarkably simple, single sleeve-valve engine, how did the Ever Onwards *feel*, and how well did this unusual, little-known engine manufactured by B&S from 1920–25 perform when compared with other engines of a similar capacity?

The first thing I noted at start-up was the almost total lack of any engine noise, for the only sound to be heard was the soft swish of the sleeve in motion and only a faint hum from the chain drive to the magneto.

The sleeve-vale's overall performance was very surprising, including the exhaust note, or lack thereof, and it reminded me at once of the very quiet approach of the Beaufighter fighter-bombers which were, of course, unsilenced, but whose exhaust was said to have been surprisingly quiet.

Acceleration was very brisk indeed, and the bike seemed very eager to stretch its wings and really take off, with no (apparent) end in sight to its engine revs. It was, in fact, quite remarkable.

The Ever Onward's large drum brakes were light in operation, and were surprisingly powerful, while the rigid frame and short-travel, undamped front suspension took some time to become used to. The suspension chattered over bumpy surfaces and did not work very well over solid bumps and/or small potholes, the sprung single saddle taking upon itself the task of absorbing much of the rough road surfaces which the rigid rear end simply could not be expected to handle. Unsurprisingly, that small saddle did the job it was designed to do very well, although the ride was still not all that great. But what would one expect from a machine built as a Bitza in 1966, using up a whole lot of seemingly ill-matched bits and pieces lying about in someone's shed?

It must be said, however, that the Ever Onward was very well bolted together and made for a remarkably good-looking machine, which performed surprisingly well.

Had the Barr and Stroud single sleeve-valve engine received even a fraction of the many decades of development enjoyed by the inferior (?) poppet-valve design, been made of lightweight alloy castings, received its rightful pinnacle of development, and been placed in a more modern frame, it would certainly have presented a very serious – and probably unanswerable – challenge to other designs, be well assured of that irrefutable fact!

The most unusual aspect of the sleeve-valve engine seemed to be that it liked to just keep on

Here is the 350cc engine in a brand-new Beardmore 'Precision' motorcycle from the mid-1920s. Note the gravity-feed oil line into the union at the base of the cylinder barrel. The oil could be pressurised to a degree by a hand-operated pump on the side of the fuel tank. The action of the sleeve and piston movement was enough to 'suck' and spray oil everywhere throughout the engine's interior. Note that the B.P. exhaust is almost identical to the Ever Onward.

keeping on, almost as though there might be no end in sight as to its engine speed. It was able to propel the machine along very smoothly at little more than walking speed in top gear, and then, as the throttle was very gently eased open (or as gently as possible!) it kept the power coming on very impressively indeed as it wound itself out. This was a real surprise, for no other motorcycle I have ridden (and there must have been many hundreds of them I have ridden over some 74 years of pounding them about the countryside) gave that odd feeling of 'never-ending' power.

I might also add that tight, feet-up U-turns were very difficult because of the tight, lever-type 'lawnmower' throttle control, which totally refused to allow the subtly offered so easily by the twistgrip control. On one occasion, after just changing back to second gear and with the gear lever knob nudging my right knee, the clutch being fed in while cranking over for a medium-paced corner, and a thumb trying hard to force open the tight throttle lever, I was about as busy at the time as a one-armed violinist!

But, overall, to have ridden this rare, one-off machine and being able to comment on the most fascinating sleeve-valve engine in such detail was really something to fondly remember. I would dearly love to ride the Ever Onward again, but only if somebody would fit the handlebars with a standard twistgrip! Oh, and a Burman CP – or Triumph – foot-change gearbox would make for an added joy, although most of the smart-looking little bike's great character would then be lost. Perhaps the great Ever Onward should be left just as it is? Oh, yes, I really think so.

Unhappily, the brilliantly conceived, single sleeve-valve B&S single-cylinder motorcycle engine from back in the 1920s was never fully exploited, probably because the Scottish factory was more into the manufacture of binoculars, rangefinders, surveyors' instruments, and submarine periscopes. But, as we have noted, similar sleeve-valve designs, some more complicated with two sleeves, were used in many other applications in motor cars over some years, since the first of its type appeared way back in 1905.

The latest news is that there are individuals out there (like the Briggs and Stratton engineer with his converted power-plant) who are very seriously looking anew at single sleeve-valve engines, and there are known to be several sleeve-valve engines fitted to small model aircraft, so we may hear yet again of a new series of these quite interesting, if mostly forgotten, powerful engines. Let us all hope it is sooner rather than later, for I can hardly wait!

Turning a sharp corner was an interesting exercise. I had just changed back to second gear, the lever nudging my right knee, while easing the clutch home, and juggling with the too-tight throttle lever, while trying the line the corner up as well. It was quite a test. Oh, for the subtly of a simple twistgrip!

www.ingramcontent.com/pod-product-compliance
Lightning Source LLC
Chambersburg PA
CBHW061535010526
44107CB00066B/2876